Practical Reason in Historical and Systematic Perspective

Berlin Studies
in Knowledge Research

Edited by
Günter Abel and James Conant

Volume 19

Practical Reason in Historical and Systematic Perspective

Edited by
James Conant and Dawa Ometto

DE GRUYTER

Series Editors
Prof. em. Dr. Günter Abel
Technische Universität Berlin
Institut für Philosophie
Straße des 17. Juni 135
10623 Berlin
Germany
e-mail: abel@tu-berlin.de

Prof. Dr. James Conant
The University of Chicago
Dept. of Philosophy
1115 E. 58th Street
Chicago IL 60637
USA
e-mail: jconant@uchicago.edu

ISBN 978-3-11-221479-4
e-ISBN (PDF) 978-3-11-098133-9
e-ISBN (EPUB) 978-3-11-098230-5
ISSN 2365-1601

Library of Congress Control Number: 2023940066

Bibliographic information published by the Deutsche Nationalbibliothek
The Deutsche Nationalbibliothek lists this publication in the Deutsche Nationalbibliografie; detailed bibliographic data are available on the internet at http://dnb.dnb.de.

© 2025 Walter de Gruyter GmbH, Berlin/Boston
This volume is text- and page-identical with the hardback published in 2024.
Printing and binding: CPI books GmbH, Leck

www.degruyter.com

Table of Contents

Dawa Ometto
Two Perspectives on Practical Reason and Practical Knowledge —— 1

Part I: **Action & Practical Reasoning**

John McDowell
Self-Consciousness in Acting —— 27

Sebastian Rödl
The Practical Syllogism —— 43

Jason Bridges
The Unity of a Practical Inference —— 61

Jennifer Ryan Lockhart
Kant on Practical Necessity —— 97

Part II: **Ethics and Meta-ethics**

Rory O'Connell
Against the Possibility of a Merely Instrumentally Rational Agent —— 135

Douglas Lavin
Rousseau's Conscience in Modern Moral Philosophy —— 171

Anastasia Berg
Kant and the Freedom to Do What We Want —— 211

Part III: **Political Philosophy**

Anton Ford and Benjamin Laurence
The Parts and Whole of Plato's Republic —— 239

Wolfram Gobsch
Philosophizing as Dying: Self-Knowledge and Reconciliation in Hegel —— 281

Alec Hinshelwood
The Work of Human Hands: Marx on Humanity as Solidarity —— 321

Index —— 353

Dawa Ometto
Two Perspectives on Practical Reason and Practical Knowledge

1 Introduction

Practical philosophy in the analytical tradition is largely dominated by a set of views that, although it certainly contains much room for disagreement, still constitutes a fixed perspective. Endorsement of this perspective appears to be a matter of course, so that it is rarely recognized *as* a distinctive perspective at all. As we will see in the course of this introduction, this perspective is rooted in a particular conception of practical reason—one that is not only historically contingent, but also deserves to be systematically interrogated and juxtaposed to a different one. However, it is one symptom of the dominance of the prevailing conception that alternatives to it (be it in the historical tradition, or in certain subcurrents of analytic philosophy itself) often go unrecognized: such alternatives are either declared to be incomprehensible, or else are consciously or unconsciously domesticated—reinterpreted in such a way as to fit the mold of the prevailing conception. Providing a proper antidote to the blind spots of contemporary practical philosophy must therefore involve work that is at the same time historical *and* systematic—work that draws on historical figures for inspiration, but that also gives us ways of understanding their positions as cogent systematic alternatives. That is what this volume attempts to do. Before we turn to the alternative perspective that our contributors exhibit, as well as the strong disagreements to be found within it, it will be helpful to sketch the prevailing conception of practical reason, and the ways it influences contemporary work in the philosophy of action, ethics and meta-ethics, and political philosophy.

The prevailing conception closely associates reasoning about action to reasoning about theoretical matters, and so assimilates (I submit) practical knowledge—both knowledge of what one *is* doing, and of what one ultimately *ought* to do—to theoretical belief. It is, as Anscombe (1963, 57) calls it polemically, an "incorrigibly contemplative conception of knowledge." On this conception, the thought is that insofar as practical deliberation is a form of *reasoning*, it must be a matter of operating on one's attitudes in such a way as to achieve a certain kind of consistency in one's mental economy, e. g., between what one desires will happen and what one believes about the world.¹ This process is taken to yield new attitudes (desires or intentions) which may then go on to cause the corresponding action. In the lucky case in which the action is successfully produced, the agent may be in a position to take themselves to be engaged in it—i.e., the process of practical reasoning may generate a licensed *belief* that one is doing what one intends. And if one is a realist about value, one may also insist that the agent has *ethical* knowledge if the attitudes that form the premises of her practical reasoning somehow track the independent facts about what is good. Even such a value realist, however, will agree with Hume (whose legacy should be obvious in the approach to practical deliberation sketched above) at least to this extent: grasping what is ultimately good or valuable is not an exercise of an intrinsically practical form of reasoning. The purview of the latter is restricted, as it is for Hume, to instrumental reasoning, while the realist supposes additionally that there is such a thing as having true or false beliefs *about* value. Knowledge of the good, then, is a species of *theoretical* knowledge, in so far as it does not *eo ipso* entail any *practical* commitments.² And accordingly, what *is* good—what it is to act well, individually or as a society—cannot itself be partially constituted by the presence of a form of practical wisdom or knowledge in it.³ That all this (save perhaps the optional commitment to value realism) may sound like a truism is testament to the overwhelming dominance in contemporary analytic philosophy of the paradigm described here. Value realism and full-blown Humeanism oppose each other only as two species of this broader paradigm, which rejects the possibility of a truly practical form of knowledge.⁴ And

---

1 This tendency is apparent in much canonical mainstream work on practical reasoning, e.g., Broome (2013) and Wallace (2020).
2 Of course, the realist may insist that some kind of necessity operates in those who have acquired beliefs about what is good, leading them to acquire corresponding practical commitments. The present point is just that however we understand this necessary link, it cannot be a form of reasoning.
3 As we will see below, this is the hallmark of theoretical knowledge, which is, in Anscombe's (1963, 87) translation of Aquinas, "derived from the objects known."
4 Here a remark is perhaps in order about so-called constructivism in meta-ethics, most famously defended, of course, by Christine Korsgaard, e.g., in her (2009). Constructivism explicitly attempts to provide an alternative to both value realism and Humean non-cognitivism, and it does so by making practical reason partially constitutive of the object of moral knowledge (i.e., the good). To that extent, we can view constructivists as allies in opposing the prevailing paradigm (and indeed in the way in which Korsgaard and others interrogate the historical tradition). However, more critically, it is unclear whether the constructivists succeed in fully leaving behind the Humean paradigm. This query is especially salient when it comes to the constructivist's conception of *desire* as a capacity that is entirely the same in rational beings and in non-rational animals, and, connected to this, the question how practical reason can be *productive* of action (and not just helpful in "stepping back" from bad desires, as Korsgaard (2009, 19) sometimes puts it). Such a critical exami-

given the prevalence of this conception of practical reason and the good, I submit, it is certainly no accident that consequentialism—the philosophy *par excellence* that separates the object of moral knowledge from the activity of practical reasoning, and treats the good (in the guise of utility or preference-satisfaction) as a given —still enjoys such a good reputation in both normative ethics and political philosophy.

The purpose of this volume is to throw into relief the contingency of this near consensus view by gathering together a number of essays that develop a different philosophical outlook, unified by the idea that to take seriously the topic of practical reason, and to make progress in understanding it, is to be in a dialogue with a historical tradition that spans from classical to medieval philosophy (e.g., Aristotle, and Aquinas), further onwards to modern times (e.g., Kant, Hegel, and Marx), and perhaps more recently, to Wittgenstein and a certain strand of analytical philosophy. Following Stephen Engstrom, we can call this alternative tradition *practical cognitivism*. As he argues, we can see that the aforementioned historical figures (for all their occasionally momentous disagreements) indeed all belong to it by contrasting this tradition to the broadly Humean strand of thinking described above. Where the latter rejects the idea that there is an intrinsically practical use or species of reason and attempts to reduce practical reason and knowledge to their theoretical counterparts, practical cognitivism holds fast to the idea that there is a *sui generis* form of reason and knowledge that concerns the question what to do, or how to live. Engstrom describes the most important unifying features of the practical cognitivist tradition, with all its internal divisions, as follows:

> ... shining through these differences are certain unmistakable marks and characters revealing membership in a common family line: the arresting insight that all good things depend for their goodness on knowledge and wisdom; the consequent recognition of these latter as basic to virtue; the associated appreciation that the several virtues are bound together in one, giving unity to a virtuous life as a whole, both for an individual and for society; and above all the recognition that the principles of ethical life lie in form and activity (Engstrom 2009, vii).

Unified in their acceptance of these basic insights, the contributions in this volume can be seen as attempts to pursue a deeper understanding of the following three questions:
- What is practical knowledge?
- What is virtue or good action?

---

nation of Kantian constructivism is present in some of the contributions to this volume (e.g., those of Berg and Gobsch).

- What is a sound way of living together for us, beings who possess practical reason?

These three questions correspond to the three parts into which this book is divided: *Action and Practical Reason* (Part I), *Ethics and Meta-Ethics* (Part II), and *Political Philosophy* (Part III). The contributions seek to open up for systematic philosophical thought certain perspectives on these questions that are inspired by various historical representatives of the practical cognitivist tradition—perspectives the very possibility of which are often obscured by our tendency to bring our own contemporary assumptions and preoccupations to our attempts to interpret historical texts. In the next section, I will sketch in some more detail how these three questions, and so the three parts of this volume, relate to each other, and to the practical cognitivist tradition at large. In the course of doing so, I will also say more about the mentioned need for systematic philosophy to draw inspiration from the history of the discipline.

2 The Parts of the Volume

I. Practical Reasoning and Action. Practical cognitivism's distinctive outlook on knowledge of the good (as identified above by Engstrom) is rooted in a distinctive understanding of practical reasoning and action that diverges from the standard story in several crucial respects. These differences can best be understood by considering the following central idea, shared by all the contributions to this volume: that intentional action is to be understood as an exercise of a self-conscious capacity for *practical knowledge*. That is to say that it is impossible to understand intentional action except through considering the agent's own understanding of what they are doing, and why. And this agential self-consciousness is to be contrasted with third-personal, theoretical, or *contemplative* knowledge of what one is doing—i.e., knowledge that is paradigmatically acquired through observation and inference. For in acting intentionally, we do not represent ourselves as engaged in some movement *anyway*, i.e., independently of our representing ourselves *as* engaged in it. And our knowledge of *why* we are doing it, similarly, is not a representation of a tendency or causal principle that we discover to be independently operative in us: it is not knowledge of a causal principle that (until we discovered it) was operating in us behind our back. Instead, when we act intentionally, we understand ourselves to be doing something, φ, precisely *in* representing it as *to be done*, or as *good to do*—perhaps with a view to some other goal we are aiming at, or perhaps as good in itself.[5] Our knowledge of being engaged in a certain action—i.e., our understanding of φ *as* our answer to the question what is to be done, here and now—is thus part of what it is to be acting intentionally at all. Intentional action, as opposed to animal action or mere physical movements, then, is to be understood as a *form* of happening that essentially involves self-consciousness. As Eric Marcus puts it, intentional actions are "moves in the space of reasons" (Marcus 2018, 320): they are an agent's response to the question what to do, as determined by her capacity for practical reasoning or practical thought. Unlike in the standard story, then, practical reasoning does not conclude in an attitude or mental state, but instead in action itself.

An understanding of action along these lines can be found in various historical representatives of the practical cognitivist tradition. However, it has arguably only re-entered analytical philosophy of action in recent decades through the reception of G. E. M. Anscombe's *Intention*.[6] Anscombe's attempt to recover the idea of practical knowledge constitutes a common touchstone for the essays of this volume (and especially in Part I), even if the authors, of course, may also disagree with her in important ways. However, the way in which her thought has been received in recent analytic literature also provides an example of the way in which systematic philosophy can go awry when it shows insufficient interest in its own history.

Following Aquinas, Anscombe puts the thought that intentional action is a *sui generis* form of movement characterized by agential self-consciousness by saying that practical knowledge is the "cause of what it understands," where …

> [t]his means more than that practical knowledge is observed to be a necessary condition of the production of various results; or that an idea of doing such-and-such in such-and-such ways is such a condition. It means that without it what happens does not come under the description—execution of intentions—whose characteristic we have been investigating (Anscombe 1963, 87–88).

That practical knowledge is "the cause of what it understands"—as opposed to "speculative knowledge, which 'is derived from the objects known'" (Anscombe 1963, 87)—thus means that *what* is known cannot be separated from this very knowledge. And it is this thesis that separates the practical cognitivist from contemporary attempts to account for the phenomenon that agents, by and large,

---

5 On the difference between representing one's action as instrumentally and non-instrumentally good, see the discussion of Part II of this volume below.
6 Anscombe (1963). For the reception, see for example the essays in Ford (2011).

seem to know (without having to look or think about it) what they are doing from within a broadly neo-Humean framework.[7]

On such neo-Humean views, acting intentionally is analyzed, roughly, as doing φ while *believing* that one is being caused to φ (by a certain desire, say, and perhaps also by this very belief). Now, if, following Anscombe, we understand speculative or contemplative knowledge as knowledge that is "derived from the objects known"—i.e., as knowledge of an object that is what it is *anyway*, independently of being known—we can see that these accounts are attempts to reduce practical knowledge as just described into a (peculiar) kind of contemplative knowledge. Someone like Velleman, for instance, holds that such knowledge is a true belief —i.e., an *accurate reflection*—of an event or state of affairs that is not essentially or formally such as to *be* known by the agent. Such beliefs are peculiar in that they do not require an act of explicit inference or observation, and therefore give rise to epistemological difficulties: e.g., how could an agent *know* that she is doing φ merely on the basis that, say, she strongly desires to φ?

From the perspective of the practical cognitivist, however, the attempt to answer such questions is misguided: it arises from a dogmatic adherence to what Anscombe calls a "incorrigibly contemplative conception of knowledge,"[8] a refusal to take seriously the idea that there might be a form of knowledge that is "the cause of what it understands," and therefore irreducibly practical. Here is not the time or place to argue against such reductive accounts: suffice it to say that, as many defenders of what we are here calling practical cognitivism (including some of the contributors to this volume[9]) have argued, it is a consequence of such a reduction that the agent will always relate to what is happening in an external or alienated way—in thinking "I am making such-and-such-movements because I am mental states X, Y, and Z," the agent does not, as such, *endorse* the action as *theirs*. The essential point, for now, is that understanding practical knowledge, on the practical cognitivist conception, will not be an exercise in *epistemology*, at least as this field is now normally conceived of. Rather, it will be to understand the unity of our capacities to reason about the good, and to bring about changes in the world. This nominal definition of the topic leaves open many questions. For instance, we may ask: is there any kind of *necessary connection* between the premises from which a practical reasoner begins, and her (knowledge of her) action? Is an action to be thought as in some way *deriving* from these premises? What forms, instrumental and otherwise, can such premises take? Exactly how does practical

---

7 The most prominent examples of this tendency are perhaps Velleman (2004), Setiya (2008), and Schwenkler (2019).
8 Anscombe (1963, 57).
9 For example, Lavin (2013).

reasoning put an agent in a position to know what they are doing, if not indirectly (as on the prevailing conception)? As we will see, there is considerable disagreement amongst our contributors about such questions. Nevertheless, I believe that this nominal definition accurately describes the problematic that they (and, of course, others whose work is responsive to the importance of agential self-consciousness) see themselves as grappling with.

Moreover, it is worth pointing out that contemporary attempts to read Anscombe herself in terms of a contemplative conception of knowledge—that is, as insisting that practical knowledge must be a special variety of ordinary true belief—is an interesting example of the aforementioned tendency to "domesticate" attempts to spell out what is parochial and perhaps false in the prevailing conception by reinterpreting such attempts in terms more friendly to it. To our minds, drawing attention to the history of the practical cognitivist tradition, against the background of which Anscombe's claim that practical knowledge is "the cause of what it understands" is to be placed, is essential to counter this tendency. Perhaps this may at least give pause to such attempts at domestication. The contributions in Part I exemplify an alternative approach, by adding to recent attempts to take seriously Anscombe's thought on its own terms (the contributors' disagreements with Anscombe notwithstanding).

II. Ethics and Meta-Ethics. Given this broad conception of practical knowledge, and of practical reasoning as issuing in action, an array of questions opens up that remains out of view on the prevailing perspective. To think of practical reasoning and action as essentially self-conscious in the way set out above is to embrace the insight Engstrom mentioned, "that all good things depend for their goodness on knowledge and wisdom." After all, the conclusion of practical reasoning, i.e., the answer to the question "what to do?" or "what is good?" has shown itself to be formally characterized by our knowledge of it. Now, if that is right, it becomes important to inquire into the meaning of this phrase "our knowledge"—*what* knowledge and *whose* knowledge is it, exactly, that formally characterizes the good?

To begin with the "what": it immediately follows, given our starting point, that consequentialism of all kinds is already ruled out—knowledge of what consequences (described without reference to the agent's practical thought) an action would realize is not knowledge that could formally characterize good action as such. But various alternatives, notably neo-Aristotelian and Kantian, remain open and have in recent years been developed.[10] And these broadly Aristotelian and Kantian accounts in turn offer diverging answers to the question "whose knowledge?" Whereas the former claims that the relevant practical knowledge is in some sense limited

---

10 Cf. Foot (2001) and Engstrom (2009), respectively.

or specific to the form of human living (and so tied to a set of virtues that play a special role in *human* life), the latter claims that it is fully universal—such as to characterize the sound practical reasoning of *any* rational being. The essays in Part II struggle with the question how to make sense of the relevant alternatives. They ask, for instance: is our essentially human capacity for desire somehow informed by (our human?) practical reasoning, or do reason and desire stand fully opposed to one another? And can we so much as entertain the idea of a different species of practical reason, or ask the question whether *our* reason is indeed such as to require conformity with virtue? It is testament to the originality of the contributions that they each complicate and blur the lines between canonically Kantian and Aristotelian answers to these questions, thus opening up new terrain.

III. Political Philosophy. Whereas much modern political philosophy departs from quasi-consequentialist considerations about how to realize certain pre-reflectively intuitively desirable goods on a societal scale (even if the result of this procedure is, as in Rawls' case, a certain regard for equity over pure maximization), the practical cognitivist perspective opens up another way of thinking about the question what a sound way of living together would be. In particular, as Engstrom puts it, it opens up the possibility that a sound form of living together might be characterized by a certain *form*—a form essentially understood, in the ideal case of a good society, to be actually realized in that society. An example of this would be the idea that *freedom* might be a matter of living according to principles that *constitute* our independence as practically reasoning subjects, rather than being a mere tool for the unimpeded realization of our desires—as recently developed in certain strands of Kantian political philosophy.[11] The contributions to Part III develop this general practical cognitivist approach to political philosophy in new and original directions, inspired by Plato, Hegel, and Marx. The fundamental question they raise, and attempt to answer in the different ways summarized below, is what it might mean to say that the good of members of a human society is *shared*, and this in such a way that the actual realization of this good depends on their ability to understand it to be realized in their form of life.

---

11 See, e.g., Ripstein (2010).

3 The Contributions

Part I: Action and Practical Reasoning

John McDowell—Self-Consciousness in Acting. McDowell's essay begins with a detailed examination of Anscombe's account of practical knowledge—an account which has been hugely influential on many of the contributions in this volume, as well as on recent discussions of practical reason and action more generally. McDowell seeks to show how Anscombe's account of "the knowledge a man has of his intentional actions" (Anscombe 1963, 50–51), i.e., the non-observational and indeed non-*contemplative* knowledge that agents typically have of what they are doing, can be seen to fit in with a more general understanding of self-consciousness. The idea is that in general, a subject's self-knowledge of the fact that a certain predicate applies to her is essential to what it is for the predicate to apply: for instance, it is essential to my *believing that p* that I know myself (without observation, or again non-contemplatively) to believe that *p*. McDowell here cites approvingly Rödl's dictum that self-knowledge and its object are "the same reality" (Rödl 2007, 14). According to McDowell, when Anscombe agrees with Aquinas that practical knowledge is the "formal cause" of action, this is therefore not to distinguish practical knowledge from other forms of self-knowledge. That distinction is to be made simply in virtue of the *object* of the agent's self-knowledge: not a thought or experience, but an action—a happening formally characterized by the "order" that Anscombe elucidates through the notion of the practical syllogism.

McDowell draws two important lessons from this account. First of all, according to his reading, an Ansombean theorist of action need not claim (as Anscombe may seem to claim) that agents necessarily or always have practical knowledge of what they are doing intentionally. Or more precisely: they need not claim that always when an agent has practical self-knowledge, the *object* of her self-knowledge is an ongoing action. For instance, in familiar cases, it seems as if an agent cannot know whether she is really, say, painting a wall yellow without being in perceptual contact with the object she is working on. Assume that something is going wrong, and the wall is therefore not turning yellow. In such a case, McDowell argues, we should simply say that the object of the agent's self-knowledge is not an ongoing action ("painting the wall yellow") but instead something else—and moreover something we can explain only as a *defective* case of what is self-known in a successful attempt. McDowell can here be seen to apply the *disjunctivist* strategy he famously applies to theoretical knowledge.[12]

Second, McDowell argues against the idea that practical reasoning requires what Rödl calls a "measure": a general standard (which Rödl identifies with a "practical lifeform") from which the *necessity* of particular acts of the will can be derived.[13] McDowell argues that a quasi-deductive picture of practical reasoning would skirt dangerously close to the idea for which Anscombe warns us, that what we accept in practical reasoning are *thoughts* (Anscombe says: propositions). And he suggests that we may avoid such a picture if we distinguish between practical thoughts *off* and *on* "active service": it is only when a consideration about the good of a prospective action is "on active service" that the conclusion follows with any kind of necessity from the premise—when we are committed to φ'ing because of ψ, then of course this "active" premise implies that we are doing φ.

This distinction between premises on active and passive service thus means that, for McDowell, one can determine one's answer to the question what to do not by *beginning* from what Rödl calls an "infinite end"[14] (a first premise about the good), but simply by judging that it is good to do A, where that is a means to B, and thereby coming to want to do B (that is, bringing the premise B into "active service"). And it is precisely because, for McDowell, practical knowledge does not *always* accompany *all* movements that are formally characterized by the order of practical reasoning (see above), that he has room to distinguish between premises off and on "active service."

Sebastian Rödl—The Practical Syllogism. In his essay, Rödl develops the idea of a practical syllogism in a way meant to counter McDowell's worries about the (alleged) importance of *necessity* to practical reasoning (see above). Rödl insists that to say that a practical syllogism is genuinely a form of inference is already to say that there is a *non-accidental* (and so necessary) connection between premises and conclusion. For, he argues, the conclusion of any inference expresses a consciousness of the premises as constituting *sufficient* grounds for the action. The question is how to understand this in the practical case. Rödl focuses on the calculating or instrumental form of the practical syllogism, although he insists that this is to be viewed as only one (obviously limited) sense in which one practical judgement can be a sufficient ground for another.

---

[12] See McDowell (1996). He similarly suggests such a strategy in McDowell (2010, 431).
[13] For both the idea of such a measure, and the idea that it is constituted by a practical lifeform, see Rödl (2007, Chapter 2). McDowell's present disagreement with Rödl, and the latter's response to it in his contribution, show how discussion of the form and necessity of practical reasoning bear on the topic of Part II of this volume.
[14] Rödl (2007, 34).

Against Anscombe, who claims that "[t]he role of 'wanting' in the practical syllogism is quite different from that of a premise,"[15] Rödl argues that the premise of a calculating syllogism must be an act of the will, or of wanting—something expressible by "I want to do A." Otherwise, the *presence* of an act of wanting would be a necessary condition of action not itself contained in a practical syllogism, and so the syllogism or its conclusion could not express an understanding of the premises as *sufficient* for the conclusion. Or if we say that an act of *wanting* the premises is not itself a premise, but instead something along the lines of an *inference principle*, then it would follow that the validity of the inference can only be recognized by someone who has the relevant desire.

From this point of departure, Rödl critically interrogates McDowell's argument (in this volume) that practical reasoning need not be conceived as deriving an action from an ultimate or non-instrumental end, and argues that this is in fact a mistake by McDowell's own lights (insofar as the latter insists that a premise of practical reasoning must be not just wanted, but *intelligibly* wanted, i.e., is itself apt to be the conclusion of a practical syllogism). As we have seen above, McDowell insists that a practical reasoner need not *start* from the premise that a certain action is good, instead letting a judgement about its goodness depend on what means would be necessary to achieve it—a question answered in practical reasoning where one's premises are not "on active service." However, Rödl insists that a judgement about whether taking up some means is good will still depend on other acts of the will—be they finite or infinite ends, in his terminology (e.g., "I can't do B, because the only way of doing B is doing A, and A will make it impossible for me to X," with X a finite *or* infinite end). He reiterates that both instrumental and non-instrumental forms of reasoning (such as Anscombe's backward-looking motives) must be understood together, as parts of a single logical whole. In addition, he grants McDowell the possibility of what the latter calls a determination of the will *de novo*—i.e., a determination of the will not through previous acts of willing—but insists that this possibility (which Rödl professes to find essential, but also confounding) does not obviate the possibility or necessity of determinations of the will through others acts of will (i.e., through *wanting*).

Rödl closes by giving an argument derived from Anselm Müller's essay *How theoretical is practical reasoning?*[16] that is intended to show that practical reasoning must proceed from what McDowell would call premises "on active service." That practical reasoning is *practical* means that it is "for the sake of" acting, in a manner that involves seeing one's reasoning *as* contributing to the realization

---

15 Anscombe (1963, 66).
16 Müller (1979).

of an end. If this is right, there will be no room for practical reasoning from premises that are merely potentially on active service—nor indeed for practical reasoning that identifies more than one suitable means to achieving an end.

Jason Bridges—The Unity of a Practical Inference. The idea that the conclusion and premises of practical reasoning must be tied together "by necessity" is also the point of departure of Jason Bridges' contribution. Bridges main target is what he calls "practical Fregeanism," according to which this necessity is in some sense logical or conceptual. The latter takes its name from Frege's thesis that when it comes to theoretical inference, at least, judging the premises is necessarily to judge the conclusion.[17] Rödl's account, according to Bridges, is a prime example of the latter. And Bridges argues that practical Fregeanism is not able to overcome the "problem of singularization": the problem, already introduced above, that there are often alternative means available to an agent, so that cases in which a judgement about means is *necessary* to establish the conclusion are a rare exception, and not illustrative of the form of practical reasoning. Bridges argues that many theories of practical reasoning are caught up in a dichotomy between Fregeanism on the one hand and empiricism on the other—both of which Bridges sees as misguided attempts to assimilate practical and theoretical inference.

Bridges discusses various ways of spelling out practical Fregeanism. Here I mention only his discussion of Anselm Müller's argument, which we have already seen in the discussion of Rödl's paper above. Rödl appeals to Müller's insight that practical reasoning is *for the sake of* action in order to diffuse the problem of singularization. But Bridges argues that the Müllerian thought is flawed. He insists that the fact that a judgement that doing A is a means to doing B is "for the sake of acting" need not be understood as entailing that such a judgement leads (with any necessity) to an action of doing A, and can instead be understood as a *potential* to act. He therefore insists that practical reasoning must be "more than holding thoughts together in consciousness," i.e., grasping means-ends connections in thought, and is instead "actualizing the potential the conjoined premise-thoughts represent". Acting, that is, essentially involves a moment of "singula-

---

[17] Frege (1979, 3) famously holds that "judging, being conscious of other truths as justifying grounds, is called inferring." In recent years, this claim has often been discussed in discussion of the so-called "taking condition" on inference: the idea that inference requires a subject to be in some sense aware of her reasons for drawing the conclusion. In this literature, a subject's consciousness of justifying grounds is often treated as causally necessitating the conclusion. Bridges calls the analogous view in the practical domain "empiricism," and opposes it to what is arguably closer to Frege's own view: the idea that there is a logical or conceptual connection between judging the premises and judging the conclusion.

rization," i.e., of making our ends ever more concrete in reality, that has no analogue in theoretical reasoning.

Now, Rödl and Müller would perhaps counter that on their conception, truly identifying something *as a means* already involves more than a mere *readiness* to act. Our purpose here is not to settle this dispute. But Bridges' argument certainly challenges us to better understand the *efficacy* of practical thought, or what he calls its "singularizing" character. He offers his own account of the latter which he styles "intentionalism": the idea that the act of mind needed to *take up* a means that one has identified in thought is just the intention to "do A in order to B," where this "in order to" is *itself* part of what is intended. Bridges closes by considering what this means for the prospects of empiricists approaches to action. If as he argues the teleological connective "in order to" cannot be understood except as itself falling into the scope of what is intended, he argues, it is no surprise that such theories always run into the problems of causal deviance.

Jennifer Ryan Lockhart—Kant on Practical Necessity. Lockhart's paper provides a novel interpretation of Kant's concept of "practical necessity," and of *rational* necessity more generally. Although Lockhart thus develops her conception of such necessity as a reading of Kant, it bears precisely on the systematic questions raised by the other essays in Part I of this volume: whether, and in what sense, practical reasoning necessitates its conclusion, and so what it means for an action to be justified. Lockhart starts by identifying the "standard view" of practical necessity, which equates it with the *overridingness* of a reason: if an agent has such a reason for φ'ing, she "cannot but" φ on pain of, say, irrationality (such a view is often imputed to Kant), or of "losing oneself" (on, e.g., Bernard Williams' view). According to many of readings of Kant, the categorical imperative provides reasons that are "necessitating" in this sense: it makes all but one action morally speaking impossible. But Lockhart points out that this has the awkward consequence of making nonsense of the concept of an *imperfect duty* (paradigmatically, duties of benevolence). Moreover, Kant also speaks of the *hypothetical* imperative as grounding "practical necessity." On the standard reading, the scope of this claim must be limited to cases in which there is a single necessary means (and not multiple sufficient ones) available—but Kant does not seem to limit it this way.

Lockhart then develops an alternative to the standard view that is not plagued by these difficulties. Moreover, Lockhart argues, this alternative view promises us, first, a way out of what is often perceived as the *rigorism* of Kant's moral philosophy, and second, to provide a satisfactory account of both the *unity* and the specific difference of theoretical and practical rational necessity. She does so by taking up Kenny's attempt to formalize practical inference, and showing what role the notion of rational necessity plays in such a formal system.[18] As Lockhart argues, rational necessity is the necessity, or guarantee, that a particular conclusion is *justified:* justified as *true* in the theoretical case, and justified as *good* in the practical. In a good inference, truth or goodness is "transmitted" from one premise to another, so that given a certain set of premises, the conclusion can be *shown* to be justified. Lockhart shows that it is this understanding of practical necessity that underlies Kant's account of both the categorical and hypothetical imperative, arguing that this has gone unnoticed because commentators have implicitly worked with a too contemplative picture of reason. On the resulting account, we can make sense of imperfect duties not as somehow imperfectly necessary, but simply as contrasting with duties that provide (in particular cases) an overriding reason in the sense of the standard picture. As Lockhart argues, an account of the way in which *perfect* duties require a single, specific action needs to go beyond the idea of practical necessity and into the "formula" of the categorical imperative. We can therefore appreciate Kant's moral philosophy as one that recognizes that there is often *not* a single action that is called for but instead makes room for the importance of "playroom for free choice in following ... the law" (Lockhart, this volume).

Part II: Ethics and Meta-Ethics

Rory O'Connell—Against the Possibility of a Merely Instrumentally Rational Agent. This paper takes up an important question at the interstices of action theory and meta-ethics: whether rational agents that possess the capacity for instrumental reasoning—and *not* for any kind of knowledge of the good—are possible. One context in which this question has recently emerged as a topic for discussion is the debate about *constitutivist* theories in meta-ethics. Constitutivists of various kinds (Humean, Kantian, neo-Aristotelian) argue that moral norms can be justified by showing them to derive from the very nature of agency. But where Kantians like Korsgaard claim that a commitment to the categorical imperative can be derived from the very idea of instrumental reasoning, others have argued that Korsgaard's argument begs the question by presupposing that a merely instrumental reasoner would not deserve the label "rational agent"—and thus, that she reads facts about *our* capacity for rational agency (which, let us assume, *does* involve a commitment to non-instrumental norms or principles) into the concept of rational agency in general. Lavin and Thompson, for example, have therefore suggested that we should leave open the *possibility* of merely instrumental agency, but simply insist

---

18 Cf. Kenny (1966).

that this possibility is not *actual* in the case of human agents:[19] why would an argument that acting on considerations of, e. g., justice is practically rational require us to establish this fact *for all rational beings*, rather than just for those we are interested in—ourselves?

O'Connell's intervention in this debate seeks to accomplish two things. First, he aims to provide an argument against the possibility of instrumental agency that does not rely on a contentious view of what we are willing to call rational agency (like, arguably, Korsgaard's). Instead, his argument proceeds by investigating what is involved in the very idea of an *end*—something to be realized in practical reasoning. O'Connell argues that ends are "instrumentally malleable," i. e., that any given action-concept (like "visiting N in France") leaves undetermined, by itself, what would constitute a proper means to its realization. For such a concept to function as a *standard* by which we can judge the soundness of a particular piece of practical reasoning, we must know *with a view to what good* the end is being pursued.[20] But of course, such a further purpose is itself an end, and will therefore exhibit the same instrumental malleability. In this way, O'Connell argues that the very idea of a rational pursuit of an end requires the agent to have some *good* in view—a good which cannot itself be understood as of merely instrumental value. He further develops and defends this argument by applying it to three distinct conceptions of merely instrumental agency that can be extracted from the literature: Thompson's conception of "naïve agency," a contemporary Humean account of rational agency, and Engstrom's Kantian account of a capacity for mere "practical thought."

In the course of this argument, O'Connell shows that the very idea of a specifically self-conscious form of causal *efficacy* (which we have seen is central to the idea of practical reason) requires an agent to have some conception of their (non-instrumental) good in view. Without this, he argues, the very idea of rational efficacy, as opposed to the mere pursuit of desire, falls apart. This helps accomplish his second aim: to show that even to leave open the *possibility* of merely instrumental agency leads to a misunderstanding of the nature of our own practical rationality. For to leave open that possibility suggests that our capacity for rational action consists, so to speak, of a capacity for rational efficacy that we would share with a merely instrumental agent *and* a capacity for knowledge of the good. Instead, O'Connell suggests, we should take seriously the alternative view

---

[19] See Thompson (2008) and Lavin (2017).
[20] For instance, only the further purpose at which one aims in visiting France can determine whether, say, walking there slowly or only getting on the speediest flight counts as a realization of the end.

(which he attributes to Aristotle) that practical deliberation—the capacity to find means to ends—is itself already thoroughly ethical.

Douglas Lavin—Rousseau's Conscience in Modern Moral Philosophy. Lavin aims to reassess traditional understandings of the importance of Rousseau's moral philosophy. While all agree that Rousseau's work constitutes a step towards the development of a typically modern conception of practical philosophy (for instance, in the importance of autonomy to his political philosophy), the consensus has been that this influence was merely indirect, through providing a certain rhetorical inspiration to Kant—and that it was only with the latter that the connection between the *freedom* or self-determining character of human action and moral requirement was made. However, Lavin argues that it was Rousseau who "already made the crucial 'Kantian' move [of taking] conscience to be not merely a source of sympathetic motivation … but rather the fundamental principle of the free human will". In so doing, Lavin presents a compelling case for the rehabilitation of Rousseau as an important theorist of moral requirement and action in his own right. And this is not merely of historical, but also of great systematic interest. For as Lavin suggests, if we appreciate the fact that Rousseau already had a theory that grounded the idea of moral requirement in conscience—and that is, he argues, in the autonomy of the human will—this reveals that not every such theory needs to be Kantian in nature, or be responsive to specifically Kantian concerns.

Lavin argues that like Kant, Rousseau rejects both "empirical naturalism" (e. g., Hume and contemporary expressivists) and "rational intuitionism" (e. g., Price and contemporary value realists) about moral requirement. Roughly, for the former, morality requires acting out of a sentiment or motive (for instance sympathy) that must be understood independently of an appraisal of the goodness of the action (indeed, goodness will itself be a function of what agents are in this way motivated to do). Rational intuitionism, balking at the empirical naturalist's apparent rejection of the idea that there is such a thing as *objective* moral requirement, insists instead that there is no essential connection between the moral qualities of actions and our motivational faculties: moral requirements are knowable objectively, through a power to perceive or intuit them. Through a detailed investigation of Rousseau's moral psychology (specifically, his distinction between *amour-de-soi* and *amour propre*—i. e., roughly, between natural and rational appetite) Lavin argues that Rousseau accepts the rationalist's commitment to the idea that moral requirements can be known objectively, and the empirical naturalist's insistence that moral action must be performed for the right kind of motive. The relevant source of motivation, it emerges, is what Rousseau calls conscience. Although some interpreters have been misled into thinking of Rousseau as an empirical naturalist because of his reference to conscience as a *sentiment* or *instinct*, Lavin shows that Rousseau thinks of conscience as an irreducibly rational and social faculty that essentially characterizes human beings. And the groundbreaking move often attributed only to Kant, which Lavin identifies already in Rousseau, is to insist that good action simply *is* action that accords with conscience. But unlike Kant, Lavin argues, Rousseau remains unfazed by what he calls "the problem of content": that (as argued by Hume) an analysis of good action as action performed *because it is good* threatens to leave us without a principle allowing us to identify good actions. Where the Kantian feels pressure to show how contentful moral norms can be derived from the (seemingly empty) idea of agreement with practical reason, Lavin shows that Rousseau rejects this felt philosophical urge for *ethical* reasons. As Lavin explains, Rousseau's response to the moral skeptic is thus thoroughly *quietist:* "Rousseau is not worried about discovering something horrible—that there is no principle, and so no morality. He is concerned about what he would have to be like to want to investigate such things".

Anastasia Berg—Kant and the Freedom to Do What We Want. Berg takes up the question of how, on a Kantian understanding of practical reason and action, to make sense of the possibility of free action that is not action from duty. It is a given that we often perform many actions that are neither morally required nor prohibited, and perform them freely—but how can this be, if freedom is supposed to consist in an action having its source in the moral law? Berg argues against the received interpretative and systematic solution to this problem, which relies on the so-called Incorporation Thesis: the idea that the desires on which one acts, in cases of non-moral free action, must first be incorporated into a maxim that conforms with the moral law. Berg not only argues that the Incorporation Thesis is insufficiently substantiated by the relevant texts—for Kant arguably does not speak of *individual* desires being incorporated into a maxim on every particular occasion of action—but also that it saddles Kantians with a systematically unconvincing view of *both* moral and non-moral free action. This is because the Incorporation Thesis cannot explain how particular desires, thought of as extra-rationally "given," could so much as provide *candidates* for reasons to be acted on: from the point of view of pure practical reason, it seems, the mere fact that something is desired cannot recommend it as an end to be pursued. On the alternative reading Berg defends, what is admitted into one's maxim— which she argues is not the maxim governing a particular action but instead a general, "supreme," or character-defining maxim—is not a particular desire but a *Triebfeder*.[21] Berg argues that we may then see agents as admitting both moral and non-moral *Triebfedern* into their will, i.e., as recognizing two kinds of princi-

---

21 While this term is often translated as "incentive," Berg explains it may be best to leave it untranslated.

ples on which they might act. The possibility of acting on *material* principles is then always already provided for by practical reason: there is no need to somehow rationally sanctify certain particular, extra-rational desires. If this is right, it also has profound repercussions for the way we understand moral action: rather than viewing ourselves as having to decide which extra-rational principle to "endorse" reflectively, the question instead becomes which *Triebfeder* of practical reason we give priority over the other.

Part III: Political Philosophy

Anton Ford and Benjamin Laurence—The Parts and Whole of Plato's Republic. In this essay, the authors address a fundamental question about the interpretation of Plato's *Republic*, the answer to which they argue has far-reaching consequences for systematic moral and political philosophy. The question is how to interpret the relation between Socrates' (or Plato's) account of justice as a characteristic of the individual human *soul* (*psychic* justice), and of justice as a characteristic of the city or political community (*civic* justice). Socrates, challenged by his interlocutors to provide the former account, famously insists that to do so, it is necessary to investigate the latter: the account of the just and happy city is developed, it seems, as a way to reach clarity on justice as a virtue of individual human beings. Many 20th century interpreters have tried to understand Socrates' move as an appeal to an analogy, and as a result have considered the argument unsatisfactory: why assume that psychic justice is in any way *like* civic justice? Moreover, even if we accept the principle that like justice in the city, justice in the soul consists in a certain harmony of its parts, this still seems to leave open the very question that Socrates' interlocutors began by pressing him on: whether justice (understood as the disposition to, say, not cheat, steal or harm one's fellow citizens) benefits the individual human being.

Ford and Laurence argue that Socrates' account of civic justice is not at all intended to provide an *analogy* to psychic justice. Instead, they propose, Socrates is insisting that the two justices are in fact *one*—in the same way that when we ask after what constitutes the health of a human body and of a human hand, we are not asking after two *different* things. For when it comes to *natural* unities, like that of a living body, an account of the well-functioning of the whole is presupposed by, and will itself contain, an account of the well-functioning of the part. And Socrates holds precisely that human beings are *by nature* part of a city, the function of which is a form of cooperation or partnership in pursuit of the good. On such an understanding, it will be no mystery why an account of psychic justice requires one of civic justice. But at the same time, it will explain why (as Socrates also insists) our understanding of the good of the whole can be *influenced* by our understanding of the good of the parts (just as a better understanding of how the hand functions may influence our understanding of what constitutes a healthy body).

Why has this interpretative option (which, as Ford and Laurence point out, was common sense until the second half of the 20th century) remained unnoticed by so many modern readers of the *Republic?* Ford and Laurence show how a tendency to read a certain kind of *individualism* into Plato's political philosophy has muddied the waters. Roughly, the assumption is that, since Socrates says that the function of the city is to promote the good of its members, the good of the individual members must be *prior to* the good of community—and so, that the good of each involves no reference to the good of the others. But, they argue, this assumption is alien to the *Republic*, and the insistence to project individualism onto the *Republic* keeps us from taking seriously an attractive *systematic* position. Ford and Laurence argue that on a correct reading, Plato's *Republic* can help us see that the demand to show justice to belong to the good life should be rejected, if it is posed in such a way as to assume that the good of the individual must be opposed to that of others—i.e., if the demand is "to be shown that justice pays in a coin that does not already bear its stamp".

What we can learn from the *Republic* is that we do not have to construe the activity of living together in those terms: instead, the good of each member of the *polis* may be intertwined with that of each other. But to accept this is not necessarily to commit to the substance of Socrates' account of what good living consists in: we may accept the *form* of the Platonic account while rejecting its content, thus for instance rejecting the idea that for human beings, a good society can be one which exhibits the class distinctions Socrates insists on.

Wolfram Gobsch—Philosophizing as Dying: Self-Knowledge and Reconciliation in Hegel. Gobsch's aim is to reconstruct and defend Hegel's conception of philosophy through reflection on the latter's understanding of the relation between philosophical knowledge and knowledge of the good. The central challenge is that of reconciling two characterizations of philosophical knowledge, which according to Hegel is at once knowledge of the absolute, as well as *self*-knowledge—i.e., knowledge of the finite subject who philosophizes, or equally "its own time comprehended in thought." Gobsch explains that these two characterizations of philosophy, for Hegel, can be held together insofar as in philosophy, "the finite spirit of its time" is comprehended, in its "passing away," as "the presence of the absolute". That is, as self-knowledge, what philosophy comprehends is that the activity of the subject (her living according to a particular form of "ethical life") is "unconditionally necessary"—but precisely *in* doing so, comprehends it as essentially finite, limited, and thus "corrupted." Philosophy offers a form of reconciliation with the finite spirit of our times: it allows us to see the necessity of the way things are, and of its passing away. But precisely for that reason, philosophical self-understanding offers no practical orientation: *"the modality of philosophical insight is ultimately not a modality of practical knowledge"* (Gobsch). Instead, philosophical comprehension *is* the demise of the spirit of the time, and in that sense, the *dying* of the philosophizing subject—Minerva's owl, we will remember, flies only at dusk.

In this understanding of philosophical knowledge as distinct from practical knowledge, Hegel's philosophy distances itself from a great variety of thinkers to whom the highest point of philosophy (arguably) *is* a form of knowledge of the good, or at least a way of removing obstacles to a sound form of living: figures as diverse as Aristotle, Kant, Marx, Adorno and Wittgenstein. Accordingly, the conception of philosophy that Gobsch develops distinguishes itself not only from other forms of idealism, but also from so-called philosophical *quietism* (roughly, a Wittgensteinian or therapeutic conception of philosophy). At the same time, this is not to simply do away with the very idea of practical knowledge. Indeed, the point of departure for Gobsch's systematic defense of the Hegelian conception is the idea that philosophy is an attempt to answer the question "Who am I?" and thus an attempt to reach *self*-knowledge. And the "self" known in philosophy, Gobsch argues, is essentially one capable of free *self-determination:* a subject of intentional action, and thus of practical knowledge.

However, the notion of self-determination is threatened with a contradiction: to determine ourselves means *both* to view ourselves as acting out of an unconditional "practical law," *and* as distinguishing ourselves from that purely formal principle as a subject with particular, contingent desires. The key to resolving this contradiction lies in the notion of *mutual recognition*, in which two subjects are simultaneously *distinguished from* and *identified with* the practical law. The answer to the philosophical question "Who am I?" thus points towards "the reality of a shared practical life" (Gobsch): in Hegel's terms, "objective spirit," which is eventually revealed to be *ethical life* (*Sittlichkeit*). Although it would go too far to reconstruct Gobsch's meticulous argument in its entirety, we can already begin to see that for the Hegelian, self-determination requires the existence of an *objective* "spirit of the times." And if an objectively existing ethical life is the source and condition of our thought of the good, it follows that it is "impossible for us even to think a higher good apart from the good of our own ethical life" (Gobsch). For the Hegelian, there can be no thought of the good that is not thought of *actuality*. As Gobsch argues, this accounts for both philosophy's inability to provide practical orientation, and for the need to view ethical life as *passing away*, since a philosophical comprehension of our ethical life will reveal the ground of its existence to lie outside of itself, in the absolute.

Alec Hinshelwood—The Work of Human Hands: Marx on Humanity as Solidarity. It is precisely the Hegelian understanding of the self-conscious particularity of the subject of action and, as a consequence, of philosophy's inability to provide practical orientation that is challenged by Alec Hinshelwood in *The Work of Human Hands*. Hinshelwood's aim is to reconstruct a problematic to which, he argues, we can view both Hegel and Marx as being responsive—and argues that only the latter's response can be successful. Hinshelwood's contribution therefore not only articulates a powerful criticism of the Hegelian conception of self-conscious particularity and ethical life, but also paves the way to a renewed understanding of the specifically *philosophical* importance of Marx's work.

The problematic in question is what Hinshelwood calls "the problem of practical solipsism," which he initially develops as a problem for neo-Aristotelian ethical naturalist views.[22] On the Aristotelian view, the good at which we aim in action is determined by the *lifeform* that we fall under (in our case, *human being*). And according to at least some neo-Aristotelians, we possess (at least in the ideal case of a virtuous agent) a specifically self-conscious, non-empirical, and *practical* knowledge of the good. However, Hinshelwood argues, since the good that we are supposed to know in that manner is a *natural telos*, the neo-Aristotelian cannot make good on that promise. The worry is that the sense in which a lifeform might make it no accident that we act in certain ways cannot explain the possibility of first-personal knowledge of those ways of acting. In order for our thoughts about what to do to amount to knowledge, we would have to understand them as holding true of an empirical object (i.e., the lifeform). And Hinshelwood argues that there would then be no way of applying them self-consciously to *ourselves*. It would follow that the very idea of a manifold of practical thinkers to which we belong would fall apart: we could not view ourselves as being one particular among many subjects who fall under one and the same principle of goodness (what Gobsch called a "practical law").[23]

As Hinshelwood, echoing Marx's *Theses on Feuerbach*, explains the resulting insight: the manifold to which subjects of practical thought belong cannot be "an inner, mute general character which unites the many individuals *in a natural way*" (Marx 1998, 570). And in a manner similar to Gobsch, Hinshelwood argues that we can understand the Hegelian account of recognition as responding to this difficulty concerning the particularity and generality of the practical thinker. But Hinshelwood disagrees with the Hegelian about the right way to develop this insight. He argues that the Hegelian conception of recognition is as unable to solve

---

22 Again, see, for example, Foot (2001) and Thompson (2008).
23 The resulting predicament is a form of solipsism in a sense similar to the solipsism of the Tractarian thinker, who Wittgenstein famously denies is *in* the world—even if in the present context (in contrast to the *Tractatus*) this is taken as a problem rather than insight, since Hinshelwood argues that the resulting solipsism would render practical thought impossible.

the problem of practical solipsism as the Aristotelian, insofar as it relies on the assumption that we can understand the particularity of the subject *first* in terms of her possessing a certain range of arbitrary, merely natural or *given* desires—a givenness or particularity which must then be corrected or rectified by the habituating influence of institutions of ethical life that, as *objective*, stand over and above the subject. And so Hinshelwood argues that this assumption is untenable. Following Marx, he sketches the contours of a different view, on which human sociality from the start permeates the particularity of our desires—a view on which the tie that binds us is neither simply natural, nor an ethical life that has its source outside of our practice, but lies instead within our own hands.[24]

Together, the essays by Gobsch and Hinshelwood thus illustrate how Hegel and Marx's different answers to the question of how philosophy relates to practice, or to *life*, depend on their respective conceptions of what it means to know ourselves as particular, but self-consciously desiring subjects. And both positions can in turn be seen to relate in different ways to the Platonic (and perhaps also Aristotelian) model proposed by Ford and Laurence. Like the latter, Hinshelwood rejects the assumption that the good of a particular human being can be understood without reference to the good of her fellows. But unlike them, he insists that certain forms of societal organization (e.g., a distinction between a Platonic class of guardians and producers) are ruled out not on the level of the *content* of our theory of the human good, but at the level of its form. In this insistence on the importance of mutual recognition and the demand for certain forms of equality that flows from it, it seems the Marxist and the Hegelian both reject an understanding of the relation between our individual and collective good as a merely natural bond.[25]

References

Anscombe, Gertrude Elizabeth Margaret (1963): *Intention*. Cambridge: Harvard University Press.
Broome, John (2013): *Rationality Through Reasoning*. Malden: Wiley-Blackwell.
Engstrom, Stephen P. (2009): *The Form of Practical Knowledge: A Study of the Categorical Imperative*. Cambridge: Harvard University Press.
Foot, Phillipa (2001): *Natural Goodness*. Oxford: Oxford University Press.
Ford, Anton, Hornsby, Jennifer, and Stoutland, Frederick (Eds.) (2011): *Essays on Anscombe's* Intention. Cambridge: Harvard University Press.

---

[24] To echo Marx's (1998, 570) *Theses on Feuerbach* again: "human essence" would then be "the ensemble of the social relations."

[25] I would like to thank Jesse Mulder and my co-editor James Conant for helpful conversations and comments on this introduction. For their work on the manuscripts in this volume, the editors would like to thank Stephen Cunniff, Melinda Johnston, Amy Levine, and Michael Powell.

Frege, Gottlob (1979): "Logic (1879–1891)." In: Frege, Gottlob: *Posthumous Writings*. Hans Hermes, Friedrich Kambartel, and Friedrich Kaulbach with the assistance of Gottfried Gabriel and Walburga Rödding (Eds.). Peter Long and Roger White with the assistance of Raymond Hargreaves (Trans.). Oxford: Basil Blackwell.
Kenny, Anthony (1966): "Practical Inference." In: *Analysis* 26. No. 3, 65–75.
Korsgaard, Christine (2009): *Self-Constitution: Agency, Identity, and Integrity*. Oxford: Oxford University Press.
Lavin, Douglas (2013): "Must there be basic action?" In: *Noûs* 47. No. 2, 273–301.
Lavin, Douglas (2017): "Forms of rational agency." In: *Royal Institute of Philosophy Supplements* 80, 171–193.
Marcus, Eric (2018): "Practical Knowledge as Knowledge of a Normative Judgment." In: *Manuscrito* 41. No. 4, 319–347.
Marx, Karl (1998): "Theses on Feuerbach." In: Marx, Karl and Engels, Friedrich: *The German Ideology*. New York: Prometheus Books, 569–571.
McDowell, John (1996): *Mind and World*. Cambridge: Harvard University Press.
McDowell, John (2010): "What Is the Content of an Intention in Action?" In: *Ratio* 23. No. 4, 415–432.
Müller, Anselm Winfried (1979): "How theoretical is practical reason?" In: Diamond, Cora and Teichman, Jenny (Eds.): *Intention and Intentionality: Essays in Honour of G. E. M. Anscombe*. Ithaca: Cornell University Press, 91–108.
Ripstein, Arthur (2010): *Force and Freedom*. Cambridge: Harvard University Press.
Rödl, Sebastian (2007): *Self-Consciousness*. Cambridge: Harvard University Press.
Schwenkler, John (2019): *Anscombe's Intention: A Guide*. New York: Oxford University Press.
Setiya, Kieran (2008): "Practical knowledge." In: *Ethics* 118. No. 3, 388–409.
Thompson, Michael (2008): *Life and Action: Elementary Structures of Practice and Practical Thought*. Cambridge: Harvard University Press.
Velleman, J. David (2004): "Précis of The Possibility of Practical Reason." In: *Philosophical Studies* 121. No. 3, 225–238.
Wallace, R. Jay (2020): "Practical Reason." In: Zalta, Edward N. (Ed.): *The Stanford Encyclopedia of Philosophy* (Spring 2020 edition). https://plato.stanford.edu/archives/spr2020/entries/practical-reason, last accessed April 19th, 2023.

Part I: **Action & Practical Reasoning**

John McDowell
Self-Consciousness in Acting

Abstract: This essay considers Anscombe's account of practical knowledge, the non-observational and non-contemplative "knowledge that a man has of his intentional actions" (Anscombe 1963, 50–51), and investigates how such knowledge can fit into a more general conception of self-consciousness. Doing so will allow us to see that, as self-knowledge generally is "the same reality" (Rödl 2007, 14) as its object, the idea that practical knowledge is the (formal) "cause of what it understands" (a dictum that Anscombe adopts from Aquinas) does not as such constitute a mark distinguishing self-knowledge of action from other forms of self-knowledge. This in turn allows us to avoid a pitfall: the idea that action, as the conclusion of practical reasoning, must be necessitated by the premises—as well as the accompanying idea that every action must be derived from a final or "infinite" end (Rödl 2007, 38).

1. My topic is what G. E. M. Anscombe in *Intention*[1] calls "practical knowledge" or, at one point, "the knowledge that a man has of his intentional actions" (Anscombe 1963, 50–51). Anscombe does not explicitly describe practical knowledge as a case of self-consciousness, but I think putting what she says in that context helps to make sense of it. But first, I will spend some time working through Anscombe's discussion.

2. First, knowledge of one's actions is not observational.
Anscombe singles out intentional actions by whether the question "Why?" in a certain sense has application.[2] The relevant sense is one in which the question asks for someone's reason for doing something. But in Anscombe's project, that explanation of the question is off limits. It would presuppose that we understand the idea of reasons for acting, which is part of the conceptual region she wants to elucidate. So, she explains the question in a roundabout way, which includes listing kinds of case in which it does *not* apply. And one way of rejecting the question is to say "I knew I was doing that, but only because I observed it" (Anscombe 1963, 14). So, knowledge of one's actions is not observational.

---

1 Anscombe (1963).
2 See Anscombe (1963, 9).

3. Second, practical knowledge is not just not observational but also not contemplative. Contemplative knowledge owes its being knowledge to the independent actuality of what is known. Observational knowledge is contemplative in that sense, but not all contemplative knowledge is observational. So, it could be that practical knowledge is not observational but still contemplative in some other way. Anscombe argues that it is not.

She arrives at this by a train of thought that starts with a skeptical question about the claim that knowledge of one's intentional actions is, as she sometimes puts it, "without observation": "is it reasonable to say that one 'knows without observation' that one is [for instance] painting a wall yellow?" (Anscombe 1963, 50). And she responds:

> When knowledge or opinion are present concerning what is the case, and what can happen—say Z—if one does certain things, say ABC, then it is possible to have the intention of doing Z in doing ABC; and if the case is one of knowledge or if the opinion is correct, then doing or causing Z is an intentional action, and it is not by observation that one knows one is doing Z; or in so far as one is observing, inferring etc. that Z is actually taking place, one's knowledge is not the knowledge that a man has of his intentional actions. By the knowledge that a man has of his intentional actions I mean the knowledge that one denies having if when asked e. g. "Why are you ringing that bell?" one replies "Good heavens! I didn't know *I* was ringing it!" (Anscombe 1963, 50–51).

The claim that knowledge of one's intentional actions is "without observation" might have seemed to imply that there is *no* room for observational knowledge when one is, e.g., painting a wall yellow, and the question expresses a well-placed skepticism about that. But here she concedes that someone who is doing Z (e.g., painting a wall yellow) *may* be observing that Z is actually taking place (in that case, that the wall is actually becoming yellow).³ It is just that in so far as he does have observational knowledge of what is happening to the wall, *that* knowledge "is not the knowledge that a man has of his intentional actions."

And now the question becomes: how can conceding that the painter may have observational knowledge of the relevant happening on the surface of the wall cohere with claiming that that happening is *also* an object for non-observational knowledge of it as something he is intentionally effecting? As she puts it:

> If there are two *ways* of knowing here, one of which I call knowledge of one's intentional action and the other of which I call knowledge by observation of what takes place, then must there not be two *objects* of knowledge? How can one speak of two different knowledges of *exactly* the same thing? (Anscombe 1963, 51).

---

3 "Z" shifts, in Anscombe's presentation, between what one is doing and what one is causing.

Confronted with this difficulty, one can be tempted to conceive objects of practical knowledge as inner items, distinct from any observable happening. But Anscombe dismisses such conceptions as nonsense.[4] They make it unintelligible how a public happening can be the execution of an intention.

The source of this trouble, Anscombe suggests, is a failure to realize that knowledge of a happening as the execution of one's intention is not contemplative:

> Can it be that there is something that modern philosophy has blankly misunderstood: namely what ancient and medieval philosophers meant by *practical knowledge?* Certainly in modern philosophy we have an incorrigibly contemplative conception of knowledge. Knowledge must be something that is judged as such by being in accord with the facts. The facts, reality, are prior, and dictate what is to be said, if it is knowledge. And this is the explanation of the utter darkness in which we found ourselves. For if there are two knowledges—one by observation, the other in intention—then it looks as if there must be two objects of knowledge; but if one says the objects are the same, one looks hopelessly for the different *mode of contemplative knowledge* in acting, as if there were a very queer and special sort of seeing eye in the middle of the acting (Anscombe 1963, 57).

Recall Anscombe's case of the person who was unknowingly ringing a bell. Imagine a case like hers except that the person knows he is ringing the bell. There is a happening consisting in the bell's ringing, which (since the case is like Anscombe's) the person knows through hearing it, so observationally. And that same happening is also known to the person as his doing. Anscombe's point is that if contemplative knowledge is the only kind under which we can bring this second bit of knowledge, we are stuck with the plainly hopeless picture of "a very queer and special sort of seeing eye in the middle of the acting."

4. At this point, Anscombe says we need to understand practical reasoning before we can understand practical knowledge.[5] And she embarks on a discussion of Aristotle on practical syllogisms.

The discussion is complex, but for my purposes the essentials are enough. The conclusion of a practical syllogism is acting in a certain way—not coming to accept a proposition. There is a premise that specifies something that, when the syllogism issues in an action, is revealed as an end for whose sake the agent is acting; and another premise or set of premises in the light of which the action that is the conclusion can be seen to be a means to or way of pursuing that end.

It would be absurd to think there is practical syllogizing whenever there is intentional action. "The interest of the account is that it describes an order which is

---

4 See Anscombe (1963, 51–53).
5 See Anscombe (1963, 57).

there whenever actions are done with intentions" (Anscombe 1963, 80). And Anscombe notices that the order brought out by Aristotle's account of practical reasoning is the same as an order she described earlier in terms of a succession of questions "Why?" and answers to them: "Why are you moving your arm up and down?"—"In order to work the pump" or "Because I am pumping."—"Why are you pumping?"—"In order to replenish the house water supply" or "Because I am replenishing the house water supply" (Anscombe 1963, 37–47). And so on.

The topic of intentional action can seem an unmanageable multiplicity. But this order makes it manageable: "Aristotle's 'practical reasoning' or my order of questions 'Why?' can be looked at as a device which reveals the order that there is in this chaos" (Anscombe 1963, 80).

5. When Anscombe returns to practical knowledge, she exploits the order that has emerged from her discussion of practical reasoning, to explain "a *form* of description of events."[6] (By "events" she means what I have been calling "happenings.") If a description has the form, it describes, or at least purports to describe, a happening as intentional on the part of an agent. The mark of the form is that a description can have "in order to …" or "because …" (in one sense) attached to it. Adding "in order to …" locates a description in Aristotle's version of the order; adding "because …" locates a description in Anscombe's version of it.[7]

She gives an example: "I slid on the ice because I felt cheerful." If I can say that "my sliding on the ice" has the form she is explaining; it describes the sliding as intentional on my part. "Because I felt cheerful" explains the action in a way that could also be done by saying, e.g., "in order to express my cheerfulness." Not so if I slid on the ice because, e.g., I lost my footing.

Some verbs or verb phrases, e.g., "marrying," are unlike "sliding on ice" in that one can know that a description of a happening has the form just on the basis that one of those verbs or verb phrases figures in it. Others, e.g., "offending," are unlike "sliding on ice," and like "marrying," in that their sense depends on their being able to figure in descriptions that have the form; but unlike "marrying" in that a description of a happening in which one of them figures may or may not have the form, depending on whether it admits of supplementation with "in order to …" or "because …" in the relevant sense.

The point of saying "the term 'intentional' has reference to a *form* of description of events" is to insist that being intentional is not "an extra property" of the

---

6 See Anscombe (1963, 84).
7 "Because (in one sense)" obviously points to answers to the question "Why?" in the sense she explained earlier in the book.

happenings of which it is true: a property possessed by happenings that would be the happenings they are even if they were not intentional on the part of the relevant agent (Anscombe 1963, 84). Being intentional is *intrinsic* to the happenings of which it is true.

6. Anscombe now makes two remarks as a preliminary to her explanation of practical knowledge.[8]

First: "a great many descriptions of events effected by human beings are *formally* descriptions of executed intentions" (Anscombe 1963, 87). They are descriptions that have the form she has explained.

Second: if someone intends to be doing something in particular, it is exceptional for there not to be a happening that is that intention getting executed, at any rate if we consider "a man's performance in its more immediate descriptions."

What one is doing intentionally may have the form of a *kinēsis:* one will have done what one intends only if one reaches a certain terminus. And one can be, e. g., painting a wall yellow even if one is not going to finish painting it yellow. Anscombe's point in the second remark is not the obviously false claim that failure to bring projects to completion is exceptional, but that it is exceptional, if someone intends to be doing something, for there not to be a happening consisting in that intention's being in the course of getting executed: in that case, a happening that includes the wall's being in the course of becoming yellow.

And now she gives her explanation of practical knowledge:

> If we put these considerations together, we can say that where (*a*) the description of an event is of a type to be formally the description of an executed intention [and] (*b*) the event is actually the execution of an intention (by our criteria) then the account given by Aquinas of the nature of practical knowledge holds: Practical knowledge is "the cause of what it understands," unlike "speculative" knowledge, which "is derived from the objects known." This means more than that practical knowledge is observed to be a necessary condition of the production of various results; or that an idea of doing such-and-such in such-and-such ways is such a condition. It means that without it [that is, without practical knowledge] what happens does not come under the description—execution of intentions—whose characteristics we have been investigating (Anscombe 1963, 87–88).

As she said in the second preliminary remark, when someone intends to be doing something in particular, there usually is a happening that is that intention getting executed. In these terms, the point she made by invoking a distinctive form of description was that the happening's being the intention getting executed is intrinsic to it. Nothing could be *that* happening if it was not that intention getting executed.

---

8 See Anscombe (1963, 87).

And that can be expressed by saying the happening's being that intention getting executed is its *formal cause.*

But a happening's being an intention getting executed is the *same* fact as its being an object for the agent's practical knowledge: that is, its being available to the agent to be known as being effected by her under the description that gives the content of her intention. So, we can say being an object for the agent's practical knowledge is the formal cause of the happening. That is the thesis Anscombe finds in Aquinas.

7. Anscombe applies the formula from Aquinas to happenings that are intentions getting executed. That is the significance of conditions (*a*) and (*b*). We might wonder what we should say about knowledge in intention in the cases—she has said that they are rare but not that they are non-existent—in which someone intends to be doing something but there is no happening that is the intention getting executed: no happening of which the person's knowledge in intention could be the formal cause.

When Anscombe first returns to practical knowledge after the intervening discussion of practical reasoning, she considers a case of this. She is writing "I am a fool" on the blackboard in her lecture room with her eyes shut. She has knowledge of a happening consisting in the words appearing on the blackboard. That knowledge can only be practical: she knows the happening as being effected by her, and she has no contemplative knowledge of it. But, as she notes, "intentions [can] fail to get executed" (Anscombe 1963, 82). The words might not have been appearing, because something might have gone wrong with the chalk or the surface. In that case she would still have had an intention to be writing those words on the blackboard with her eyes shut, but there would have been no happening consisting in that intention getting executed. There would have been happenings consisting in other intentions getting executed: for instance, her moving the chalk, in intermittent contact with the surface of the blackboard, in the ways required for writing those words. But there would have been no happening consisting in the words appearing on the blackboard.

In a puzzling remark, Anscombe says her knowledge "would have been the same even if this had happened." The remark is puzzling because it seems right to protest in a way she immediately acknowledges:

> If then my knowledge is independent of what actually happens, how can it be knowledge of what does happen? Someone might say that it was a funny sort of knowledge that was still knowledge even though what it was knowledge of was not the case! (Anscombe 1963, 82).

What can she mean by saying her knowledge would have been the same?

In the alternative possible world in which the words do not appear, her intention to be writing those words on the blackboard with her eyes shut is the same. So, her knowledge is the same insofar as it is her self-consciousness in, as she supposes, executing that intention.

But knowledge that one has in, as one supposes, executing an intention comes in two forms. In the alternative possible world, her knowledge is a defective form of a kind of thing whose non-defective form is this: having available to one to be known as one's doing a happening whose description matches the content of one's intention. Her knowledge in the alternative possible world stands to the knowledge she credits herself with in the actual world, knowledge of the happening consisting in those words appearing on the blackboard, as failure to be doing what one intends to be doing stands to actually doing it.

And defective forms need to be understood precisely as defective forms of what they are defective forms of. In the alternative possible world, there is no happening that could have as its formal cause the knowledge in intention whose content is given by her intention to be writing those words on the blackboard. We have to understand her knowledge in intention in that case as a defective form of what Aquinas says practical knowledge is in its non-defective form.

8. Anscombe's example of writing with her eyes shut is paired with a parallel example of someone directing the building of a house without observing or getting reports of what is going on at the site. His knowledge of the happenings at the site can only be practical; he knows them as effected by him, and he has no contemplative knowledge of them.

In both these examples practical knowledge figures as an agent's *only* knowledge of some happenings. It would be wrong to interpret this as indicating that in Anscombe's view practical knowledge is in general a way of knowing that the happenings that are its objects are actually happening.

Near the end of her treatment of practical knowledge Anscombe reverts to the example of the building director and says:

> Naturally my imaginary case, in which a man directs operations which he does not see and of which he gets no information, is a very improbable one. Normally someone doing or directing anything makes use of his senses, or of reports given him, the whole time: he will not go on to the next order, for example, until he knows that the preceding one has been executed, or, if he is the operator, his senses inform him of what is going on. This knowledge is of course always "speculative" as opposed to "practical." Thus in any operation we really can speak of two knowledges—the account that one could give of what one was doing, without adverting to observation; and the account of exactly what is happening at a given moment (say) to the material one is working on. The one is practical, the other speculative (Anscombe 1963, 88–89).

Normally, then, an agent needs speculative knowledge of happenings that are thereby available to her to know as her doing. ("Speculative" is another way of saying "contemplative"; Anscombe has switched to Aquinas' term.) It is only in special cases, as perhaps when a skilled writer writes short strings of words with her eyes shut, that practical knowledge might be sufficient by itself for knowing the actuality of a happening that its agent can know, not contemplatively, as effected by her.

The doctrine Anscombe finds in Aquinas is that the formal cause of a happening intentionally effected by an agent is its being an object for the agent's practical knowledge. That does not require that the agent actually knows it as her doing. What it requires is, as I have occasionally put it, that it is *available* to her to be known as her doing. She may need contemplative knowledge of the happening for the potentiality implicit in that use of "available" to be actualized.

Donald Davidson imagined someone setting out to make ten copies of a document all at once by interleaving ten sheets of paper with carbon paper and writing firmly on the top sheet.[9] If the words are appearing on all the sheets, the person is intentionally making ten copies all at once, but he cannot know he is doing that without looking.

This is often thought to be a counterexample to a doctrine of Anscombe's, but it is not. If the person is getting the words to appear on all the sheets in writing firmly on the top sheet, he is doing that intentionally; the case meets Anscombe's requirements, set out in a passage I quoted in §3 above, for a phrase of the form "doing Z in doing ABC" to describe an intentional action. But contrary to the idea that the example tells against Anscombe, the happening that consists in the words appearing on all the sheets is an object for the agent's practical knowledge in the only sense Anscombe needs. It is available to the agent to be known as his doing; if he finds out by looking that there has been such a happening, he knows, not contemplatively, that it has been intentionally effected by him.

Anscombe's list of ways of rejecting the question "Why?" starts with "I was not aware I was doing that" (Anscombe 1963, 11). This might seem to imply the doctrine to which Davidson offers his case as a counterexample, that someone cannot be doing something intentionally unless she knows she is doing it. But it does not. Davidson's agent cannot know he is writing on all the sheets at once until he checks whether the requisite things are happening, by observation or other contemplative ways of knowing. But if he has not checked and so does not know the words are appearing on all the sheets, he will not invoke his lack of knowledge to reject the question "Why?" This lack of knowledge does not disqualify "making ten copies all at once" from being a description of an executed intention.

---

9 See Davidson (2001, 92).

Practical knowledge is knowledge, concerning a happening whose actuality one may need to know contemplatively if it is to figure in one's knowledge at all, that it is one's intention getting executed. Even if one knows only contemplatively that the relevant thing is happening, one's knowledge, concerning that happening, that it is one's intention getting executed is not contemplative. It is an instance of the self-knowledge of an agent.

9. In the last few pages, I have begun to frame practical knowledge as a species of self-consciousness.

The idea of knowledge that is the formal cause of its object is not special to practical knowledge. It fits *all* varieties of self-knowledge, in this sense: knowledge expressible in the first person, not mediated by an identification of oneself with an item about which one knows the relevant thing otherwise than first-personally. My knowledge that I have an ache in my knee is self-knowledge in that sense; it is not mediated by knowledge that a certain person has an ache in his knee plus knowledge that I am that person. Contrast my knowledge of how much I weigh: it is not self-knowledge in the relevant sense, even though I can express it in the first person, because it is mediated by my knowing, e.g., how much the person who was standing on a certain scale weighed plus knowing that I was that person.

My self-consciousness in feeling an ache in my knee is intrinsic to the state of consciousness that my feeling the ache is. And my self-consciousness in believing something is intrinsic to the believing. Sebastian Rödl says that in self-consciousness in all its varieties knowing and what is known are "the same reality" (Rödl 2007, 14). We can express Rödl's idea by saying knowledge in self-consciousness is the formal cause of its objects.

If knowledge that is the formal cause of its objects is not restricted even to self-consciousness in acts of reason, let alone to self-consciousness in acts of practical reason, intentional actions, that may seem to cast doubt on how I have interpreted the formula from Aquinas. Should not the formula specify what is *practical* about practical knowledge?

No. Practical knowledge is practical not by virtue of being the formal cause of its objects, something it shares with all varieties of self-consciousness, but by virtue of the form of the descriptions under which its objects are known: what Anscombe explains, in effect, as the form that belongs to descriptions of conclusions of practical reasoning. We can set aside self-consciousness in such things as bodily feelings. Self-consciousness in an act of reason, theoretical or practical, is consciousness of its object as the act of reason it is. And descriptions of practical and theoretical acts of reason—the descriptions under which they are objects for the self-consciousness of their subjects—differ in form according to the form of the reasoning of which the acts they describe are such as to be conclusions;

or, what comes to the same thing, the form of the explanations that explain those acts as the acts of reason they are.

I said "the reasoning of which the acts they describe are *such as to be* conclusions"; I am not implying that any act of reason *is* a conclusion of some reasoning. As Anscombe says, the interest of Aristotle's account of practical reasoning does not require the idea that intentional action always issues from reasoning. The point is this: a description that represents an act as an act of, say, practical reason has a form by virtue of which it represents what it describes as belonging to a sort that conclusions of practical reasoning belong to. That is in effect how Anscombe explains the form of description under which objects of practical knowledge are known.

Self-consciousness in general is the formal cause of what it knows. Practical knowledge, self-consciousness in acting, is *practical* self-consciousness. It is the self-consciousness of someone who is effecting a happening describable in the form Anscombe explains in terms of the form of practical reasoning.

10. I have found in Anscombe the claim that intentional actions figure in the self-consciousness of their agents under descriptions that represent them as belonging to a kind instantiated by conclusions of practical reasoning. And about the distinctive character of practical reasoning, Anscombe follows Aristotle. We can summarize her account like this: a practical syllogism has a premise through the good and a premise (or perhaps a set of premises) through the possible, and its conclusion is acting.[10]

What I have said about self-consciousness in acts of reason in general comes from Rödl. But according to Rödl, to say practical reasoning concludes in acting "is no account of practical reasoning" (Rödl 2007, 19). Not that practical reasoning does not conclude in acting, but he thinks we must understand practical reasoning as concluding in a *thought* that "joins a subject with an action-form in a manner that represents the latter as to be done"; we must comprehend the unity of the movement that the acting is with a thought of that form. He uses "I * do A" (or less abstractly "I should do A") to express what he calls "this form of predication." And he argues that on pain of putting in doubt the unity of our topic, we must expound a *system* of forms of answers to the question practical reasoning addresses.

Anscombe, in contrast, seems content to say a practical syllogism concludes in acting, that is, effecting a happening describable in the form she explains. And the sort of system Rödl demands is conspicuously absent from her discussion of prac-

---

10 The terminology "premise through the good" and "premise through the possible" is from Aristotle, *de Motu Animalium*, VII.

tical reasoning, and her characterization of the same order in terms of the question "Why?" Rödl criticizes Anscombe on this score:

> Anscombe delimits the question "why?" that asks for an action explanation by a list of ways of answering it. She does not explain how these spring from a principle and constitute a system. Thus, she fails to establish that they define one sense of "why?" and thus one concept of action, as opposed to many (Rödl 2007, 44).

11. Rödl's exposition of a system of forms of answers to the question addressed by practical reasoning culminates in this claim: the question is defined by a measure given by a unity of infinite ends, a practical life-form.[11] Self-consciously exemplifying a practical life-form would be an ethical stance. So, according to Rödl, the question addressed by practical reasoning is defined in terms of the way practical reasoning relates to acting on ethical grounds.

Contrast Anscombe, who says: "the practical syllogism is not as such an ethical topic" (Rödl 2007, 78).

Rödl's system starts with instrumental reasoning, which he conceives as reasoning from a thought of the form "I am doing B" to a conclusion of the form "I * do A," where doing A is a means to doing B. In beginning with "I am doing B," this reasoning begins with something that is already an answer to the question what to do. Reflecting about such reasoning cannot tell us what it is to answer the question. We need to consider reasoning that answers the question *de novo*.

As a candidate to meet that need, Rödl first considers reasoning from a desire or a set of desires. But he argues that the question addressed by practical reasoning cannot be explained by some concept like "doing what would best satisfy my present relevant desires taken together." That has the wrong temporality to give the principle of unity of an answer to the question what to do. My desires might change while I am engaged in the intentional action that is my answer to the question.

Only "adherence" to infinite ends has the right temporality. That is how Rödl arrives at his claim that the question is defined by the measure of reasoning with a view to infinite ends.

12. Rödl conceives the first premise of a practical syllogism as an act of will: if not already an answer to the question what to do, as in his conception of instrumental reasoning, then a desire in a sense that includes "adhering" to an infinite end.

For Anscombe, the first premise of a practical syllogism is a specification of something that might be intelligibly desired, not the desiring of it that would be

---

11 See Rödl (2007, 38).

the act of will Rödl envisages as a first premise. She says: "The role of 'wanting' in the practical syllogism is quite different from that of a premise. It is that whatever is described in the starting point of the argument must be wanted in order for the reasoning to lead to any action" (Anscombe 1963, 66). If someone concludes a practical syllogism by acting in a certain way, the good mentioned in its first premise is an end she is pursuing in her action. But that is not to say the first premise of her reasoning was already an act of her will.

Anscombe says the premises are "so to speak, on active service" when they issue in acting (Anscombe 1963, 60). Rödl's idea that the first premise is an act of will applies to premises on active service.

There is a similar point about second premises. In Anscombe's examples they typically state facts in the light of which the action that is the conclusion can be seen to be a means to the end that figures in the first premise. ("Means" here need not be restricted to instrumental reasoning.)[12] Rödl distinguishes second premises from statements to the effect that doing such-and-such would be a means to an end one may or may not decide to pursue. About "Doing A is a means of doing B" as the form of the second premise of an instrumental syllogism, Rödl says: "It is internal to the second premise—it is its form—that through it I am doing A" (Rödl 2011, 223). Again, this remark applies to premises on active service.

Now with premises of the good, the distinction between active service and the potential for it undermines Rödl's progression from instrumental reasoning to reasoning with a view to infinite ends. Doing A as an instrumental means to doing B *can* issue from reasoning that starts from the subject's being engaged in doing B anyway, independently of this reasoning. But it need not. Doing B may *become* an object of the agent's will only when reasoning that starts from B's being worth doing, not yet what she is doing, concludes in her doing A. She settles the question whether to do B only in the act of settling the question whether to do A. So, doing A as a means to doing B can be answering the question what to do *de novo*. There is no need to move to a different form of answer. Rödl's progression need not begin.

13. Rödl's demand for a measure that defines the sense of the practical question reflects his idea that practical reasoning is reasoning towards a thought about what one should do in a certain sense; the required measure is the measure of that "should."

Anscombe says we obscure practical reasoning if we treat it as reasoning towards the truth of a proposition, even one that is somehow "practical," e.g., by

---

12 *Contra* something Rödl implies in *Self-Consciousness* (2007, 18, n. 2).

being about what one ought to do.[13] Does Rödl's conception of reasoning towards thoughts of the form "I * do A" respect this? A thought of that form predicates of its thinker being such that a certain action-form is to be done by her. Surely it is true just in case the action-form *is* to be done by her. How could reasoning towards it not be reasoning towards its truth?

Rödl says: "A term of reasoning is an act of applying concepts, i.e., a thought in the broad sense in which we speak of practical and theoretical thought" (Rödl 2007, 19). But are all acts of thinking in that broad sense acts of *applying* concepts? In the thinking that acting is, the thinker does not apply an action-form to herself. She *realizes* one.

Rödl did not intend to contradict that remark of Anscombe's. He says (in conversation) that if his talk of a form of predication imports the idea of reasoning towards the truth of a proposition, it was inept. With the form "I * do A," he was aiming only to express this thought: if practical reasoning is *reasoning*, self-consciousness in its conclusion must be consciousness of that act as *necessitated* by the reasoning.

There is something right about this. But it does not warrant the demand for a measure.

It is part of what it is for me to be doing A as the conclusion of some reasoning that I conceive A as, if you like, to be done by me on the grounds that figure in the reasoning. But that is not to say the reasoning is towards the thought that A is to be done by me, so that it would need to be governed by a measure for a "should" implicit in that "to be done." The conclusion of my reasoning is doing A, and to say I conceive A as to be done by me is just a way of saying my self-consciousness in doing A is consciousness of doing A as my conclusion from the reasoning.

What does that mean? Here is something Rödl says:

> Inferring something from other things is not just thinking it because one thinks those other things, but thinking it in recognition of the fact that those other things provide sufficient grounds for thinking it. This describes reasoning in general. It is by recognizing this manner of dependence, this form of unity, among acts of the mind in the form of thought that constitutes the unity of actions that we are licensed to speak of practical reasoning: when I want to do *B* because I want to do *A*, and this nexus is constituted by reasoning from a will to do *A* to a will to do *B*, then not only is it the case that my wanting to do *A* explains my wanting to do *B*. It does so on account of my recognition that there is sufficient ground to do *B*, lying in the fact that doing it is a means to doing *A* (Rödl 2011, 233–234).

If we abstract from the exclusive focus on reasoning from what is already an act of will, this is exactly right. Self-consciousness in the conclusion of reasoning of any

---

[13] See Anscombe (1963, 57–58).

kind is consciousness of that act as the conclusion of the reasoning, that is, as sufficiently grounded, by the lights of the relevant kind of reasoning, by its premises.

The conclusion of a theoretical inference is an act of believing, and consciousness of it as the conclusion of the reasoning is consciousness of it as rationally compulsory in the light of the premises, provided one stays committed to the premises. That is what "sufficiently grounded" comes to here. Not that the reasoning is towards the thought that it is rationally compulsory to believe such-and-such; the reasoning is towards believing such-and-such. Even so, it would be reasonable to demand a measure for that rational compulsoriness, and to count that measure as defining the sense of the question what to believe.

If we conceive a practical syllogism as constituted by premises on active service, it can have only the conclusion it has: it necessitates that conclusion. That is Rödl's thought. But this does not imply, as in theoretical reasoning, that the corresponding reasoning makes the conclusion rationally compulsory. The reasoning does that only if it is rationally compulsory for the agent to put those premises on active service, and that is so only in special cases. It is only in special cases that acting in a certain way is rationally compulsory in the light of the reasoning of which it is the conclusion; that is not in general what "sufficiently grounded" comes to in practical reasoning. But in all cases, not just those special cases, consciousness of acting as the conclusion of some reasoning is consciousness of it as sufficiently grounded by the premises. As Anscombe puts it, "the conclusion is an action whose point is shewn by the premises" (Anscombe 1963, 60). That is enough for the reasoning to be reasoning.

I argued that the distinction between active service and the potential for it shows that Rödl's progression need not begin. What we see here is that the point has a wider significance. The relation between practical premises and acting comes into view for Rödl only with premises on active service. That restricts his attention to what it is for an answer to the question what to do to *have been* determined. Practical reasoning, as *determining* answers to the question, goes missing. When one is determining what to do, practical premises are figuring in one's reasoning but not yet on active service. That is true of second premises no less than first premises. If one is doing A in order to do B, the premise that doing A is a means to doing B is on active service: as Rödl says, it is internal to the premise —it is its form—that through it one is doing A. But one gives the premise that form only in the act of determining A as what to do. Rödl's thought does not touch practical reasoning as a procedure for arriving at that act.

The necessity that belongs to actions as answers to the question what to do is irrelevant to the idea of a measure for reasoning that determines those answers. There are as many measures as there are kinds of point acting can have; they need no more unity than is expressed by Anscombe's idea that the premises of practical reasoning show the point of the action that is the conclusion. It does not tell against a candidate measure, as in the second stage of Rödl's progression, that it does not have the right temporality to give the principle of unity of an answer to the question what to do. The principle of unity of an intentional action is given by whatever it is that one is intentionally doing; it is unproblematic that the point of embarking on an intentional action can be lost during the doing. It is not just at its beginning that Rödl's progression to infinite ends reflects a misconception of what practical reasoning is.[14]

References

Anscombe, Gertrude Elizabeth Margaret (1963): *Intention.* Cambridge: Harvard University Press.
Davidson, Donald (2001): "Intending." In: Davidson, Donald: *Essays on Actions and Events.* Oxford: Clarendon Press, 83–102.
Rödl, Sebastian (2007): *Self-Consciousness.* Cambridge: Harvard University Press.
Rödl, Sebastian (2011): "Two forms of practical knowledge and their unity." In: Ford, Anton, Hornsby, Jennifer, and Stoutland, Frederick (Eds.): *Essays on Anscombe's* Intention. Cambridge: Harvard University Press.

---

14 The point here at the end might be put by saying that deciding what to do, answering the question what to do, is not in general to be conceived as coming to *know* what to do. The "practical inference" is not in general a way of acquiring *knowledge.*

Sebastian Rödl
The Practical Syllogism

Abstract: Aristotle framed the idea of a practical syllogism: an act of the mind that is a syllogism and is practical. In this essay, I expound the idea of a practical syllogism, consider a central form of it, the calculating syllogism, and explain how its premises must be conceived if it is to conform to the general concept of a syllogism.

1 The Conclusion of a Practical Syllogism

Not only the idea of a practical syllogism originates with Aristotle. Aristotle also is the first to describe the syllogism in general. It is, he explains, a unity of three acts of the mind such that the first two, the premises, are sufficient for the third, the conclusion. Conversely, the conclusion is necessary on account of the premises.[1] This is the converse, for if the conclusion were not necessary given the premises, then the premises would not be sufficient for the conclusion; something in addition to the premises would be needed. Moreover, the conclusion is conscious of the premises as sufficient for it; it is conscious of itself as necessary on account of the premises.

A theoretical syllogism is one whose conclusion is a judgment that things are so, a judgment of fact. A practical syllogism is one whose conclusion is an action. As the conclusion of a syllogism, this action is conscious of itself as resting on the grounds that are thought in the premises. So, it is conscious of itself: it is a first-person thought, the first-person thought of that very action, "I am doing A." Since it is conscious of itself in the manner of understanding itself to be necessary on account of the premises, it can be expressed in a manner that gives voice to that understanding. So does Aristotle when he calls "I must do A" the conclusion of the syllogism.[2] Furthermore, since I am doing A intentionally when I am doing it in conclusion of a syllogism, the conclusion can be put in a way that makes that explicit: "I want to do A", "I intend to do A." In common discourse, these phrases cannot always take each other's place. Yet they are the same in expressing the conclusion of a practical syllogism in its different aspects: as self-consciousness of the

---

1 Cf. the *Prior Analytics* (Aristotle 1984, 24b19–26).
2 Cf. the *Movement of Animals* (Aristotle 1984, 701a20).

action, as consciousness of it as resting on sufficient grounds, and as will to act, respectively.[3]

It may be said that "I want to do A" does not express an act of will, but a judgment that things are so: they are so that a certain person wants to do a certain thing. Yet it is an unusual use of "I want to do A" in which it does not express one's will to do A, but a judgment of fact. Usually, one uses these words to speak one's will, from the inside, as it were. So they are used when they express the conclusion of a practical syllogism.

Again, it may be said that "I must do A" expresses a judgment, a normative judgment, perhaps. Now, perhaps there is a judgment that can be expressed by this form of words. Even if there is, the usual use of these words is to express an act of will, namely, one that concludes a practical syllogism. To vary an example of Aristotle's: I need Sushi. Sakura delivers. I must call Sakura. Straightaway, I call.[4]

A further way to express the conclusion of a practical syllogism is: "It is good to do A." The term "good", so used, expresses the manner in which an action is conceived in the conclusion of a practical syllogism: it expresses the understanding of one's doing A as resting on sufficient grounds and thus necessary. So, in this use, "good" expresses a consciousness of practical necessity. Just as "I want to do A" does not express a judgment that things are so, when it gives voice to the conclusion of a practical syllogism, so "It is good to do A" does not express a judgment, specifically not an evaluative judgment.

It has been noted that the term "true" can be used as a pro-sentence, standing in for a sentence expressing a judgment that things are so. You say: "It is so:___." I answer: "True." So used, "true" is not a predicate, but a variable. As a variable, it signifies not a property of things, but a form, namely, the form shared by the values of the variable. In the given case, that form is the general form of judgment. There is a use of "good" parallel to that use of "true", a use of it as a prosentence. You say, "Let us plant the tree here." I answer, "Good." The sentence from which my "good" receives its meaning does not articulate a judgment of fact, but an act of will. Again, "good", so used, is not a predicate but a variable, and it signifies not a property but a form. It signifies the form of the will.[5]

This observation may be said to be deflationary in the sense that it deflates an imagined property signified by "true" or "good." In so doing, it is inflationary in the sense that it reveals "good" and "true" to signify the concern of philosophy.

---

3 I understand this to be the result of Michael Thompson's (2008, Part II) seminal paper "Naïve Action Theory."
4 Cf. *Movement of Animals:* "The conclusion 'I must make a coat' is an action" (Aristotle 1984, 701a20).
5 Cf. Rödl (2010).

What is truth? What is goodness? These questions ask for an understanding of what it is to judge and what it is to will. Thus, they articulate the aim of philosophy: self-comprehension of thought in its two species, judgment and will.

This explains the philosophical interest of the syllogism. Inferring, when theoretical, is judging something being conscious of the premises as showing the judgment to be true. (Cf. Frege's explanation of what is meant by "inferring.")[6] Principles of the theoretical syllogism therefore are laws of truth, which need to be understood by her who seeks to know what truth is. (Frege says these laws define the meaning of "true.")[7] Inferring, when practical, is doing something, being conscious of the premises as showing it to be good to do. Hence, principles of the practical syllogism are laws of the good, which she will want to know who wants to know what the good is.

2 The Calculating Syllogism

The premises of a practical syllogism give sufficient grounds for its conclusion. The logical form of the premises must provide for this capacity of theirs: what is thought in them must be such as to give sufficient grounds for doing something. Anscombe says of the practical syllogism that its premises show the point of acting as one does in conclusion of that syllogism.[8] Using this locution, we can say that we need to describe the premises in a way that reveals them to be such as to provide such a point.

Here I will discuss one form of practical syllogism, one kind of point: a syllogism that gives sufficient grounds for doing something by representing doing it as realizing a finite end, a syllogism, that is, that represents the point of doing something as residing in a finite end that doing it serves. In order to distinguish it from other forms of syllogism, I refer to it as the calculating syllogism.

An end is something general that explains what realizes it.[9] A finite end is the terminus of a change. It is finite in the sense that what realizes it brings itself to an end in the end's being realized. In this way a finite end is external: it is external to, it is other than and lies outside, what realizes it. (Finite ends contrast with infinite ends, which are internal: what realizes an infinite end is nothing but itself, and

---

6 See Frege (1979, 3).
7 Frege (1979, 3): "It would not perhaps be beside the mark to say that the laws of logic are nothing other than an unfolding of the content of the word 'true.'"
8 See Anscombe (1963, 60).
9 Cf. Kant's definition of an end in the Critique of the *Power of Judgment*, at §10 (Kant 2000).

hence there is no end to an infinite end.[10] I think there is reasoning that gives grounds for doing something by representing it as realizing an infinite end, reasoning that shows the point of doing something to reside in that end. But that shall not be my topic.)

An end explains the means to it. And in general, what explains something renders necessary what it explains. Now, a calculating syllogism is a thought of doing something in which doing it is recognized as necessary given the end and given that doing it is a means to this end. (Below I shall discuss a doubt directed at the idea that a calculating syllogism represents doing something as necessary, which, given how Aristotle explains "syllogism", doubts the understanding of it as a syllogism. The doubt arises from the observation that it is by accident if doing something is the only, and in this sense a necessary, means to a given end. I set this doubt aside for now.) A calculating syllogism thus is a consciousness of the means as necessary, given the end; equivalently, it is a consciousness of the end as explaining the means to it. It is not a contemplative consciousness of this explanatory nexus. Rather, the nexus obtains in and through that consciousness of it. My end of getting a Jersey cow explains the means to it: it explains why I am headed to Hereford market. It does so as I understand that they have Jersey cows there. So, the calculative syllogism proceeds from the representation of a finite end, this is its first premise. (I shall discuss an objection to this in a moment.) The second premise is a representation of doing something as realizing that end.[11] The conclusion is doing it, in the consciousness of it as realizing the end.

I said we need to describe the premises of the practical syllogism in such a way as to reveal how, in virtue of their form, they suffice for, that is, render necessary, the conclusion. We have done that: the calculating syllogism is a consciousness of an end's explaining the means to it, a consciousness in and through which an end explains sufficient means to it. That consciousness holds together the thought of the end with the thought that doing such-and-such realizes it. Holding these thoughts together is understanding doing such-and-such to be necessary and is doing it in and through so understanding it. Hence, these thoughts are premises of a syllogism whose conclusion is an action.

As this description of the calculating syllogism shows that its premises provide sufficient grounds for the conclusion, it provides a specification of what is meant

---

10 Stephen Engstrom argues that only infinite ends are true ends. True ends, he says, do not come to an end. See Engstrom (2009, 48).
11 I take this to be Aristotle's meaning when he says, of the premises of a practical syllogism, that one relates to the good, the other to the possible *Movement of Animals*, Aristotle (1984, 701a24). For what is wanted is represented as good in the act of wanting it. And representing something as a means to an end is to represent the end as possible through that means.

by "point": the point of doing something may reside in the end in the service of which one is doing it. Equivalently, it provides a specification of "good": something may be good to do on account of its serving a certain end; it is good to do it in the manner of being good for that end.

3 The First Premise of a Calculating Syllogism

Anscombe denies that a calculating syllogism proceeds from a premise of the form "I want to do B."[12] The syllogism, she thinks, has only one premise, a judgment of fact. It reads, not "I want to do B. Doing B is a means to doing A. So, I'll do A," but "Doing B is a means to doing A. So, I'll do A."

Anscombe notes that she who reasons "Doing B is a means to doing A. So, I'll do A" wants to do B. The act of the will is there; and it is there as a condition of the conclusion. Yet it is not a premise. "The role of 'wanting' in the practical syllogism is quite different from that of a premise. It is that whatever is described in the starting point of the argument must be wanted in order for the reasoning to lead to any action" (Anscombe 1963, 66). The starting point of which she speaks is the first and only premise: "Doing A serves the end of doing B." It describes what is wanted with respect to how it may be realized. In her example, "Dry food is suitable" is the starting point; what is wanted is suitable food; it is described in the starting point as attainable by attaining dry food.

Anscombe acknowledges that it is a condition of the conclusion that the end be wanted. Yet that act of will is not a premise. This may seem a contradiction; in any case, it entails that that the practical syllogism does not conform to Aristotle's account of a syllogism, which requires that nothing beyond the premises be necessary for the conclusion. Indeed, without an act of will as a premise, the syllogism disintegrates; there is no unity to its alleged premise and its alleged conclusion. "This is the way to Larissa. So, I'll take it"—so someone may reason who wants to get to Larissa. "This is the way to Larissa. So, I won't take it"—so someone may reason who wants to avoid Larissa. There is nothing in "This is the way to Larissa" that joins it any closer to "I'll take it" than it does so to "I won't take it."

This point is not affected when the judgment of fact that is to be the starting point deploys evaluative terms, as in "Dry food is suitable. So, I will have some of this" (supplementing "This is dry food, hence suitable") or in "Vitamin X is good for me. So, I'll have some pigs tripes" (supplementing "Pigs tripes provide plenty of vitamin X"). Anscombe recognizes this. She says of "Dry food is suitable. So, I will

---

12 See Anscombe (1963, 66).

have some of this" that it "will go on only in someone who wants to eat suitable food" (Anscombe 1963, 66). People usually want to live healthy, eat suitable food and take care of themselves. (These are infinite ends.) And thus, we have no difficulty following someone who says, "Dry food is suitable. So, I will have some of this." But we have no less difficulty understanding her who says, "This is the way to Larissa. So, I'll take it." And again, "Dry food is suitable. So, I won't have some of this", may go on in someone who wishes to avoid suitable food.

It is a condition of the conclusion that the end be wanted, yet the act of wanting the end is not a premise. I said this may seem a contradiction. Anselm Müller discusses and rejects a way to answer this objection, namely, the following. She who draws an inference recognizes the principle by which her inference is valid. This recognition is necessary for the conclusion, yet not as a premise. One may argue that wanting the end is present in someone who reasons from an end to the means to it in this way: not as a premise, but as a principle by which the premise necessitates the conclusion. Müller rejects this answer on the ground that it entails that only she who wants the end recognizes the validity of her reasoning. – It may be said that the thought entails, instead, that a calculating syllogism is valid not absolutely, but relative to her who reasons. I recognize that my reasoning is valid for me, and so may you. Yet this undermines the idea of reasoning to a conclusion. Judging that an inference is valid for someone is not the same as drawing the conclusion. This does not change when she who so judges is the same as she for whom she judges the inference to be valid. For that is accidental to that judgment. Conversely, if it is not accidental, then we are back at Müller's point.

I said that the calculating syllogism is the consciousness of an end as explaining the means to it, a consciousness in and through which this explanatory nexus obtains. So, a calculating syllogism and the corresponding action explanation exhibit the same order, as Anscombe notes.[13] Action explanations of the relevant form can be expressed in various way: "Why is he eating this?"—"It is suitable food." "It is dry food." "He wants some suitable food." The representation of practical reasoning enjoys the same flexibility. "Dry food is suitable. So, I'll eat this", "I want to eat suitable food. So, I'll eat this", "This food is dry. So, I'll eat this"—all of these may express the same calculating syllogism. The elements that must be present—in the syllogism, in the explanation—are: wanting an end, recognizing something as means to that end, taking those means.[14]

---

13 See Anscombe (1963, 80).
14 Compare Müller (1979, 100–101 and 103).

There is a further reason to represent wanting the end as a premise, as opposed to akin to the consciousness of a principle of inference. Theoretical syllogisms may be joined together in a chain, in which the conclusion of one syllogism is the first premise of another (pro- and epi-syllogisms, respectively). Now, calculating syllogisms may be joined in a chain in which the conclusion of one calculating syllogism is the act of wanting from which a further syllogism proceeds. Such a chain can be perspicuously represented when that act is represented as a premise.

The premise of a calculating syllogism may be a conclusion and a conclusion a premise because means are ends and ends means. A means to an end, as a means, is an end. And a finite end, as an end, is a means: it is explanatory of what realizes it by being in turn explained by an end. It would lead too far afield to elaborate this in a general account of teleology.[15] It suffices to see how it is reflected in the form of consciousness of an end as explaining what realizes it that is a calculating syllogism. First, a means is an end: until I have reached something I can simply do, my conclusion does not lead to action until I reason from it to more specific means. For example: Dry food is suitable. Food of such a kind is dry. This is food of such a kind. The intermediate conclusion, I'll have food of such a kind, is a will that must be present if I am to reason from the recognition that this food is of such a kind to having this. Second, a finite end is a means: the end from which I reason must have a point if it is to provide grounds for taking the means to it. Hence it must be such as to be the conclusion of a line of thought that shows the point of that conclusion: a practical syllogism.

We can find this last point in Davidson. He says that the premise of a calculating syllogism is not that I desire something, but that that it is desirable. In the same way, he says, the first premise of a theoretical judgment is not that I believe that things are so, but that things are so.[16] Now, a judgment in which a syllogism concludes is conscious of itself as resting on grounds that show it to be true. The judgment's consciousness of itself is expressed by "I judge that things are so", its consciousness of its truth by "It is true that things are so" or "Things are so." Conversely, the statement "Things are so" expresses the consciousness of the truth of judging that things are so, and therewith the consciousness of judging it in the consciousness of its truth. So, Davidson's point is the same as the one Frege makes when he says that premises of a syllogism are truths, indeed, truths recognized as such, or known truths.[17] If this point applies to the practical syllogism, then the end in the first premise not only is wanted, but is wanted in the

---

15 The first part is developed by Thompson (2008, Part II). Both parts are developed by Hegel in the *Science of Logic*.
16 Davidson (2006, 31).
17 Cf. once again Frege (1979, 3).

consciousness of grounds that show what is wanted to be good, or, in Anscombe's locution, show the point of wanting it.

We can find the same thought in McDowell: "The first premise of a practical syllogism is a specification of something that might be intelligibly desired."[18] This is the same thought if the intelligibility in question is the intelligibility provided of the conclusion of a syllogism by that syllogism and if "might be" means "is such as to be", if, that is, the modality is governed by the logical form of the term.[19]

An end that figures in a calculative syllogism not only is wanted, but is intelligibly wanted, the kind of intelligibility being the one that a syllogism confers on its conclusion. It follows that reasoning that proceeds from finite ends is not the only form of reasoning to a finite end. The calculative syllogism is a moment of a larger whole of practical thought.

McDowell finds fault with this. But it is unclear that he should, by his own lights. Of course, someone may want something without having a reason for wanting it. Why do you want to do A? No reason, she answers. This may happen. But it is not the case through which we understand the practical syllogism. For it makes no sense to suppose that it is the only case. It makes no sense if, first, the premises of a practical syllogism show the point of acting as one does in conclusion, and if, second, something pointless cannot be the point of doing anything. McDowell affirms the first, and he appears to affirm the second when he requires that the end must

---

[18] He attributes that thought to Anscombe. That strikes me as not quite right. Anscombe's only premise is a judgment that states or implies that something is a means to something. For example, the judgment that dry foods are suitable implies that eating dry food is a way to eat suitable food.
[19] It appears McDowell has a different point in view. When he says that the syllogism proceeds from an end that might be intelligibly desired, he means to speak of a case in which she who reasons does not (not yet, anyway) desire it (although, as she understands, she might). This appears in Anscombe as the "idle syllogism": reasoning from something which one does not want, but which might intelligibly be wanted. The idle syllogism does not lead to action, and it may go on in someone who does not want the end. Since Anscombe deletes what I call the first premise, and since the idle syllogism has no conclusion, it shrinks to the intermediate premise. It is in its entirety a judgment of fact. Not much of a syllogism, really.—An idle syllogism is a practical syllogism *in potentia*, since the end that figures in it is a potential end: someone might want it. Its potential is actualized as the end is taken up in an act of will. Then the syllogism yields a conclusion and becomes a syllogism proper. We can bring out the character of the idle syllogism as a potential syllogism by representing it in this way, adapting Anscombe's example: Suppose someone wanted to eat suitable food: how might she proceed? She might eat this, for this is dry food, and dry food is suitable. Someone who wants to eat suitable food can make use of the knowledge that this is dry food and dry food suitable in a syllogism proper: Dry food suits any man. This is dry food. So, I'll have this. (Compare: Suppose all Fs were G. What would follow? Well, all Gs are H. So, it would follow that all Fs are H. Someone who knows that all Fs are G can make use of this, inferring that all Fs are H.)

be intelligibly wanted. For it is not intelligible that someone should want something that has no point. The point of something wanted may be a finite end that it serves. But that cannot be the only meaning of "point." Hence, reasoning from a finite end is not the only form of syllogism. It is not the only way of showing the point of doing something.

In a practical syllogism as I have described it, willing the end, which is a premise and thus a condition under which the judgment that doing something serves this end leads to action, is prior to, for it is the basis of, the will to take the means. McDowell thinks this need not be so. He imagines a case in which I reason from an end I do not, not yet, want, but which I come to want upon seeing that doing A is a sufficient means to it. He writes:

> Doing A as an instrumental means to doing B can issue from reasoning that starts from the subject's being engaged in doing B anyway, independently of this reasoning. But it need not. Doing B may become an object of the agent's will only when reasoning that starts from B's being worth doing, not yet what she is doing, concludes in her doing A. She settles the question whether to do B only in the act of settling the question whether to do A. So, doing A as a means to doing B can be answering the question what to do *de novo* (McDowell, this volume).

It may happen that I am not sure whether I want to do B, as it depends on what it takes to do it: I want to do B, but only if doing it (doing what it takes to do it) satisfies certain further conditions. (For example, I want to do it, but only if I can be done by noon, when I need to do something else, or only if doing it is not too unpleasant.) Seeing that doing A, which is a sufficient means to doing B, satisfies these conditions, I decide to do B. In this case, my recognition that doing A is a means to doing B does not suffice to explain why I am doing A. It suffices only together with my recognition that doing what is sufficient to do B satisfies further conditions. These may be provided by finite ends or by whatever else may be the point of doing something (for example, its being pleasant to do).

McDowell speaks of "answering the question what to do *de novo*." In the case as I have described it, the will need not be determined *de novo*. Whether it is or not will depend on the conditions under which I want B and on whether they include determinations of my will. But we can consider the idea of a determination of will *de novo* independently. McDowell seems to think that reasoning determines the will only if it determines it *de novo*. He writes:

> When one is determining what to do, practical premises are figuring in one's reasoning but not yet on active service. That is true of second premises no less than first premises. If one is doing A in order to do B, the premise that doing A is a means to doing B is on active service: as Rödl says, it is internal to the premise—it is its form—that through it one is doing A. But one gives the premise that form only in the act of determining A as what to do. Rödl's thought

does not touch practical reasoning as a procedure for arriving at that act (McDowell, this volume).

Premises are on active service when I want the end. So, McDowell seems to say, I do not touch reasoning as a procedure for arriving at wanting to do something because the reasoning I touch proceeds from wanting to do something. This appears to imply that we touch practical reasoning as determining the will only when we describe it as determining the will *de novo*, that is, in a manner that does not proceed from a determination. In that case, speaking of the calculating syllogism is not touching reasoning as a procedure for arriving at a determination of the will. What would be touching it?

In *Self-Consciousness*, I do not recognize any form of practical reasoning that determines the will *de novo*. All principles by which the will determines itself in reasoning I describe in that book are determinations of the will: pursuit of a finite end, adherence to an infinite end, practical consciousness of a practical life-form.[20] A determination *de novo* would proceed from a consciousness which is no act of will, yet leads from that consciousness to an act of will without therein depending on any prior determination of the will. I now think (as I did not in *Self-Consciousness*, where I exclude determination *de novo*) that it is fundamental to the human will that it may be so determined, and therefore I would be glad if I saw clearly how to understand this manner of determination. (I shall say that it seems to me that the consciousness from which the determination *de novo* proceeds is illimitable in its content, wherefore the manner in which action arises from it is not discursive and no reasoning.) In any case, even if the will may be determined *de novo*, that does not do away with its determining itself on the basis of a prior determination: in a calculating syllogism, for example.

Or in other forms of practical reasoning. There are other forms of reasoning leading to action, proceeding from other forms of willing. Anscombe describes several, notably reasoning from a motive and from a desirability characterization. She gives evidence of wanting to find them not a haphazard bunch, but a whole, as she exhausts the temporal extases through backward-looking motives, interpretive motives, and forward-looking motives. I think she is right in wanting to apprehend a whole, for only in a whole of forms is any logical form determined. If there is a form of syllogism, then this form is contained in any of its potential terms; it can-

---

20 So, McDowell is wrong to think that I seek forms of practical reasoning distinct from the one that puts means to a finite end because I think reasoning must determine the will *de novo*. My "progression" is to determinations of the will proceeding from different forms of willing, not from no willing. (Kant does not recognize determination of the will *de novo*. The moral law is an a priori determination of the free will.)

not be an accident that a term be capable of figuring in reasoning of a form in which it is indeed capable of figuring. This is so because a potential term of reasoning of a form is an understanding of itself as a potential term of reasoning of that form. Therefore, forms of reasoning as such form a whole; the thought of that whole is internal to any act of reasoning. (Wittgenstein makes that point in the *Tractatus*: "2.011 Es ist dem Ding wesentlich, der Bestandteil eines Sachverhalts sein zu können. 2.012 In der Logik ist nichts zufällig: Wenn das Dinge im Sachverhalt vorkommen kann, so muß die Möglichkeit des Sachverhalts im Ding bereits präjudiziert sein." He fails to mention that nothing is accidental "in logic" because logic is the self-consciousness of thought.)[21] Therefore, recognizing, as Anscombe does, that there are higher forms of practical reasoning is recognizing that the question, "What is action?" is not answered by describing an order of finite ends (her A-to-D-order). It is recognizing that there is no such thing as action theory, if this is to be an understanding of human action that is not ethics.[22]

4 The Second Premise

The second premise puts means to an end, "Doing A is a means to doing B." "Is a means to" may be specified in various ways: prepares, removes an obstacle to, enhances the chances of success of a further means, contributes to, is a step of, etc. Here I focus on the fundamental case, in which doing A is sufficient for doing B. This case is fundamental because—and this is the main thought of this section—practical reasoning serves the end from which it reasons. It is for the sake of this end. Therefore, the central case of practical reasoning is that in which its end is realized, which it is when the means taken are sufficient.

---

21 McDowell writes: "Anscombe, in contrast, seems content to say a practical syllogism concludes in acting, that is, effecting a happening describable in the form she explains. And the sort of system Rödl demands is conspicuously absent from her discussion of practical reasoning, and her characterization of the same order in terms of the question 'Why?'" (this volume, p. 36) Anscombe does not call an answer to the question why that cites a backward-looking motive a practical syllogism. Yet that answer understands itself to show the point of acting as one does so from that motive. As Anscombe proposes to elucidate what it is to act intentionally by identifying a sense of the question why, all ways of answering the question in that sense that she lists form part of her account of what it is to act intentionally. It follows that, as long as we do not understand the unity of these ways of answering the question, we do not understand that there is one sense of the question, hence one sense of "intentional action."
22 This is Michael Thompson's definition of action theory in "Naïve Action Theory" (Thompson 2008).

There usually is, and it is an accident if there is not, more than one way to realize an end, more than one sufficient means to it. This may make it seem as though there can be no practical unity of the mind that conforms to Aristotle's description of a syllogism: the premises are sufficient for the conclusion, the conclusion necessary on account of the premises.[23] For we have

1st premise: I want to do B.
2nd premise: a) Doing A_a is sufficient to do B.   b) Doing A_b is sufficient to do B.
Conclusion   a) I'll do A_a.   b) I'll do A_b.

The first premise and the second premise a) are sufficient for the conclusion a). By the same token, the first premise and the second premise b) are sufficient for the conclusion b). Let us assume I hold true, even know, both second premise a) and second premise b). Then it seems that both conclusions are necessary. But this cannot be. For the conclusions may be incompatible. And even when they are not, it is false that it is necessary to take more than sufficient means, as I would doing both A_a and A_b.

We might try saying that while both means are sufficient, one may be better than the other. Or one may be outright bad. However, both means are equal as ways of realizing the end of doing B: both are sufficient. Hence, if one is better than the other or one bad, then it is so not on account of its relation to that end. It can be so in the light of further ends or indeed in the light of any kind of ground one may have for wanting something. We set consideration of such grounds aside.

Or we might try saying that the calculating syllogism is valid only when there are means that are not only sufficient, but also necessary. (Kant restricts his discussion of instrumental reasoning to the case in which means are recognized to be "indispensably necessary."[24]) This would mean that it is an accident if conditions are such that it is possible to reason from a finite end to an action. The concept of a calculating syllogism would have no place in a clarification of what it is to act.

A calculating syllogism represents doing something as necessary by showing it to be sufficient for the end from which the syllogism proceeds. Unless we understand how this is so, we have no concept of a practical syllogism. We do understand it through the idea above: a practical syllogism is for the sake of the end re-

---

[23] I discuss this issue in Rödl (2008, 22), where I refer to Müller's essay as providing the insight that I seek to convey there.
[24] Cf. Kant (2012, 4:417).

alized by the action in which it concludes. This idea has been expounded by Anselm Müller in "How Theoretical is Practical Reasoning?" What follows everywhere depends on this essay, a high point of action theory *avant la lettre*.

The first premise of a calculating syllogism represents an end as an end. As an end explains what realizes it, the first premise represents an end as explaining what realizes it. Now, an end represented in a syllogism explains what realizes it through an understanding of this explanatory nexus, which understanding is that syllogism. Hence, an act of wanting understands itself as explaining the attainment of what it wants,[25] understanding it to be attained through the syllogism of which it is the first premise. This understanding informs the syllogism as a whole. The second premise, then, a judgment that specifies means to the end, understands itself to serve that end.

So, this is what it is to represent an end as an end: Reasoning from my end, I reason for the sake of that end; I specify means to my end in order to realize that end. I understand this purpose of my judgment of means, and understand it not in a separate act, but in specifying those means. In this way—here I use an example of Müller's (cf. 1979, 98–99)—"I specify means to eating suitable food in order to eat suitable food" differs from "I am sweating in order to cool down." My sweating is ordered to the end of cooling, and I understand this. Yet my understanding the function of my sweating is not the same as my sweating. The end of cooling does not realize itself through thought. I do not sweat in conclusion of a syllogism that proceeds from a representation of that end.

When I specify means to an end within a syllogism through which I realize that end, then this thought of mine, the second premise of the syllogism, serves the end to which it specifies means. It serves it in and through my understanding of it as serving it. If it did not serve this end, or did so independently of my understanding it to do so, I would not represent the end as an end. So, this understanding is not a further thought, different from and additional to the thought whose purpose it understands. If it were, there would be no practical syllogism. For that further thought would bear the same form as the one it concerns: it would be a thought that specifies means to an end. Hence the same consideration would apply to it. It would follow that a thought is the second premise of a calculating syllogism in virtue of a different thought that is the second premise of a different syllogism. Which would show that there is no such thought, hence no calculating syllogism.[26]

---

25 As Engstrom puts it: it is efficacious through the understanding of itself as efficacious.
26 Cf. Müller (1979, 97): "But, of course, if, quite generally, thinking could be practical, i.e., for the sake of some goal, only on account of a thought which relates it to this goal, there would be no end

This line of reasoning shows, Müller says, that "the content of a practical consideration cannot be separated from its practical function" (Müller 1979, 103). The function of the second premise—its serving the end to which it specifies means—is "somehow internal to its own content" wherefore the distinction of function and content "is of limited validity only."[27] I want to try and say something about how it is internal.

A thought is conscious of itself as the thought it is. That is, I am conscious of thinking what I do not in a further thought, distinct from the thought of which I am conscious, but in this very thought. So, thinking that things are so is thinking oneself to think this; one and the same thought is expressed by "I think things are so" and by "Things are so." This means that the distinction of what is thought from the act of thinking it is of limited validity only. As "Things are so" and "I think things are so" express but one thought, it is internal to what is thought that it be thought.

Were it a further thought in which I think myself to think what, thereby, I think, there would be no such thing as my understanding myself to think anything, hence no such thing as my thinking anything. I will not go through that here.[28] I want to consider briefly an idea that may be proposed by someone who recognizes this. She may affirm that it is not in a further thought in which I think myself to think what I do. It is not a further thought in the sense that it is not a further act of thinking. Yet, what I think thinking snow is white is not the same as what I think, thinking I think snow is white. The first concerns snow and predicates of it whiteness. The second concerns me and predicates of it thinking snow is white. A different topic altogether. So, we distinguish thought as the act of thinking from thought as what is thought. Having made this distinction, we are in a position to acknowledge that thinking oneself to think something and thinking it are but one thought, namely, when "thought" means the act of thinking. Yet there are two distinct thoughts, namely, when "thought" means what is thought. There is one act with two contents.

---

to the chain of such thoughts presupposed by any practical thinking, or rather, there would be no practical reasoning and no reasoned practice."

27 Müller (1979, 99): "If ... I consider, with a view to acting, how such-and-such can be taken across [a river], my consideration being conducted with a view to this end must be treated as somehow internal to its own content. (One might even say that the distinction between the content and the employment of a thought is of limited validity only.)" Cf. Müller (1979, 100): "Problems arise when, in a philosophical analysis of practical reasoning, one tries to reduce expressions of practical thinking to a component expressing propositional contents and a component reflecting its practical function."

28 Cf. Rödl (2018, Chapter 3).

This is not a way to appreciate the self-consciousness of thought, but a way to deny that thought is self-conscious. It deploys the distinction of what is thought from thinking it, which, on account of the self-consciousness of thought, "is of limited validity only." A way to see this is to consider how I would know that it is in the same act in which I think that things are so and think that I think this.[29] It would seem that I know this because thinking something is knowing oneself to think it; an act of thinking is known by her who is the subject of this act and is known by her to think what it does. Yet now we must remember how we propose to comprehend that, namely, in this way: thinking something is thinking, in the same act, that one thinks it. Applying this, we say that thinking, in one act, that things are so and that one thinks this, is thinking, in that very act, that one thinks, in one act, that things are so and that one thinks they are. Now there are three things thought in one act of thinking. Yet the addition of a third content does not explain how I know that third content. That I think this content in the same act which figures in it does not explain how I recognize its truth. Unless, of course, I know that my act of thinking a certain act of thinking of mine was the same as the one of which therein I think. Yet we are trying to understand how I might know this. (This entails that it is a fraud when, in that proposal, what is thought —in the same act as something else—is rendered by the first-person pronoun, "I think.") The self-consciousness of thought is not a content thought.[30]

In reasoning from something I want, my thought that specifies means to what I want understands itself to serve that end. It may be thought this means that, in the same act, I think two things: first, doing such-and-such serves my end, second, my thinking this serves my end. Yet, whether it be thought in the same act or a different one, my thought that my thinking serves my end serves my end does so only in and through my understanding it to do so. Hence, we need to postulate a further thought. We may add that it is but one act in which this, now third, content is thought. That does not save the idea of such a thought from dissolving into unintelligibility.

---

[29] I mention but do not discuss this proposal in Rödl (2018, 21). But it is straightforward to adapt the point presented there (Rödl 2018, 22) in relation to a variant of it, which is what I do here.
[30] In Kant's words, the "I think", which accompanies all my thoughts, cannot be accompanied by any thought (see Kant (2013), the Critique of Pure Reason, at B132). (I find it common for people to say that Kant asserts, not that all my thoughts are accompanied by the "I think", but that all my thoughts must be able to be accompanied by the "I think." In truth, Kant says that the "I think" must be able to accompany all my representations because, if it did not, there would be something represented in me which could not be thought at all. This presupposes what Kant in this line of reasoning treats as universally known because known through itself—that the "I think" does accompany (in distinction to: is able to accompany) all my thoughts.)

The second premise is an understanding of itself as serving the end to which it specifies means. This means that it is internal to its content, to what is judged in this judgment, that it serves that end, the end that figures in it. It is internal to it as its self-consciousness. Since the self-consciousness of a judgment is its formal cause, or form, we may say that it is the form of the second premise that it serves the end to which it specifies means.[31] However, this must not encourage the idea that there is a content here which may or may not bear this form and which may be given that form.[32] A bit of clay may be given a form it did not have prior to being given it. And Hegel asserts that a human being, declaring an animal her property, takes out that animal's soul and puts her own soul into it.[33] Since an animal's soul is the form of its body, this would be a body being given a form it did not previously possess. Whether this makes sense or not, in any case, it is meaningless to speak of something's being given a form it did not yet possess when that form is the form of a thought. For the form of a thought is that thought's understanding of itself. Hence, what is thought is that understanding of itself, or its form. (Again, that is Wittgenstein's point in the passage mentioned above: a logical form cannot be added to that whose form it is.)

A judgment of fact need not figure in a calculating syllogism. Not every judgment does. This does not mean that it is given a form it did not possess when it is taken up in a syllogism. A judgment of fact is such as to be the second premise of a practical syllogism. This is its form and hence understood in any such judgment. This means that theoretical knowledge, as such, is ordered to practical thought. (It may be thought that this means that the entirety of nature is *a priori* matter for the specification of my will. This seems wrong to me. Instead, it seems to me to mean that the principle of nature is the good. Following this thought will lead to a point where it makes contact with an idea that came up above: determination of the will *de novo*.)

It remains to make explicit how the Müllerian account of the calculating syllogism explains why the availability of two or more equally sufficient means does not prevent a representation of the end and a representation of sufficient means to that end from providing, held together, sufficient grounds for the conclusion, namely, the action of taking the means. When I have specified means that are sufficient for my end—means that reside in things I can do straightaway—then I have done everything necessary in terms of thinking in order to realize my end. It would be pointless to think up further means, even if these were equally sufficient.

---

31 So McDowell puts it (this volume).
32 McDowell speaks of my giving something that form, which—one must infer—did not possess that form prior to my giving it that form.
33 Hegel (1991, §44).

Consequently, no further thought of means can be a second premise of a calculating syllogism that proceeds from that end, for no such further thought could understand itself as serving this end.

References

Anscombe, Gertrude Elizabeth Margaret (1963): *Intention*. Cambridge: Harvard University Press.
Aristotle (1912, 1984): *Complete Works of Aristotle*. Jonathan Barnes (Ed.). Oxford and Princeton: Oxford University Press and Princeton University Press.
Davidson, Donald (2001): "How is weakness of the will possible?" In: Davidson, Donald: *Essays on actions and events*. Oxford: Oxford University Press, 21–42.
Engstrom, Stephen P. (2009): *The Form of Practical Knowledge*. Cambridge: Harvard University Press.
Frege, Gottlob (1979): "Logic (1879–1891)." In: Frege, Gottlob: *Posthumous Writings*. Hans Hermes, Friedrich Kambartel, and Friedrich Kaulbach with the assistance of Gottfried Gabriel and Walburga Rödding (Eds.). Peter Long and Roger White with the assistance of Raymond Hargreaves (Trans.). Oxford: Basil Blackwell.
Hegel, Georg Wilhelm Fredrich (1991): *Elements of the philosophy of right*. Cambridge: Cambridge University Press.
Kant, Immanuel (2000): *Critique of the Power of Judgement*. Cambridge: Cambridge University Press.
Kant, Immanuel (2012): *Groundwork of the Metaphysics of Morals*. Cambridge: Cambridge University Press.
Kant, Immanuel (2013): *Critique of Pure Reason*. Cambridge: Cambridge University Press.
Müller, Anselm Winfried (1979): "How theoretical is practical reason?" In: Diamond, Cora and Teichman, Jenny (Eds.): *Intention and Intentionality: Essays in Honour of G. E. M. Anscombe*. Ithaca: Cornell University Press, 91–108.
Rödl, Sebastian (2007): *Self-Consciousness*. Cambridge: Harvard University Press.
Rödl, Sebastian (2010): "The form of the will." In: Tenenbaum, Sergio (Ed.): *Desire, practical reason, and the good*. Oxford: Oxford University Press, 138–160.
Rödl, Sebastian (2018): *Self-Consciousness and Objectivity. An Introduction to Absolute Idealism*. Cambridge: Harvard University Press.
Thompson, Michael (2008): *Life and Action: Elementary Structures of Practice and Practical Thought*. Cambridge: Harvard University Press.

Jason Bridges
The Unity of a Practical Inference

Abstract: This essay seeks to hold together two fundamental ideas. The first idea is that an inference between thoughts is itself a thought: inferring one thought from another is nothing other than thinking a connection to lie between them. The second idea is that practical justification is teleological: a reason for an action derives from its potential to serve an end. The second idea poses a problem for the first, here called *the challenge of singularization*. Ideas that might seem equipped to solve this challenge—such as that of a special category of means, of an "all-things-considered" assessment of justification, and of a distinctively practical mode of means-end judgment—fail to do so. The right solution is to understand practical inference as a logically complex form of intention. The essay concludes by considering the import of this *intentionalist* solution for the "standard causal story" of rational action.

In this essay, I argue against one account of practical inference and for another. The account I will reject opposes the empiricism which is mainstream in the current literature on the topic. It may seem, indeed, to be the only possible alternative to empiricism. That is not so. There is space for another alternative. In this space, I will argue, lies the correct account.

I begin with some stage-setting to get our topic into view.

1 Theoretical and Practical Inference

An inference is one thought depending upon others. You think some things, and on the basis of these things, you think some further thing. The philosopher seeks to understand the nature of this dependence. She asks, "In what does it consist that the one thought is inferred from, based on, other thoughts?"

Frege writes, "Judging in the consciousness of other truths as justifying grounds is called inferring" (1979, 3).[1] This remark is usually interpreted as specifying one essential element of inference, one element among others that must be present if the thinker is to count as inferring (Boghossian 2014, 4). What Frege is

---

[1] Here, I follow the translation suggestion in Rödl (2020). It will be evident the present discussion is indebted to Rödl's essay in other ways, despite my departure from its main idea.

pointing out, it is supposed, is that if a judgment is to count as inferred from some premises, then among other conditions, the one who judges must regard the premises as justifying the conclusion.

But Frege does not represent himself this way. He represents himself as giving an account of what is "called inferring." One speaks like this when one is purporting to define a concept. You do not define a concept merely by giving a necessary condition for something to fall under it. "A triangle is a plane figure," is not a definition. You define a concept by saying what it is for something to fall under that concept. This requires that the things one says be not only necessary but sufficient.

Let us take Frege's remark in the way he evidently intends and see what account of inference may be drawn out of it so understood.

So understood, Frege says inferring is nothing other than judging in the consciousness of other truths as justification for so judging. But inference is one thought depending upon others. Therefore, the dependence of one judgment on others which is characteristic of inference consists in nothing other than the inferrer's being conscious of the truth of the latter as justifying the former. You recognize some things you judge to justify judging some further thing, and it is simply in your recognizing this that you infer this judgment from or base it upon the others. It is widely held that an inferential connection requires more than the recognition of justification. It is thought to require in addition that one's recognition of that justification play a special role in the production of the concluding judgment, a role the fulfillment of which is not entailed by the mere presence of the recognition. The philosopher's task is to explain this role and give its conditions. To accept the Fregean account is to deny there is any such task.

On the Fregean account, the inferential dependence of the concluding judgment on the premise judgments—the way in which the concluding judgment is derived from the premise judgments—consists in nothing other than the consciousness of the truth of the premise judgments as justifying the conclusion. This implies that this consciousness is logically sufficient for reaching the concluding judgment. The prevalent contemporary view is to reject this. Recognition of a conclusion's justification is held to yield the drawing of the conclusion not by entailing it but by causing it. Whereas on the Fregean account, to be conscious of a judgment's justification by other truths already *is* to draw that conclusion, already is to so judge. The consciousness of justification, as we might put it, contains the conclusion. There is no gap for a causal connection to bridge.

Finally, it is not merely one's thought of the conclusion of the inference that is contained within the consciousness of justification which, on the Fregean account, provides for the inferential connection. It is also one's thought of the premises. For one can be conscious of certain truths as justifying something only if one judges those truths to be so.

Putting these points together, we have it that an inference is nothing other than a thought of a judgment as justified by other truths one judges. Inferring r from p and q = being conscious of judging r as justified by the truth of one's judgments p and q. This consciousness gives us everything we need: it gives us that we judge the premises, that we judge the conclusion, and that we infer the latter from the former. If we accept Frege's report on what is called inferring, the consciousness of justification is not one element among others in the inferential nexus. It is the inferential nexus.

This account is uncluttered. From the perspective of the contemporary literature, it will seem absurdly austere. But it will nonetheless pay to separate out two ideas contained within it.

The first idea is that an inference is nothing other than a thought. What binds thoughts together in the manner of an inference is nothing but a thought of them as bound. You think the judgment p to bear a connection to some other judgments, and it is simply in thinking this that you infer the former judgment from the latter. I will call this idea *Frege's principle.*

If we accept Frege's principle, then we will think that for every inference, there is a thought that constitutes it. Call such a thing an *inferential thought.* The question arises what this thought may be. The second idea gives an answer to this question: it says that the inferential thought linking premises and conclusion is the consciousness—the recognition or understanding—of the conclusion as justified by the premises. You are conscious of a judgment as justified by some truths you judge, and it is this consciousness which is your inferring this judgment from these truths. This idea, which goes beyond Frege's principle to offer a candidate for the thought the principle posits, I will call *the Fregean account of theoretical inference.*

Now, I say "theoretical" inference. As Frege defines inferring, an inference concludes in a judgment. This fits ordinary use of the word "inference." But a judgment is not the only thing we say we "base" on something we think. We also speak of acting on the basis of reasons, these reasons being things which we grasp in thought. So, it looks harmless to widen the use of the word "inference" accordingly. In what we may call a "practical inference," one draws a conclusion from things one thinks. What is special about a practical inference is that the conclusion is an intentional action—or at least, as in cases of inference directed toward future occasions for action, an intention to later act.

What account should we give of practical inference? We might, for a start, take it that Frege's principle extends to this domain. We might take it that drawing a practical conclusion—acting or intending to act for certain reasons one has in view—consists in nothing more than thinking a thought which links the action with those considerations.

Supposing we accept this answer, it generates a new question: what is the character of the practical-inferential thought? Here, too, we might propose to extend Frege's definition of the theoretical case. We might hold that that the relationship between a reason and an intentional action or intention to act, when one acts or intends to act on the basis of that reason, lies in this: that one is conscious of the reason as justifying the action. Doing or intending to do M for reason R = being conscious of R as justifying doing M. I will call this the *Fregean account of practical inference*—or, more pithily, *practical Fregeanism*—not because Frege endorses it, but because it borrows the shape of what he does say.

Frege's principle is widely rejected in work on inference in both the theoretical and practical sphere. We may call the denial of Frege's principle *empiricism*. An empiricist can (and generally will) accept that the presence of a thought akin to the one Frege identifies is necessary for an inference. But they will deny that it is sufficient. The inferential connection between thoughts is not guaranteed merely by one's thinking the one thought to be justified by the others. Indeed, it is not guaranteed by anything one thinks about the relation between these thoughts. The inferential connection is external to the things one thinks, tying them together, as it were, from the outside.

The usual template for pursuing an empiricist account of inference is to suppose that thoughts are states of an object (perhaps a human being, perhaps a "mind") and that an inferential connection between thoughts is a transition over time between such states. Just as a physical mechanism's entering into one state may, in virtue of how the mechanism is disposed, lead it to enter into another state, so the mind or human being entering the state of having a certain thought or set of thoughts may lead it, in virtue of how it is disposed, to enter into another such state. Some of these state transitions count as inferences. The philosopher's job is to explain the principle of this class. If we adopt this point of view, Frege's principle will look nonsensical. The consciousness of one thought as justifying another is just another mental state. As such it may need to be present for an inferential transition to transpire. It cannot be the transition itself.

I think it can be shown that empiricism is untenable and so that Frege's principle is correct. Showing this is not my aim here. Possession of a compelling argument against empiricism would not mean the work of achieving a philosophical understanding of inference is finished. Even if we are convinced that Frege's principle must be true, it cannot be denied that there are difficulties in seeing *how* it can be true. In this essay, I will consider one such difficulty. And I will endeavor to solve it.

The difficulty I will discuss is limited in an important respect: it bears on the Fregean analysis of practical inference only. For the difficulty arises as a consequence of a distinctive feature—indeed, *the* distinctive feature—of practical reasoning: its teleological character.

Defenders of practical Fregeanism are aware of a problem in the vicinity of what I will describe, and they propose various measures to handle it. We will see that these measures fail. The only solution to the problem is to abandon the Fregean account of practical inference.

The alternative I will propose—what I will call *intentionalism*—holds to Frege's principle. But it rejects practical Fregeanism's way of specifying the practical-inferential thought. On the intentionalist account, the thought which unifies a practical inference is a thought which goes beyond consciousness of justification. It is a thought that realizes what, in the consciousness of justification, is thought of only as potentiality. This thought, we will see, is a form of complex intention.

The intentionalist account entails a deep difference between theoretical and practical inference. That might seem worrying. In fact, it is at it should be. Theoretical reasoning is coming to understand what one is justified in thinking. It is bringing what it is right to think into view. Practical reasoning is different. To reason practically is not to bring what one is justified in doing into view; it is to bring it into being. Its mandate is not to apprehend reality but to make a reality of what it apprehends. This difference between theoretical and practical reasoning is, or ought to be, a given. A satisfactory treatment of practical inference should do it justice. The present essay is a contribution to this project as well.[2]

2 The Challenge of Singularization

Frege's principle, applied to a given form of inference, entails the existence of an inferential thought, a thought whose thinking just is the drawing of an inference of that form. An inferential thought must entail the thinking of all of the thoughts that go into the inferential nexus. This includes the conclusion—the thought that

---

[2] Here, I flag an issue I will not be addressing directly: one might worry that Frege's principle cannot have application in the practical domain, on the ground that the conclusion of a practical inference is an action, and that an action is not a thought. Now, in fact, one who held this view of action could try to hold Frege's principle by modifying their idea of the conclusion of a practical inference. An intention is a thought. So, one might hold that it is an intention, and not an action, that is the conclusion of a practical inference. Rather than say, as I did, that a practical inference concludes either in an intentional action or an intention to act, one with this view would rather have to say that all practical inferences conclude in intentions to act. I will often talk this way myself. But I do so as a way of covering different cases synoptically, not as a way of accommodating an expulsion of action from the sphere of thought. One form an intention to act can assume, I take it, is that of an intentional action. The arguments to come will offer support for this assumption.

is inferred from, or based upon, other thoughts. If thinking thought I is not logically sufficient for thinking thought C, it cannot be the thought constituting an inference concluding in C.

For example, Lewis Carroll's tortoise claims that he accepts that truths A and B establish the truth of Z but does not accept Z.[3] If it were really possible for a thinker to do this, it would rule out identifying the theoretical-inferential thought with the consciousness of a judgment as established by other truths. Reading Carroll's tale, I presume we feel rather that the tortoise (or Carroll) is engaged in a pretense with a view to making a philosophical point. Indeed, the palpable absurdity of the tortoise's avowal, taken at face value rather than as an object lesson for some philosophical purpose, serves to solidify our doubts about the possibility of what is avowed.

On the Fregean account of practical inference, a practical inference is constituted by consciousness of the action as justified by reasons for it. This consciousness is held to be logically sufficient for the action. Thus, the account precludes the possibility of an agent who possesses the requisite consciousness but, when the time comes, does not act.

On its face, this putative possibility seems rather more possible than the tortoise's parallel claim on the theoretical side. For one thing, as Müller observes, the success of practical reason is distinctively vulnerable to "impediments beyond its ken" (Müller 1979, 104). However conscious you may be of your reasons for making a dinner date, you still might get in a car accident on the way. A practical Fregean might rejoin that there was at least the intention to make the date in this case, and that this is all the account requires. But even the intention does not seem to be present in a case of *akrasia*. Can I not be clear on my excellent reasons for engaging in physical exercise, but not form the slightest intention to do so?

There are various things practical Fregeans might and do say about how to reconcile their view with the phenomenon of *akrasia*. We will have occasion to refer to one possible solution later. But the challenge *akrasia* raises for practical Fregeanism is not my topic here. I mention it only to distinguish it from what will be my real concern. This is *the challenge of singularization*. It arises as follows.

Some thoughts preclude each other. Aristotle gives the fundamental case of this: one cannot together judge p and judge *not-p*. Of course, we do not need Aristotle to inform us of this principle. Judging that p, I know that I have set myself against judging *not-p*. This comes out, for example, when I acknowledge that I cannot hold to my judgment that p and further judge something else I recognize would

---

[3] See Carroll (1895).

commit me to *not-p*. No thinker can fail to grasp such things. Such knowledge is internal to, or inseparable from, the act of judgment.

There is a parallel opposition on the side of practical thought. One cannot simultaneously intend to do *A* and intend not to do *A*. I can intend to go out tonight or to stay in. But knowing that doing one of these would mean not doing the other, I cannot intend to do both. And again, this negative point about what I cannot think, when it comes to intending, goes along with a positive point about what I do think in intending something. Intending to do *A*, I know myself to foreclose on taking any action incompatible with doing *A*. It is just because this understanding is inseparable from intention that it is appropriate to speak of every intention as a choice. A choice is a selection from among alternatives. Sometimes one makes this selection by weighing the merits of given options, and this scenario tends to be what we have in mind when we speak of a person as "making a choice." But even when such comparative reflections are not involved, what remains is this: one who decides to do something knows that she denies herself the possibility of doing any other incompatible thing. In this sense, she selects; she chooses.

An account of inference for a given sphere of thought must respect whatever incompatibilities obtain within this sphere. A Fregean account of a form of inference finds *being conscious of premises as justifying a thought T* logically sufficient for *thinking T*. We are led to the following requirement upon such an account: wherever *thinking T* is incompatible with *thinking U*, so must *being conscious of premises as justifying thinking T* be incompatible with *being conscious of premises as justifying thinking U*. Moreover, as the thinker herself will know thinking *T* to be incompatible with thinking *U*, so must she recognize the incompatibility in the corresponding thoughts of justification. A Fregean view of inference must conceive one's consciousness of a thought as justified as at once a consciousness of the absence of such a justification for any thought incompatible with the thought in question.[4]

It looks relatively straightforward to meet this requirement on the theoretical side. Suppose we say that a judgment is justified by other truths only insofar as those truths establish the truth of the judgment. Whatever ensures the truth of the judgment *p* simultaneously ensures the falsity of the judgment *not-p*. And if *not-p* is not a truth, then of course nothing can establish its truth. One who judges *p* knows all this. It follows that one who is conscious of other truths as justifying

---

4 Later, we will consider an attempt to deny this in the practical case.

judging *p* knows this to preclude consciousness of other truths as justifying judging *not-p*.[5]

What about practical inference? Suppose I know doing *A* to preclude doing *B*. Intending to do *A*, I know I cannot intend to do *B*. Is it also so that if I am conscious of doing *A* as justified by reasons for it, I know I cannot also be conscious of doing *B* as justified by reasons for it? The matter can be put this way. When we intend to do something, we single out that action from all possible alternatives to it, as the one we shall pursue. Our question is whether we can understand an agent's consciousness of an action's justification to similarly *singularize:* to exclude consciousness of any alternative to that action as justified.

I will argue that this demand cannot be met. There are singularizing forms of consciousness of practical justification. But these are special cases. The *general* form of consciousness of an action's justification does not singularize. This is not an incidental feature of the form but fundamental to it. Consciousness of an action's justification is not merely such as to fail to rule out alternatives; it is such as to invite them.

3 Ends, Means, and Practical Justification

A Fregean account of inference identifies an inference with the thinker's recognition of the premises as justifying the concluding thought. This equation can make sense only if the recognition of justification singularizes, only if it precludes recognition of thoughts incompatible with the conclusion as justified. We saw that a natural idea about the justification of judgments appears to secure singularization in that case. We now need to consider whether the same may be so on the practical side. Let us ask: how are actions justified?

The first thing to be said on this matter—a point so basic it can be hard to get into focus—is that justification for actions emerges in consideration of what will be accomplished in doing them. To see a reason, a potential justification, for an action is to see a point to that action. And to see a point to an action is to see something positive in whose accomplishment the action will or may be expected to figure.

This is a truism. It may not sound like one. It may sound like taking sides in the dispute between the "teleological" and the "deontological" view of moral rea-

---

[5] It is a tricky question whether the theoretical Fregean can extend this idea to a defeasible notion of theoretical justification, as may seem to be required to understand various kinds of theoretical inferences.

sons. Is it not only a proponent of the former who thinks that what matters about an action lies solely in what it will accomplish? No: whatever the distinction between these two views is supposed to be, it is not this. One philosopher says that we should keep a promise only if doing so will contribute to overall happiness. Another says we must keep our promise regardless because it is the moral law. The latter does not thereby maintain that there is no point to keeping a promise. On the contrary, she tells us what she thinks the point is: it is to obey the moral law. Keeping a promise, I manifest obedience to the moral law. It is in its accomplishing this that I have a reason—and indeed, the only reason I require—for taking this action. True, the relationship between my keeping a promise and my manifesting obedience to the moral law is not the same as the relationship between that action and a future state of affairs of increased overall happiness to which it may lead. The former relationship is more, as we say, intrinsic. This does not show that only the latter of these relationships speaks to what the action may accomplish. It shows that we will need to do philosophical work if we want to isolate what might be distinctively "teleological" (or "consequentialist," as we are wisely now inclined to say) about the latter.

The point can be put this way. There is no seeing a reason for an action of doing *M* in the absence of a judgment expressible with the schema *by doing M, I will (or may)* …. What can go into the ellipsis is various. It may be a specification of an action using a different action-concept than that by which we specify *M*, e. g., *by kicking this garden gnome, I will knock it over*. It may reference what Rödl calls an "infinite end," e. g., *by throwing out this bag of chips, I will serve my health* (2007, 37 ff.). In a case likely to be of especial interest to a "consequentialist," it may be of the form an instance of which is *by planting the bloody knife in the parlor, I will bring it about that suspicion falls on the butler*. These judgments all exhibit different forms. But they are all forms for specifying what one may accomplish with an action. They articulate different kinds of thing for one's action to, in the manner suitable to the kind, *realize*—to make or keep real, to bring into, or sustain in, being.

In philosophy, the words "means" and "end" are sometimes held in reserve for the special topic of "instrumental reasoning," conceived as one, but not the only, form of practical reasoning. There are various reasonable ways to draw boundaries around a topic for which the "instrumental" label might seem particularly suited. But there is no special topic of reasons for action that concern what, by performing an action, one may accomplish—or, as we may also say, what one may realize. There is nothing else for a reason for action to be. And since ordinary English does not discriminate between speaking of what one may accomplish "by" an action and what that action may be a "means" to, it is within our rights to say that all reasons for action concern ends to which these actions are, or may be, means.

It is said the agent's question, the question which sets the general topic of practical reasoning, is "What am I to do?" This is not wrong, but our truistic point equips us to note an important difference between two forms this question may assume depending upon the context in which it arises. Sometimes an agent is presented with a set of options, and their task is to choose among them. In such a context, the agent's question assumes the guise, "Am I to do M, or O, or…?" You answer this question by considering and weighing things that may be expected to come of these various options. You were going to stay home for the evening, but your friend suggests the two of you check out a new bar. Are you to go out or stay in? Going out, you will probably have fun. Maybe you will also nurture a friendship that, as it happens, could use it. It is true that you would have a chance to relax if you stayed home, but on reflection, what will come of going out seems most important. You decide to do that.

Due, I take it, to the influence of decision theory, we tend nowadays to see cases like this, in which one's options are given, as paradigmatic. They are not. The primary context for practical reasoning is that in which what is given is one's end, and one's task is then to *find* a suitable option, to find a means to one's end. Here the agent's question takes the form, "How am I to realize E?" I seek, say, to raise my neighbor's spirits, and so I ask how I may do so. In this context, it is still more manifest that the reasons one may find for this or that action will have to do with what it may accomplish. What such an action would need to accomplish, for one to have a reason for it in the context, is given in the question itself.

Of course, it is not a new idea in practical philosophy that practical reasoning, in its primary employment, proceeds from an end to the finding and taking of a means to that end. On the contrary, it is the oldest idea. Insofar as we have lost track of it, so has it become more difficult to keep the point I am insisting upon in view.

Two further issues arise at this juncture, which I flag now but can defer discussion of until later.

First, not just anything that might be anticipated to come of an action generates a reason for doing it. Some potential ends are worth pursuing, and some are not. So having a reason for an action, derived from the action's capacity to realize or help realize an end, requires that the end be pursuit-worthy—that it be, as we may put it, good or valid or correct. The goodness of an end may in turn derive from the realizing of this end being a means to a still further end. But such a sequence cannot go on forever. At some point, it would seem, we must come to an end that generates reasons for means to it without itself being justified as a means to something else. No further reason is required to make this end worthy of pursuit; it is worthy of pursuit on its own account. Perhaps I make my neighbor a cake to raise his spirits, and that to render him open to rational suasion, and that to ensure passage of a proposal at my condo-board meeting, and that, finally, for the sake of justice. A complete treatment of practical reasoning must explain the logic of this final (or, going the other way, first) step.

Second, it is widely held that reasons for action are facts.[6] Prima facie, this view seems equipped to accommodate the present point. We can hold that the only facts that can be reasons for action are those which speak to what that action may accomplish. But our discussion so far at least hints at the prospect of a different idea: that reasons for action need not be facts at all, but ends. A reason for an action might be *to knock over the gnome*, or *that suspicion should fall on the butler*, or, simply, *honor*. Vindication of this idea will need to lie in an account of the logic of practical inference which shows its necessity. Toward the end, I will say just a bit about how the account I propose may do that. In the interval, I do not wish to prejudge the issue between the factualist view and this potential alternative.

So, let us say, neutrally, that a reason for an action arises from the action's potential to realize or help realize a valid end. This is our *first observation*.

To this observation, we may add another. It is possible for two incompatible actions to each have the potential to realize, or help realize, a given end. That my doing M will help realize E does not preclude that there be an action O, incompatible with doing M, which would similarly further E. This is our *second observation*.

An action that does not in itself provide for the realization of an end, but which may nonetheless help realize the end, we may call a *contributory means*. An action or course of action that, relative to the occasion, fully realizes the end is called a *sufficient means*. One may or may not need recourse to the first category in reasoning about how to achieve a given end; one always needs recourse to the second. In relation to that category, the second observation is particularly clear and familiar. There is nothing in general to prevent more than one sufficient means to the same end. I seek to raise my neighbor's spirits. I judge I can do so by making him a cake. The truth of this judgment does not entail that I can raise his spirits in no other way. Why should it? The judgment is true, if it is, in virtue of features and implications of the action of making my neighbor a cake that suit it to raising his spirits. No doubt these factors have primarily to do with my relationship to my neighbor as well as his tastes and character. And their existence will leave open the possibility of other such factors which speak to the suitability of an alternative means. They leave open the possibility, say,

---

6 C.f. Scanlon (2014) and Schroeder (2008).

that I might raise his spirits by using the time available to me to instead buy him a nice bottle of wine.

Let us put the first and second observations together. That an action is a means to an end does not in general preclude an alternative, incompatible, action being a means to that end. Thus, consciousness of a given action as a means to one's end does not in general rule out consciousness of an incompatible alternative as a means to that same end. But actions are justified as means to good ends. Thus, consciousness of an action as justified does not, in general, singularize. Coupling this argument with that of the previous section, it follows that the Fregean account of practical inference is incorrect.

Or so it seems. Over the next three sections, we will consider strategies for rescuing the account.

4 Best Means and Necessary Means

One strategy is to promote as central to practical reason a category of means other than the sufficient, and in particular a category that would provide for a singularizing consciousness of justification.

One candidate is that of the *best means* to one's end. We might ask: would a perfectly "rational" agent really be content with any old sufficient means to their end? Does not rationality demand choosing that which is best? To find the best means, it will not suffice to just consider how a given action relates to the end. As judgments of best-ness are comparative, one must consider other alternatives. It may be held that such a comparative assessment will single out one unique alternative in any given situation, and thus solve the challenge of singularization.[7]

I think it is a mistake to hold that practical rationality is a matter of choosing what is best.[8] But in fact this issue is moot here. Assessments of best means would not solve the challenge of singularization anyway. That is because the logic of bestness is not intrinsically singularizing. For the question "What is best?" to have meaningful application in a context, it is not necessary that there be only one cor-

---

7 This is the gist of Nussbaum's (1987, 191) interpretation of Aristotle, on which "the desire statement (major premise)" of a practical syllogism contains "a criterion for selection among possible alternatives." Aristotle's actual examples of practical syllogisms do not explicitly reference such criteria but, according to Nussbaum, "Aristotle would probably say that if we make the contents of the major premise precise enough [via a criterion of selection], we will always get an action as conclusion via some one appropriate minor premise" (1987, 191).
8 I discuss this in Bridges (manuscript).

rect answer to it. What is necessary is that there be a measure which enables a ranking of candidates. Such a measure can allow for ties in the top position.

We might try to claim that there will, in fact, always be a measure of quality of means which ensures uniqueness in the top spot. But this is a fantasy. Since what counts as a better means in a given case will depend upon the nature of the end, there is no general way to specify such a criterion. And there is manifestly no reason to expect one to be forthcoming in all specific cases—or indeed even in any but rare cases. Even criteria for assessing achievement as fine-grained as those used in the Olympics do not preclude ties.[9]

A different candidate for promotion is the category of a *necessary means*. Here we might reference Kant, who organizes his treatment of purposive reasoning around the "analytic" truth that "whoever wills the end also wills (insofar as reason has decisive influence on his actions) the indispensably necessary means to it that are within his power" (Kant 2012, 4:417ed).[10]

A necessary means for realizing E is an action without which E cannot be realized. So long as we stipulate that only achievable ends can have necessary means, it follows that incompatible actions cannot both be necessary means to the same end. Consciousness of an action as justified as a necessary means to E would then singularize. If we hold that such consciousness is the primary form of consciousness of practical justification, we open space for the Fregean account.

This line does not seem far from Kant's own. He frames his examination of the grounds of action as an inquiry into the source of the "imperative"—a.k.a., "ought"-involving, "necessitating"—character of rules for action. In the "hypothetical" case, these rules concern ends that an agent may or may not happen to possess; in the "categorical" case, we find an end present in the very idea of practical reason and as such inescapable. But in either case, that the rules in question are "imperatives" for us—that they "necessitate" our actions, or tell us what we "ought" to do—comes to this: while we are in fact imperfectly rational beings who cannot be counted upon to act appropriately for the sake of our ends, "if reason completely determined the will the action would without fail take place in accordance with this rule" (Kant 2015, 5:20).

This conception of the operations of practical reason requires that we suppose, as Kant does, that the envisioned "rules" specify necessary means for the

---

9 The point I am making here is acknowledged by at least some philosophers who adopt a comparative conception of practical rationality. Of special note is Chang (2016), who argues for a strongly "comparativist" conception of the grounds of "objective rationality" while emphasizing the possibility of multiple best alternatives.
10 For more recent examples of the tack of centering necessary means in practical reasoning, see Hare (1971), Wright (1963, 1974, and 1989), and Broome (2002).

ends they concern. The governing force of a rule identifying a sufficient means, by contrast, could not be understood in Kant's way. The idea of a reasoner who without fail takes every sufficient means to their ends does not specify an ideal, achievable or otherwise, but is mere nonsense. It is nonsense precisely because consciousness of a means as sufficient to a given end does not singularize.

But there is a decisive problem with this vision of reasoning toward the achievement of ends. The category of necessary means is simply less fundamental than that of the sufficient. There is no getting around the fact that in seeking to achieve an end, we seek to do something, or a series of things, by which that end is realized. And this is just to say that our concern is to find and take a sufficient means.

Of course, it can be important to identify necessary steps to one's end. But even when it is, we had better find a sufficient means to our end or the necessary steps will be for naught. There is no point in turning on the oven if you do not have ingredients to make the cake. Kant's "analytic truth" is not even true except given the proviso that one who "wills" an end is one who sees and pursues a sufficient means to that end. Hence, his truth is at best a special application of a more fundamental "analytic" truth: that *whoever wills the end also wills (insofar as reason has a decisive influence on their actions) a sufficient means to the end that is within their power.* Here, the shift to the indefinite article—*a* sufficient means—bespeaks the lack of singularization.[11]

Engstrom, in his reconstruction and defense of Kant's account of practical reasoning, recognizes that Kant's treatment of purposive reasoning might seem to overlook the essential role of sufficient means.[12] His rejoinder, in effect, is that the two analytic truths I am contrasting are really equivalent. For "it is necessarily true that doing everything necessary to achieve some object or end is identical with doing something sufficient." This purported equivalence does have an air of plausibility. Obviously doing something sufficient entails doing everything necessary. And in support of the converse entailment, we might, with Engstrom, offer this apparent contrapositive reformulation: "until one has done something sufficient there is more that needs to be done."

But Engstrom's equivalence is correct only if we allow as description-forms of actions "done to achieve some object or end" such things as "achieving E" or "tak-

---

11 Kant's derivations of *moral* obligations characteristically rely on two claims of necessity. The first is that the necessary end for all rational finite beings is obedience to the moral law. The second is that a certain kind of action—say, keeping a promise or telling the truth—is a necessary means for such obedience in every context in which the question arises whether to perform an action of that kind. Anscombe's (1951, 2) famous objections target both steps.

12 All quotations in this paragraph are from Engstrom (2009, 41, n.).

ing some sufficient means to achieve *E*." So interpreted, the claim of equivalence would be not merely correct; it would be tautologous. And as such, it would have nothing to say about practical reasoning. Consider that while we can say, if we like, that achieving *E* is sufficient for achieving *E*, we cannot say that achieving *E* is a sufficient *means* for achieving *E*. We cannot say this, at any rate, if to identify a sufficient means for achieving *E* is to find a description of an action which answers the question, "How am I to achieve *E*?" An answer to this question must reflect a substantive piece of knowledge, not a mere shuffling of identical or otherwise logically equivalent descriptions.

Similarly, if by "doing everything necessary to achieve some object or end" is meant that the agent takes every necessary *means* to their end, in the sense of "means" just identified, then their doing this does not entail their "doing something sufficient." Suppose there are just three courses of action which are sufficient means for doing *E*: doing *A* then *B* then *C*, doing *D* then *B*, or doing *B* then *F* then *G*. In this case there is one necessary means for doing *E*: doing *B*.[13] To take every necessary means for doing *E* is thus only to do *B*. But that one does *B* does not entail that one takes a sufficient means for doing *E*. This shows that when interpreted as a claim about necessary and sufficient means—as it must be if it is to serve in defense of Kant's approach to purposive reasoning—Engstrom's equivalence does not hold.

5 Justification All-Things-Considered

A reason for an action derives from its capacity to realize, or help realize, an end. As ends may be multiply realized, consciousness of an action as justified as a sufficient means to a given end does not singularize. As the latter consciousness is the fundamental form of consciousness of an action as justified, it belongs to the form of consciousness of practical justification as such that it does not singularize.

---

13 Can we say that in this case there is a disjunctive necessary means, namely, to either do *A* then *B* then *C or* to do *D* then *B or* etc.? To see why this suggestion is useless, consider (a) that a specification of means should be a specification of an action under which it is to be intentional; and (b) that if we can be said to act intentionally under disjunctive specifications at all, it will be as an implication of our acting intentionally under one of the disjuncts. Perhaps we can allow it is intentional of me that I am either making a cake or going to the moon, but such talk is at best a trivial consequence of my knowing myself to be making a cake. Thought about means must make direct contact with the disjuncts which describe particular actions if it is to imply our intentionally satisfying disjunctive descriptions thereof.

So I have argued. But one may wish to object to the final step. Granted, reasons for action derive from consideration of the ends the action is fit to serve. But it is one thing to see a particular reason for an action, and another thing to see that action as justified, full stop. Choosing an action, for a conscientious agent, means taking into account everything that pertains to the respective merits of the options. Such an agent does not identify a particular good end that a particular option serves and then calls it quits; they choose on the basis of a comprehensive assessment of all salient reasons pro and con. They act, as it is said, in light of an "all things considered" judgment about what to do.

From the fact that consciousness of the form *doing M is a sufficient means to my good end* fails to singularize, it does not follow that consciousness of the form *doing M is justified all things considered* fails to singularize. So, it looks open for the practical Fregean to solve the challenge of singularization by taking the practical-inferential thought to be a consciousness of the latter form. Of course, this will require a more complicated conception of the premises of a practical inference than is envisioned in the literature on the "practical syllogism." But our account should answer to the facts on the ground, not to a desire for elegance.

We find this idea, too, in Engstrom's reconstruction of Kant. At the heart of Engstrom's account is the idea of a "practical judgment," a judgment of what it is good to do which may be identified with an intention to do the thing judged good. Engstrom appreciates the point I have made here—that this identification can be sustained only if the envisioned judgment of goodness singularizes. But he thinks we can meet this condition, and that we can do so precisely by understanding the judgment in question to be all-things-considered. As he puts the idea, if a judgment of goodness is to have "the efficacy of an intention," then it "must deem the action good, not just in this or that respect, but on the whole, or on balance, since to judge merely that an action is good in some respect is not to imply that its opposite is unworthy of choice, or bad" (Engstrom 2009, 49–50). Whereas, "if one reaches a decision and judges that one of the alternatives is good on the whole, subsequent judgment that the other is good on the whole is thereby excluded" (Engstrom 2009, 102).[14]

Is this so? Is it really the case that we are excluded from judging two competing alternatives good on the whole, justified all things considered? Let us approach this question through an example. I seek, rightly, to raise my neighbor's spirits. I know I can do so by making him a cake. So much structure we have already considered. Now, let us ask: what more do I need to add to this thought to get to the

---

[14] Davidson's identification of "pure intending" with "all-out" judgments of desirability (2001, 99) is an earlier proposal of the same character as that described in this paragraph.

conclusion that my making him a cake is justified all things considered? What further considerations do I need to register if I am to be confident this action is, as Engstrom puts it, good on the whole?

This question, abstract as it is, may seem difficult to answer. In fact, we can make quick progress by examining how actual human agents, on those occasions in which they seek to be conscientious in their choices, satisfy themselves that an action is good unconditionally and not merely relative to some particular end. What we will find, as we conduct this inquiry, is that agents often rely upon a criterion that is easy to state, if not always easy to apply in the given case. The criterion is that taking the action in question does not stand in the way of their pursuit of their other good ends and obligations.

Perhaps I promised my wife that I would save her the ingredients that would be needed to make a cake. Or suppose I worry making the cake would aggravate the wrist injury I am trying to keep under control—as our electric mixer is broken and I would have to whisk everything by hand. Or perhaps I know what I really need to be doing right now is taking steps to meet a work deadline. In the first two of these cases, I have a compelling reason for opting for some alternative means of raising my neighbor's spirits; in the third case, there is a consideration that indicates that the whole matter of endeavoring to raise my neighbor's spirits should be left for another occasion. But now consider a fourth case: I see no considerations of any of these kinds to be in play. My making the cake would not run up against my other ends or obligations in any way I can see. Then, I suggest, I will find that this action, simply on this basis, has survived the crucible of all-things-considered assessment.

My thinking on this occasion reveals my concern with meeting the following conditions: (1) that my action be a sufficient means for realizing my good end and (2) that it not interfere with pursuit of my other good ends or obligations. Call this bipartite standard *elementary rationality*. Attention to the reflection of conscientious agents will show they are very often content to determine that an action achieves elementary rationality. Evidently, they view elementary rationality as sufficient for justification all things considered.[15]

In comparison to the formulae for practical rationality proposed by philosophers in the broadly decision-theoretic tradition, the standard of elementary rationality may look unrigorous, even facile. The adjudication of this dispute is a large topic. But I can at least suggest, in broad outline, a reason to hold that it is

---

15 Sufficient but not, of course, necessary, for there will be cases in which one cannot avoid obstructing some end or other no matter what one does.

rather the other side of this disagreement that is guilty of failing to think seriously about the true character of the work of rational agency.

Formalistic principles of choice tend to treat acting itself as an afterthought. An action is modeled on placing a bet or choosing a lottery. As actions, these are exceedingly simple. The difficulty in placing a bet is not in the placing of it —one need only indicate one's intention with a word—but in calculating what bet to place. Accordingly, the formalistic principles devote themselves to an analysis of such calculations.

In real life, actions are not simple. They are not the infallible upshot of prior choices. They take time, thought, effort, and attention. One needs to ask how to realize an end not just once, but repeatedly, as the situation develops. At the limit, speaking of the agent as asking themselves this question is an idealization of processes of thought whose shape is more continuous and dynamic.

A realistic picture of agency-in-the-world will enable us to understand why actual agents should take elementary rationality as the characteristic standard of justification. For on the one hand, our practical thought must be focused on finding and then following through on a means toward achieving what we are after. And then, focused on this positive task as we must be, there are sharp limits on what other considerations we may simultaneously have in view. Occasionally when the environment cooperates, we can find a single course of action in which we may respond to several different positive considerations at once. But because different ends demand different means, different exploitations of the affordances at hand, the prospects for multitasking will invariably be circumscribed. In general, we are wise to focus on getting this or that thing accomplished, attending to other ends only with a view toward holding them safe for pursuit on future occasions. And so, elementary rationality presents itself as our ideal.

It matters for our present topic that conscientious agents find elementary rationality sufficient for all-things-considered justification. For consciousness of the elementary rationality of an action does not singularize.

There are two components to the grounds for an assessment of elementary rationality. The first component encompasses thoughts which go into establishing that the action or course of action is a sufficient means to a justified end. Call this *positive teleology*. We have already seen that consciousness of positive teleology does not singularize.

The second component encompasses thoughts which bear on the question of whether the action will interfere with the pursuit of our further ends and obligations. Call this *negative teleology*. This is the new element our search for all-things-considered justification has introduced. And it does not singularize either. That doing M for the sake of E would not obstruct my pursuit of other ends or obligations does not imply that every alternative means *would* interfere with some end or obligation. The thought that it will cause no trouble for me to make my neighbor a cake sits comfortably with the thought that buying him a bottle of wine will cause no trouble either.

Granting that elementary rationality suffices for goodness on the whole, consciousness of goodness on the whole does not singularize. Engstrom's attempt to vindicate practical Fregeanism fails.

Engstrom's Kant sees judgments of goodness-on-the-whole as bipolar in the following way: thinking an action good on the whole is thinking alternative actions bad on the whole. This posited opposition parallels that of truth, as thinking a judgment true is thinking alternative judgments false. It might seem inevitable that we should draw such a parallel; we are now in a position to see why it is a mistake to do so. An action's goodness derives from its relationship to ends. The opposite of goodness thus consists in the opposing relationship to ends. As an action is good in its service to a good end, so an action is bad in its *disservice* to such an end.[16] Consideration of this prospect is just what I have called negative teleology.

Construing the opposition of good and bad in this way, we secure that an action cannot be both good and bad relative to the same end. Granting the sufficiency of elementary teleology for goodness on the whole, we are also on the way to securing that an action cannot be both good and bad on the whole. But because an action's being suited to serve an end does not imply that alternatives to the action will be hindrances to that end, goodness and badness do not pattern onto incompatible alternatives in the manner of truth and falsity.

6 Practical Consciousness of Justification

My argument has relied on the following assumption: if a justificatory status can be possessed by incompatible actions, then consciousness of an action as possessing that status cannot singularize. This might seem undeniable. An action's justificatory status is something of which we may be conscious, something we may recognize or know. If it is possible for two incompatible actions to have a given justificatory status, how then can it be impossible for us to be conscious of both as having that status?

But in fact, the matter might be held to be more complex. We can grant that it must be possible for us to be conscious, in some sense, of the justificatory status of

---

[16] An action may also be bad in its service to a bad end. This is inherited badness; the ultimate explanation of why it is bad lies with an explanation of the badness of the end. Ultimately, I would argue, this will be a matter of disservice to a good end.

any available action. But we might posit *different modes* of such consciousness, modes which can differ even while holding action and justificatory status fixed. This idea gives us an extra degree of freedom. It opens the prospect of a distinctive mode of consciousness of justification that can attach at most to only one action in any set of competing alternatives of which the agent is aware. Call this envisioned mode of awareness *practical consciousness* of justification. An agent may be aware of—may know or recognize—more than one incompatible alternative to possess the requisite justificatory status, but can be practically conscious of such a justification for only one alternative. We may thus cast practical Fregeanism as taking a practical inference to consist in the practical consciousness of the justification for the action provided by the premises.

So far, this is just a template for a solution to the challenge of singularization. A solution will mean saying what the "practical" mode of consciousness of justification is.

Marcus defends a Fregean account of practical inference, on which "acting-for-a-reason is the agent's representing one action as to be done as a consequence of the to-be-done-ness of another action" (Marcus 2012, 71). He acknowledges this account may seem belied by the fact that sometimes "we fail to act or even to be motivated by what we judge to be the right thing to do, all things considered."[17] His solution is to appeal to a distinction between "engaged" and "disengaged" deliberation, where in the former case but not in the latter, the agent's "will is on the line" and he has "given himself over to the results of his deliberation." This appeal equips him to specify the practical-inferential thought as a representation of all-things-considered to-be-doneness which is embedded in engaged deliberation. Marcus suggests that this proposal is not question-begging because we have an independent phenomenological grasp on the engaged/disengaged distinction in advance of encountering Marcus' philosophical use of it.

Perhaps we do. Regardless, the distinction is in the wrong place to help with the challenge of singularization. I seek to raise my neighbor's spirits, consider that I may do so either by making him a cake or buying him a nice bottle of wine, and, as it happens, opt for the former. In all of this reflection, my thinking is "engaged," my will on the line. For I know throughout that I will conclude by choosing and pursuing some means for raising my neighbor's spirits. If there is a difference between the mode in which I was conscious of my justification for the action I chose and the mode in which I was conscious of my justification for the action I did not, it must be a difference between modes each of which are available within "engaged" deliberation.

---

[17] The remaining quotations and ascriptions in this paragraph are from Marcus (2012, 82–83).

There is a lesson here that is not particular to Marcus. "Internalism" about moral knowledge holds that such knowledge is intrinsically motivating, without the need for an independently constituted desire. Against this, anti-internalists point to the many cases in which people are not moved to act by moral views they purport to accept. A familiar style of internalist response is that such cases can be cordoned off as involving a defect of knowledge or will, with internalism then preserved for the non-defective cases. But I exhibit no defect of any kind when I do not choose to buy my neighbor a bottle of wine. On the contrary, I *have* to turn down one of my options, despite its being justified, if I am to act towards my end at all. This shows that the challenge of singularization is wholly distinct from traditional worries about motivational force.

Müller argues that a "judgment relating means to end" upon which an agent acts possesses "intrinsic teleology" (1979, 98 and 106). Such a means-end judgment does not merely identify an action which furthers attainment of the end; it is itself "intrinsically 'in the service of' the attainment of the end" (Müller 1979, 104). Here, the "intrinsically" signals that the judgment is for the sake of the end not in virtue of a further thought representing it as such. That it is for the sake of the end is internal to the judgment that it is: its possession of this teleology "must be treated as somehow internal to its own content" (Müller 1979, 99).

Müller says, "there seems to be a close link between what I call the intrinsic teleology of practical reasoning and the rationality of inferring non-necessary conditions as practical conclusions." Appreciating intrinsic teleology will help us to see why, "*pace* Buridan's ass," it is no "impediment" to action "when a given end leaves us a choice of equally acceptable means...." This is because a means-end judgment's having such teleology "implies that it results in an action conducive to [the] end when such an action is possible" (Müller 1979, 104). A practical Fregean might wish to extend this idea in a bid to solve the challenge of singularization: consciousness of an action's justification may be intrinsically teleological or it may not, and it is only when it is that it entails the determination to act.

If the solution is to work, we must be able to hold that when I consider that I might buy my neighbor a nice bottle of wine to raise his spirits but instead I make him a cake, my consciousness of the justification for the former action is not intrinsically teleological. And it is difficult to understand how that can be so.

One obstacle is that Müller's own attempts to bring the idea of intrinsic teleology into view for us do not help us achieve this understanding. For example, he writes,

> If I consider the possibilities of taking something across a river, in order to distract myself, my awareness (or the thought, if it occurs) that I am doing this to distract myself is in no way constitutive of what I am considering. If, on the other hand, I consider, with a view to acting,

how such-and-such can be taken across, my consideration's being conducted with a view to this end must be treated as somehow internal to its own content (Müller 1979, 99).

On what side of the contrast here implied should we locate my judgment that I can raise my neighbor's spirits by buying him some wine? My consideration of this possibility for action is not for the sake of distracting myself or any other extrinsic end. So, it seems we should rather say that I "conduct this consideration with a view" to achieving the very end the thought concerns. And, of course, this *is* the right thing to say—assuming, at any rate, we are using these words with their ordinary meaning. But then this judgment would possess intrinsic teleology no less than the judgment upon which I actually act, and intrinsic teleology would not after all provide for singularization.

We might try to hold that there are two degrees of intrinsic teleology that a means-end judgment can possess. One is possessed by any such judgment "conducted with a view to the end" in the sense just illustrated, whether one acts upon it or not. The second degree is possessed only by the judgment upon which the agent actually acts. It is only possession of intrinsic teleology of the second degree which "implies [the judgment] results in an action conducive to [the] end when such an action is possible," and so is such as to singularize.

But this idea is, I think, difficult to make out. A means-end judgment, a judgment of the form *doing M is a means of doing E*, is a judgment of potentiality. It may be reformulated with "can": *I can do E by doing M*. By contrast, a determination, an intention, to do E by doing M contains a judgment of actuality: *I will do E by doing M* or *I am doing E by doing M*. The question is how the former judgment could be construed to have a content which entails or contains the latter. Certainly, the thought that I *must* do A—or, à la Kant, that it is "practically necessary" to do A—could intelligibly be held to entail the determination or choice that I *will* do A. (This is just what the moral internalist maintains.) But the thought that I *can* do A has no such implication. The implication goes rather in the opposite direction. Müller himself treats this matter as dark: "there *seems* to be a close link...," "...must be treated as *somehow* internal..." I think this is a sign we will do better to try a different tack.[18]

---

[18] In conversation, Müller reports that he now conceives the unity of the practical inference as involving a distinctive practicality in the inference considered as a whole. This may move his picture closer to the one I will offer here.

7 Solving the Challenge of Singularization

Seeking to elaborate Frege's principle for the practical case, we must identify the practical-inferential thought, the thought which, per the principle, constitutes the drawing of a practical inference. The Fregean account of practical inference offers a candidate for this thought: it is the consciousness of an action as justified by reasons for it.

This may seem a natural, even inevitable, idea. It mirrors what Frege says we mean when we speak of inference in the theoretical case. But it cannot be sustained.

An intention to act precludes intentions to perform incompatible actions. Intending to do A, and knowing that to be incompatible with doing B, I accept that I have foreclosed on my doing B. Consciousness of an action as justified, by contrast, does not rule out consciousness of incompatible actions as justified. This failure of singularization is a consequence of the teleological form of practical justification: reasons for action derive from the ends these actions may serve. There is no avoiding this result. It is not circumvented by appeal to special notions of means, the idea of an all-things-considered assessment, or the hypothesis of a distinctively practical mode of consciousness of practical justification.

The upshot is that the Fregean account is unsustainable. To hold to Frege's principle, we will need to articulate an alternative understanding of the form of the practical-inferential thought, one which exhibits the necessary congruence with the logic of intention.

What sets the terms of our problem, I suggest, also provides its solution. We seek a thought that singularizes in the manner of intention. The right conclusion is that the thought we seek is itself an intention.

A practical inference concludes in an intentional action or otherwise an intention to act. The concluding intention is to do M, say. Of course, this intention considered as such is not what we are looking for. We do not reveal the thought constituting a practical inference on my part by saying I intend to do M. A specification of the practical-inferential thought must represent not merely the conclusion of the inference but also its premises, as well as a connection between the conclusion and premises. I am doing M, let us say, for the sake of end E and in the judgment that doing M is a means of realizing E. The practical-inferential thought must provide for the whole of this nexus. What intention could meet this condition?

Again, the question contains its answer. The intention we seek just is the intention to do M for the sake of E. A practical inference from an end to a means consists in an intention to take the action for the sake of the end.

The practical-inferential thought, the thought that provides of the unity of a practical inference, is an intention of the form:

I (will) do M for the sake of E.

I will call this view the intentionalist account of practical inference or, a bit more pithily, inferential intentionalism.

If inferential intentionalism can be adequately explained and shown otherwise objectionable, it is evident that it will solve the problem of singularization. The intention *to do M to for the sake of E* entails the intention to do M. Indeed, it just is (a more determinate form of) that intention. And so, it cannot fail to singularize in the manner of that intention. Knowing doing M and doing O to be incompatible, I can simultaneously recognize both to be justified as means toward realizing end E. But I cannot simultaneously intend *doing M for the sake of E* and *doing O for the sake of E*.

8 Practical Inference as Realization

The fundamental form of practical inference is the taking of a sufficient means to an end. To so infer, I must have an end I am pursuing, and I must deem the action I take to be a sufficient means to that end. There are two different thoughts here: an intention to realize the end, and the judgment that by the action in question I may realize that end. The conclusion—my determination to take the action—depends upon both of these thoughts taken together. It cannot issue from just one alone.

We may represent the thoughts that are joined together in a practical inference as follows:

Reasoning to a sufficient means

(1) I seek to realize E.

(2) Doing M is a sufficient means of realizing E.

(3) Therefore, I will do M.

Here (1) and (3) represent intentions, and (2) a judgment about how one may achieve an end.

According to Frege's principle, these three thoughts are joined in an inferential nexus by being thought as joined. What more can we say about the thought which so joins them? A proponent of practical Fregeanism might suggest it is this:

> (F1) I am conscious that *my seeking to realize E coupled with doing M being a sufficient means of realizing E justifies my doing M.*
>
> Or perhaps:
>
> (F2) I am conscious that *its being good to realize E coupled with doing M being a sufficient means of realizing E justifies my doing M.*

It is not to present purposes to examine the differences between these options, or between others a practical Fregean might conceivably propose. What matters is a feature common to all such proposals: that they will explicitly represent me as joining thoughts (1) and (2) together to (3). Contrast the intentionalist proposal:

> (I) I intend I (will) do *M* for the sake of *E*.

This thought explicitly represents me as joining thought (1) to (3). But (2), the means-end judgment, seems to have dropped out of the picture. That doing *M* is a sufficient means of realizing *E* is not explicitly represented within the content of (1) as something I think. To take (I) as the practical-inferential thought seems to falsely represent the inference as proceeding from (1) alone.

In fact, (I) does represent my doing *M* as grounded in judgment (2). You cannot intend to do something unless you judge it possible for yourself to do it.[19] If I think I am incapable of climbing the John Hancock Center, I cannot intend to climb the John Hancock Center. The point is general; it holds of all intentions regardless of content. It holds in particular for an intention *to do M for the sake of E*. I cannot intend *to do M for the sake of E* unless I think it possible for me *to do M for the sake of E*. To think this possible is not just to think it possible to do *M* and possible to realize *E*. It is to think it possible to realize or contribute to realizing *E* by doing *M*. This, of course, is what I think possible when I judge doing *M* a means of doing *E*.

We have just noted that intending to do something entails thinking it possible for oneself to do it. But we can say more than this. In principle, this entailment could hold if the agent understood the intention to justify the judgment of possibility. But agents do not think this way. I do not think, "I know I can climb the Han-

---

19 The degree of possibility required is debated in the literature. It may be weak. Perhaps there are contexts in which it is enough for intending to do *A* that one deem that one does not know that one is incapable of doing *A*. This is not a matter we need to pursue here.

cock, for that follows from my intention to do it." I think rather, "It is open to me to form the intention to climb the Hancock, for I have the ability and the resources to do it." Here the judgment of possibility is justified prior to the intention. It has a ground independent of my so intending. We all know, at least in rough outline, the character of such a ground. It will consist in knowledge of one's capacities and skills, and of the affordances of the situation.

The priority of judgment of possibility to intention is, again, general: it holds regardless of the content of the intention. If I intend *to raise my neighbor's spirits by making him a cake*, I must take myself to have a reason, independent of my intending this, to judge it possible for me to raise his spirits in this fashion. (2) is not merely required for (I) but is prior to it in the order of justification. In that sense, it is a necessary ground for the intention.

All of these things are known by the one who intends. Intending *to do M for the sake of E*, I know not just that I seek to do M and to realize E. I know that I judge, on prior grounds, that it is possible for me to realize E through doing M. This judgment is not explicitly represented in my intention. But, as we are now observing, it lies just below the surface.

One may still find a reason to worry here about inferential intentionalism. What does it signify that (1), but not (2), is explicitly represented in the practical-inferential thought? Does that not still suggest that (1) gives the inference's only real premise, with judgment (2) playing some other, subsidiary role?

The answer to this question will depend upon what we mean by "premise."

Let us say that a "syllogism" is a representation of a possible course of reasoning with the following features: it is a list of n things one might think; each of the first n-1 thoughts (a.k.a., the "premises") could intelligibly be thought without thinking any of the other thoughts on the list; but thinking the first n-1 thoughts together guarantees thinking the final nth thought (the "conclusion").

Theoretical reasoning of the *modus ponens* form would appear to admit of such a representation:

The modus ponens syllogism

(i) p

(ii) *if p then q*

(iii) q

When p and q are logically independent, I can judge (i) without judging (ii) or (iii), and I can judge (ii) without judging (i) or (iii), but I cannot judge (i) and (ii) together without judging (iii). (Carroll's tortoise says he can, but we know he is bluffing.)

A proponent of the Fregean account of theoretical inference can accommodate the syllogistic character of this reasoning. Indeed, she can try to give an account of it. She can say that one who judges (i) and (ii) together, understanding what she thus judges, cannot but recognize the justification they provide for judging (iii). And recognizing this justification, she thereby judges (iii).[20]

Reasoning to a necessary means is sometimes thought (e.g., by the thinkers listed in footnote 13) to provide a practical example of a syllogism:

The necessary-means syllogism

I seek to realize E.

(2N) Doing M is a necessary means for realizing E.

(3) I will do M.

One who intends (1) and judges (2N), it might be held, is guaranteed to intend (3). (We may wish to add the proviso, with Kant, that the agent be one for whom "reason completely determined the will.") And again, a practical Fregean might purport to offer a natural explanation of this guarantee.

In reasoning that admits of a syllogistic representation, the conclusion comes immediately of holding the premises together in consciousness. The premises, as it were, wring the conclusion from us. It is tempting to think that all reasoning, at bottom, is like this. Sometimes the premises a person offers in support of a conclusion they draw do not seem to us to render the conclusion inevitable. We tend to think this means that their accounting of their premises is incomplete. There must be a suppressed premise or two at work in the person's thinking. Once these are brought to light and added to the list, we will find ourselves with reasoning admitting of a syllogistic representation (or, perhaps, a linked chain of such representations).

Whether or not this is so of theoretical reasoning as such, it is not true of reasoning as such. For it is not true of practical reasoning in its most characteristic employment. A practical inference from an end to the taking of a sufficient means does not admit of a syllogistic representation. Were we to allow the definition I gave of a syllogism to fix the meaning of "premise," then (2) would not be a "premise" of a practical inference to the taking of a sufficient means. Indeed, such an inference could not be said to have any "premises" at all.

But this is puzzling, for, as we have observed, (1) and (2) do together provide a ground for an inference to (3). This ground, moreover, is sufficient: no further con-

---

20 See, for example, Marcus (2021).

siderations are needed to justify drawing this conclusion.[21] How can we hold onto this truth while acknowledging the non-syllogistic character of reasoning from (1) and (2) to (3)? Inferential intentionalism shows how. No thoughts beyond (1) or (2) are needed to provide grounds of the inference to (3). But a further thought, not contained within or otherwise guaranteed by these two thoughts, *is* needed to infer (3) from (1) and (2). *The inference itself is this further thought.* The inference adds something that is not present in the conjunction of the thoughts which constitute its basis. It adds, precisely, that one draws the inference—that one takes the action deemed a means to one's end.

Practical inference is more than holding thoughts together in consciousness. It is actualizing the potential the conjoined premise-thoughts represent. The judgment that an action is a means to one's end is a judgment of opportunity. Recognizing an opportunity is necessary for taking it. But it is not sufficient. The potential must be not just recognized but realized. That is why the means-end judgment is beneath the surface of the inferential thought, instead of represented explicitly therein. What the judgment represents as a potentiality must be represented in the inference as actuality. Judging *doing M is a means to E* gets taken up as actually *doing M for the sake of E*.

There is no such thing as recognizing an opportunity to judge something truly but not judging it. I cannot think: *I can judge truly by judging that p, but I will refrain from doing so*. Recognizing this supposed "opportunity" is already to judge that *p*. By the same token, it means nothing—except as a jokey way of asserting that *p*—to say, "I can judge truly by judging that *p*, and I will take the world up on that opportunity." The thought that an opportunity is taken must add something to the thought that the opportunity obtains.

But of course, there is such a thing as recognizing a means to realizing one's end and not taking it. We must distinguish between recognition of an opportunity and its pursuit. Practical inference is the latter. As such, it depends upon the former. But it goes beyond it. Pursuing an opportunity is work. It must be carried through. The inference is the carrying through.[22]

Disquiet with this picture may remain. Are not the grounds upon which one infers a conclusion supposed to provide a complete explanation of one's doing so? And how can that be if, because the reasoning is not syllogistic, the agent's

---

[21] Here, I follow work in the tradition of the "practical syllogism" in bracketing the prospect of a role for negative teleology.

[22] In the course of putting an opportunity into action, one will likely face more particular questions of how to proceed. One will need to find and take a more particular way forward. The gap between potentiality and actuality explains why practical reasoning has a tendency to grow ever more fine-grained. There is no parallel on the theoretical side.

grasp of these grounds sometimes does and sometimes does not yield the intention to act? Suppose I aim to realize *E* and judge I may do so either by doing *M* or *O*. As it happens, I opt to do *M*. What accounts for this difference? Do we not need to specify a further element, present with respect to my thought of doing *M* but not doing *O*, which completes the explanation of my choice?

In fact, there is a complete explanation of why I do *M*. The explanation is that I do it in order to realize *E*. This explanation implies that I judged doing *M* a means of doing *E*. But it does not imply any particular thoughts or attitudes on my part toward alternatives to doing *M*. Because the explanation is in terms of the end for which the action is undertaken, precisely the same explanation remains available whether we stipulate that I am or am not aware of other potential means of realizing the end.

It is true that if I were aware of other such options, you could ask me why I went in for doing *M* rather than one of the others. I might have something to say to this. Or I might not. If I do not, this would not show my original explanation of doing *M* is incomplete. It would show it is teleological.

9 Practical Inference as Reasoning

Practical inference is reasoning. It is acting on or in light of a reason or justification. The agent recognizes the reason, and act on its basis. An account of practical inference must make room for a role played by the agent's consciousness of her reason, her justification. Otherwise, it loses contact with its subject matter.

The Fregean account does not lose contact with its subject matter (at least not in this way). For the inference is said just to *be* the consciousness of justification. What about inferential intentionalism? I spoke in the last section as if the inferential intentionalist were entitled to speak of the agent's grounds for action. But how do grounds—justifying grounds, reasons—get into the intentionalist picture at all? Is a thought of a ground contained in the intention to do something for the sake of an end?

The answer to this question is yes.

Let us be more explicit about two aspects of consciousness of justification, as it is to figure into practical inference. First, the consciousness of justification is to ensure that a practical inference, as McDowell puts it, manifests not merely "responsiveness to reasons" but "responsiveness to reasons as such" (2009, 128). Perhaps it is possible for a creature to be aware of something which is in fact a reason do something without thinking of the reason in that way. But one who practically infers does conceive her reason *as* a reason. The consideration figures in her thinking in the guise of—under the concept or category of—a reason, a justifying ground.

Second, to know the reason to which an agent responds, conceiving it as the reason it is, is to have an explanation of her action. The explanation is distinctive—so it is earmarked as a "rational" or "reason-involving" explanation. As a first pass at giving its distinctive character, we may note this equivalence: what I say, in "rationally" explaining *why I do (or did) A*, is exactly the same as what I say when I ask myself, in advance of acting, *why do A? Why do A?* speaks to the agent's question, *what am I to do?* which sets the topic of practical reasoning. The *why do A?* is apropos when doing *A* has been indicated as an available option on an occasion for choice, and one seeks to assess what can be said for taking that option. But an action may also be indicated as salient by the fact that it is something the agent is doing or has done. Now the agent's question is not to the point. We ask rather the rational-explanatory question, *why is S doing A?* These questions have a different point. But for the agent they receive the same answer. She gives the same reasons, conceived in just the same way, in answer to both. We can say: *why to do A* becomes *why I do A* upon one's decision.[23]

The specification of the intention *I (will) do M for the sake of E*, we worried, seems not to make use of the concept of a justifying ground. What is undeniable is that it makes use of the concept of an end. An end of an action is just that for the sake of which the action is undertaken. *I do M for the sake of E = I do M to realize E = I do M with the end of E*. Moreover, we are using these constructions to describe the agent's activity not from the outside, but from the inside. We are giving the content of the agent's own intention. The suggestion is not that the agent intends *to do M* and intends *to realize E* and that some fact external to the agent's thought of what she is up to fixes the one thing as done for the sake of the other. The suggestion is that the agent intends not merely *to do M* and *to realize E*, but *to do M with the end of E*.

Shortly, we will consider the relevance of this point to the philosophy of action. For the moment, the pertinent implication is that the inferential intention represents the agent, in practically inferring, as acting for an end conceived *as* an end. When I *intend to do M for the sake of E*, *E* figures into my thinking under the concept of end. In parallel with McDowell's formulation, we may say that inferential intentionalism at least shows us how to understand practical reason as responsiveness to *ends as such*.

---

[23] This is not to say, as a proponent of practical Fregeanism might, that the agent's finding a satisfying answer to the question why to do *A* *is* for her to decide to do *A*. It is to say that *if* she does act upon the reasons of which she is conscious, then the content of this consciousness will be the rational explanation of her action.

Now, suppose I go out with my friend with the end of having fun. My intention is *to go out with my friend in order to have fun.* Knowing my own intention, I have an answer to the question why I go out. The answer is: to have fun. This is precisely the same answer I give when I ask myself earlier whether to take up my friend's suggestion. "She asks me to go out. Why do that? Well, to have fun!" My explanation of why I go out is thus "rational" by the measure earlier observed: what explains why I go out is precisely my answer to the question why to go out. The latter question, as it is a form of the agent's question, is answered by giving reasons for action, understood as such. It follows that the explanation of my action available to me in knowing my intention is an explanation in terms of reasons for action, understood as such. As my inference is in the consciousness of an end as an end, so, we see, it is in the consciousness of a reason as a reason.

It may seem that this argument has to be unsound. It purports to establish that understanding oneself to act for the sake of an end just is to understand oneself as acting for the sake of a reason or justification. But surely it is an observable fact that human beings can act for ends they view as worthless and, as such, as not justificatory. "It is true I am kicking this garden gnome so as to knock it over," I might say. "But as to why I seek to knock it over, I can give no reason. I allow it is a pointless pursuit. I'm not interested in causing trouble. And I am not even enjoying the activity. I just cannot help it." So much seems possible for a human being, if, admittedly, "irrational." There is thus a difference between acting for an end as such and acting for a reason as such. The categories come apart.

An answer to this objection will require leaving the topic of practical inference strictly conceived. What needs to be seen is how a practical inference from a given end depends for its full intelligibility on an explanation of the pursuit of the end—and how cases of "irrationality" depend parasitically on cases of full intelligibility.

An explanation of the pursuit of an end may relate the end to a further end for which it is itself to be pursued. But ultimately, we must come to an end which explains its own pursuit. This would be an end such that in understanding what it is, we understand why it can be cited in answer to the question what to do. Such an end will not merely be a reason for action. It will be, for us, what a reason for action is.[24]

---

[24] Kant thought such a reason must arise from reason alone, without any contribution from experience. I think this idea is untenable and so that an inquiry into ultimate ends will need to explain why we do not need it.

10 Practical Inference as Intention

According to inferential intentionalism, doing something for the sake of an end is intentional. When I do M for the sake of E, it is not merely my doing M and my pursuit of E that count as objects of my intention, but my doing the one for the sake of the other. If such an intention really does provide the key to practical inference, one will wonder why contemporary philosophers of action, who spend a lot of time thinking about intentions, have shown almost no inclination to appeal it in explaining any of the things they seek to explain.[25] In this final section, I will offer a hypothesis for this neglect.

The neglect, I think, is not because the idea is somehow unintuitive. Let us return to our example. I make my neighbor a cake to raise his spirits, and that to open him up to rational persuasion, and that to ensure passage of my condo-board proposal, and that to serve justice. Did I do one thing intentionally, or four? We give the first answer if we want to emphasize that it was from my making the cake that, as I conceived it, all else followed. We give the second answer if we want to emphasize the full complexity of my design. Either way, we should not overlook that my plan is not merely that I should do the four things in this order of means and ends, but that the means should *serve as means* in just the way the order lays out. My plan could not be said to have been executed if, while it is true that I baked my neighbor a cake and raised his spirits, it was not by the cake that the spirits were raised. That my making him the cake should be the vehicle of raising his spirits was itself something I sought, something that I meant or intended.

This point can be brought out in a different way. Suppose I say, "In a few moments, I am going to create a distraction," and you ask, "Where do you intend to do that?" You are not asking where my intention is (as one might try to determine when doing cognitive science), nor where I go to do my intending (as if it were a kind of meditating). The location you seek is not the location of my intention or intending, but the location *in* my intention—the location I intend. It is internal to the content of the intention. Just the same, if you ask "How do you intend to do that?" you are not asking for my means of forming and maintaining this intention (as if, say, it took a special act of willpower). The means you seek is not the means

---

[25] The glaring exception to this is Wilson (1980) and, following Wilson, Ginet (1990). Unfortunately, Wilson and Ginet's use of the idea of an intention to act for the sake of a further purpose turns on their analysis of such an intention as making a *de re* reference to an action considered as a "token event." This is untenable (McDowell 2011; see also Thompson 2008). But the failure of this analysis does not impugn the idea it seeks to analyze.

of my intending but the means in my intending—the means I intend, my intended means. Here, too, my answer to this question will identify something internal to my intention's content.

One of the three kinds of statement about intention identified at the beginning of Anscombe's *Intention*[26] is that in which we say "with what intention the thing was done." What we are now observing is that something's being done with an intention is itself something the agent intends. To say that I bake my neighbor a cake with the intention of raising his spirits is, on the use to which Anscombe is drawing our attention, the same as to say that I bake him the cake in order to raise his spirits.[27] And that I bake him the cake to raise his spirits, we are noticing, means that I intend *to bake him a cake to raise his spirits*. That the one act is for the sake of the other itself falls within the scope of my intention. But then that I do the one thing with the intention of doing the other, being the same link otherwise described, also falls within the scope of my intention. In this way, intending is itself revealed to be intentional.

This may seem paradoxical. The appearance of paradox here, I take it, is a version of the paradoxical appearance which Anscombe pointed out in the case of actions for which "it is essential...that someone who is doing it should think he is doing it" (Anscombe 1981, 10). Her example is marriage. You cannot get married except in the thought of doing so.[28] This simple point seems, paradoxically, to make it impossible to explain what marrying is. Seeking to say what goes into getting married, we will need to note as one condition that the people involved think they are getting married. But what is it that a person who thinks this thinks they are up to? This is just a reappearance of our original question of what marrying is. So, we need to go back to beginning, and immediately we stumble again upon the fact that the act we seek to explain requires the thought of itself. We are trapped in a tiny explanatory circle. It seems we have no understanding of marriage at all, that we simply lack a determinate concept.

---

26 See Anscombe (1963, 1).
27 As Wilson (1985, 32, n.) points out, there are uses of talk of "the intention with which" other than the one Anscombe had in mind. "I took a nap with the intention of getting to my chores later" is an example. But such uses are not as distinct as Wilson seems to think. I think the remark about the nap may be analyzed in terms of the idea of negative teleology.
28 This is, among other things, a legal fact. In my state of Illinois, as I presume is true elsewhere, a supposed marriage is annulled if the supposed act of getting married is shown to have been nonconsensual for one of the parties. This does not mean, of course, that a marrying ceremony is valid if it is consented to under some description or other. It means that one who marries must consent to doing just that.

I do not think Anscombe's line of thought really shows this. What it shows is that *if* an "explanation" of an idea is not allowed to exploit the understanding of the idea of one who possesses it, then the idea of marriage has no explanation, is inexplicable. From this conditional we need not conclude that its consequent is true; we can conclude rather that its antecedent is false. Say that a "reductive" or "naturalistic" explanation of a concept seeks to explain it in terms that do not rely upon the understanding of the concept we already have in advance of giving the explanation. Then what has been shown impossible is a naturalistic explanation of the idea of marriage.

According to the "standard story" of rational action, an action is done for a reason in virtue of being caused in the right way by desires and other related "mental states." This idea is naturally understood, among other things, as proposing a template for an account of acting with an intention: to do M with the intention of doing E, by the lights of the "standard story," is for one's doing M to be caused in a certain manner by one's desire to do E along other mental states. It is a condition on the account that we are not to specify the requisite manner of causing through appeal to the notion of an *intention with which*—as that is among the phenomena we seek to explain—but rather in other terms.

As Davidson predicted, no account of this kind has been found.[29] Davidson's ground for his prediction had to do with the justificatory character of a rational explanation of action. Our current reflections support this general line (if not the particular details of Davidson's elaboration thereof). Practical inference, acting in light of a reason, is acting with the intention of realizing an end. Acting with such an intention is itself intentional. It follows that, like getting married, it does not admit of a naturalistic explanation. But it is such an explanation that the standard story directs us to find. Inferential intentionalism is irreconcilable with the standard story.[30]

References

Anscombe, Gertrude Elizabeth Margaret (1958): Modern Moral Philosophy. In: *Philosophy* 33, 1–19.
Anscombe, Gertrude Elizabeth Margaret (1981): "On promising and its justice, and whether it needs be respected in foro interno." In: Anscombe, Gertrude Elizabeth Margaret: *Ethics, Religion, and Politics*. Minneapolis: University of Minnesota Press.

---

29 Davidson (2001a).
30 I would like to thank Anton Ford, Matthias Haase, Eric Marcus, Anselm Müller, Dawa Ometto, Will Small, Nora Titone and participants in workshops and seminars at the University of Chicago in 2022–2023 for extremely helpful comments on drafts of this paper.

Anscombe, Gertrude Elizabeth Margaret (2000): *Intention*. Cambridge: Harvard University Press.
Boghossian, Paul (2014): "What Is Inference?" In: *Philosophical Studies* 169. No. 1, 1–18.
Bridges, Jason (Manuscript): "Practical rationality: comparison vs. purpose."
Broome, John (2002): "Practical reasoning." In: Bermúdez, José Luis and Millar, Alan (Eds.): *Reason and Nature: Essays in the Theory of Rationality*. Oxford: Oxford University Press, 85–111.
Chang, Ruth (2016): "Comparativism: The grounds of rational choice." In: Lord, Errol and Maguire, Barry (Eds.): *Weighing Reasons*. Oxford: Oxford University Press, 213–240.
Davidson, Donald (2001a): "Freedom to act." In: Davidson, Donald: *Essays on Actions and Events: Philosophical Essays*. Oxford: Oxford University Press, 63–81.
Davidson, Donald (2001b): "Intending." In: Davidson, Donald: *Essays on Actions and Events: Philosophical Essays*. Oxford: Oxford University Press, 83–102.
Engstrom, Stephen P. (2009): *The Form of Practical Knowledge: A Study of the Categorical Imperative*. Cambridge: Harvard University Press.
Frege, Gottlob (1979): "Logic (1879–1891)". In: Frege, Gottlob: *Posthumous Writings*. Hans Hermes, Friedrich Kambartel, and Friedrich Kaulbach with the assistance of Gottfried Gabriel and Walburga Rödding (Eds.). Peter Long and Roger White with the assistance of Raymond Hargreaves (Trans.). Oxford: Basil Blackwell.
Ginet, Carl (1990): *On Action*. Cambridge: Cambridge University Press.
Hare, Richard (1971): "Practical inferences." In: Hare, Richard: *Practical Inferences*. Berkeley: University of California Press, 59–73.
Kant, Immanuel (2012): *Groundwork of the Metaphysics of Morals*. Cambridge: Cambridge University Press.
Kant, Immanuel (2015): *Critique of Practical Reason*. Cambridge: Cambridge University Press.
Marcus, Eric (2012): *Rational Causation*. Cambridge: Harvard University Press.
Marcus, Eric (2021): *Belief, Inference, and the Self-Conscious Mind*. Oxford: Oxford University Press.
McDowell, John (2009): "Conceptual capacities in perception." In: McDowell, John: *Having the World in View: Essays on Kant, Hegel, and Sellars*. Cambridge: Harvard University Press.
McDowell, John (2011): "Some Remarks on Intention in Action." In: *The Amherst Lecture in Philosophy* 6, 1–18.
Müller, Anselm Winfried (1979): "How Theoretical is Practical Reasoning?" In: Diamond, Cora and Teichman, Jenny (Eds.): *Intention and Intentionality: Essays in Honour of G. E. M. Anscombe*. Ithaca: Cornell University Press, 91–108.
Nussbaum, Martha (1978): *Aristotle's De Motu Animalium: Text with Translation, Commentary, and Interpretive Essays*. Princeton: Princeton University Press.
Rödl, Sebastian (2007): *Self-consciousness*. Cambridge: Harvard University Press.
Rödl, Sebastian (2020): "Nature and the Good." In: *Analytic Philosophy* 61. No. 4, 281–296.
Scanlon, Tim M. (2014): *Being Realistic About Reasons*. Oxford: Oxford University Press.
Schroeder, Mark (2007): *Slaves of the Passions*. Oxford: Oxford University Press.
Thompson, Michael (2008): *Life and Action: Elementary Structures of Practice and Practical Thought*. Cambridge: Harvard University Press.
Wilson, George M. (1980): *The Intentionality of Human Action*. Stanford: Stanford University Press.
Wilson, George M. (1985): "Davidson on intentional action." In: Lepore, Ernest and McLaughlin, Brian (Eds.): *Actions and Events: Perspectives on the Philosophy of Donald Davidson*. Oxford: Basil Blackwell.
Wright, Georg Henrik von (1963): *The Varieties of Goodness*. Abingdon: Routledge and Kegan Paul.

Wright, Georg Henrik von (1974): "Explanation and Understanding." In: *Philosophy and Rhetoric* 7. No. 3, 187–190.
Wright, Georg Henrik von (1989): "Reply to Anscombe." In: Hahn, Lewis Edwin and Schilpp, Paul Arthur (Eds.): *The Philosophy of Georg Henrik von Wright*. LaSalle: Open Court.

Jennifer Ryan Lockhart
Kant on Practical Necessity

Abstract: Contemporary discussions conflate two understandings of practical necessity: according to one, an action is practically necessary when there are overriding reasons in favor of it such that the agent cannot do otherwise without opening himself to criticism; according to the other, to say that an action is practically necessary is to say that the demand that the agent perform the action is unconditioned, stemming from reason itself or from the agent's constitution, without making reference to some purpose that the agent could fail to have. The first notion of practical necessity is relatively straightforward, while the second notion is more difficult to understand. In this paper, I distinguish between these two ways of understanding practical necessity, arguing both that they are conceptually distinct and that an unconditioned demand may not be overriding. I argue that it is useful not only to distinguish these notions but also to reserve the term "practical necessity" for the second since, contrary to first appearances, this captures the sense in which necessity within a practical context functions analogously to necessity in a theoretical context. Although my claims can be generalized, I argue for them by reference to Kant's practical philosophy, making the case that Kant employs the term "practical necessity" in the second sense; failure to distinguish these notions has contributed to a great deal of confusion in the secondary literature on Kant. The proper understanding of the notion of practical necessity within Kant's philosophy allows us to appreciate how practical and theoretical reasoning are unified but distinct—unified because reasoning seeks to produce and to preserve *justification* (of action on the one hand and belief on the other) yet distinct because practical reasoning is governed by its own characteristic patterns of inference.

1 Practical Necessity

What does it mean to say that an action is practically necessary? Since Kant, moral philosophers have often spoken of "practical necessity" when characterizing their views. Talk of practical necessity arises not only within the Kantian moral framework. It is also crucial to some of its harshest critics. Bernard Williams, for example, maintains that our character is fundamentally revealed through what is, for each of us, practically necessary.

It is easy to take for granted that we know what this talk of practical necessity means. We see the term "practical" and take it that our topic is action, and we see the term "necessity" and assume that we are now talking about an action that, in some sense, the agent cannot but perform. We could put the same point by saying that there are overriding considerations speaking in favor of the action. I will call this the **standard view of practical necessity**, according to which an action is practically necessary if and only if there are overriding considerations in favor of the action such that the agent, in some sense, cannot do otherwise. To the extent that there has been recent debate about practical necessity, it has concerned not whether these slogans properly characterize the concept, but instead, what exactly the slogans amount to. Thus, we are told, for example, that for Kant, to say that an action is practically necessary for an agent is to say that he cannot on pain of *irrationality* do otherwise.[1] Williams, on the other hand, offers a different reading of the "cannot," contending that when an action is practically necessary for an agent, he cannot on pain of *no longer being who he is* do otherwise. This dispute yields two species of the generically standard view.

Contemporary discussions of practical necessity only dimly intimate that there might be another sense of practical necessity that has little to do with an action which the agent cannot but perform. These perturbations in the rhetoric of the standard view, which generally go unnoticed, are especially prevalent in treatments of Kant on practical necessity (a phenomenon that, I will argue, is a symptom of the fact that Kant's understanding of this notion cannot be made to square with the standard view of practical necessity). For the purposes of this investigation, therefore, I will carry out a general inquiry into the concept of practical necessity within the context of Kant's practical philosophy. In what follows, when I discuss the standard view of practical necessity, I will consider the specific version of this view most commonly attributed to Kant according to which the agent cannot but perform the action on pain of *irrationality*.

It is uncontroversial that, according to Kant, moral actions are those actions that are practically necessary. Rawls, for instance, notes that "whatever is required by the categorical imperative (via the CI-procedure) is practically necessary for us" (2000, 248). This is fine as far as it goes, and countless other examples from the secondary literature could be adduced, which are, as they stand, similarly inoffensive

---

[1] In this paper, I am using the term "rational" in a broad way to include what John Rawls calls the "rational" and the "reasonable." As Rawls himself points out: "The distinction between the reasonable and the rational goes back, I believe, to Kant: it is expressed in his distinction between the categorical and the hypothetical imperative in the *Foundations* and his other writings. The first represents pure practical reason, the second represents empirical practical reason." See Rawls (1993, 48–49).

explications of Kant's view of practical necessity.² But in what does this necessity consist?

One possibility is, of course, the understanding of practical necessity articulated by the standard view. However, commentators cannot fail to notice that Kant speaks of practically necessary actions as those which are rationally unconditioned. For instance, Kant says of the categorical imperative that it is "limited by no condition and, as absolutely although practically necessary, can be called quite strictly speaking a command" (Kant, *G* 4:416). Unlike the hypothetical imperative, which gets its grip on the agent on the condition that he is pursuing some end, the categorical imperative issues from reason and is, in this sense, ultimately not conditioned by an end that the agent pursues.³ I will call this the **unconditioned view of practical necessity**, according to which an action is practically necessary if and only if the considerations in favor of the action are unconditioned.⁴ Exactly how to understand this view of practical necessity and why we should think of it as a form of necessity at all—these are delicate matters. Making sense of them is one of the central tasks of what follows.

---

2 Here are a few further examples of the sort of thing that is said about practically necessity, which, while not strictly speaking false, can invite the misunderstanding with which I am here concerned:

But Kant thinks it is just a contingent empirical fact that you have the desires you have. If so, then on these views it is a matter of happenstance whether or not someone is bound by any moral necessity. Obligation becomes a matter of what one wants to do. But true moral necessity, Kant held, would make an action necessary regardless of what the agent wants (Schneewind 1992, 313).

What Kant means by "necessity" in moral contexts is that rational principles do not apply to us merely because we have some desire (G 4:389). Whether we are speaking of moral or nonmoral principles of reason, these principles "necessitate" in the sense that they constrain (or should constrain) me to do what they prescribe irrespective of what I may otherwise desire to do at the moment (Wood 1999, 57).

Obligation requires practical necessitation independent of desire... (Herman 1993, 209).

I will say more about the ambiguity that haunts these formulations in §7.

3 Here, I am drawing on Kant's discussion of imperatives, which apply to beings whose wills are "not necessarily determined by" them. When such a being's will is determined by an imperative, Kant calls this "a necessitation." (*G* 4:413) One might be tempted to confuse the concept of *necessitation* [*Nötigung*] with that of practical *necessity* [*Notwendigkeit*]. While necessitation pertains to the relation of an imperfect will to the law, practical necessity, for Kant, is a matter of the character of the practical law itself. The practical thought of a holy will (which does not experience the law as an imperative) is determined by practical *necessity* although this is not a matter of *necessitation*. (See *G* 4:414).

4 Like the standard view, the unconditioned view here is articulated in a generic form which I go on to specify in the Kantian way. We could imagine a version of the unconditioned view that Williams might endorse where the considerations in favor of the action stem directly from constitutive features of the agent's character.

The standard view and the unconditioned view articulate two different conceptions of practical necessity. A Kantian commentator who, until now, has been conflating these two notions might try to console himself with the thought that although the standard and the unconditioned view are different descriptions of practical necessity, they in fact pick out the same actions. He might begin by trying to reason along the following lines: if the considerations in favor of an action are unconditioned, issuing from reason alone, then they hold no matter what; therefore, if the agent is to act rationally, he cannot but perform the action. This line of reasoning, I will argue, is faulty, but to see why we need to have a better grasp of the unconditioned view of rational necessity. By the end of the paper, I will have demonstrated that some actions which are practically necessary in the second sense are not practically necessary in the first.

The aim of this paper is to recommend the unconditioned view of practical necessity both as a view and as a reading of Kant. Since neither contemporary Neo-Kantians nor non-Kantians have recognized it as a distinctive position in its own right, a proper development of it will enable a new understanding of the difficulties at the heart of certain debates surrounding Kant's practical philosophy. One consequence of this transformed understanding of Kant is that the charge of rigorism sometimes leveled against his moral thought will be seen to be completely misplaced.

Recognizing this distinction also has far-reaching consequences for debates concerning practical reason. I will make the case that the standard view gets much of its appeal (appeal which has worked to make the unconditioned view of practical necessity virtually invisible) by imposing on *practical* reason an implicitly contemplative and theoretical understanding of reason itself. This theoretical distortion of practical reason prevents one from appreciating the true commonality between practical and theoretical reason. The basic moves of this paper tend, therefore, in two opposite but complimentary directions: first, singling out what is distinctive about rational necessity when it functions as a concept governing practical rather than theoretical reason; second, once these differences are appreciated, giving a properly generic description of rational necessity so that we can understand both practical and theoretical necessity as species of a single genus. It is only the unconditioned view of practical necessity that allows us to carry out both of these tasks.

2 Imperfect Duties and Practical Necessity

The more clearheaded one is in one's endorsement of the standard view of practical necessity, the more difficult it becomes to make sense of the concept of an imperfect duty. In this section I bring forward two proponents of the standard view, Marcia Baron[5] and Bernard Williams, who serve as specific examples of commentators, friendly and critical, who explicitly endorse the standard view of practical necessity. With these articulations of the standard view in hand, we can see how this view threatens the very coherence of the concept of an imperfect duty, saddling interpreters with only two possibilities, each of which faces both philosophical and exegetical difficulties.

Marcia Baron, in her defense of Kant, takes it that performing an action from duty is performing the action because it is morally required. She writes, "Duty is not the sort of thing one can act from only halfway. Duty is to trump all competing considerations. Acting from duty is an all or nothing affair: you do not act from duty if you regard the fact that the action is morally required as less than decisive" (Baron 2006, 26). Williams, in his criticism of Kant, claims that a deliberative conclusion is one of practical necessity when it "embodies a consideration that has the highest deliberative priority and is also of the greatest importance (at least to the agent)" and becomes "the conclusion not merely that one should do a certain thing but that one *must*, and that one cannot do anything else" (1986, 188). Williams claims that Kant,

> was concerned with the recognition of an *I must* that is unconditional and goes all the way down, but he construed this unconditional practical necessity as being peculiar to morality. He thought that it was unconditional in the sense that it did not depend on desire at all: a course of action presented to us with this kind of necessity was one we had reason to take *whatever we might happen to want*, and it was only moral reasons that could transcend desire in this way (Williams 1986, 189).

On the face of it, this standard view of practical necessity sits uneasily alongside another feature of Kant's moral thought: that we have imperfect duties such as the duty of beneficence, the duty "to promote according to one's means the happiness of others in need, without hoping for something in return" (Kant, *MM* 6:453). I may help my neighbor Sara by lending her my car, and I may do this from duty. That is, I may act in this case for moral reasons, but it seems odd to say that the moral considerations that ground my action are overriding or that, rationally speaking, I cannot do otherwise but lend her my car. In many cases like this I do not say with Luther, "Here I stand. I can do no other." Kant, of course, recognizes that our moral lives have this feature. He writes, "if the law can prescribe only the maxim of actions, not actions themselves, this is a sign that it leaves a playroom (*latitudo*) for free choice in following (complying with) the law, that is, the law can-

---

5 Lockhart, Jennifer Ryan (2017).

not specify precisely in what way one is to act and how much one is to do by the action for an end that is also a duty" (Kant, *MM* 6:390).

The Kantian who endorses the standard view of practical necessity is faced with an inconsistency: on the one hand, moral actions are actions such that we cannot rationally do otherwise, while, on the other hand, many moral actions are optional. While endorsing the standard view of practical necessity, there are two basic strategies on offer for accounting for such actions. Each of these strategies, in its own way, vitiates the concept of an imperfect duty.

The first strategy is to try to assimilate imperfect duties to perfect ones by arguing that although imperfect duties are duties to perform particular actions, these duties are not, in fact, as imperfect as we might be inclined to think and actually do prescribe actions that the rational agent cannot but perform. In order to motivate the idea that there are particular beneficent actions of this sort, Baron gives the example of a situation in which "help is desperately and immediately needed, no one else is on the scene, and one needs only to (say) phone on one's cell phone for an ambulance" (Baron 2006, 27). While there are examples like this in which an imperfect duty is such that, rationally, speaking one cannot do otherwise, these hardly exhaust the category of beneficent actions. One could try to force all beneficent actions into this mold by claiming that we are under an obligation "to help whenever we can, unless certain conditions obtain..." (Baron 2006, 27–28). As an interpretation of Kant, this is not a very cheery exegetical prospect when one has to square this view with passages like the one above about the latitude involved in complying with the law. Philosophically, this strategy makes Kant's moral thought out to be distastefully rigid. It would have to attribute to Kant the idea that in the final analysis, once everything is taken into consideration, even those cases which appeared at first to leave room for the playful involvement of choice are fully determined with unrelenting specificity by reason alone.

Baron rejects this first strategy for reasons similar to the ones I have just rehearsed and puts forward a second strategy. The second way to account for imperfect duties is to abandon the idea that most beneficent actions are actions done from duty at all (with the exception of those cases like the one above of the urgently needed cell phone call) and to conclude that they are therefore not practically necessary. According to this interpretation, strictly speaking, one only has a duty to adopt the happiness of others as one's end; one does not, strictly speaking, have a duty to perform any particular beneficent actions. On this view, the imperfect duty is to adopt the end of the happiness of others, and, like perfect duties, this is something which an agent cannot fail to do without opening himself to rational criticism.

However, this way of understanding Kant on beneficence also faces serious exegetical difficulties. As Baron notes, in the discussion of the downcast philanthropist from the *Groundwork*, Kant says that the man, "tears himself out of this deadly insensibility and *does the action* without any inclination, simply *from duty*" (Kant, *G* 4:398).⁶ Baron can account for this passage only by claiming, "that Kant should not have said what he said" and instead should have "said that he adopted a maxim of beneficence from duty" (Baron 2006, 30). She attempts to mitigate the effect of having to attribute such a mistake to Kant by claiming that because the *Groundwork* is early, Kant "had not worked out at the time... exactly how imperfect duties differ from perfect duties" (Baron 2006, 29).

Such a solution, while inelegant, might be plausible, were it not to fly in the face of the account of imperfect duties Kant gives later in his career when he returns to this topic in *The Metaphysics of Morals*. There Kant does emphasize that there are ends (such as the happiness of others) which one has a duty to adopt. However, although the adoption of this end makes possible imperfect duties, it is not itself an imperfect duty. As Korsgaard points out, "The general duty to *adopt* morally good ends—the duty of moral perfection—is perfect" (1996, 21). To fail to see this point is to run roughshod over the very concept of an imperfect duty, for imperfect duties are such that, "Fulfillment of them is *merit (meritum)* ... but failure to fulfill them is not in itself *culpability (demeritum)*..." (Kant, *MM* 6:390). It is the duty to perform particular beneficent actions, not the duty to adopt the end of the happiness of others, which one is not culpable for failing to fulfill, and which can therefore occupy the conceptual space of an imperfect duty.

Philosophically, this second strategy allows one latitude in one's choice of beneficent actions and thereby avoids the rigorism of the first strategy. However, many particular actions which are intuitively moral are situated outside of the realm of morality. Although Baron pays lip service to what is clearly Kant's position, that there is such a thing as an imperfect duty and that one has latitude in fulfilling it, she ends up with a view according to which there is no room for such an imperfect duty, since when there is latitude in acting, one cannot, after all, act from duty: "Because acts of helping another are not, as individual acts, generally morally required, it does not make sense to speak of someone performing them from duty..." (Baron 2006, 28). Allen Wood sharply marks what is awkward in Baron's position: "If Baron were correct, then there could be no imperfect duties at all, regarded as consequent upon a *command* of reason, carrying with it a practical *necessity*" (2008, 309).⁷

---

6 Here, I follow Baron's italicization.
7 I am largely in sympathy with what Wood says on this matter. He writes, for instance that "there would be something the matter with your character if you could not *make yourself* do something,

In what follows, I will argue that this problem is symptomatic of a deeper issue. What has been making mischief for Kantian commentators when it comes to imperfect duties is their unreflective adoption of the standard view of practical necessity. Kant's conception of practical necessity is intimately related to a number of other key Kantian concepts such as duty, obligation, law, and the imperitival ought. In the case at hand, commentators are well aware that "duty is the necessity of an action from respect for law" (Kant, *G* 4:400). However, if the necessity of an action is understood, as it is on the standard view, as meaning that the agent cannot but perform the action, otherwise he opens himself to rational criticism, then rationally speaking, such an action is not optional. And yet Kant recognizes duties (necessary actions) that are optional; when one holds the standard view of practical necessity, it is hard to see how an optional duty can amount to anything more than an oxymoron. In what follows, I will show how we can avoid these problems by rejecting the shared presupposition of each of the strategies I have considered: that what it means for an action to be practically necessary is for there to be overriding reasons speaking in its favor. That is, I will reject the idea that to say that an action is practically necessary is to say that, rationally speaking, one cannot do otherwise.[8]

---

or decide you *had to do it*, on moral grounds, unless you were afraid you would be blamed (or blame yourself) if you *didn't* do it." However, I am interested in giving an account of the logic of practical reasoning that underwrites an intuition such as this. One way of highlighting how my discussion goes beyond Wood's is to point out that he is here concerned with duty, a concept which brings with it the idea the relation of "an objective law of reason to a will that by its subjective constitution is not necessarily determined by it (a necessitation)" (*G*, 4:413). By the end of this paper, we ought to be able to see that a holy and perfectly rational will (a will to which the concept of duty does not apply) may also fail to perform some actions which it would be a merit to have performed. (This will obtain at least in the case where it performs some other equally meritorious action which is practically incompatible with the first.)

8 As we go along, it should become clear that my reading can preserve the idea that Kant's position is a radical departure from Hume's. We do not need to appeal to the overridingness of moral reasons to explain the difference between Hume and Kant. It is an open question whether a good Humean can recognize the kind of practical inferences I will discuss in §§4 and 5, but no Humean will be able to recognize practically necessary actions as I will go on to represent them in §6, where I discuss the schema of a categorical imperative [henceforth, the CI schema]. Even if we were n*ever* to have overriding reasons to perform moral actions and actions that could be justified morally were limited to, for example, cases where we could help someone out with practically no skin off our own nose, the way of representing the justification of such actions displayed in the CI schema would not be one that the Humean could accept. Even if morality never gave us an overriding reason to act, we would still be committed to the thought that pure reason has a practical employment, and this the Humean will not countenance.

In §4, I will reject this idea as an account of the practical necessity of hypothetical imperatives before moving on in §6 to reject it as an account of the practical necessity of categorical imperatives. Before doing so, however, I will briefly digress in §3 to highlight the issues at stake here and to remove some possible obstacles to understanding.

3 Three Issues Concerning Practical Reason

My interpretation of Kant on practical necessity takes a stand on three issues to do with practical reason. This section will be concerned to foreground those issues, both because being clear on these points will make it easier to understand my interpretation of Kant, and because keeping them in mind will bring to light some of the broader implications of this view. The first issue is the nature of the *conclusion* of practical reasoning. The second issue is the question of the *sufficiency of the middle term* of instrumental reasoning. The third issue has to do with whether we should understand practical reasoning as *inferential*.

What is the conclusion of a piece of practical reasoning? Is the conclusion a judgment, an intention, or an action? Is practical reasoning a species of theoretical reasoning insofar as it issues in a judgment, but a judgment the content of which concerns what we ought to do?[9] Or is practical reasoning practical not because of the content of the reasoning, that it is about what to do, but rather because of the form of the reasoning, that the reasoning's issuing in action is internal to the form of the reasoning itself? For the purposes of this paper, I am assuming that the conclusion of a practical reasoning is, paradigmatically, an action.[10] Keeping in mind

---

9 Anscombe quips that if this is what we mean by practical reasoning, then "one might easily wonder why no one has ever pointed out the mince pie syllogism: the peculiarity of this would be that it was about mince pies, and an example would be 'All mince pies have suet in them—this is a mince pie—therefore etc.' Certainly ethics is of importance to human beings in a way that mince pies are not; but such importance cannot justify us in speaking of a special sort of reasoning" (1963, 58).
10 There is some skepticism about the possibility of practical reasoning concluding in action, arguing for this view is beyond the scope of this paper. See, for instance, Dancy (2009). Dancy's argument that practical reasoning cannot conclude in action begins from the observation that there is a distinction to be made between "inference-as-process and inference-as-structure" (2009, 278). In the case of theoretical reasoning, the inference-as-process has as conclusion a belief while the inference-as-structure has as conclusion the thing believed. Dancy argues that there is no suitable analogue to this distinction between belief and thing believed to be found for the action and the thing done. So, action cannot be the conclusion of a chain of practical reasoning. In what follows, I take the first approach that Dancy puts forward and argues against, "that we could take

the claim that practical reasoning concludes in action allows us to attend to the differences in the ways in which we think of actions and judgments *as justified*. Actions are justified by showing what good there is in doing them. Judgments, on the other hand, even judgments about what it would be good to do, are not justified in this way, by showing the good in doing them. This denial, that judgments are not justified by showing the good in doing them, hardly makes sense. Judgments about what it would be good to do, like other judgments, are justified by showing the grounds on which we hold them to be true. It is only by getting into view the way in which we seek to justify our *actions*, that we can understand the legitimacy of the distinctively practical inferential structures involved in practical reasoning.

Second, do cases in which an agent takes a sufficient but not indispensable means to his end count as cases of valid practical reasoning? Or is practical reasoning valid only when an agent takes an indispensable means to his end?[11] I will be assuming for the purposes of this paper that there are clearly cases of valid practical reasoning which conform to what Robert Audi calls "sufficient condition schemata" that represent an agent as taking some means which is sufficient for achieving his goal (1982, 25).

Third, is practical reasoning inferential? Or does practical reason traffic in reasons without being a matter of inference? Jonathan Dancy holds this latter view, claiming that it would "be wrong to suppose that all handlings of reasons involve inference."[12] While I will not, for the purposes of this paper, assume that all

---

what is known by the agent in knowing what she is doing, and use that as the "content" of the action ..." (2009, 284). This is a proposal for how to make a distinction between the action and the thing done (here the content). Dancy dismisses this possibility quickly, saying, "It makes little sense to suppose that one acts because one recognizes that this sort of thing known—that I am Φ-ing—follows suitably from premises about the situation. If it does follow, it seems that I ought to be acting already. That is, the conclusion of the inference should be true *because* I am acting, rather than the action occurring because the agent recognizes some inferential relation between premises and the conclusion that he is acting in a certain way. So I don't see that this first approach delivers the goods" (2009, 284). Dancy's objection is predicated on the thought that this content can only stand in one sort of inferential relation, a theoretical one. However, the rest of this paper provides the materials for a reply to Dancy, since I will be arguing that the same content, with a different force, can be caught up in a uniquely practical set of inferential relations. If I can vindicate this thought, then Dancy's argument fails.

11 For example, Georg Spielthenner holds that instances of practical reasoning that follow what he calls "Sufficient condition schemata," according to which committing an action can be sufficient for achieving an end, are *not* cases of making a practical *inference* in which the conclusion follows "deductively" from the premises (Spielthenner 2007, 140).

12 "So my view is that whether we are thinking of the move from reasons to decision or of the relation between rightness and the right-makers in the case, we should not suppose that what

practical reasoning is inferential, I will assume that those instances of practical reasoning which satisfy a sufficient condition schema are inferential.

How do these three issues bear on one another? On most contemporary understandings of the terrain, the second two questions, concerning the sufficiency of the middle term and whether or not practical reasoning is inferential, cut against one another such that it is difficult to give the most natural answer to both. On the one hand, if we recognize, as I urge we do, that there are cases of valid practical reasoning which conform to sufficient condition schemata, it is hard to see how this reasoning is inferential, since the inferential relationships among the propositional contents, considered theoretically, do not support drawing the conclusion in these cases. Holding on to the idea that sufficient condition schemata are valid forms of practical reasoning seems to force one into the position that these stretches of practical reasoning are non-inferential. The next three sections, §§4–6, make the case that once we recognize that the conclusion of practical reasoning is an action, then we can hold both that valid reasoning can conform to a sufficient condition schema and be genuinely inferential.

4 Hypothetical Necessity

Kant makes use of the notion of practical necessity no less in his explanation of a hypothetical imperative than in his discussion of the categorical imperative.[13] In this section, I follow Kant's lead and articulate a conception of how necessity is at work in practical inferences which have a hypothetical form. In §5, I will explore in more detail how we can apply this understanding to the case of moral actions structured by the categorical imperative.

Kant says of both the hypothetical and categorical imperatives that "Since every practical law represents a possible action as good and thus as necessary for a subject practically determinable by reason, all imperatives are formulae for the determination of action that is necessary in accordance with the principle

---

is called "practical reasoning" is inferential. At this point, its status as reasoning might even be challenged. We are, however, always dealing with reasons here, and drawing our conclusions or making our decisions in the light of those reasons. So there can be nothing wrong with talking of reasoning, since we are involved in the handling of reasons. What would be wrong to suppose that all handlings of reasons involve inference" (Dancy 2004, 105).

13 In drawing attention to the importance of imperatives, I do not mean to be endorsing the idea that one should understand the conclusion of a practical syllogism to be a proposition that asserts the imperative. I take it that the importance of imperatives in Kant's philosophy is reconcilable with the idea that practical inference concludes in action.

of a will which is good in some way" (Kant, *G* 4:414). Here, Kant links *necessity* with the rational representation of the action merely as *good*, not with talk about the agent having an overriding reason to perform the action. He continues, "Now, if the action would be good merely as a means *to something else* the imperative is *hypothetical*; if the action is represented as *in itself* good, hence as necessary in a will in itself conforming to reason, as its principle, *then it is categorical*" (Kant, *G* 4:414). Notice, once again, that the action is said to be rationally necessary merely by having been represented as good, and once again, this does not have to do with there being overriding considerations in favor of the action.

Interpreters who take the standard view of practical necessity might not see much significance in this point, for they will simply take this aspect of the characterization of necessary actions (that they are those which are represented as good) as compatible with their own understanding of necessary actions as those which we have overriding reason to perform. But what about the fact that Kant uses necessity to explain both the categorical and the hypothetical imperative? The standard view tries to articulate a position according to which the necessity which attaches to the hypothetical imperative also has to do with overriding reasons for action. The standard view does this by appealing to the idea of indispensably necessary means to one's end. Kant writes, "Whoever wills the end also wills (insofar as reason has decisive influence on his actions) the indispensably necessary means to it that are within his power" (Kant, *G* 4:417). On the standard view, the way that necessity enters into hypothetical reasoning is intuitive enough: non-moral practical reason can also conclude in actions that are necessary in just those cases where there exists some indispensably necessary means to one's end. When one of the premises of the reasoning involves a given goal and there is some means that must be taken (that is, insofar as one pursues this end, one cannot do otherwise) in order to achieve the goal, then rationality dictates that the agent who has the goal take this indispensably necessary means. The reasoning in this case appears to follow the same inference rules as theoretical reasoning: A (the goal); if A then B (since B is indispensably necessary to A); so B.[14]

The standard interpretation, however, overlooks what, by its own lights, ought to seem strikingly strange about what Kant says: that he speaks here of indispens-

---

[14] Bernard Williams is not satisfied even with saying that taking the indispensably necessary means to some given end is itself a necessary action since, "if A wants X, and if it is true that if he wants X he must do Y, it does not follow that he must do Y; that will follow only if, further, X is the thing that he must pursue" (Williams 1982, 125). But Williams misses the point that the kind of necessity at issue here is *hypothetical* necessity. Just as believing q is not of itself necessary, still if one believes p and believes if p then q, one is justified in believing q with the force of necessity.

ably necessary [*unentbehrlich nothwendige*] means. While it is possible that Kant's formulation simply contains a redundancy, we need not attribute to him such carelessness, on my view. I will be arguing that we ought not understand the necessity of taking the means to one's ends in terms of the indispensability of those means. Kant's language suggests that there could be, in effect, a dispensably necessary means to one's end. If we take seriously the way in which "indispensably" functions as an adverb modifying "necessary," then this might lead us to conclude that, for Kant, the indispensability of some means comes apart from its necessity. I will be arguing that there are both dispensably necessary means and indispensably necessary means and that the necessity of the latter ought not to be confused with their indispensability. When some means is indispensable, this will produce an overriding reason (at least with respect to the end at hand) to take the means, but the overridingness of this reason for action ought not be confused with the necessity of the action. I will say much more about this in what follows; here, I merely note the way in which the standard view must ignore certain aspects of Kant's own exposition for which my view can account.

Another peculiar consequence of the standard understanding of Kant on hypothetical reasoning is that his remarks about the hypothetical imperative seem to describe only a small subset of our instrumental reasoning. We can pursue most of our goals in a variety of ways using a variety of means.[15] Consider this example from Aristotle as it is schematized by Anthony Kenny:

> This man is to be healed
> Iff his humors are balanced he will be healed
> If he is heated, his humors will be balanced
> If he is rubbed, he will be heated
> So I'll rub him (Kenny 1966, 65).[16]

Rubbing is not indispensably necessary to heating the patient. I might, after all, wrap him in a down blanket, or place him by a fire. Most of our lives with practical reason have this shape; very seldom is there some means that is absolutely indispensable to my end. So, the standard view ends up confining Kant's remarks about the hypothetical imperative and its rational necessity to a small subset of our actions. While a proponent of the standard view may resign himself to this limita-

---

[15] Likewise, most of the moral actions we undertake, like the example from above of my lending Sara my car, are hardly instances where we say "Here I stand. I can do no other." In this way, the problem I am identifying here with the standard understanding of the role of necessity in the hypothetical imperative mirrors the problem I identified at the end of §2 with understanding the way in which certain moral actions for Kant, like those of beneficence, are in some way optional.
[16] The example is modified from Aristotle's *Metaphysics*, 1032b19.

tion, on my view, Kant's remarks about the necessity involved in hypothetical reasoning have a much broader application.

It is worth noting that the example above, unlike the case involving indispensably necessary means, does not have the form of a valid piece of theoretical reasoning. As Kenny remarks, "'S, iff R then S, if Q then R, if P then Q, so P' commits twice the fallacy of affirming the consequent" (1966, 67). In fact, because proponents of the standard view think that when Kant talks about necessity with respect to hypothetical reasoning he means "indispensably necessary," they are only willing to call the conclusion of a piece of practical reasoning practically necessary (with respect to the given end) when that piece of practical reasoning can also be represented as a valid piece of *theoretical* reasoning. Instead, in what follows, I make the suggestion that we consider the conclusion of a piece of practical reasoning practically necessary (with respect to the given end) when the piece of practical reasoning can be represented a valid piece of *practical* reasoning. On this understanding, we may properly call my rubbing the patient practically necessary (with respect to my end of healing him), although I might have rationally done otherwise. On the face of it, this may seem strange to some, but my aim here is to argue that this appearance of strangeness is itself a consequence of a certain distorted picture of practical necessity, a picture which is governed by the assumption that the validity of a stretch of practical reasoning should be assessed by its conformity to canons of reasoning drawn from theoretical reasoning. The aim of this paper is to demonstrate that the way of employing the terminology which I am putting forward is elegant, useful and Kantian, because it highlights the fact that rational necessity is a matter of guaranteeing and preserving justification. In the theoretical case what is justified is belief, in the practical case, action. Therefore, getting clear on the logical structure of the justification of action will allow us to appreciate the *sui generis* manner in which rational necessity functions in the practical sphere. This is, so far, highly schematic and it is the task of the rest of this paper to make it plausible and intelligible.

This leaves us with two tasks. First, we need to come to grips with the understanding of practical inference and the place of necessity in this form of inference, such that we can see there to be an overarching genus of rational necessity that covers both the practical and theoretical case (§§5 and 6). Second, we need to understand why it is that interpreters who hold the standard view of practical necessity try to shoehorn the rational necessity of practical reasoning into the mold of theoretical reasoning (§7).

5 Representing Instrumental Reasoning

Now we turn to the representation of practical inference in order to clarify the role that rational concepts, such as necessity, play in practical reasoning. This section presents the core idea of Kenny's system of practical inference which he develops in the paper "Practical Inference," although I have modified much of the terminology and notation. Kenny's formal system of practical inference is motivated by the insight that when we are engaged in practical reasoning, our starting point is often some goal that we aim to bring about, and we reason about how to achieve this goal. His idea is that a formalized stretch of practical reasoning represents the way in which a particular action is satisfactory in light of one's goals and the facts of the situation. When reasoning theoretically, we might begin with the thought of some fact, for instance that the door is shut. When reasoning practically, we might begin with the thought of something that we aim to bring about, for instance that the door be shut. According to one familiar way of using the terms, these two thoughts have the same content but different force. The force is, in the first case assertoric and in the second case optative; the content is what is shared in common by the two thoughts.[17]

We can abstract from differences in practical and theoretical reasoning to such a degree that we introduce a notion of content such that the following will hold of it: any such content capable of being expressed as a sentence in the assertoric mood can also be expressed as a sentence in the optative mood.[18] To take the example we were using above, "I rub him" is a sentence in the assertoric mood, while "Would that I rub him" is a sentence in the optative mood. I will follow Kenny in calling sentences in the optative mood "fiats." Fiats exhibit "a perfect par-

---

17 This way of putting things has the advantage of being helpfully clear-cut, but it does raise some questions which will eventually matter. If all one means by putting things this way is that one can abstract from these two forms of reasoning a level of content such that stretches of theoretical and practical reasoning can be seen to share a common topic, it is certainly unobjectionable. If, however, in distinguishing between force and content this way, one assumes both that all that a force operator indicates is an attitude towards an inferentially individuable content and that the validity of the inference itself is not affected by whether the operator here is of a theoretical or practical nature, then one has, of course, simply lapsed back into the central assumption that it is the aim of this paper to expose.
18 In the spirit of the previous footnote, it does not follow from what I have said here that such a notion of content is to be identified with inferential content in the sense that it and only it matters to the validity of inference. We are able to abstract this level of content because of the systematic relations between practical and theoretical reasoning; but when such content is further specified with an assertoric or optative mood operator, these further specifications of content will not be inferentially interchangeable.

allelism with assertoric sentences" since they can be created by attaching the "would that" locution to the corresponding assertoric sentence (Kenny 1966, 69).[19] Let us introduce a symbol that we can add to the usual repertoire of first-order logical notation to indicate that a sentence is in the optative mood. Suppose that A is an ordinary sentence in some language of first-order logic. Let us write A followed by "!" to indicate the sentence that we get when we express the thought-content of A (according to the particular semantic interpretation at hand) in a sentence in the optative mood.

In the theoretical case, when there is a derivation from a set of sentences Σ to a sentence A we can write $\Sigma \vdash A$. If the system of logic in which such a derivation is possible is a good system, then it preserves truth. We can think of the derivation as putting on display a way in which the conclusion follows with rational necessity from the premises; the truth of the sentences in Σ necessitate the truth of A. We can think of the derivation as allowing us to see how this is so by representing a justification of A on the basis of Σ.

Kenny suggests that we can use a derivation system for ordinary logic to generate at least one of the inference rules for a system of inference designed to capture practical reasoning. The logic of practical inference, as Kenny develops it, has the remarkable feature that its inference rules are the "mirror image" of the truth preserving inference rules which govern assertoric sentences. We can state the main inference rule of Kenny's practical system as follows:

> A practical inference is valid if the assertoric sentence which correspond' to the conclusion conjoined with the assertoric sentences corresponding to the other premises logically entails the assertoric sentence corresponding to the goal.[20]

Now let me consider some examples to illustrate how this inference rule works. I will use "p," "q," etc. to represent atomic sentences. Suppose that I aim to go to school. I can bike or walk. The following seems to be a good piece of practical reasoning:

Goal: Would that I go to school. (q!)
If I cycle then I go to school. (p→q)
Therefore: Would that I cycle. (p!)

---

19 Kenny (1966, 69).
20 It is worth noting that a fully formalized satisfactory logic will be a form of non-monotonic logic: adding premises can reduce the set of conclusions. Once we start to represent an agent with various fiats, some conclusions that can be inferred from only one of her fiats will not be able to be inferred from the set of all her fiats.

This is a valid inference since
p& (p→q) ⊢ q.

The intuitive idea behind Kenny's inference rule is this: given what you know about the possible means to your end, it had better be the case that the course of action you select is one which allows you to achieve your end.

Here is another example using a quantified sentence: I aim to consume one of my five daily fruits. Here in front of me is a piece of fruit, so I eat it.

Goal: Would that I eat a piece of fruit. ((∃ x)(Fx & Cx)!)
This is a piece of fruit. (Fa)
Therefore: I eat it. (Ca!)

Although this is not a valid piece of theoretical reasoning, it is an intuitively valid piece of practical reasoning, and it will indeed be valid in Kenny's system because:

(Ca & Fa) ⊢ (∃ x)(Fx & Cx).

Let us consider one final example: My goal is to post the letter or burn the letter, so I post it.

Goal: I post the letter or I burn the letter. (p v q)!
Therefore: I post the letter. p!

This is a fine piece of practical reasoning, which is valid in Kenny's system since:

p ⊢ p v q.

I will introduce the practical turnstile ("⊢$_p$") to indicate entailment in a system of first order logic which is extended by the inference rules designed to capture practical reasoning. Kenny's practical inference rule is a good candidate for an inference rule that would have to be added to first order logic in order to develop such a system. Let Ψ be a set of fiats including the practical goal and Σ be a set of assertoric sentences.[21] Then the practical turnstile will be used as follows: If A! is a conclusion of a piece of practical reasoning that has all of the members of Σ and Ψ as premises, then we write:

---

[21] These sentences ought to correspond to the relevant set of facts I am taking into consideration. In the examples above, for instance that this is a piece of fruit and that if I cycle then I go to school.

$\Sigma, \Psi \vdash_p A!$.

In theoretical reasoning, the goal is to preserve truth. If the premises are true then, necessarily, the conclusion is true; the conclusion follows with the force of necessity from the premises. However, including Kenny's inference rule will, as we have seen, allow inferences which are valid but not truth-preserving. So far, we have been working with the intuitive idea that the reasoning above is good practical reasoning, but now we need to ask: What property is it, if not truth, of which these inferences are supposed to guarantee the preservation? Kenny's answer to this question is what he calls "satisfactoriness." Since a fiat in the premise expresses a purpose, goal, plan, etc., the new system ensures that we never pass "from a fiat which is satisfactory for a particular purpose to a fiat which is unsatisfactory for that purpose" (Kenny 1966, 72). Kenny remarks that "the preservation of satisfactoriness, therefore, has in practical inference that place which the preservation of truth has in theoretical inference" (1966, 73).

I want to depart from Kenny on this score and make a suggestion that is perhaps bold but certainly not without precedent: that it is goodness which serves the role in practical reasoning that truth serves in theoretical reasoning. We can see Kenny's inference rule as "goodness-preserving" in the sense that representing a stretch of practical reason in this way puts on display the way in which the goodness of the end is rationally passed along to the means to that end. By formalizing a stretch of practical reasoning in this way one is able to put on display a possible answer to the question, "What's the good of it?" asked about an action, and therefore to put on display a justification for the action.[22]

As we saw before, Kant holds that, "every practical law represents a possible action as good and thus as necessary for a subject practically determinable by reason..." (Kant, *G* 4:414). As I noted before, Kant here links the necessity of an action to the action's being rationally represented as good. We can think of Kenny's inference rule as providing us with a way to understand this connection between necessity and goodness by giving us a way to formalize how it is that a hypothetical imperative could be a principle that represents an action as good. If the original fiat is good, these inference rules guarantee that we pass to other fiats that are also good.

But what are we to make of Kant's claim that such a law not only represents the action as good but also represents it as necessary ("for a subject who is practically determinable by reason...")? The worry might arise at this point that, although I have found something for the words "practical necessity" to mean in

---

[22] This way of putting it is indebted to G. E. M. Anscombe. See Anscombe (2002).

Kant that solves certain exegetical problems, what my account in the end delivers is not the sort of practical necessity that we should be after. Given the particular way in which I have unpacked the idea of practical necessity (namely, by locating it in the idea that the rational necessity of an action has to do with the way in which it is justifiable in the light of certain premises), one might worry that I have seized upon a way of understanding practical reason which, from another point view, can be seen as, in effect, highlighting the *lack* of necessity of practical conclusions. After all, if warming the patient is good, I can conclude my deliberation by placing him by the fire. On the other hand, I might conclude by wrapping him in a blanket or by rubbing him. Goodness is passed along to any of these means, but none of them, so this worry goes, is therefore necessary.

This objection is, I think, motivated by two related mistakes. First, there is a tendency to think that the sort of rational necessity that characterizes theoretical reasoning is the only sort of rational necessity there is. This is to mistake characteristics of the species of theoretical rational necessity for characteristics of the genus of rational necessity. Once we assume that practical rational necessity, if it is to be rational necessity at all, must have all the features of theoretical rational necessity, it appears that we are forced to make a choice between two unappealing alternatives: either the rational necessity of practical reasoning is *just like* the rational necessity of theoretical reasoning (the standard view of practical necessity), in which case it is difficult to account for much of what seems to be practically rational; or practical reason does not involve rational necessity at all (the objection I am considering now). The first mistake, therefore, is trying to shoehorn practical rational necessity into the mold of theoretical rational necessity, trying to understand one species of rational necessity according to the particular characteristics of another species. The second related mistake is that of failing to give a properly generic characterization of the genus rational necessity such that both theoretical and practical rational necessity can be understood as species falling under a single genus.

So far, this section has been emphasizing the way in which practical reason is importantly different from theoretical reasoning by showing the way in which a formal system designed to preserve goodness is different from a formal system designed to preserve only truth. The aim of this section has thus been to combat the first mistake, that of trying to shoehorn the rational necessity of practical reasoning into the mold of the rational necessity of theoretical reasoning. However, what we still need in order to counter the objection just raised, that practical reasoning does not involve rational necessity at all, is a properly generic characterization of rational necessity.

The components of such a generic characterization of rational necessity are already in place. In fact, I gave such a generic description in characterizing the rational necessity of the theoretical reasoning above. Recall that we can think of Σ ⊢ A as making a claim that there is a derivation which can put on display a way in which the conclusion follows with rational necessity from the premises; the truth of the sentences in Σ rationally necessitate the truth of A. We can think of the derivation as allowing us to see how this is so by representing a justification of A on the basis of Σ. Likewise, we can think of Σ, Ψ ⊢$_p$ A! as making a claim that there is a derivation which can put on display a way in which the conclusion follows with rational necessity from the premises. While attending to what is specific about the case of practical reasoning, we can say that the goodness of the sentences in Ψ and the truth of those in Σ necessitate the goodness of A!. Generically, we say just the same thing: The derivation allows us to see how this is so by representing a justification of A! on the basis of Σ and Ψ. Generically understood, rational necessity is the necessity of justification. It cannot be the case that Σ is true, Ψ is good and A! happens to be unjustified.[23]

What is passed along with rational necessity in the case of practical reasoning is goodness. This gives us a way to understand why Kant thinks that rationally representing an action as good represents it as necessary, and also a way to understand how there could be dispensably necessary means to one's end. Practical rational necessity does not have to do with the idea that the action, rationally speaking, must come about, or even that it is true that it ought to come about. That would be to miss what is crucially *practical* about practical reasoning. Instead, the necessity here is the rational necessity that attaches to the action because it is justified through an exercise of reason. If I do act, the formalized reasoning puts on displays why I am, of necessity, justified in so acting. It could not turn out that I happen to be unjustified, so long as the premises are good.

What practical reasoning preserves is not the truth of the propositional content of its conclusion but, we could say, the propositional content's goodness or its worth-doing-ness. Beliefs are justified by showing that they are true. Actions

---

[23] One might worry that the non-monotonicity of such a system poses a problem for this understanding of practical necessity. An action which is justified given one set of premises may turn out not to be justified given the addition of premises. The first response to this worry is that what is put on display is the justificatory force of certain considerations which remain in place even with the addition of other premises. This is therefore not contingent. However, given a certain view of the "silencing" function of moral considerations, one might worry that in some cases it falsifies practical reasoning to represent considerations which one does not act upon as nonetheless having justificatory force. Briefly, I have so far proposed only one rule of inference that would be needed to capture practical reasoning. Were we to give more inference rules, it might be the case that these would rule out certain goal fiats which would, then, not be eligible to contribute justificatory force. This is compatible with the thought that so long as we do represent the person as having certain goal fiats, they function to justify the conclusion with the force of necessity.

are justified by showing the good in doing them. The practical inference preserves justification of the action (it preserves the goodness in it) and it does this with the force of necessity, in spite of the fact that other actions might be equally justified and that the inference is in no straightforward way connected to the truth of the proposition that the action is performed or even the truth of the proposition that it ought to be performed. The fixation with the case of indispensably necessary means to one's ends and the misunderstanding that looks for the rational necessity of practical inference in this way stems from a failure to appreciate this central difference between theoretical and practical reasoning and from a failure to appreciate the generic notion of rational necessity that spans both sorts of reasoning. If there are indispensably necessary means, this line of thought went, then we could hope that the premises might, somehow, rationally preserve the truth of the proposition of the conclusion or at least the truth of the proposition that it ought to be done. But we are mistaken to look for the necessity of practical inference in the premises guaranteeing the truth of the conclusion. This is to overlook that we are dealing with *practical* inference.

Kenny begins his quest for a system of practical inference by noting that when we are dealing with practical reasoning, "the conclusions are actions or plans of action" (Kenny 1966, 65). However, the conclusions of the formal system of practical inference that he develops are, as we saw, sentences in the optative mood. One might worry that since Kenny's system in the end only allows for conclusions which are *sentences*, albeit in the optative mood, he has failed to develop a system of truly practical inference, a system the conclusion of which can be an action. There is, however, a reply to this worry that I take to be in the spirit of Kenny's project. A formal system of practical inference will, by its nature, govern sentences since it is an attempt to represent practical thought formally. But the thought that is thereby represented is itself genuinely practical and can be, therefore, the thought embodied in an action. It would be a mistake to assume that what it is to think the conclusion of some practical syllogism is to hold a belief, although to hold the belief with a peculiar force. To think the thought represented by "Would that I rub him" is not a matter of whispering such a sentence to oneself or being willing to "assert" it (whatever it would mean to assert a sentence in the optative mood) to someone else. It is not a matter of holding a *true belief* about what ought to be done. Rather, one of the ways in which one can think a thought in the optative mood is by performing an action with that thought content. Another way in which one might entertain such a practical thought would be to engage in active planning, for instance, the drawing up of blueprints for a building that one is building. It will be important in what follows that the conclusion of a practical inference is a practical conclusion, paradigmatically, an action. As long as we are inclined to think about A! as representing a peculiar belief, we will still be prone to the fantasy that there is some fuller justification required for A! to be practically necessary than is in fact required or available.

6 What About the Categorical Imperative?

At the beginning of the last section, I suggested that before turning to the way in which moral actions are necessary for Kant, we ought to consider the role that necessity plays in the hypothetical imperative. In the last section, we saw that Kenny's inference rule is an attempt to formalize the rational connections between conclusions and premises in instrumental practical reasoning. I suggested that the necessity involved in this practical inference is what Kant has in mind when he says of a hypothetical imperative that it, "represents a possible action as good and hence as necessary for a subject who is practically determinable by reason" (Kant, G 4:414).

Given the inference rules of first-order logic, it turns out that there are theorems: sentences that can be derived from the null set and that can therefore appear on the right side of the ordinary turnstile while on the left side is only the null set. I define a "practical theorem" as a sentence in the optative mood derived from the null set and Σ, a set containing only sentences in the assertoric mood. If we expand first-order logic to include Kenny's inference rule, we will not be able to derive any practical theorems.[24] I introduced the practical turnstile to indicate entailment in a system of first-order logic which is extended by the inference rules designed to capture practical reasoning. There may be inference rules besides Kenny's that are needed to capture practical reasoning fully.[25] Without taking as stand on this issue, however, we can still say something about what would be the case were there such inference rules that allowed one to derive practical theorems. We know how we would represent such theorems using the practical turnstile:

CI schema: $\Sigma \vdash_p $ A!

Kant says, "Now, if the action would be good merely as a means *to something else* the imperative is *hypothetical*; if the action is represented as *in itself* good, hence as

---

[24] This is clear since the inference rule requires there to be a first order logical derivation of the content of the goal sentence (considered assertorically). Clearly, if there is no goal sentence, there will be no such derivation.
[25] The view that some rule like Kenny's is the only one that would be needed to capture practical reasoning is itself a substantive philosophical view about practical reasoning, the truth of which I will not address in this paper.

necessary in a will in itself conforming to reason, as its principle, *then it is categorical*" (*G* 4:414). Kant's remark here about the nature of the categorical imperative suggests that we might represent an action which is justified as good in itself (not good as a means to some end) as a limiting case in which the set of fiats, designated in our practical symbolism by Ψ, is the null set. A sentence in the optative mood representing an action required by the categorical imperative would be, therefore, a practical theorem.[26] Although the set of fiats is the null set, practical theorems are nevertheless derived from some set of facts Σ, since this captures the way in which action is situated in the world and hence must make reference to the relevant facts.

But what does this suggestion amount to? If an action could be the conclusion of a practical inference which takes the form displayed in the CI schema, then we could say that the action is rationally justified without respect to any of the agent's contingent goals. We can see the good of it without appealing to any of these. Practical inference, I argued, preserves goodness with the force of necessity. When it comes to instrumental reasoning, the means is necessarily good relative to the goodness of the end. When A! is a practical theorem, A! is justified with the force of necessity but not relative to the goodness of some end. It is practically necessary *simplicter*. We might think of logical theorems as rationally necessary. If we give a properly generic characterization of the rational necessity of logical theorems, it will permit us to see how practical theorems are rationally necessary. In both the theoretical and the practical case, theorems are rationally necessary since they cannot fail to be justified; theorems are justified with the force of necessity.

Nothing about this analysis of a practical theorem, however, requires that, rationally speaking, there is only one thing the agent can do. It could turn out, incidentally, that the inference rules are such that whenever a practical theorem is generated it is the only action that is rationally justified under the circumstances, that, rationally speaking, the agent cannot do otherwise. But following our analysis of the necessity of practical reason from the previous section, we can see that the practical *necessity* of the action is not a matter of this incidental feature. Kant does not think that practically necessary actions have this incidental feature, which is why he recognizes that particular benevolent moral actions are optional. The practical necessity of such actions can be seen by observing that answering the question, "What's the good in it?" does not rely on an appeal to any of the agent's con-

---

[26] According to Kant, there are some ends that we must adopt. For each of us at any time, the set of fiats will not be the null set. However, this end, which one must adopt, can itself be represented as derived from the null set. Any action, therefore, that can be represented as derived from such an end can be represented as derived from the null set of fiats.

tingent goals; this is an answer that could be given by any rational being. Notice that this account of practical necessity (as having nothing to do with the overridingness of the considerations in favor of the action) lines up well with the way in which Kant himself actually characterizes the necessity of moral action. Kant writes, "Everyone must grant that a law, if it is to hold morally, that is, as a ground of an obligation, must carry with it absolute necessity; that, for example, the command "though shalt not lie" does not hold only for human beings, as if other rational beings did not have to heed it, and so with all other moral laws properly so called..." (Kant, *G* 4:389). Kant does not understand the necessity of the moral law in terms of the overridingness of moral reasons (that, rationally speaking, a person cannot do otherwise) but in terms the fact that the reason-giving force of the moral law operates simply in virtue of the *rationality* of the agent. When unpacking the necessity involved here, Kant does not insist that, no matter what else the agent is up to, he must not lie (although he may think this too). Rather, he elaborates the necessity by saying that this reason gets a grip on any rational being, that is, its justificatory force is not in virtue of any contingent goals of the agent.

In order to see that an action's being practically necessary does not mean that I have an overriding reason to perform the action, imagine that I have $50. Suppose that I donate the money to a homeless shelter and that this action is a moral action. This does not mean that I have an overriding reason to give the money to the homeless shelter, since, after all, I might have given it to an equally deserving battered women's shelter, and this too might have been a moral action. Either giving the money to the homeless shelter or giving it to the women's shelter could be a moral action, but I do not, in this case, have an overriding reason to do either.

This allows us an elegant solution to the problem I raised in §2. Recall the problem I discussed there: On the one hand, Kant characterizes moral action as practically necessary while, on the other hand, he recognizes moral actions, such as benevolent actions, which are optional. Commentators who are in the grip of the standard view of practical necessity are forced to play down either the practical necessity and rational requiredness of *particular* benevolent actions or the sense in which there really is latitude for the agent in choosing which benevolent actions to perform. However, once we see that the practical necessity of an action lies in the fact that its justification does not rely on the contingent goals of the agent (not in the fact that the agent, rationally speaking, cannot do otherwise), the tension between Kant's two claims simply disappears.

One might worry that severing the tie between practically necessary actions and those actions that an agent has an overriding reason to perform means that practically necessary actions become indistinguishable from merely permissible actions. According to this objection, if an agent has a reason to perform an action without needing to invoke his contingent goals but does not have a reason to perform the action no matter what his contingent goals, then the action is perhaps merely permissible, not necessary. However, the point of representing the action as *justified* in the way I did above is to represent an answer to the question, "What's the good in it?" To say that an action is permissible is not to say that it is justified at all or that there is anything good in it (although when we are interested in permissibility, it is usually with respect to those actions that we do have some reason to perform). Still, to say of an action that it is permissible is to say that we do not have a reason not to do it; it is not yet to show that there is any reason to do it. In this respect, permissible actions contrast with practically necessary actions as I have characterized them.

7 The Allure of the Standard View

Once we see that there is a difference between an action's being rationally justified without relying for its justification on the contingent aims of the particular agent and an action's being such that, rationally speaking, one cannot do otherwise, we may be struck by the question: how is it that Kant commentators have failed to note this distinction and have for so long run together these two notions under the heading of practical necessity?

One reason for this is that most of what is said about Kant on this score is not, strictly speaking, false but simply ambiguous. Williams gives a fairly representative description of a practically necessary action when he says it is an action which we have "reason to take *whatever we might happen to want*" (Williams 1986, 189). This could mean either of the following two things:
(1) that the necessity of moral action rests in the fact that all of our other wants ought to be thrust aside by the overridingness of the moral ought;
(2) that when it comes to moral action, we have a justification for the action which does not depend on what we happen to want; that is, even if we wanted totally different things or happened to want nothing in particular at the moment, the justification for the moral action would still stand.

The first interpretation of Williams' statement is an articulation of the standard view of practical necessity. The second interpretation of what Williams' says captures the sense of practical necessity which I have been arguing for in this paper, and it is in this sense that there is some truth in what he says about practical necessity.

A similar ambiguity plagues much of what is said in the secondary literature about practical necessity in Kant. My diagnosis of this confusion is that commentators hit on what can be a correct formulation of Kant's view—that when we act for moral reasons, we have these reasons regardless of what our contingent aims are. This can express (2), as we saw. But then, trying to square this with what it is that we are explaining, the way that, for Kant, moral actions are practically *necessary*, leads these commentators back towards (1), the pernicious interpretation. One way to put the aim of this paper is to illuminate the idea of practical necessity in a fashion that lands us squarely with (2).

However, noting this ambiguity and the temptation to understand practical necessity according to the standard view only raises the specter of a deeper misunderstanding. Why does it seem, after all, so difficult to square my reading of practical necessity with the thought that these actions are genuinely *necessary*? The short answer to this question is, I think, that we are tempted by a thoroughly contemplative understanding of reason, and hence, of rational concepts generally. Our confusion with regard to the specific concept of rational necessity is ultimately to be traced to this deeper tendency to conflate practical with theoretical reason. A person in the grip of this contemplative conception of reason, might summarize what I have shown in this paper as follows: "Philosophers who read Kant have been wrong insofar as they conflate the idea of the necessity of moral actions with the idea that there are overriding reasons for moral actions. But all that this shows is that Kant uses the term 'necessity' in a strange way in the practical case." This response, however, misses the force of what I have been arguing so far. The point of giving a generic description of rational necessity, as I have done, is to demonstrate that the conception of practical necessity which I have been developing is not necessity in name only, but is the rightful heir to that title in the practical sphere.

What does it mean to say that we are tempted by a thoroughly contemplative conception of reason which prevents us from making a genuinely practical application of rational concepts? Let me illuminate this charge by way of considering a particular discussion of rational necessity by Korsgaard and the way in which the unspoken assimilation of practical reason to theoretical reason distorts this discussion. Korsgaard's stated ambition in a way mirrors mine, in that she attempts to show the way in which the notion of rational necessity gets a purchase in both practical and theoretical contexts. Korsgaard gives this example: "If I *believe* that all women are mortal, and I *believe* that I am a woman, then I *ought* to conclude that I am mortal. The necessity embodied in the use of "ought" is rational necessity. If I am guided by reason, then I will conclude that I am mortal" (2008, 34). Korsgaard notes that she may nevertheless fail to draw the conclusion, since, after all, she may fail to be guided by reason.[27] Korsgaard introduces this example in an attempt to illuminate the way in which rational necessity functions in instrumental reasoning. According to Korsgaard, insofar as an agent is rational in reasoning about the means to her ends she is *"guided* by reason, and in particular, guided by what reason presents as necessary," just as the rational believer is guided by what reason presents as necessary (2008, 33).

So, Korsgaard's analysis purports to give an account of rational necessity that is suitable for spanning both theoretical and practical reasoning. However, this analysis does not illuminate, in general, what is involved in being guided by reason when one reasons instrumentally. It cannot, therefore, give a general account of necessity as it functions in practical reasoning. Recall from §4 that often it turns out that there are multiple suitable means to my end. For instance, if I aim to warm the patient, I may wrap him a blanket or sit him by the fire. Whichever of the means I choose to take, it seems fair to say that I am *guided* by reason in taking the means to my end. But notice that Korsgaard has no way to account for reason's guidance in this case. She unpacks the rational necessity of belief in her theoretical example by saying, "If I am guided by reason, then I will conclude that I am mortal." But it is simply not true of the practical example at hand that "If I am guided by reason, then I will wrap the patient in a blanket." Korsgaard has gotten it backwards: what may be true is something like the converse of her statement, "When I wrap the patient in a blanket, I am guided by reason."

Korsgaard's account can pretend to explain the rational necessity of reasoning only in those cases where there actually are indispensably necessary means to one's ends. It does so by picking out a feature of these cases that is shared by theoretical cases. If there is an indispensably necessary means to an agent's end, then it will be true that if the agent is guided by reason, then he will take the means.

---

[27] Of this difficulty that beings who are imperfectly rational can fail to be moved by rational considerations, Korsgaard writes, "there seem to be plenty of things that could interfere with the motivational influence of a given rational consideration. Rage, passion, depression, distraction, grief, physical or mental illness: all these could cause us to act irrationally, that is, to fail to be motivationally responsive to the rational considerations available to us. The necessity, or the compellingness, of rational considerations lies in those considerations themselves, not in us: that is, we will not necessarily be motivated by them. Or rather, to put the point more properly and not to foreclose any metaphysical possibilities, their necessity may lie in the fact that, when they do move us —either in the realm of conviction or in that of motivation—they move us with the force of necessity. But it will still not be the case that they necessarily move us" (Korsgaard 1996, 320). I think that Korsgaard's analysis here is insightful. I want to consider what it could mean to say that moral reasons "move us with the force of necessity" and whether this needs to involve the idea that the reasons are overriding.

This suggests, however, that rather than explain rational necessity in general, Korsgaard has incorporated into her generic description of rational necessity features that are peculiar to one species of this genus, namely, theoretical rational necessity.[28] In order to give a properly generic description of rational necessity we need to appreciate that theoretical reasoning aims at and preserves truth while practical reasoning aims at and preserves goodness. Practical reasoning will exhibit patterns of inference that differ from those of theoretical reasoning. These patterns of inference nonetheless preserve the rational justification of an action by representing it as good. The properly generic notion of rational necessity is one according to which a belief or an action is rationally necessary if in holding the belief or performing the action, I am guided by reason. Given the premises of the theoretical or practical syllogism, I am, of necessity, justified in holding the belief or performing the action, since those premises constitute my justification. Given the premises, it will not turn out, accidentally in this case, that I am unjustified in drawing the conclusion. Here, following Korsgaard, I have been discussing hypothetical reasoning, but this generic notion of rational necessity applies equally to practical and theoretical theorems.

I imagine that someone in the grip of the contemplative conception of reasoning will not yet be satisfied and might ask, "If reasoning allows that I can rub the patient or sit him by the fire, how can reason be guiding me if I choose to rub him? I see that reason guides me up to the point where I decide that I will do one thing or the other, but reasoning does not offer me any particular guidance in my choice of rubbing him." As I have been arguing, in order to answer this objection, we need to attend to the way in which the action can be fully rationally justified, even if some other action might have been equally justified.

Consider the following two examples:

(a) Imagine I am playing Clue. The player of such a game must perform various bits of theoretical reasoning about who committed a certain crime, what weapon they used and in what room they used it. Imagine further that I have reached a point in the game at which, having successfully narrowed down the weapon to the candlestick and the room to the library, and having also eliminated all possible suspects but two, I am still not yet in a position dispositively to assert whether the murderer is Reverend Green or whether he is Colonel Mustard. From the vantage of theoretical reason, I am equally, though in neither case fully, justified in judging that the murderer is Green and justified in judging that he is Mustard. Of course, if

---

28 It is possible that Korsgaard thinks that purported reasoning in which the agent takes some means to her end which is not indispensable will not count as practical reasoning at all. If this is Korsgaard's view, she is not up front about this perhaps unwelcome implication of her account.

what I am doing is *playing the game* of Clue, my aim in declaring to the other players that the murderer is Green or is Mustard is guided my understanding of what is required in order to attain the practical end of winning the game. If, for instance, I suspect that someone else will make a correct accusation before I can if I do not accuse someone on this turn, then if I am reasoning practically, I may simply choose to accuse either Green or Mustard. From the point of view of theoretical reason, however, I have no reasons, not even any hunches, to support the theoretical judgment that one of them is the murderer rather than the other.

(b) Imagine I have handed out class evaluations at the end of term. For purposes of anonymity, I need one student to collect the evaluations and to return them to the office. I ask the students if there are any volunteers, and both Rena and Tito raise their hands. I have no reason for preferring one student to the other for the task. It is not, for instance, more convenient for one than for the other. I charge Tito with returning the evaluations to the office.

What I want to do now is to focus on the stretch of theoretical reasoning in which, while playing the game, I engage (when I try to arrive at an objective judgment about who committed the murder) and to contrast this with the stretch of practical reasoning in which I engage in the second example. The first example is a case of my reasoning theoretically which seeks to issue in a judgment about who performed the murder. The second example is a case of my reasoning practically issuing in an action—charging Tito with returning the evaluations. In both cases, I am fully justified in judging or performing the *disjunction* ("Green or Mustard," "Rena or Tito"), but only in the second case am I justified in moving beyond the disjunction to one of the disjuncts. As long as I remain within the sphere of purely theoretical reason, if simply opt for one of the disjuncts and conclude, for instance, that Mustard is the murderer, theoretically speaking, I am unjustified in arriving at this judgment; such a judgment opens me to rational criticism. If I move to one of the disjuncts, however, in the second case and charge, say, Tito with returning the evaluations, I am *fully justified* in doing so. It is precisely this difference between theoretical and practical reason which Kenny's system so perspicuously represents. It is in this sense that, in the practical case, reason guides me all the way to my choice of the particular disjunct, even if it does not tell between choosing one disjunct or the other.

Someone might object by saying: "Surely, there must be something that tells between charging Rena and charging Tito? Just as in the case of the Clue player faced with his last chance to win, perhaps in this case too one needs to make a decision with relative haste for pragmatic reasons. But as in the purely theoretical case, so too here such a judgment, therefore, lacks full rational justification." This objection is predicated on a claim that seems patently false—that there must always be some reason to prefer one action over another. Consider the case of standing in a grocery store isle and buying a can of soup. It hardly seems plausible that there must be reasons for picking up one can of soup over and above any of the others. In real life cases, things will be complicated and there may often be reasons to prefer one way of acting to another. For instance, walking and taking the bus may both be justified with respect to my end of getting to school, however, taking the bus may have the additional advantage of preventing me from getting sweaty. Adducing such cases, however, does nothing to support the claim that my objector needs, since his claim is that *in every case* there is some reason to prefer one action to another. The burden, in any case, lies on the objector to show why we ought to endorse this implausible claim. It is possible that in a case similar to (b) there would be reasons that tell in favor of charging Tito over Rena. I have stipulated, however, that this is one of those cases where there are no such reasons. Practical reason therefore fully justifies me in my charging Tito with returning the evaluations. There is no further justification that is lacking, as there would be in the purely theoretical case described above, if I tried to find a way to get theoretical reason to allow me to move from my grounds for making the theoretical judgment "Green or Mustard is the murderer" to a ground for judging "Mustard is the murderer" or judging "Green is the murderer." Practical reason, by contrast, in the second case described above, fully guides me in my choice of Tito, even though it might equally have guided me in choosing Rena.

This response may engender another worry: if I am fully justified in charging Rena and charging Tito then, if I am to follow the dictates of reason, I must charge them both. Such a concern fuels Spielthenner's worry that

> sufficient condition schemata raise paradoxes... You want to buy your favorite mineral water. There are fifty bottles of it on the shelves in the supermarket. If you take the first bottle, this is sufficient for your aim and therefore you should take it. But if you take the second bottle, this is also sufficient, so you should also take this one, and so on, for all fifty bottles. If "you should buy the first bottle" and "you should buy the second (etc.) bottle," then it follows that you should buy all fifty bottles, even though you wanted only one. One might reply to this line of argument that also the disjunction (bottle one *or* bottle two ...) is a sufficient condition for your aim. But this raises the next paradox. If the disjunction is sufficient, the conjunction is too, and therefore you should do both, buying at least one of the bottles and buying all of them (Spielthenner 2007, 141–142).

As it stands, Spielthenner's point is ambiguous with respect to the scope of the fiat operator. Let b_1 be "I buy the first bottle" and b_2 be "I buy the second bottle," etc. The first way to take Spielthenner's criticism is as a complaint that in Kenny's system, I could conclude my reasoning with (b_1 & b_2 & ...& b_{50})! Kenny considers a similar objection and replies that

From the command "open the door" one can, however, infer the fiat "[(opening of the door and smashing of the window)!]"; someone who did execute such a plan would indeed obey the original command and satisfy the desire which that command might vent. By executing the command in such a manner, the agent would no doubt annoy the commander; but this would be because he would be acting against the commander's tacit desire that the window should not be broken. If this tacit desire were made explicit, the fiat expressing the commander's state of mind would be of the form [(p& ¬q)!]; from which there is no inference in the logic of satisfactoriness to [(p & q)!]. Thus the paradox here is only apparent (Kenny 1966, 74–75).[29]

Kenny here responds to the way in which that inference rule seems unintuitive which allows one, when reasoning practically, to continue to add conjuncts to one's conclusion. His response hinges on the non-monotinicity of the system of practical inference he has established. By adding new premises one can change the inferences one is licensed to draw. We have been dealing with practical reasoning at some level of abstraction. To return to Spielthenner's example, if the buying a bottle of water were the only fiat in Ψ, then it would make no difference whether I buy one bottle or fifty. Either action is a way of buying a bottle of mineral water. But in ordinary circumstances, we work a huge number of fiats. In real life, I probably also have the fiat that I do not spend more money than I need to and that I do not buy more than I can carry. The reason that buying fifty bottles rather than one is not a valid practical inference does not have to do with its not being a legitimate way of buying a bottle of water, but with the fact that the set of fiats from which one makes the inference, in ordinary circumstances, contains more than this single fiat.

This brings us to the second way of hearing Spielthenner's worry. Notice that there is a dissimilarity between the case which Kenny considers and that which Spielthenner puts forward. In Kenny's case, the conjunct "(I break the window)" is ruled out by a fiat which says "(I do not break the window)!" In the examples of the bottles of water, there is no possibility of adding a fiat like this; even if, for reasons of economy, buying all of the bottles is ruled out, there is still a valid inference to $(b_1)!$ and a valid inference to $(b_2)!$—etc. We might take Spielthenner as claiming that this means that in Kenny's system, we must be able to conclude: $((b_1)! \& (b_2)! \& \ldots \& (b_{50})!)$. However, on this way of taking the objection, the charge turns out to be false, since such a string is not well-formed in Kenny's system. There are no rules for conjoining fiats with truth-functional operators. This strikes me as a felicitous consequence, since what the fiats represent is action

---

[29] I have altered Kenny's notation so that it matches that in the rest of this paper.

which, unlike a judgment about action, is not truth-evaluable. There is no reason that we should expect actions to be connected by truth-functional operators. The intuition that one can, of course, do more than one thing at once is accommodated by conjunctions falling within the scope of the fiat operator.[30]

Attending to the fact that the conclusion of practical reasoning is action allows us to appreciate the way in which a particular action can be *fully* justified without the reasoning that justifies it representing it as better than some other action. It also enables us, on the other hand, to see why the potential for the full justification of several options need not justify doing all of these.

8 Overriding Reasons, Perfect Duties

I have been arguing that for Kant, a practically necessary action is not one that an agent has overriding reason to perform; instead, a practically necessary action is an action the justification of which has its ultimate source in reason itself, so that the action is thereby unconditioned by the subjective, material ends of the agent. I now turn to two possible lingering worries. First, one might assume that Kant's general rhetoric surrounding duty and the moral law invokes the overridingness of the reasons involved. For instance, in the *Groundwork*, he writes:

> Only what is connected with my will merely as ground and never as effect, what does not serve my inclination but outweighs it or at least excludes it altogether from calculations in making a choice—hence the mere law for itself—can be an object of respect and so a command (Kant, *G* 4:400).

Later, he says:

---

[30] The view that I have been advancing is like non-cognitivism in that the conclusion of practical reasoning, action, is not truth-evaluable. However, this view is like cognitivism in that it holds on to the idea that action is a form of practical *cognition*. Such practical cognition is rational insofar as it is goodness-evaluable. On the view of practical reasoning presented in this paper, one can, of course, make judgments about whether actions are good (are justified), and such judgments themselves can be truth-evaluable. The point here, however, is that one needs to pay careful attention to what falls within the scope of such claims of justification. If I claim that I am justified in buying the first bottle and that I am justified in buying the second bottle, it does not follow that I am justified in buying the first and in buying the second bottle. This stands in contrast to the way in which the scope of justification functions when involved in judgments made about beliefs. For instance, if I am justified in believing that there is a first bottle and I am justified in believing that there is a second bottle, then I am justified in believing that there is a first bottle and there is a second bottle.

For, only law brings with it the concept of *unconditional* and objective and hence universally valid *necessity*, and commands are laws that must be obeyed, that is, must be followed even against inclination (Kant, *G* 4:416).

It is not uncommon, I think, for people to imagine passages such as these to speak in favor of the standard view of practical necessity by suggesting that an action complies with the law only insofar as one cannot do otherwise without opening oneself to rational criticism. In fact, these sorts of passages support no such claim. In order to see how this is so, let us consider an example: I donate $50 to a homeless shelter ($50 that I could have donated to a battered women's shelter), in spite of the fact that I have an inclination to use the money to buy a sequin tank top. If we stipulate that I do act for moral reasons, then this case is compatible with the first passage since it is the law that serves as the ground of choice and does outweigh and exclude my inclination to buy the tank top. It is so compatible even though I have latitude in complying with the law since the particular action is optional. Likewise, this example is compatible with the second passage since my reason is unconditional and (as I have been arguing) a matter of objective universally valid necessity. Again, the action does amount to complying with the law even against inclination, since inclination supports buying the tank top. The sense in which these passages support the idea that moral reasons are overriding is only the sense in which they serve as an unconditioned ground of action independent of inclination, not in the sense that the proponent of the standard view of practical necessity needs, according to which there must be only one action such that the agent cannot fail to perform it without opening himself to rational criticism.

Second, it is also well known that Kant holds that morality does give us some overriding reasons to perform particular actions; specifically, we have overriding reasons to fulfill our perfect duties. How does my account, which severs the connection between moral action and overriding reasons, explain the overridingness of reasons in the case of perfect duties?

The short answer is that the view of practical necessity I have offered here does not entail any account of the overridingness of the reasons to fulfill perfect duties. Rather than serving as fodder for criticism of my view, however, this is one of its virtues. I have been mainly concerned with giving an analysis of a central Kantian concept, practical necessity. One of the advantages of this analysis is that it does not make nonsense out of the category of imperfect duty. This is because practical necessity has little to do with reason homing in on a particular action in such a way that this particular action is the only one that the agent can perform without opening himself to rational criticism. The rationally non-optional simply does not play a role in understanding the concept of practical necessity. However, it is a further feature of the Kantian view that sometimes reason does home in on a particular action that is not optional; these are the cases of perfect duties, and if one fails to perform the particular action, one opens oneself to rational criticism. In order to account for why some duties are perfect, one would have to go beyond the "mere concept of a categorical imperative," which is all that I invoked above in representing formally an unconditioned reason for action, to "its formula containing the proposition which alone can be a categorical imperative" (Kant, *G* 4:420). Given that how to understand the categorical imperative and the way in which it generates content are much debated topics in the secondary literature, it is a virtue of my view that it will be compatible with many understandings of the actual workings of the categorical imperative.

It is worth drawing out one consequence of this discussion: the perfection of perfect duties is a feature which is incidental to their being duties. Perfect duties are not perfect in the sense of being paradigmatic, nor are imperfect duties imperfect in the sense of being defective. The distinction between perfect and imperfect duties was a conventional division that Kant would have been familiar with. There is little reason to think, on the basis of these labels alone, that this classification marks a deep division in Kant's concept of duty or is a particularly helpful guide in determining what duty *really* is. Just as we drew the distinction between dispensably and indispensably necessary means, so we could draw a distinction between actions which are dispensably necessary and indispensably necessary simpliciter. In each case, the division into the dispensable and the indispensable is one which runs orthogonal to concerns about practical necessity.

Allen Wood remarks that despite Kant's "notorious reputation for moral strictness and his preoccupation with rational architectonic," his ethics "as compared with many fashionable theories, is far more permissive and leaves a lot more to the free volition of individuals in determining what their own duties are" (2008, 169). A proper understanding of the generic notion of rational necessity and the way in which it ought to be specified when involved in practical and theoretical reasoning allows us a deep understanding of why this should be so.

Abbreviations

Kant's Works

All citations of Kant's works are given in the notes as abbreviation, volume number, and page number as per the *Akademie Ausgabe* (AA), *Kant's Gesammelte Schriften*, edited by the Royal Prussian (later German) Academy of Sciences (Berlin: Georg Reimer, later Walter de Gruyter, 1900–). All translations are from *Practical*

Philosophy, edited by Mary J. Gregor (Cambridge: Cambridge University Press, 1999). I use the following abbreviations:
G   Groundwork of the Metaphysics of Morals (1785)
MM The Metaphysics of Morals (1797)

References

Anscombe, Gertrude Elizabeth Margaret (1963): *Intention*. Cambridge: Harvard University Press.
Anscombe, Gertrude Elizabeth Margaret (2002): "Practical Inference." In: Hursthouse, Rosalind, Lawrence, Gavin, and Quinn, Warren (Eds.): *Virtues and Reasons*. Oxford: Clarendon Press, 1–34.
Audi, Robert (1982): "A Theory of Practical Reasoning." In: *American Philosophical Quarterly* 19. No. 1, 25–39.
Baron, Marcia (2006): "Overdetermined Actions and Imperfect Duties." In: Schönecker, Dieter and Kühn, Manfred (Eds.): *Moralische Motivation: Kant und die Alternativen*. Hamburg: Felix Meiner, 23–37.
Dancy, Jonathan (2004): *Ethics Without Principles*. Oxford: Oxford University Press.
Dancy, Jonathan (2009): "Action, Content and Inference." In: Glock, Hans-Johann and Hyman, John (Eds.): *Wittgenstein and Analytic Philosophy*. Oxford: Oxford University Press, 278–298.
Herman, Barbara (1993): *The Practice of Moral Judgment*. Cambridge: Harvard University Press.
Kenny, Anthony (1966): "Practical Inference." In: *Analysis* 26. No. 3, 65–75.
Korsgaard, Christine (1996): *Creating the Kingdom of Ends*. Cambridge: Cambridge University Press.
Korsgaard, Christine (2008): *The Constitution of Agency*. Oxford: Oxford University Press.
Lockhart, Jennifer Ryan (2017): "Kant on the motive of (imperfect) duty." In: Inquiry 60. No. 6, 569–603.
Rawls, John (1993): *Political Liberalism*. New York: Columbia University Press.
Rawls, John (2000): *Lectures on the History of Moral Philosophy*. Cambridge: Harvard University Press.
Schneewind, Jerome B. (1992): "Autonomy, obligation, and virtue: An overview of Kant's moral philosophy." In: Guyer, Paul (Ed.): *The Cambridge Companion to Kant*. Cambridge: Cambridge University Press, 309–341.
Spielthenner, Georg (2007): "A Logic of Practical Reasoning." In: *Acta Analytica* 22. No. 2, 139–153.
Williams, Bernard (1982): *Moral Luck*. Cambridge: Cambridge University Press.
Williams, Bernard (1986): *Ethics and the Limits of Philosophy*. Cambridge: Harvard University Press.
Wood, Allen (1999): *Kant's Ethical Thought*. Cambridge: Cambridge University Press.
Wood, Allen (2008): *Kantian Ethics*. Cambridge: Cambridge University Press.

Part II: **Ethics and Meta-ethics**

Rory O'Connell
Against the Possibility of a Merely Instrumentally Rational Agent

Abstract: Can we coherently conceive of an agent whose practical rationality is limited to merely instrumental reasoning? I argue that we cannot. Existing arguments to this effect have focused on what is required in order to have reasons to take means to our ends—or on what is required in order to be bound by the so-called 'instrumental principle'. By contrast, I argue that consideration of the special kind of concept-use characteristic of instrumental reasoning reveals that a merely instrumentally rational agent would not be so much as able to *identify* means to ends in the first place. I then elucidate this line of thought by testing it against three different conceptions of merely instrumentally rational agency found in the literature. I conclude by highlighting a risk associated with remaining agnostic concerning the possibility of merely instrumentally rational agents: namely, that we arrive at a false conception of our own capacity to identify means to ends as somehow isolated from our conceptions of the good.

1 Introduction

Philosophers often have cause to consider some being the very possibility of which may be considered dubious. The being that forms the topic of this paper holds a special position among the usual suspects. In the case of swamp men, philosophical zombies, disembodied Cartesian egos, or logical aliens, we are not normally prone to think that we or our interlocutors are potential instances of the topic in question. However, in the case of the merely instrumentally rational agent— an agent whose practical reason exclusively comprises the calculation of means to ends—arguments for or against its possibility generally aim at settling whether the form of agency in question is exemplified by *us*. Some claim that such agents are the *only* kind of rational agent of which we have a fully intelligible conception —and thus that *we* are likely such agents—while others claim that the very idea of such an agent is ultimately incoherent and thus that *we cannot be* such agents.[1] The issue at stake in these disputes is thus always that of our own practical nature.

---

[1] See Drier (1997), Street (2010 and 2012), and Vogler (2002) for—very different—examples of accounts of the former variety; see Korsgaard (2008 and 2009), Rödl (2007), Smith (2015), and Velleman (2009) for—very different—examples of accounts of the latter variety.

In this article, I shall make a novel argument against the possibility of a merely instrumentally rational agent. I take my leave from the following question: what are the prerequisites for agents to be so much as capable of identifying what the means to their ends are in the first place? My central claim in answering that question is that nothing less than a rational appreciation of the non-instrumental good of our ends is a prerequisite for the identification of means in instrumental reasoning.

In taking this question as my starting point, I avoid the different question of which *principles* govern instrumental reasoning—in particular, I will not have anything to say about the "instrumental principle" ("take the necessary means to your ends"). Nor will I be concerned with the question of what needs to be in place if agents are to count as having reasons to take means to their ends—nor, indeed, will I say much about acting for a reason in general. The focus of my argument thus differs from existing ones, including Christine Korsgaard's well-known argument.[2] Korsgaard argues that agents are not subject to the instrumental principle unless they possess a further form of non-instrumental practical rationality. Her argument turns on the contention that in order to be subject to a rational principle one must be capable of violating it. Violating the instrumental principle is impossible for an agent whose ends are not governed by rational principles since, she argues, we cannot distinguish in a principled way between the agent failing to take means to its ends from its simply having adopted different ends. The agent in question is therefore not subject to the instrumental principle and so, according to Korsgaard, is not instrumentally rational.

Partly in response to the alleged limitations of that kind of argument—most notably the concern that it presupposes a demanding notion of instrumental rationality that its opponents will happily reject—some philosophers who are unsympathetic to instrumentalism have urged that we should remain officially agnostic about—or indeed positively *affirm*—the possibility of merely instrumentally rational agency.[3] According to this approach, we need not claim that the kind of rationality instrumentalists ascribe to human beings is unintelligible—merely apparent form of rationality that, as it were, collapses entirely when placed under sufficient philosophical scrutiny. All we need claim is that it is not *our* form of rationality. Douglas Lavin—couching the central dispute in question as one between "Kantians" and "anti-Kantians"—thus suggests that "The anti-Kantians might be

---

[2] See Korsgaard (1997). See Lavin (2004) for an illuminating discussion of the so-called "Error Constraint" that is central to Korsgaard's argument.
[3] See Lavin (2004, 2017) as well as Thompson (2008, 2–3). Tenenbaum (2021) is another example of a philosopher who rejects Korsgaard's argument and who is also happy to leave open the possibility of a merely instrumentally rational being, but who also rejects instrumentalism.

right that the very concept of a capacity to act for reasons does not imply any further requirement beyond the instrumental principle, while the Kantians might be right that our actual capacity to act for reasons takes a form that implies the existence of unconditional practical norms."[4]

Agnosticism with respect to the possibility of merely instrumentally rational agency is tempting since it eases the argumentative burden in opposing instrumentalism. As Michael Thompson puts it, "We are anxious to oppose *Humeanism* in ethical theory, but setting out to disprove it *analytically* of *whatever applies thought to action* seems a hopeless task" (2013, 773). However, the case I make below should—in addition to showing that the burden might be shouldered—also reveal a hidden danger of agnosticism. If the possibility of merely instrumentally rational agency is not ruled out, it is almost inevitable that a philosopher will conceive of the rudimentary form of practical rationality attributable to such an agent as constituting a *component* in our more-than-instrumental form of practical rationality. In countenancing that possibility we risk corrupting our own practical self-conception within ethical theory. In particular, we are quickly led to an account of what it is to determine means to our ends that renders instrumental reasoning a merely "technical" achievement—one that need not draw on our conception of our ends' goodness. This in turn precludes us from appreciating the ethical dimension of what is then understood as "mere" instrumental reasoning. In countenancing the *possibility* of merely instrumentally rational agency, we therefore make room for a corrupted conception of the *actuality* of our own practical rationality.

I shall begin making my case against the possibility of merely instrumentally rational agency by exploring how means-end reasoning should be distinguished from theoretical reasoning, with special focus on the way in which an agent's ends constitute what I call "standards of success" within their instrumental reasoning (§2). I will then outline a preliminary argument against the possibility of a merely instrumentally rational agent (§3). In order to test the argument's strength and elucidate its import, I shall consider three different conceptions of a merely instrumentally rational agent from the literature. A "naïve agent," drawn from Michael Thompson's naïve action theory (§4.1); a form of "Humean

---

[4] Lavin (2017, 185). Lavin locates Korsgaard's argument—as well as those of some of her opponents—in the context of wider debates concerning constitutivism. According to Lavin, if we reject the assumption that the standards constitutive of our form of agency are necessarily constitutive of *all* forms of rational agency, we can grant the intelligibility of Humean practical rationality while blocking its application to our case. This "pluralistic" approach has the advantage that we can undermine instrumentalism about (our) practical reason without begging the question against its proponents (as Lavin argues Korsgaard is in real danger of doing).

agent" recognizable from various contemporary accounts of agency (§4.2), and finally, the "practical thinker," whom we encounter in the course of Stephen Engstrom's account of Kant's notion of practical knowledge (§4.3). In each case, consideration of the agent in question will help to bring out problematic assumptions that help to prop up the ultimately illusory notion of merely instrumentally rational agency. I conclude by returning briefly to the danger of remaining agnostic with respect to the possibility of a merely instrumentally rational agent, and by outlining the idea of a "non-technical" conception of instrumental reasoning (§5).

2 The Productive Character of Instrumental Reasoning

Instrumental reasoning takes as its point of departure something the agent aims to realize—an end—and when successful concludes, at least, in a conception of *how* they can realize it or, less minimally, in the action or actions they have identified as a means to their end.[5] We can depict the general shape such reasoning takes via the following schema:

1. Do *A*
2. In order to do *A*, do *B*
3. Therefore, do *B*

Although the exercise of the agent's capacity for means-end thought can consist in a deliberative episode—i.e., a course of reasoning exhibiting temporal duration—the capacity is exercised whenever an agent performs an intentional action that exhibits a means-end structure.[6]

Although the subject matter of instrumental reasoning is intentional action, what distinguishes it as genuinely practical is that it aims at actually realizing

---

[5] Many philosophers follow Aristotle in holding that the conclusion of practical reasoning is not merely an intention or judgment about what to do but intentional action itself. Although I share this view, the argument I present in this paper is officially neutral on whether the conclusion of practical reasoning is an action or an intention, etc. See Fernandez (2016) for a helpful discussion of this issue.

[6] This is shown by the fact that, barring contingent impediments to articulateness, agents are able to explain why they are doing/have done each of the actions they are performing/have performed. No episode of deliberation need occur in order for instrumental rationality to be operative in intentional action. See Anscombe (2000, 79–80) on this point. For ease of exposition, I shall nevertheless often speak in terms of episodes of deliberation.

an agent's end. Its concern with action is therefore intrinsically *productive*, as opposed to merely reflective. A mark of this fact is that instrumental reasoning, when it is not merely an idle or speculative exercise, is subject to distinctive constraints. As Aristotle notes, we deliberate not just about anything but about things that "are in our power and can be done," which is why "no one deliberates about the past but about what is future and is capable of being otherwise" (*NE* 1112a31–2 and 1139b11).[7] Furthermore, instrumental reasoning is generally assessed—like the very actions undertaken in pursuit of our ends—in terms of how well it serves a given end. Instrumental reasoning that proceeds from time-consuming deliberation or that arrives at a needlessly complex way of doing something can be said to fail by its own lights if in exhibiting those characteristics it thereby frustrates the realization of the agent's end.

That it is in virtue of bearing this essentially productive relation to its subject matter that practical reason is distinguished from theoretical reason is an old idea, one that has been articulated variously throughout the tradition.[8] Kant writes in the preface to the first *Critique* that:

> ...knowledge can be related to its object in two ways, either merely to determine this object and its concept (which must be given from elsewhere), or also to make it actual. The former is theoretical and the latter practical knowledge of reason (Bix–x; cf. *KpV* 46 and 89).

Much later, Anscombe expresses a similar insight (employing a phrase borrowed from Aquinas):

> Practical knowledge is "the cause of what it understands," unlike "speculative" knowledge, which "is derived from the things known" (Anscombe 2000, 87).

Anscombe and Kant are in fact addressing different aspects of practical reason. Kant is speaking of practical knowledge of the good. Anscombe's topic is not knowledge of the good but the agent's distinctive knowledge of their own intentional action.[9] But common to both is the idea, articulated by Aristotle, that what makes

---

[7] People often *think about* what they could have done differently, but no one *deliberates* about what they could have done differently—unless, of course, they are deciding what to do next time.
[8] Contemporary philosophers tend to distinguish practical from theoretical thought in terms of the different kinds of *attitude* involved in each. My focus on practical reason's productive character should not be understood as a rejection of that idea, though I should want to argue that any difference in the sorts of attitudes involved must be understood through the lens of what I describe here as practical reason's "productivity."
[9] Rödl (2010) offers a unified account of these two different senses of practical reason and knowledge.

practical thinking *practical* is precisely its productive or efficacious character. My goal in the remainder of this section will be to show how the productive character of practical reasoning determines the form its standards of success must take.

In paradigmatic acts of theoretical reason, a particular object—in a broad sense of the word "object"—is brought or "subsumed" under a concept.[10] One may, for example, judge that the bus was late, that Jerry's head is hurting or that the sky is pink. In each of these cases, the particular objects in question play a privileged role in determining whether or not the judgment is true. The judgments are true if and only if they accurately represent how things stand with the object in question. (By contrast, we do not speak of the judgments capturing how things stand with "lateness," "pain" or "pink.") In a paradigmatic act of instrumental reasoning a certain action is identified as being a means to the agent's end. Just as the sky plays a privileged role in determining whether thoughts that describe it as, for example, "pink," are true, it is apparently my end of, for example, "getting to Paris" that determines whether it is true that "in order to get to Paris, I can take the Eurostar." For it is the character of my end—what *it* is—that determines whether "taking the Eurostar" is a correct means to it or not. The means must fit the end.

This suggests a certain parallel between particular objects, as they figure in paradigmatic acts of theoretical thought, and the agent's ends, as they figure in paradigmatic acts of practical thought. Both can be said to serve as "standards of success" against which the judgments concerning them are to be assessed insofar as the truth of thoughts involving them depend on them in crucial ways.[11]

However, although they occupy analogous roles at one level of abstraction they otherwise differ considerably. Instrumental reasoning's essential task is *not* to accurately *represent* objects whose existence is independent of the agent's reasoning —though it will no doubt have to involve that—but to realize an object (i.e., the agent's end) whose existence is dependent *on* that very reasoning. This is just to repeat the observation made above, that practical reasoning is distinguished in virtue of its productivity. As we shall see, this difference brings with it a difference in

---

[10] I call these particular acts of theoretical reason "paradigmatic" insofar as they are especially clear examples of thoughts that existentially depend on their object. As we shall see, they are also the kind of judgment that forms the most illuminating comparison with the practical case, at least for our purposes.

[11] Obviously *the* standard of success in each case can be correctly identified as *truth*. Truth is what each thought is aiming at. However, particular objects and ends can also be called "standards of success" insofar as attaining truth, in each case, depends on correctly characterizing them (in the theoretical case) or finding their means of realization (in the practical case).

the manner in which an agent's end forms a standard of success within instrumental reasoning.

In order to better understand the way in which standards of success differ in practical and theoretical reasoning, we must consider the special form of indeterminacy that ends exhibit. This form of indeterminacy—which, it will transpire, we can equally characterize as a form of generality—is most clearly exhibited by an end that an agent has not yet specified means to. Indeed, the generality in question is precisely what is rendered determinate *by* the agent's instrumental reasoning. For example, when I specify "taking the Eurostar" as a means to my end of "getting to Paris," I render the latter more determinate in virtue of rendering it more *specific*. My end is thereby transformed: I no longer merely aim "to go to Paris" but rather "to take the Eurostar to Paris." My more determinate end can now serve as the starting point for further specification, as when I reason that: "in order to take the Eurostar, I'll book a ticket using their website," and that "to book a ticket on the website, I'll fetch my laptop from upstairs," and so on and so forth until I reach a specification of an action that I can perform without further ado.[12]

Concerning this point the disanalogy between the practical and theoretical is significant. Since practical reason takes as its "object" something which is to be realized or "made actual," this object—that is, the agent's end—*must* at the outset be something general, and which does not yet possess the concrete determinacy of a completed act. Were this not the case, the agent's end would already have been realized and would no longer be a possible object of practical reasoning. Ends in practical reasoning—by contrast to the particular objects that feature in theoretical reasoning—can therefore be said to be *inherently* general.[13]

---

12 To simplify exposition, I am passing over several different aspects of the kind of generality distinctive of ends. As Ford (2016) emphasizes, practical reasoning involves rendering one's end more *specific* (as when a trip to France becomes a train journey to France), as well as rendering it more *particular*, as when my trip becomes a train trip to France vis-à-vis *this here train*. In each case, the generality of the agent's end is determined along a different axis. In addition to noting the aspects of determination Ford describes, we can further note it is only when the agent *acts* that the remaining vestiges of indeterminacy are in fact shed from the agent's end. As I take each step from the station's entrance to the platform for my train, my end becomes increasingly "concrete," insofar as what could have been realized by many other steps, taken at different speeds or in slightly different directions, has now been realized in the steps I have actually taken. This final "moment" of determination will lie outside the scope of our discussion, since my argument is neutral on whether action is the conclusion of practical reasoning or not, and therefore on whether this final mode of determination falls with the ken of the agent's instrumental reasoning.

13 Of course, sometimes my end is already relatively determinate. For example, upon spotting a piece of halva on the other side of the room, I may immediately pursue it. In which case there is no need for me to determine what to eat, or where to find it, etc. Nevertheless, even if what I intend is relatively determinate, until I settle how I shall do so—what path to take across the room, whether

There is much to be said about the special practical form of generality that characterizes ends.[14] For the moment, however, we can turn to the question of how it bears on ends' role as *standards of success* in instrumental reasoning. It is clear that ends do not form standards of success in virtue of possessing determinations or properties which it is the agent's task to, somehow or other, discover. I do not *find out* that my going to France is, in fact, a trip by Eurostar (unless, perhaps, someone has arranged the trip on my behalf as a surprise—but then the practical reasoning has been taken out of my hands); to think as much would be to attempt to understand practical reason on the model of theoretical reason. It would be, in other words, to treat the object of practical reasoning as having its existence independently *of* that very reasoning. By contrast, we need to articulate a notion of a standard of success that fits the non-theoretical, productive character of practical thought.

At the outset of instrumental reasoning, when an agent's ends are general in the sense we have outlined, their contents would appear to be exhausted by the action concepts through which they are thought. Once I am actually in the process of, for example, "going to France," my action—my partially realized end—takes on many characteristics not captured by that initial specification. Already the realization of my end will have involved such acts as: shooting out the front door, running to the train station and studying the schedule. Nevertheless, before the pursuit of that end has begun in earnest, before it has even been partially realized, its content would appear to simply mirror that of the action concepts through which it is thought. If so, we can understand the standards of success for the realization of those ends as being set by the action concepts used in their initial specifications. What will count as a means to my end of "going to France" will be decided by the very action concept which, as it were, captures the content—the "what it is"—of that particular end. In other words, it will be decided by the act-types expressed by those action concepts. Whether taking the Eurostar is a correct means of going to France will depend on the character of those two act-types: namely, "going to France" and "taking the Eurostar," such that the latter genuinely "fits" the former.

---

to grab it with a napkin or my bare hands, etc.—my end will be general (though not *as* general—or rather, not as general in every respect—as when I decide I would like some halva but do not yet know where some might be found).

14 For example, more needs to be said about the way in which the realization of "practical generalities"—which is just to say the realization of ends—runs along two internally related axes: On the one hand, the agent realizes their end through making it progressively more specific; on the other hand, the end *qua* generality is made "concrete" or fully determinate through the intentional movements of the agent (see footnote 12).

The attraction of this proposal, its simplicity aside, is that it is difficult to see where else to locate standards of success for the realization of ends. As we noted, the question of what would count as realizing one's end is not decided by any kind of theoretical investigation into one's end—i.e., an inquiry into a self-standing object whose properties await discovery. The only other alternative, it can then seem, is that the question is answered in terms of the general concepts—expressive of different types of action—through which the content of that end is articulated. However, although there is more than a grain of truth to the claim that the kind of action one is realizing has a role to play in determining the standards of success for its realization, we shall see it is seriously mistaken to think that mere concepts of act-types through which agents specify their ends are an adequate measure of what will count as means to those ends.

Consider two ends, both of which can be said to fall under the same general act-type. In the first, I am going to France in order to enjoy a pleasant weekend away from the stresses of work. In the second, I am also going to France, but now in order to reach the deathbed of a revered philosopher. In the latter case, waiting for the next available train will take too long—but I can hop on a nearby plane that is about to leave. In the former case, taking the Eurostar would be perfect: I am in no rush whatsoever and moreover—given that I hate plane journeys—doing that would make a poor start to a relaxing weekend. Consider, however, that if my understanding of what it is to "go to France" were, in each case, confined to the general act-type in question—an act-type that, *ex hypothesi*, determines the standards of success for its realization—I would consequently be blind, within my instrumental reasoning, to the fact that what constitutes a correct means of going to France cannot be the same in each case.

The natural response to this line of thought is that I have simply failed to properly specify the ends using the relevant act-types. I should have specified the two ends as: "going to France for a pleasant weekend" and "going to France to reach the esteemed philosopher's deathbed." The need for differing means in each case would then be obvious and the claim that the act-types themselves cannot settle the issue would be entirely undermined.

This response is fine as far as it goes, but it covers up a deeper problem with the account in question. To see why, it will be necessary to examine more closely the behavior of action concepts in instrumental reasoning.

The variation in what constituted correct means to the two ends in our example is best explained by the fact that, in each case, the further end to which "going to France" is itself a means is different. This is an utterly pervasive feature of instrumental reasoning. Action concepts that are used to specify means are instrumentally "malleable" or "plastic": which actions (or types of action) count as falling under those concepts, as deployed on given occasions, is liable to shift radically according to which further ends they themselves are specified as being a means to. These shifts are explained by the fact that what counts as a correct realization of an end is largely determined *by* the further end to which it is a means. That is why what counts as "going to France"—and thus what actions will count as a correct *means* of going to France—will differ radically depending on what end "going to France" is specified as a means to: whether for example it is to spend a pleasant weekend or to reach a philosopher's deathbed. Consequently, the very same action concepts can be used, within different pieces of instrumental reasoning, to specify ends that have *radically different* standards of success. This is what ultimately undermines the proposal that the standards of success governing the identification of means to ends are determined merely in terms of the action concepts used to identify them. The action concepts in question are not associated with any fixed standards of success which determine what it would be to correctly realize those ends on any given occasion.

In my initial example, I indeed failed to specify the two cases of "going to France" such that their differences were clearly revealed. But we have seen that the deeper explanation for these differences is that, in each case, "going to France" was specified as a means to a different end. We can indeed instead specify them as: "going to France for a pleasant weekend" and "travelling to France to reach the esteemed philosopher's deathbed." Thus specified, it is clearer that different means are appropriate. Nevertheless, what will constitute "spending a pleasant weekend" or "reaching the esteemed philosopher's deathbed" will differ radically depending on what further ends they *themselves* are a means to. So, the proposal is still undermined insofar as the action concepts deployed do not, just by themselves, set standards of success for the selection of means.

Now, since *final* ends are not beholden to any further end which determines which means correctly realize them, it is tempting to think that the proposal might at least capture the way in which their standards of success are determined. However, specifications involving final ends will still need to employ action concepts which are, in general, "instrumentally malleable"—and which, as such, can be used to specify many different kinds of action depending on the presence of further ends. They should not therefore be thought capable, just by themselves, of specifying a standard against which we can judge which actions will or will not realize the ends they describe, even when those ends are final.[15]

---

15 This claim will come under some scrutiny in §4.1, where we consider the proposal that despite their malleability, action concepts nevertheless come—or at least could come for a different kind of rational agent—with "core" or "default" standards of success.

Something more than a mere grasp of act-types is required in order to determine what will count as realizing one's ends on particular occasions—but what more? We have observed that what determines what will count as a means to any given end is in large part the further end or ends to which it itself is a means. The obvious explanation is that those further ends reveal what *the good* of, for example, going to France is. In virtue of knowing that the good of going to France is that it is a way of passing a pleasant weekend I am positioned to know what will or will not count as a means of getting there.

This explanation is, however, of limited usefulness. The good of every end cannot consist in its being useful with respect to some other end. Some ends are final; if we are to expand the insight so as to cover those ends, we must admit that in order to know what constitutes the means to my final ends—and of any action that promotes my final end—I require a conception of its intrinsic, or non-instrumental goodness. Ultimately, all of an agent's subsidiary ends will be oriented toward the intrinsic good of the final end they are pursuing, since their goodness, as means, is dependent on its non-instrumental goodness.[16] For example, my conception of the good of reaching the philosopher's deathbed (which might be hard for me to articulate but which I grasp in acting as I do) enables me to determine the correct means of doing do, as well the correct means of realizing the subsidiary ends undertaken in its pursuit. If, for example, the good of reaching the philosopher's deathbed is bound up with honoring them, that understanding of the action's intrinsic value will determine what will and will not count as the means to my getting there (as well as my conduct on arrival, etc.).

Absent any conception of the good of their ends, an agent is thus incapable of correctly finding means to those ends, for it is only when conceived as in some sense good that ends are capable of constituting standards of success in instrumental reasoning. I cannot attempt give a substantive account here of agents' conceptions of the good of their final ends—but I do claim that whatever account we should adopt will have to be consistent with the fact that an agent's conception of the good of their final ends enables those ends to form standards of success within instrumental reasoning. Many may find this conclusion surprisingly strong. This is no doubt due to the fact that we are accustomed to conceiving of the identification of means as a technical task—one that is accomplished, by and large, through the offices of theoretical reason—and that is thus bereft of any practically "normative" significance. The grip of this assumption should be eased, however,

---

16 A characterization of the good of a means action as consisting in its "usefulness" is always partial. The specific goodness attaching to a means action is always tied to the final end it promotes. If A is a means to B, then A can be thought good insofar as it promotes B—but only on the condition that B itself is thought good.

precisely by the considerations that have been brought to bear thus far. In practical reasoning, we aim to make actual, or realize, an inherently general end. The question as to what will realize an end is not decided by a theoretical inquiry into an extant object, even if answering it depends on the possession of much theoretical knowledge.[17] We have seen, moreover, that we cannot deduce the correct means to our ends simply in virtue of grasping those general action concepts we use to specify them. What goes missing in that case is precisely a conception of that in which the good of the ends that those action concepts describe consists.

The argument of this section has attempted to articulate, from one perspective, the connection between the *efficacy* or *productivity* of practical reason—its role in making actual, or realizing, what it represents—and goodness. Because practical reason does not, in the first place, aim to represent the world as it already is, but to change it, its standard of success is not *what is*, but that which *is to be done* (or what is the same: the good). Lacking such a standard—lacking any conception of goodness—the idea of productive or efficacious reason falls to the ground, for nothing—or so I claim—distinguishes success or failure within it.

3 A Preliminary Case Against Merely Instrumentally Rational Agency

We can now outline a preliminary case against the possibility of a merely instrumentally rational agent. A prerequisite for success in instrumental reasoning is knowledge of what constitutes a means to one's end. We have seen both that knowledge of one's end is knowledge of something inherently general and also that this knowledge cannot consist in knowledge of "bare" act-types, i.e., act-types understood in isolation from an agent's conception of the good of the end they serve to characterize. We established the latter point through the observation

---

17 I do not mean to deny the essential role theoretical knowledge plays in answering the agent's question as to whether one action will in fact serve as a means to another. All I wish to claim is that such knowledge must be understood as bearing on this question only in the light of the agent's conception of the goodness of their end. Whether taking the Eurostar is a way of going to France depends, among other things, on whether the Eurostar drivers will be on strike in near future, on clement weather, and so on and so forth. Nevertheless, the *relevance* of such things—which indeed affect the truth of the agent's instrumental thought that taking the Eurostar is a way of going to France—depends on its being the case that taking the Eurostar would be a correct means to my end even if the drivers were *not* on strike. As we have seen, *that* is not something determined merely by theoretical considerations—but instead by the character of my end of going to France, which character cannot be grasped in isolation from its purported goodness.

that action concepts deployed in instrumental reasoning are "instrumentally malleable": what they denote shifts from occasion to occasion, such that they do not, by themselves, determine what will count as the means to their realization on given occasions. What is required, in addition to knowledge of general kinds or types of action, is a conception of the point, or the good, of one's end. The good of one's end can be revealed by one's further end or ends, but only on the condition that the good of those further ends is itself grasped. An agent therefore needs, in addition, a conception of their final ends as intrinsically, i.e., non-instrumentally, good. Only against the backdrop of such knowledge does the very possibility of success and failure in instrumental reasoning arise. As a consequence, merely instrumentally rational agency is only apparently possible.

I shall consider challenges to different aspects of this preliminary argument that are implicitly raised by each of our three purported examples of merely instrumentally rational agency. Before doing so, however, it will be helpful to highlight four points on which the argument depends. First of all, I assume that something must determine whether a given means action does or does not constitute a realization of a given end. If nothing determines this or if it is utterly arbitrary, then there is no such thing as instrumental reasoning, for where there is reasoning there must be a possibility of success or failure. Second, the standards of success must themselves be grasped through reason, since nothing less than a rationally comprehended standard can play the role of a standard of success within what is, after all, reasoning.

Proponents of the possibility of merely instrumentally rational forms of agency should, in principle, be willing to accept both these points. They do not obviously introduce elements of practical rationality that go beyond what a merely instrumentally rational being would have to be understood as possessing. The same is not true for our third and fourth points. The third point is that the agent's grasp of standards of success in instrumental reasoning must be had, not just through reason, but through *practical* reason. We have seen that instrumental reasoning is the realization of something inherently general, and that what governs this realization is the agent's conception of the practical point, or good, of that generality, i.e., of their end. If that is so, then it should in principle be hopeless to seek a standard of success that is provided by theoretical reason. This is precisely because, as we have shown, ends are not in the first place the objects of theoretical reason.[18] (This leaves entirely open what account of practical reason—and its "formal object," the good—should ultimately undergird an agents' conception of their ends

---

[18] We shall nevertheless have cause to consider attempts to specify standards of success for an agent's end through the resources available in theoretical reason in §4.1 below.

as good.) The fourth point is that the standards of success presupposed by instrumental reasoning are not established *by* instrumental reasoning. We cannot arrive at a conception of the goodness of our final ends through the very rational activity in which we specify means, simply because the good of our final ends does not lie in their being useful (i.e., in their being means). To be sure, instrumental reason depends on—indeed, actively involves—a conception of the goodness of our final ends insofar as that conception is a prerequisite for having a stable standard of success against which the identification of means can proceed. But instrumental reasoning by itself does not *establish* that conception.

4 Three Attempts to Represent Merely Instrumentally Rational Agency

4.1 First Attempt: The Agents of "Naïve Action Theory"

The first and most rudimentary agent we shall consider is featured in Michael Thompson's "Naïve Action Theory." This agent can be justly characterized as "sub-Humean" insofar as its practical self-consciousness need not comprise desire or indeed any other conative attitude. What I shall call the "naïve agent" will thus serve as our thinnest possible conception of a merely instrumentally rational agent. As we shall we see, all the naïve agent grasps (or at least, needs to grasp) is the kind of action (or "event-form," to adopt Thompson's terminology) that it is in the process of realizing. In order to assess the prospects for this form of agency, we need to introduce some elements of Thompson's account.

According to Thompson, in the most fundamental form of action explanation what serves to "rationalize" intentional actions are simply other intentional actions. For example, if you want to know why I am *breaking eggs*—in Anscombe's special sense of the question "why?" that applies to intentional action—then it is *my making an omelet* that explains it. Action explanations of this form do not mask the true etiology of my action, where that would be better couched in terms of psychical attitudes, as when I say that "I'm breaking eggs because I desire an omelet." These latter explanations, which Thompson calls "sophisticated," are explanatorily posterior to the "naïve" forms of rationalization to which he draws our attention. Their relative posteriority is due to the fact that naïve forms of rationalization are transparent, as it were, to the form of intentional action itself:

The nature of intentional action, or of the kind of being-subject-of-an-event that characterizes a rational agent and a person, resides in the peculiar "synthesis" that unites the various parts and phases of something like house building, for example, mixing mortar, laying bricks, hammering nails etc. This synthesis is rendered explicit in naïve rationalizations, which brings them successively to the one formula "I'm building a house" (Thompson 2008, 91).

Action explanations always feature, in the position of the explanans, something *in progress*, and which is therefore the kind of thing that admits of the distinction between progressive and perfective aspect ("I am *A*-ing" vs. "I have *A*-ed"). In naïve action explanations, an action is explained in terms of its being the part or phase of *another* which is in progress. In this way, actions can be said to "rationalize" other actions without adverting to conative states—desires, appetites, and so forth—that lay behind those actions.

What is crucial for our purposes is that in the course of his argument Thompson articulates a conception of a merely instrumentally rational form of agency. Thompson's strategy for demonstrating that naïve rationalizations are prior to sophisticated rationalizations involves the claim that we can coherently conceive of a community of agents whose action explanations are entirely limited to the naïve kind—as well as showing how "sophisticated" rationalizations can be seen to develop out of these forms of explanation. Naïve agents, as I shall call them, only explicate their own and others' actions by citing further, unfolding ends that those actions are parts of. They lack the capacity to explain their own actions in terms of psychical states. They also lack any explanation of their actions (either their own or others') that appeal to or otherwise imply the presence on their part of a conception of the good of their final ends.[19] Naïve agency thus presents us with a very rudimentary form of practically rational agency—one that does not even require consciousness of a non-rational form of desire or appetite.[20]

---

19 In fact, Thompson officially brackets the "intellectual aspect" of his discussion—which includes "matters of belief, practical thought, practical calculation and so forth" (Thompson 2008, 93). He nevertheless admits that in order to properly isolate the species of object of explanation "through the imperfective" that he is interested in (i.e., intentional action as opposed to, for example, the movements of non-rational living substances) would necessarily involve making referring to the "intellectual aspect." I will be bracketing Thompson's bracketing of the "intellectual aspect" and will assume that the structure of naïve agents' actions is due to this means-end calculation that Thompson ignores for his purposes.

20 It might be that in order to conceive of a naïve agent coherently, we must posit something like animal appetite so that we can explain *why* it has any ends in the first place. Nevertheless, even if that is so, it will have to be the case that this appetite plays no role whatsoever within the agent's instrumental reasoning since the self-consciousness characteristic of a naïve agent is limited to an understanding of action which precludes reference to such things as appetites, etc.

On what grounds do we contest the possibility of naïve agency? Consider a naïve agent doing *A* because it is doing *B*. What standard determines whether *A* is genuinely a realization of *B*, and thus whether the naïve agent is succeeding or failing? A central consequence of §§2–3 was that it is impossible to generate a standard of success for a naïve agent's instrumental reasoning simply by placing an action concept, say, that of "making an omelet," in the position of a final end. What it is to make an omelet—what will count as doing that correctly or incorrectly on a given occasion—needs to be determined. Absent some conception of the non-instrumental good, or point, of pursuing this end, nothing will determine what will count as making an omelet, and so nothing decides whether the naïve agent is in fact realizing their end through any given means. The possibility of naïve agency is, therefore, merely apparent.

This line of thought may meet with strong resistance simply because, in the attempt to consider any concrete example of naïve agency, we necessarily do so using action concepts drawn from our own conceptual repertoire; it is therefore all too easy to project standards of success from our own reasoning onto naïve agency. "Isn't it just *obvious*," we find ourselves thinking, "what does and does not count as making an omelet?" To us, it is pretty obvious, but unlike the agent under discussion, we have a conception of what the good of such an act might consist in, and thus of what would, in general, count or not count as making an omelet.[21] We cannot allow whatever knowledge we possess to contaminate our examination of the naïve agent's cognitive constitution.

However, there are two more principled sources of resistance to our conclusion regarding naïve agency that must be confronted. The first challenges the significance of instrumental "malleability" as described in §2; the second claims that we can supply standards of success for the naïve agents' instrumental reasoning through the aid of theoretical thought. I shall consider each objection in turn.

We observed in §2 that what counts as successfully performing ends specified through a given action concept changes, case by case, depending on the further

---

21 Of course, one might doubt that that *we* need a conception of omelet making as good, on a given occasion, in order to determine means to the end of making one. Once we know what an omelet is, can we not just set about making one regardless of whether, or why, it is a good thing to do? In reality, however, the very idea of an omelet is intimately bound up with various goods—mainly those associated with basic nutrition, convivial dining, cookery and so on and so forth. If we attempt to abstract the end of "making an omelet" from *all* such goods what will count as making an omelet is no longer clear. We cannot make up this deficit by reference to, for example, recipes and methods for making omelets, for what it is to follow or execute a recipe on a given occasion is itself undetermined absent a conception of the good of doing so. (The idea that we could, in doing this, utilize a merely theoretical standard of what an omelet is will be considered later in this section.)

ends to which they are in turn means. Precisely because such concepts are "malleable" in this regard, they are not by themselves capable of setting standards of success in instrumental reasoning. They only do so in conjunction with an agent's conception of what the point of pursuing their end is. We can conclude from this that in the *absence* of any further end which reveals the good of pursuing a given end—and ultimately, in the absence of some non-instrumental consideration which reveals the good of their final end—there is no fact of the matter as to what constitutes the end's realization.

Consider, however, an alternative attempt to respect the observation concerning instrumental malleability that stops short of drawing the same conclusion. General action concepts contain "default" standards of success. These standards are operative within instrumental reasoning in cases where the action in question is a means to a further end, as well cases in which the action concept is used to characterize an agent's final end. In order to accommodate "instrumental malleability," however, we allow that the default standards of success pertaining to a given action concept are open to modification; this explains why they are capable of being connected to different ends in different courses of instrumental reasoning. We need not conclude, therefore, that the general act-type, by itself, is entirely *incapable* of determining standards of success. If this way of accommodating instrumental malleability is viable, then naïve agents can select means to their ends in light of the default standards of success set by those action concepts, and through which they can then conceive their final ends.

The problem with this proposal is that we can always find examples of further ends which, for any proposed "core" standard of success associated with a given kind of action, reveal that standard of success to be inapplicable. That is simply an upshot of the indefinite range of ends to which actions may be framed as means. This raises the question as to why default standards of success are required in order to deploy the action concept in instrumental reasoning at all: if I can recognize that an action of such-and-such a type will realize my end without consideration of its purportedly "default" standards of success—indeed, if I can see that it will realize my end *despite* those standards—what compels us to propose such standards in the first place? They are a hindrance to instrumental reasoning if they cannot be revised or ignored—but if they *can* be revised, it would appear they are surplus to requirements.

We may, however, choose to attack the assumption that a naïve agent's action concepts are instrumentally malleable in the first place. What prevents us from stipulating that the standards of success governing *their* action concepts—or at least some of their action concepts—are fixed? After all, we must not project what is potentially a parochial feature of our instrumental reasoning onto that of the naïve agent—this would be another form of "contamination" I warned against above. It is not clear, at a first glance, why the naïve agent could not have ends characterized using action concepts that possess immutable standards of success. Perhaps this would limit the scope of its instrumental reasoning in some way, but the question is whether it is impossible, as opposed to merely not being true in our own case.

In responding to this objection, we need to recall something noted in §3, namely, that a rational standard must determine whether the movement from a general conception of an end to a given specification of it is correct or not. The current proposal of a fixed or immutable standard of success can be shown to fail to meet this requirement. To see why, a comparison with theoretical thought is instructive.

A thinker who judges that "this dog is healthy" should in principle be able to explain why the concept of health is correctly applied in this case. That may involve explaining, *inter alia*, that the dog displays the telltale signs of fitness and lacks the telltale signs of sickness that are characteristic of its breed. In giving and receiving this explanation, the thinker and their audience will require mastery of a host of other concepts. For example, the thinker's explanation of their judgment will presuppose a shared understanding of animals, *qua* living things, such that the concept of health is so much as applicable to a dog in the first place. Now compare a case in which a different concept, initially unknown to us, is asserted by someone to hold true of some object. In order to cotton on to the use of this novel concept, thereby acquiring it ourselves, we shall need to see on what basis it is and is not considered to be applicable to different objects. This will likely require seeing the concept used in a range of different cases, as well as being introduced to further concepts to which it is essentially related. If there is a relative gulf between us and the person using this concept—perhaps due to significant linguistic and/or cultural differences—this may take some time and effort on the part of both parties. If, however, it transpires that the person applying the concept simply cannot explicate their use of the concept, if no pattern or principle in their usage emerges over time—and if there is no other impediment which explains either their inability to explain or our inability to comprehend their explanations—we would be forced to conclude that the purported application of the "concept" is something else. Perhaps it is all a prank, or perhaps they are merely subject to the delusion that they are "applying" this "concept"—either way, we shall be justified in doubting that any genuine thoughts are expressed by the apparent use of the concept in question.

Now consider the relevant practical analogue. A naïve agent explaining what they are doing may indicate that one proposed action is a reliable means to their end, another action entirely useless, and so on and so forth. What would need to hold true for them to be explaining how to realize an end—that is to say, specifying means according to some actual standards of success—as opposed to stringing together action concepts arbitrarily? The agent shall have to explain why a given end,

A, is realized by a given action, *B*, but not some other action (*C or D*, etc.) by somehow explaining or gesturing at the alleged default standards of success associated with *B*. Otherwise, the naïve agent will be analogous to the person who, in the theoretical case, has nothing to say which can illuminate why a given object falls (or does not fall) under a concept they purportedly employ. The latter might persist in asserting that *this* or *that* object falls under the concept—just as our naïve agent might insist that *such and such* an action really is a realization of their end—but if nothing reveals *why* some of the actions are means to the end in question while others are not, there will be no grounds to consider what they are doing reasoning. The mere idea of "default" standards of success is, at best, a *placeholder* for an explanation as to how naïve agents are capable of identifying means to their ends. To fill the placeholder would require explicating how the posited standards actually function. In the absence of such an account, the appeal to such standards is empty.

This brings us to the second of the two objections I mentioned. It might be thought that we have overlooked the most obvious source from which standards of success for a naïve agents' ends can be derived: theoretical reason. We have no business limiting a naïve agents' capacities for *theoretical* thought. A naïve agent's knowledge of what constitutes a correct realization of their end will be provided, on this proposal, by their knowledge of what the action concepts they deploy in instrumental reasoning are used to describe in cases of ordinary theoretical thought. What will count as "*A*-ing" in instrumental reasoning is just anything that could correctly be described as such in a paradigmatic act of theoretical reason. There is thus no need to appeal to a "brute" standard of success—but also no need to appeal to anything like a conception of the goodness of their end.

In §2, we rejected the notion that the standards of success operative in practical reasoning were identical to those operative in theoretical reasoning. This followed from the fact that the central task of practical reasoning is not to accurately represent a state of affairs, but to realize an end. However, the proposal now under consideration is not that the naïve agent's end *is* the object of theoretical reason. That is to say, it is not committed to the claim that in practical reasoning the agent is merely attempting to accurately represent some state of affairs. The proposal is rather that in realizing their ends naïve agents can employ a conception of what counts as doing so that is—somehow or other—*derived* from theoretical reason. I shall consider two ways of fleshing out this proposal. The first utilizes theoretical thoughts concerning actions in order to derive standards of success in practical reasoning; the second depends on theoretical thoughts concerning states of affairs more generally.

The first attempt to flesh out the proposal starts with the following idea: An agent's capacity to identify, in paradigmatic acts of *theoretical* thought, what would count as *A*-ing, can also serve to furnish the standards of success, in *instru-*

mental reasoning, for what would count as realizing *A*. For example, a naïve agent's end of "crushing a tomato" will be realized by anything that could be truly described as "crushing a tomato" in some theoretical judgment. The standard of success for realizing the agent's end is defined in terms of the theoretical judgments in which those action concepts are deployed.

The proposal cannot be correct as stated, since much of what is describable as "crushing a tomato" does not even constitute intentional action—as when, for example, a boulder ploughs through my vegetable patch. We must stipulate, therefore, that the end of "crushing a tomato" can be realized by any *intentional action* truly describable as "crushing a tomato" in some theoretical judgment. This complicates matters. Consider an example of a theoretical judgment, the content of which includes an intentional action truly describable as "crushing a tomato": "Frank is crushing a tomato by hitting it with a mallet." Since this judgment concerns an intentional action, its truth requires that Frank is actually wielding the mallet in virtue of considering his so doing to be a means to his end of crushing a tomato. (If what Frank is doing is involuntary, it will not be a case of the requisite kind.) As such, the "merely" theoretical thought concerning Frank already presupposes that "crushing a tomato" is a means taken in view of some further end. In virtue of this, the judgment also presupposes there are some standards of success for Frank's action. The truth of the judgment "Frank is crushing a tomato by hitting it with a mallet" turns on whether Frank is actually managing to succeed (or at least making a decent attempt); this in turn will depend on what the standards of success for Frank's action are. Perhaps he is failing to crush the tomato enough; perhaps he has gone too far, perhaps he has liquified the thing! Either way, the notion of "crushing a tomato" we end up deriving from the theoretical judgment already presupposes standards of success that are operative in an agent's practical reasoning. What appeared, therefore, to be a way of specifying an agent's end in "merely" theoretical terms in fact masks a covert dependency on the practical perspective of an agent. Once we occupy that perspective, we are faced with the same question with which we started: what will count as "crushing a tomato?"—without having articulated a merely theoretical understanding of the end that answers that question.[22]

---

22 This line of thought reveals that many so-called "theoretical" judgments about another agent's intentional action are only theoretical in a limited sense. Although the judgment in our example aims to represent a state of affairs whose existence does not depend on that very judgment, it is nevertheless one whose content includes an agent who is engaged in practical reasoning; it thereby presupposes whatever notion of goodness is at play in that person's reasoning. We might express this by saying the judgment has a theoretical "form" but a practical "matter."

Perhaps it is mistaken, however, to think that the agent's theoretically derived conception of their end must be based in judgments that take intentional actions as their objects. We might do better if we think of theoretical reason as providing a conception of whatever *result* an agent is aiming at. This may be achieved through specifications of ends that employ propositions: "to make it the case that p"; "to see to it that p" or "to bring it about that p"—where "p" stands for some proposition the obtaining of which (according to the proposal) could be known merely through an agent's capacity for theoretical thought. If p is a proposition whose obtaining is discernible by any agent with the capacity for theoretical thought (and who possesses the relevant concepts, etc.), then it seems nothing prevents the naïve agent from possessing a standard for determining whether or not some means realize their end. Of course, whatever proposition p stands for will not fully specify the content of an end on this proposal. As we have seen from our example, it must be supplemented by an action concept—such as "making it the case that"—to which it is conjoined.[23] But perhaps what will count as "making p obtain" is just *any* intentional action that brings it about that p. If that is correct, then we can apparently specify a standard of success for the realization of an end through the combination of a proposition and the stipulation that the agent be the intentional cause of the proposition obtaining.

In its alleged practical use, a proposition functions not as a representation of what is the case but as a specification of what is to be brought about. If the agent's end is to make it the case that, for example, they have a glass of water, they must therefore know what would count as the proposition, "I have a glass of water" having obtained. Note, however, that the only constraint on the naïve agent's understanding of what it is for any given proposition to obtain—given the absence of any conception of the good of their end—is highly indeterminate; what counts as p obtaining is just any state of affairs that could, in some theoretical judgment, be correctly stated as "p." Yet indefinitely many different *kinds* of states of affair can be stated using a given proposition. The naïve agent is thus faced with the problem of knowing what exactly it is supposed to be realizing.

---

[23] Unless one thinks that the content of the agent's intention or end is exhaustively specified by a proposition, such that an agent can simply "intend p." This is, in fact, a popular way to conceive of the contents of intentions in the literature—though one that rarely receives much defense despite various difficulties facing it (though see Ferrero (2013) for a notable exception). See Thompson (2008) and Boyle and Lavin (2010) for an indication of the difficulties. See also Campbell (2020), who argues more generally that the propositionalist view should not be considered the default position. The essential point made here—that the content of an agent's end cannot be articulated in terms of a merely theoretical content—can also be made with respect to the propositionalist view, though doing so would involve a layer added complexity that space does not permit.

In fact, I think the problem is insurmountable. It is important to recognize first of all that the problem is not that of moving from a general end to a specification of that end (this is the anodyne form of "indeterminacy," pegged to an end's inherent generality, that we described in §2). Consider a case in which, for example, I intend "to spend a pleasant evening by myself." This end can be specified in indefinitely many ways, but whichever way it is specified, the deliberation will be guided throughout by what I take the good of spending a pleasant evening by myself to consist in. Armed with that conception, and cognizant of the practicalities of my situation, I can determine a suitable course of action. It is tempting at first to depict the naïve agent as being in a similar predicament. The problem, however, is that the naïve agent's end is not indeterminate in the anodyne sense that, being general, it simply requires further specification. The naïve agent's end is indeterminate because it lacks any unitary character, the possession of which is a prerequisite of further specification on the part of the agent. Consider that what it is for the agent to "have" a glass of water or what will even constitute "a glass"—or for that matter "water"—is subject to massive and indefinite variation depending on what theoretical thought one picks as one's guiding example. Which of indefinitely many states of affairs is to serve as a model for what the agent is aiming at in their selection of means? One in which the water is in the agent's hand, available for drinking now, or one in which it is in a safety deposit box under my name on the other side of the globe? One in which the water contains traces of lethal poison? In which the water has frozen or is scalding hot? These questions simply serve to bring out the myriad disparate ways in which it can be true that the agent has a glass of water. To respond to the question as to which of these are to be pursued by saying "any of them!" is to concede that, in fact, there is no determinate end in view.

On the other hand, it is unclear how to render the agent's conception of their end more determinate in a manner that is consistent with the proposal. We cannot simply appeal to further ends the agent may have (e.g., that they want the glass of water in order to drink it, or to water a plant, etc.) since these are, according to the letter of the proposal, to be specified in just the same way and so are equally problematic. We can, of course, add any further detail we like to the proposition that is used to specify the naïve agent's end. For example, the agent's end might be specified as bringing it about that: "I have a glass of water that is neither close to freezing, nor scalding hot." But what will constitute a realization the agent's end is still equally undetermined—for it is only restricted to the bringing about of a state of affairs which could, in *some* theoretical judgment, be characterized in those terms. As we have seen, it only takes a little imagination to see why a constraint of this kind fails to yield a determinate goal.

The initial plausibility of the proposal stems partly from the fact we can envisage an order being given: "Bring about a state of affairs that could be described in some theoretical judgment using the proposition 'the cat is on the mat!'" Although I could engage with this instruction—as strange as this scenario would be—my actual end in this case is *to comply with the instruction.* As such, my calculating how to bring about something describable as "the cat is on the mat" must be understood as having its standards of success determined by whatever I think the point of complying with the instruction is. Perhaps I am humoring a malicious prison guard who has read a bit of philosophy, or perhaps I am playing a game with friends where the point is to come up with a creative response. Either way, the sort of end specification that the proposal attributes to the naïve agent is clearly supplemented in a way that goes beyond the confines of the proposal. (The naïve agent by contrast is, as it were, acting on orders from an entirely unknown source.) As before, the danger thus remains of contaminating our conception of the naïve agent by projecting our own, more expansive practical self-understanding onto it. In reality we may well know what someone is aiming at if they say they want to make it the case that they have a glass of water (despite their somewhat stilted mode of expression). This is not due to a grasp of what might, in *any* possible theoretical judgment, be considered that proposition's obtaining. We understand their use of a proposition to specify an end against the backdrop of a supposed conception of what the point, or the good, of having a glass of water is. Yet precisely in grasping this, we exhibit capacities that outstrip those of a merely instrumentally rational being.

4.2 Second Attempt: The (Neo-)Humean Agent

A peculiar feature of naïve agents is that their capacity to realize ends does not depend on any awareness of a desire to realize those ends. All they need to be aware of in determining means to their ends are the relevant action concepts that specify the ends they are realizing. They need not be conscious of any further conative states when explaining their action. It might therefore be thought that what is needed in order to provide standards of success for an agent's ends is precisely an awareness of the desire (or other such "pro-attitudes") responsible for establishing those ends in the first place—an awareness that should therefore be understood as having a role to play in the activity of instrumental reasoning. If such desires need not be understood as constituting or otherwise presupposing a rational conception of the good of those ends, then this will in turn make plausible a form of merely instrumentally rational agency. With this proposed modification to the naïve agent, we thus "ascend" from a sub-Humean form of agency to Humean agency proper.

In a classic articulation of the contemporary Humean theory of motivation Michael Smith cites the example (originally Davidson's) of a man who has "a yen" to drink a can of paint. According to Smith:

> knowing that he has always had a yen to drink a can of paint does provide us, and him, with a partial justification of his action, albeit a justification that only justifies from the perspective of assigning value to the action of drinking a can of paint, a perspective that he himself may occupy *only to the extent* that he has a yen to drink a can of paint, a perspective that none of us may actually share (Smith 1987, 39; emphasis added).

A "partial justification" of action consists in thinking there is "something to be said" for the action from the agent's point of view, where what is to be said for the action is, for example, that an agent has a "yen" for it. This is superficially similar to Anscombe's claim that ends must be susceptible to a "desirability characterization"—and more generally to the much-discussed claim that agents necessarily think of what is desired under "the guise of the good." However, for Smith, all one needs be able to say "in favor of" one's action is *that* one desires to do it. No characterization of what makes the action desir*able* is necessary. As such the appearance of a similarity is misleading.

Smith's Neo-Humean agent is not only realizing a given end: they understand this end to be the object of a desire in the sense just described. Bracketing, once again, the question of whether we are such agents, we can ask: is such an agent so much as possible? The fact that an agent desires to do something, on this conception of desire, does not itself illuminate *what* it is they seek to do. Smith defines the desire to A as a "functional state" that is, or reduces to, a set of dispositions to A. But this functional characterization *presupposes* that an agent has a determinate conception of what A-ing consists in—it does nothing (and is not supposed to do anything) to secure or determine the content of that conception. If an agent does not already know what will constitute A-ing, then being informed that it is anyway something they are disposed to do will not help. Yet if this form of agency is to fare better than naïve agency did, what is required is precisely an account of how desire can provide standards of success for realizing an end.

The prospects for this form of agency are not improved by the introduction of further properties of desire that contemporary proponents of Neo-Humean accounts of motivation sometimes ascribe to it. [24] The fact that desires tend to direct one's attention to opportunities for acting; that they tend to increase in motivation-

---

24 See, for example, Sinhababu (2009) and Schroeder (2008).

al power the more vividly one represents their object—these and similar such features do not serve to explicate the agent's knowledge of what would count as realizing their ends—they rather presuppose such knowledge.

One might attempt to find a more direct role for desire within instrumental reasoning. In particular, one could attempt to attribute to the agent's desire some kind of guiding role in the choice of means (this role could be connected to one of the "additional" features of desire just mentioned). Where the agent's initial specification of their end fails, desire steps in to pick up the slack—the prick of passion, or some other attention-guiding influence exerted by desire, "informs" the agent that *this* action is the true means to their end. (We could even imagine desire as thus helping the agent alight on what would constitute the correct kind of "obtaining of p" that caused so much trouble in the previous section—thus coming to the aid of mere theoretical reason in setting the agent's end). However, unless the agent's desire does this by introducing an intelligible standard of success— something the agent could appeal to in explicating *why* one action is a realization of another—the proposal undermines the agent's claim to actually be engaged in reasoning (recall the second of our four points listed in §3). For a form of instinct will have taken up the reigns in the agent's activity of specification in just the place a rational standard of success is required.

It is important to note that, in ruling out any such role for desire, we are not presupposing a contentiously "thick" notion of rationality. We only require that the identification of means to ends is principled in this sense: something explicates why some selections of means are correct while others are not. The proposal that a desire simply "guides" the agent to do one thing rather than another fails to meet this requirement for a standard of success, for it does nothing to explain why "A is a means to B" may be true while another thought, "A^* is not a means to B," is false.

4.3 Third Attempt: Engstrom's "Practical Thinker"

The final attempt to represent a merely instrumentally rational being that I shall consider appears in Stephen Engstrom's elaboration of Kant's account of practical knowledge. Engstrom's account of what he calls the capacity for "practical thought" constitutes an attempt to depict a form of thought that, being efficacious with respect to its objects, relates to them in a distinctively practical manner, but that nevertheless stops short of thinking them good. Engstrom's discussion is instructive insofar as it constitutes an attempt to think through the relation between sensible (i.e., non-rational) desire and practical thought within such an agent.

For Engstrom, the term "thought" in "practical thought" is to be contrasted with "knowledge" as it figures in a Kantian conception of "practical knowledge." An agent with practical knowledge is one in whom reason is, in the fullest Kantian sense, practical: a "practical knower" can set ends for herself through the spontaneous exercise of pure practical reason and without the need for any extraneous motivations; she can determine what she should do—and not merely how she should do it—through reason alone. A "practical thinker," on the other hand, lacks knowledge of the good, yet retains the capacity to form and execute intentions. We are not supposed to be practical thinkers on the Kantian account since we are capable of practical knowledge. Engstrom nevertheless defends the possibility of such a being as part of his elaboration of Kant's general account of practical knowledge.[25]

Engstrom gives the following description of mere practical thought:

> As spontaneously efficacious, practical thinking is a type of desiderative representation in which the self-consciousness distinctive of conceptual representation belongs to the representation's very efficacy, to the striving constituting it as desire. This amounts to saying that the efficacy of practical thinking is integral to the thinking itself, so that the self-consciousness essential to thinking in general also pertains, in the case of practical thinking, to that thinking's efficacy, its productive power, and hence that the efficacy depends on the consciousness of it. Thus, practical thinking *can* make its object actual through and only through its *consciousness* that it can do so (Engstrom 2009, 30).

Practical thought consists of representations that are inherently productive, or efficacious, of their object. This form of efficacy, which is distinctively rational, is characterized by the fact that it is dependent upon the agent's consciousness of that very efficacy. Crucially, however, this capacity—which Engstrom also glosses as the capacity to form "intentions"—does not explain, by itself, why the thinker forms and executes intentions in the first place. This is just the point that in a practical thinker, reason is not properly practical—it does not itself set ends.

In a being in whom reason alone cannot motivate the formation of an intention, something else is therefore required: sensible desire. Engstrom describes sensible desire as accompanied by a

> ...form of awareness [which] falls squarely under the heading of feeling—pleasure or displeasure—rather than thinking...What is distinctive of inclination, or sensible desire, then is that the efficacy by which it works to bring the object it represents into existence is one

---

25 This is only supposed to be a logical possibility, as opposed to a "real" possibility, according to that Kantian distinction. This logical possibility is apparently affirmed in Kant's *Religion*, where a "most rational being" is discussed that can find means to the realization of its own happiness but who is ignorant of the possibility that reason itself could be practical in the full sense.

the awareness of which lies in the feeling that accompanies it, salient modes of which are pleasure in the presence of the object (the enjoyment of an apple, for instance) and displeasure or pain where that object's realization is blocked or hindered (Engstrom 2009, 30).

Sensible desires are representations of objects that agents find pleasant—or better: they are pleasing representations of an object. Such representations tend to secure the continued existence of representations of that very form (indeed, this "reproductive" tendency is what defines them as pleasurable according to Engstrom). To use Engstrom's favorite example: The agreeable sensation experienced upon biting into an apple leads the agent form an intention to take the next bite, thereby reproducing the very same sensation.[26]

Engstrom's characterization of a practical thinker includes a capacity for productive thought that is separate from sensible desire, but which is nevertheless not a capacity to frame one's ends as being in any sense good. This is promising insofar as it appears to allow more to the agent's conception of their end than the mere consciousness of desire (thus avoiding the pitfalls encountered in §4.2) but still less than would take us past the confines of merely instrumental rationality.

Indeed, it is important that sensible desires are representations whose existence depends on their objects. They are, therefore, only *derivatively* practical in the sense that they cause agents to form properly practical representations which belong not to feeling, but to the capacity for practical thought. This raises a question as to how, precisely, we should understand the relation between sensible desire and practical thought. In fact, I think it is telling of the difficulties here that when it comes to this question, Engstrom apparently wavers between two different sorts of response.

When describing an agent capable of practical knowledge, Engstrom says, describing *its* capacity for practical thought, that

> the decision to pursue the object is a formation of intention, which, though its efficacy depends on the presence of sensible desire for the object, includes *a new ingredient not originally contained in that desire*, namely, a representation of the action (Engstrom 2007, 123; emphasis added).

Here we find the idea that the capacity to form an intention—the mark of practical *thought*—introduces a novel ingredient not contributed by sensible desire. Note that whatever this novel element is, it is responsible for the agent so much as conceiving of an action. It would appear, therefore, that practical thought is a capacity,

---

[26] More accurately: the sensation in question *is* the agent's consciousness of their faculty of desire having been determined in a particular way.

among other things, to generate specifications of intentions out of the consciousness of mere sensible desire. Nevertheless, as I noted, what Engstrom is describing in this passage is the capacity for practical thought as it exists in *us*—he is not describing a mere practical thinker here. This explains why this characterization contrasts with another, given elsewhere, of the practical thinker:

> In such a being, reason would have *only* the subalternate or derivative function of *further specifying given action specifications*, never that of supporting them through providing an original, or immediate, specification (Engstrom 2009, 92; emphasis added).

This, then, appears to be the official position: whereas agents capable of practical knowledge can frame ends that go beyond what sensible desire provides, the practical thinker apparently cannot; mere practical thought can only further specify an action on the condition that an "original" given specification has already been provided.

The official position concerning the practical thinker is problematic. Sensible desires, recall, are supposed to be only derivatively efficacious. Engstrom in fact appears to register this point even when discussing the practical thinker: "a representation of an object of sensible desire can be included in intention only insofar as the subject has, in deciding what to do, taken it up into its practical thought and hence into itself, thereby appropriating (or "incorporating") it" (Engstrom 2009, 33). Engstrom notes that talk of "appropriating" (or "incorporation") is imported into his treatment of the practical thinker from the wider account of practical *knowledge*—but he apparently holds that in the case of mere practical thought there must be an analogous phenomenon. Yet this point seems at best to be in deep tension with the official position, according to which sensible desire does have to offer an original, or basic, action specification. For if sensible desire provides an original action specification, it is unclear what need there is for such "incorporation." On the other hand, it is unclear that sensible desire has any business trucking in action specifications given its character.

Faced with this tension, we may decide the official position is inferior and disregard the suggestion that sensible desire provides an original act specification. However, this leads us to a different problem: how precisely is practical thought supposed to "incorporate" sensible desire? It is hard to see how it could construct from the bare theoretical content of sensible desire a genuinely *practical* representation. Practical *knowers* may decide it is good to realize what is represented in sensible desire and, on that basis, frame a conception of an end—that is, a conception of how to pursue the desire in question. What is a practical thinker to do?

Engstrom does not answer this question, but I think the most plausible interpretation is that what practical thought adds to the "matter" of sensible desire—

and what sensible desire cannot provide itself—is the formal idea of rational efficacy. It is in virtue of introducing this idea that practical thought should be understood as "incorporating" a sensible desire. In order to assess the prospects for the practical thinker, then, we need to return to the mode of rational efficacy that is associated with practical thought. This mode of efficacy should, in principle, be capable of yielding standards of success for the realization of the practical thinker's intentions when somehow it "incorporates" sensible desires.

As we have seen, Engstrom is clear that the efficacy that characterizes practical reason is self-conscious efficacy. That is to say, it is a form of efficacy that resides in its consciousness of itself *as* efficacious.[27] In the case of practical *knowledge*, this self-conscious efficacy resides in comprehension of the good. I identify means to my end and act on those means precisely in virtue of the fact that I recognize my end to be good (in Kant's paradigmatic case, I recognize it is my duty). However, practical *thought*...

> ...just as such is not any type of cognition or judgment about anything. Being merely the efficacious specification of what one means to do, it can be arbitrary in a way that judgment and cognition never are. It includes, however, a certain self-understanding that serves as a principle for it and relates it to principles of cognition, enabling it to be regarded as a rational activity (and even to count as knowledge of a sort—"knowledge of what one is doing"—in a subject possessing the requisite know-how or skill). Since practical thought distinguishes itself from other types of thought—*principally from theoretical thought*—through being efficacious, or productive of what it thinks, this principle is at bottom just practical thought's own understanding of itself as efficacious thought (Engstrom 2009, 35; emphasis added).

Practical thought is conscious of itself as efficacious, but this consciousness is not grounded in practical judgment or cognition. At the same time, being efficacious, it is not *merely* theoretical, although it draws on theoretical knowledge in its calculation of means.

Ultimately, the attribution of a distinctive form of self-conscious efficacy to the practical thinker is problematic for two associated reasons. First, because the practical thinker *lacks* any conception of the good there is no rational principle—in the sense of a properly justificatory principle—the agent's understanding of which can be understood to constitute the productivity of its thought. Second, there is the *presence* in the practical thinker of an alternative form of efficacy that directly competes with it as an explanation for the determination of the agent's will: sensible desire. To rebut the suspicion that no form of efficacy is associated with prac-

---

27 Similar conceptions of practical reason—often taking their leave from Anscombe's account of practical reasoning in *Intention*—have been propounded by others. See Rödl (2008) and Marcus (2012) in particular.

tical thought we would need to isolate its distinctive contribution to making actual what it represents. Practical thought is supposed to be distinguished both from the sensible desires it realizes and from the theoretical knowledge it relies on *in* realizing sensible desires. We can therefore pose the challenge thus: what does practical thought introduce which is additional to the combined contributions of sensible desire and the agent's theoretical knowledge?

In fact, this question is equivalent to asking what there is, in the practical thinker, that is additional to what is found in the case of a Humean agent as it has been traditionally conceived—an agent, that is, who acts simply on the basis of a desire and an associated means-end belief. The difference is supposed to be this: while a Humean agent has a desire to A, a belief that B-ing is a way of A-ing, and in virtue of these does A, the practical thinker is supposed to comprehend the relation between these different elements and, moreover, *in* comprehending their relation, thereby make their end actual. As such—and in alleged contrast to the Humean agent—in the practical thinker these different elements are not merely causally related to the agent's action, their causal relation to the agent's action is comprehended by the agent and moreover constituted *by* the agent's comprehension of them.

The question, however, is whether we can coherently envisage a rational activity of this form using only the materials available in the capacity for practical thought. Engstrom ascribes to the practical thinker a form of self-conscious efficacy that is not associated with practical knowledge, but is nevertheless grounded in a distinctive mode of "self-understanding"—but what understanding is that? Answering this question is essential insofar as practical thought's efficacy is precisely supposed to consist in its distinctive self-understanding. While the practical thinker has a sensible desire and grasps, theoretically, that doing such-and-such will realize that desire, it cannot answer the question—indeed, cannot even pose the question—why that something *should* be pursued. If the practical thinker were to attempt to articulate its self-understanding, posing itself the question "Why am I pursuing this end?" the only answer it can give, it seems, is that a particular sensible desire has gone to work on its faculty of desire. This answer (and hence the question) is of a theoretical character. To the extent, therefore, that the practical thinker comprehends the "unity" of its desires and means-end beliefs this comprehension must be, contrary to Engstrom's characterization, theoretical. It is the observation that sensible desire and theoretical knowledge are working in tandem to produce an action. In order to attain genuine efficacy, practical thought would have to find a way, as it were, to insert itself between its sensible desires and its theoretical thoughts about means and ends; but it is granted no rational principle of its own through which to do that. Both the "why?" and the "how?" of acting have already been decided without its contribution. Absent some further conception of its ends as good, it lacks a practical grasp of its ends to which we can appeal in grounding its allegedly practical "self-understanding."[28]

I deferred the question as to whether the capacity for practical thought would allow an agent to conceive of its ends in such a way as to provide standards of success for their realization in order to clarify the form of efficacy that is peculiar to it. I did so precisely because it is in terms of its "self-understanding" as an efficacious form of thinking that practical thought is supposed to frame its ends. That self-understanding was, after all, supposed to provide the "form" in relation to the "matter" offered up by sensible desire is incorporated. It transpires, however, that there is no intelligible form of rational efficacy distinctive of a practical thinker. As such, there is no possibility that the practical thinker provides a way of thinking about its sensible desires that supplies it with standards of success for their realization.

If, like Engstrom, we are attracted to the idea that practical reason is a self-consciously efficacious capacity—that is, a capacity the efficacy of which is constituted by its own self-understanding—we must make peace with the idea that this efficacy *necessarily* depends on a conception of one's ends as good. In an agent who is capable of forming a conception of the good of their ends we (and they) can understand their actions—but also their instrumental reasoning—as occurring because of the goodness they take their ends to possess. The efficacy of their reasoning can thus be understood to derive, in general, from their conceptions of the good. In an agent with no such conception, however, the source of the reasoning's efficacy is absent and must ultimately be attributed to a non-rational source. Yet in "outsourcing" the efficacy of practical thought to sensible desire, we lose any grip on the idea of its being an *efficacious*, that is to say, practical form of thinking in the first place.

5 Conclusion

Our preliminary case against the possibility of a merely instrumentally rational agent turned on the claim that such agents, lacking a conception of the good of their ends, are not able to identify means to them. Our consideration of different

---

28 In my presentation of Engstrom's practical thinker, I have ignored the fact that Engstrom also envisages what we might call an "expanded" version of the practical thinker I have described, one which is able to think in terms of its own "happiness," where this is the idea of the realization of the totality of its desires. This expansion is ultimately irrelevant for our purposes since the idea of a "totality" of sensible desires still provides no alternative principle of rational efficacy that could oppose that of sensible desire.

attempts to envisage merely instrumentally rational agency will hopefully have now served to defuse some possible skepticism regarding this claim. By way of conclusion, I shall try to bring out the importance of ruling the possibility of merely instrumentally rational agency out of hand, as opposed to adopting agnosticism.

In §1, I described Lavin's proposed dialectical strategy with regard to the Humean (or "anti-Kantian") which consisted in granting the possibility of a merely instrumentally rational form of agency but of denying its applicability to our case. The danger of this strategy is not merely that it admits of a possibility that it should not, but that in so doing it threatens to distort our understanding of the actuality of our own practical reason. The danger specifically consists in conceiving of merely instrumentally rational agency as existing as a component in our own, more expansive, form of practical rationality.

To see the danger in question in action, we can refer to an example with which we are now familiar: Engstrom's sympathetic reconstruction of Kant. For Engstrom, although the mere capacity for practical thought characterizes an agent who lacks knowledge of the good, this very capacity nevertheless can be understood to exist in us.[29] This implies, in turn, that within the task of identifying means to our ends, we can be wholly successful even while, strictly speaking, we remain blind or simply ignore the good we otherwise take our ends to possess. This is possible insofar as the capacity that engages in the specification of means is capable of operating independently of full-blown practical knowledge. That renders the specification of means to ends akin to a merely "technical" activity: an activity whose success in no way depends on our conceptions of the good of our ends. The same point can be made with respect to Thompson's framework. Although we are not naïve agents, it is consistent with Thompson's account, as it stands, that *their* form of agency constitutes, as it were, the basic kernel of practical rationality within within our own more sophisticated form of agency. Although we may have a conception of our ends that reveals them to be the sort of thing that we should be engaged in—and not merely that we are engaged in—our capacity to realize those ends may simply be the same capacity found in the naïve agents.[30]

One may, of course, attempt to block this consequence while affirming the possibility of merely instrumentally rational agency. One strategy would involve claim-

---

[29] Engstrom cites Kant's notion of *Willkür* or the power of choice as the textual source for his reconstruction of the capacity for practical thought (Engstrom 2009, 28). This power purportedly exists both in beings with practical knowledge or a will as well as in the "practical thinker."
[30] It is worth noting that this is so despite the fact that, within Thompson's general methodological framework, "the difference between *such* an agent [i.e., an agent who grasps their ends as in some sense non-instrumentally good] and a merely Humean agent is on the present account akin to the difference between a rock and a number" (Thompson 2008, 4).

ing that the more basic form of practical rationality is somehow "transformed" when it exists alongside a capacity to conceive of one's ends as good. This response treats the two forms of rationality analogously to the way in which Aristotle has been interpreted as treating the animality in human beings as "transformed" by their rationality.[31] The analogous claim must be rejected insofar as the purportedly "basic" forms of rationality in question do not survive scrutiny. Indeed, the figure of the merely instrumentally rational agency is well-depicted as a botched insertion on the *scala naturae*. Lacking, on the one hand, knowledge of the good that their higher neighbors possess, while at the same time lacking the mere animal instincts of their lower neighbors, such agents are condemned to use reason in specifying means to ends that that same reason cannot comprehend.

Assuming such strategies are doomed to failure, the conception we arrive at is of instrumental reasoning as an activity which, even in our own case, can be engaged in entirely successfully even while we disregard any conception we may have of the value of our ends. The spirit of instrumentalism thus survives the rejection of its letter. Alternative conceptions are possible. One resource might be Aristotle. In the *Nicomachean Ethics*, Aristotle cites the capacity to "deliberate well" as the distinctive mark of practical wisdom. This implies a decidedly non-technical picture of practical reasoning—one according to which the successful identification of means involves drawing upon and preserving an understanding of the goodness of our ends. It will be noted, however, that Aristotle in fact distinguishes good deliberation from "cleverness" (*deinotes*), a capacity that is "such as to be able to do the things that tend toward the mark we have set ourselves, and to hit it" (*NE* 1144a25–27)—regardless, that is, of whether the end is good or not. As such, the danger I have been describing is capable of rearing its head once more, this time in the form of a temptation to conceive of "cleverness" as a normatively "blind" capacity to calculate means that forms a component within the practically wise person's cognitive makeup. On this conception, good deliberation ultimately results from the conjunction of two capacities, on the one hand "cleverness," and on the other hand an ability to correctly grasp which ends are actually good. This raises the question, however, of why "good deliberation" is cited by Aristotle the mark of practical wisdom at all—surely a correct grasp of the good of our ends should be considered the mark of practical wisdom, and "good deliberation" should be thought the mark of "cleverness" (or at least of cleverness and practical wisdom combined). We need instead to recover in Aristotle's conception of the practically wise agent, not merely the capacity to grasp the worth

---

31 See Boyle (2012 and 2016) for a contemporary articulation and defense of this Aristotelian view (though not as applied to this issue).

of one's ends in combination with a separate ability to calculate means to those ends, but rather a grasp of the worth of one's ends which *enables* one to identify the means to them—where this latter is more than mere "cleverness" and is missing in an agent lacking practical wisdom.[32]

The task of developing a proper understanding of the ethical character of instrumental reasoning is a considerable one. It would have to involve exploring the way in which agents conceive their ends to be good—something we have had to defer. It would also have to involve broaching another difficult question—one that tends to be obscured while the specter of merely instrumentally rational agency lingers: to what extent does success in identifying means depend on the agent's end actually being good, as opposed to merely appearing to be so? This question cannot be avoided, I think, once agents' conceptions of their ends as good are understood to enable the very of identification of means.

Abbreviations

I follow standard conventions for referring to the works of Aristotle and Kant, using the following abbreviations:
NE   Aristotle. *Nicomachean Ethics.* Translated by W.D. Ross.
B   Kant, Immanuel. *The Critique of Pure Reason*, B-edition.
KpV Kant, Immanuel. *The Critique of Practical Reason.*

Translations come from *The Cambridge Edition of the Works of Immanuel Kant*, edited by Paul Guyer and Allen Wood (Cambridge: Cambridge University Press, 1992–), and *The Nicomachean Ethics*, translated by David Ross and Lesley Brown (Oxford: Oxford University Press, 2009), respectively.

---

[32] There are a wealth of exegetical concerns that may be raised regarding such an interpretation, but I nevertheless I think we should be encouraged in our attempt to read Aristotle along these lines by the fact that he considers the relation of cleverness to practical wisdom to be analogous to that which holds between natural virtue and virtue proper. In the latter case, natural virtue is not a *component capacity* within virtue proper but is instead something that is ultimately superseded by the latter.

References

Anscombe, Gertrude Elizabeth Margaret (1963): *Intention*. Cambridge: Harvard University Press.
Boyle, Matthew (2016): "Additive Theories of Rationality: A Critique." In: *European Journal of Philosophy* 24. No. 3, 527–555.
Campbell, Lucy (2019): "Propositionalism about Intention: Shifting the Burden of Proof." In: *Canadian Journal of Philosophy* 49. No. 2, 230–252.
Dreier, James (1997): "Humean Doubts About the Practical Justification of Morality." In: Cullity, Garrett and Gaut, Berys (Eds.): *Ethics and Practical Reason*. Oxford: Oxford University Press, 81–100.
Engstrom, Stephen (2007): "Kant on the Agreeable and the Good." In: Tenenbaum, Sergio (Ed.): *Moral Psychology*. Leiden: Brill, 111–160.
Engstrom, Stephen (2009): *The Form of Practical Knowledge*. Cambridge: Harvard University Press.
Fernandez, Patricio A. (2017): "Practical Reasoning: Where the Action Is." In: *Ethics* 126. No. 4, 869–900.
Ferrero (2013) "Can I Only Intend My Own Actions?" In: *Oxford Studies in Action and Responsibility*. Oxford: Oxford University Press, 70–94
Ford, Anton (2016): "On What is in Front of One's Nose." In: *Philosophical Topics* 44. No. 1 (Spring), 141–161.
Korsgaard, Christine (1996): *Creating the Kingdom of Ends*. Cambridge: Cambridge University Press.
Korsgaard, Christine (1997): "The Normativity of Instrumental Reason." In: Cullity, Garrett and Gaut, Berys (Eds.): *Ethics and Practical Reason*. Oxford: Oxford University Press, 215–254.
Lavin, Douglas (2004): "Practical Reason and the Possibility of Error." In: *Ethics* 114. No. 3, 424–457.
Lavin, Douglas (2017): "Forms of Rational Agency." In: *Royal Institute of Philosophy Supplement* 80, 171–190.
Marcus, Eric (2012): *Rational Causation*. Cambridge: Harvard University Press.
Mueller, Anselm (1967): "How Theoretical is Practical Reasoning?" In: Diamond, Cora and Teichman, Jenny (Eds.): *Intention and Intentionality: Essays in Honour of G. E. M. Anscombe*. Ithaca: Cornell University Press, 91–108.
Rödl, Sebastian (2007): *Self-Consciousness*. Cambridge: Harvard University Press.
Schroeder, Mark (2008): *The Slaves of the Passions*. Oxford: Oxford University Press.
Sinhababu, Neil (2007): "The Humean Theory of Motivation Reformulated and Defended." In: *Philosophical Review* 115. No 4, 465–500.
Smith, Michael (1987): "The Humean Theory of Motivation." In: *Mind* 96. No. 381, 36–61.
Smith, Michael (2015): "The Magic of Constitutivism." In: *American Philosophical Quarterly* 52. No. 2, 187–200.
Street, Sharon (2010): "What is Constructivism in Ethics and Meta-Ethics?" In: *Philosophy Compass* 5. No. 5, 363–384.
Tenenbaum, Sergio (2021): *Rational Powers in Action: Instrumental Rationality and Extended Agency*. Oxford: Oxford University Press
Thompson, Michael (2008): *Life and Action*. Cambridge: Harvard University Press.
Thompson, Michael (2013): "Forms of nature." In: Hindrichs, Gunnar and Honneth, Axel (Eds.): *Freiheit: Stuttgarter Hegel-Kongress*. Frankfurt am Main: Vittorio Klostermann: 701–735.
Velleman, David (2009): *How We Get Along*. Cambridge: Cambridge University Press.
Vogler, Candace (2001): *Reasonably Vicious*. Cambridge: Harvard University Press.

Douglas Lavin
Rousseau's Conscience in Modern Moral Philosophy

Abstract: This paper argues that Rousseau's theory of conscience provides a strong alternative, not a weak precursor, to Kant's grounding of moral requirement in the nature of a free and self-determining agent. Both philosophers reject the accounts of practical reason offered by empirical naturalism and by rational intuitionism. Empirical naturalism cannot account for the universality of moral requirement. Rational intuitionism saves this universality through a dubious metaphysics, and risks severing moral knowledge from motivation. Like Kant, Rousseau avoids both positions by arguing that morally motivated actions are expressions of our practical reason. Unlike Kant, Rousseau analyzes neither the laws governing nor those given by conscience. This silence has often been seen as a philosophical failure; I argue instead that it is motivated by Rousseau's view of philosophy as rooted in practical aims that would be ill served by such an analysis.

1 Introduction

1.1

While Rousseau's influence on modern moral philosophy has been widely acknowledged by recent commentators, that influence is often portrayed as indirect, through the role of the concept of autonomy in his political philosophy, or as merely inspirational, through his championing the moral self-sufficiency of the common man. For instance, John Rawls accords Rousseau a prominent role in shaping the tradition of political philosophy that locates the legitimate source of political authority in the individual's capacity to govern herself.[1] However, when Rawls' thought turns to foundational problems in moral philosophy Rousseau's identification of self-determination and morality does not seem to resonate.[2] Or consider

---
1 See Rawls (1971, 264).
2 See Rawls (1971, 264). Here, in a footnote, Rawls says that Kant gives a deeper reading of Rousseau's famous remark: "to be governed by appetite alone is slavery, while obedience to a law one prescribes to oneself is freedom." Rawls does not simply say that Kant develops the idea contained in this remark. See also Rawls' treatment of Kant as the origin of the "idea that reason, both theoretical and practical, is self-originating and self-authenticating" (Rawls 1993, 100).

Charles Taylor's and Jerome Schneewind's respective accounts of the development of modern moral philosophy, each of which restricts Rousseau's influence to the import of his thought that moral sensitivity does not derive from esoteric sources, whether they be religious or scientific, but rather is naturally available to the common man.[3] According to these histories, it is Kant who reworks the naïve idea that morality is somehow contained in our nature into a wholly original understanding of the foundation of moral requirement. To both critics and enthusiasts, Kant is taken to be the originator of the idea that we understand how there might be actions that absolutely must or must not be done by grasping the idea of a free and self-determining agent. The present essay aims to correct a pervasive neglect of Rousseau's real innovation in modern moral theory: Rousseau had already, even before Kant, made the crucial "Kantian" move: he took conscience to be not merely a source of sympathetic motivation or a mere moral sensitivity but rather the fundamental principle of the free human will.[4] Appreciating the fundamental status of conscience for Rousseau will further enable us to see the availability of a meta-ethical viewpoint that may seem foreclosed to us, just as it seemed to some of Rousseau's most illustrious contemporaries: a viewpoint according to which motivated action is an expression of our rational nature, where that nature is characterized not by its mysterious access to an equally mysterious realm of normative fact, but rather by its social constitution and autonomous operation.

1.2

We can introduce the problem of moral requirement by setting up a dilemma. It takes as its starting point Hume's thought that "the first virtuous motive, which bestows a merit on any action, can never be a regard to the virtue of the action" (T 478) and leaves one either with the metaphysical and epistemological excesses of rationalism or with an empirical naturalism that cannot account for the necessity of the moral "must." This, of course, needs some explanation.[5] Moved in part by a distaste for appeals upward and outward to a supernatural order to understand morality, the empirical naturalist instead turns his attention forward and inward towards human beings—to what they do and why they do it, to what they approve

---
[3] Schneewind (1998, 487–492) and Taylor (1989, 355–363); Allen Wood suggests something similar in his introduction to *Immanuel Kant: Practical Philosophy* (Wood 1996, xvii).
[4] This essay contributes to Ernst Cassirer's understanding of Rousseau's place in the history of moral philosophy: See Cassirer (1945, 1951, and 1989).
[5] See Korsgaard (1989) for such an account. My sense of how to frame the concerns driving modern moral philosophy has been influenced by this essay.

of and why they approve of it. It does seem to be a necessary condition of a "non-spooky" moral theory that it proceeds in something like this manner; that is, from an understanding of what goes on in human beings, to an understanding of right and wrong. But we should note a potential equivocation in this expression "what goes on in human beings," what might be called the two senses of *action's ground*. On the first, when we ask about "what goes on in human beings" we are asking about something like the *structure* of human motivation; we are asking with Plato about the parts of the soul, or with Kant about the determining grounds of the faculty of desire, or again, and in a more contemporary spirit, about kinds of explanatory reason. In contrast, on the second interpretation, when we ask about "what goes on in human beings" we are asking about the *contents* of the various kinds of motivation. To see what I mean, suppose that we are all ultimately moved by sense appetite; it is still an open question which appetites we have. Or suppose that it is settled with Hume that all rational motivation is ultimately based on passion; it is still an open question what passions move us. Are they all self-regarding? Is there a passion for cruelty? An inquiry into what goes on in human beings that aims at an understanding of morality must consider both and must not confuse them.

It is a starting point of Hume's "that all virtuous actions derive their merit only from virtuous motives, and are consider'd merely as signs of those motives" (T 478). His thought here is not only that if a particular action is praiseworthy, then it is done from a praiseworthy motive. It is also that motives are the primary object of moral evaluation; it is in terms of these that we are to understand which actions are morally correct. That is, Hume accepts a motivational analysis of morally correct action; such an analysis proceeds by asking which motives have moral worth and then asking which actions are to be done from such motives. The morality of motive and action are linked by definition: action *A* is morally correct if and only if *A* would be done from ideal moral motives. We have independent access only to the right side of the definition. The problem, then, is to determine what the ideal motives are.

Hume's famous argument that the "first virtuous motive, which bestows a merit on any action, can never be a regard to the virtue of the action" (T 478) can be read as ruling out the possibility of a particular motivational analysis—namely, one that takes the motive of duty (or again, the motive to do what is right, good, or virtuous) as the way in. What Hume argues is that any such account will be viciously circular:

> To suppose, that the mere regard to the virtue of the action, may be the first motive, which produc'd the action, and render'd it virtuous, is to reason in a circle. Before we can have such a regard, the action must be really virtuous; and this virtue must be deriv'd from some vir-

tuous motive: And consequently the virtuous motive must be different from the regard to the virtue of the action. A virtuous motive is requisite to render an action virtuous. An action must be virtuous before we can have a regard to its virtue. Some virtuous motive, therefore, must be antecedent to that regard (Hume, T 478).

The idea is that there is nothing for the motive of duty to latch onto, if duties are fixed by motives, or again that the principle "Do what is right because it is right" is, by itself, empty. It leaves one in the dark about which actions are right and so by itself cannot direct one to perform an action or explain why one performed an action. The sort of doubt raised here is, I think, an instance of what Christine Korsgaard has called content skepticism—skepticism about the bearing of rational considerations on deliberation and action.[6] In this case, it concerns the emptiness of the principle of duty or, as we might say in a more Rousseauian spirit, the apparent emptiness of conscience.

If "the ultimate object of our praise and approbation is the motive" (Hume, T 477) and the first moral motive cannot be a regard for the morality of the action, then, as Hume sees, "no action can be virtuous, or morally good, unless there be in human nature some motive to produce it, distinct from the motive of duty" (T 479). This sets the problem for the empirical naturalist: to determine what the distinct motives are. As I understand him, the empirical naturalist appeals to thoroughly independent motives here: most commonly self-love (modified by external constraint), or *sui generis* other-regarding psychological forces. The independence of such motives has two aspects: (i) the specification of their content does not employ any fundamental moral concepts, e.g., virtuous, right, or good; (ii), there is no need to look to a wider context than an individual bearer of the motive to understand its presence in her.

In §2, I lay out Rousseau's objections to empirical naturalism, focusing on this dual independence of its candidate motives. For now, however, I simply want to mention that the rationalist response to empirical naturalism was to say that it fails to account for the universality and necessity of moral requirement. According to the rationalist, this is because on such a view there is only a contingent relation between the candidate motives and what is intuitively regarded as right action, and also because there is no obligation to have the relevant motives and so no obligation to perform the relevant action.

In accord with the constraint of Hume's "first virtuous motive" argument, the rationalist intuitionist (I will take Richard Price as a model) abandons the analysis of rightness of action in terms of motives: indeed, abandons trying to understand right and wrong by understanding what goes on in human beings. With Price,

---

6 Christine Korsgaard, "Skepticism about Practical Reason" (Korsgaard 1996, 311).

rightness becomes an intrinsic quality of actions that we have the power to perceive. To account for our intuition that moral judgment and motivation are intimately connected, Price simply asserts that awareness of the rightness of action is sufficient to motivate of duty; the first is stipulated, and when rightness is an intrinsic property of actions it is possible simply to act because of it. But all this comes at a familiar cost. Price abandons an understanding of morality as an expression of our nature—the thought behind the Humean motivational analysis—and, I think, is at great risk of severing any plausible or intelligible connection between motivation and moral judgment. At the very least, the gulf that opens between judgment and action on such a view presents an obstacle to establishing their necessary connection. And where it is only an accident that the creatures that can intuit moral qualities are equipped to be moved in accord with that recognition it will be impossible to give a satisfying answer to the question "Why be moral?" There are also familiar worries about the metaphysical credentials of moral qualities understood as primary qualities.

In short, either (a) we understand the morality of actions in terms of independently specified motives, or (b) we maintain that the first moral motive can be a regard for the morality of the action. If (a), then the motives in terms of which we account for the morality of actions must be other than a regard for the morality of the action, and then we come upon empirical naturalism and its problems. If (b), then we must abandon the thesis that the morality of actions is to be understood in terms of motives, and so come upon rational intuitionism and its problems.

1.3

I set up the question of the nature of moral requirement in this way because I take Rousseau and Kant to reject the empirical naturalist (§2) and rational intuitionist (§3) responses to the dilemma for similar reasons. Taking the first horn, the empirical naturalist cannot properly make sense of a moral requirement as applying universally and categorically—he cannot make sense of it as an object of knowledge. Taking the second horn, the rational intuitionist is committed to an unacceptable metaphysics and leaves the epistemological and motivational features of moral thought utterly mysterious—he cannot make sense of its efficacy. In rejecting both approaches, we can see Rousseau and Kant acknowledging that any adequate account of moral requirement will treat the motive of duty or conscience as that in terms of which we understand right action—the measure of acting well is internal to the will itself.

In other words, each refuses to buy into Hume's dilemma. But by what right? What grounds do Rousseau and Kant have for maintaining that we are to find our way into morality through an understanding of the motive of duty? To answer this is to look at the different ways in which Rousseau and Kant take themselves to be under a philosophical obligation to address the question of the apparent emptiness of the principle of duty (Kant) or conscience (Rousseau). Their approaches are markedly distinct. On the one hand, Kant rejects Hume's claim that the principle of duty is empty; he claims to be able to derive the supreme moral principle from common moral cognition and then show how it is that content, i.e., substantive duties, is contained in that principle by reflecting on the universalization procedure. Rousseau, on the other hand, seems not to reject but to ignore Hume's challenge. In the absence of such a response to Hume's challenge one might reasonably suggest either that Rousseau's account is a failure or take that failure to be a demand for a different interpretation of his moral theory. But I will argue (§§5–6) that the absence should not tell against an interpretation of Rousseau's moral theory according to which conscience is the fundamental principle of the free human will. Instead, his silence on this count is driven by moral considerations: he does not attempt an analysis of conscience because conscience forbids it. This point reflects a deep feature of Rousseau's philosophizing that puts him somewhat at odds with much contemporary practice: the conviction that philosophy at its heart is as much an ethical as an epistemic enterprise, and perhaps an ethically dubious one at that.

2 Against Empirical Naturalism: "Flee Those Who Sow Dispiriting Doctrines in Men's Hearts Under the Pretext of Explaining Nature" (E 312)

2.1

Rousseau's objections to empirical naturalism take a variety of forms, some commonplaces of his period and others more distinctive and innovative. I begin by considering what might be regarded as a moral objection to the sentimentalist construal of acting from duty. Then I turn to the problems that stem from what I called above the thorough independence of empirical naturalism's candidate motives. Rousseau holds that these empirically given motives—motives other than duty, conscience, etc.—bear only a contingent relation to right action. As I will characterize this familiar objection, it is directed towards the *content* of the favorite motives of the empirical naturalist. Bearing in mind our two senses of *action's ground*, I then develop a different and perhaps less appreciated line of Rousseau's thought. Here, the empirical naturalist is charged with being unable to explain the essentially relational character of morality—or at least that part of morality which has to do with what Kant calls the "practical relation of one person to another, insofar as their actions, as deeds, can have (direct or indirect) influence on each other" (MM 230)[7], i.e., private right. The basis for this charge, in my reading, is already contained in Rousseau's well-known criticism of Hobbes in the *Discourse on Inequality*. As I will characterize it, this more metaphysical objection is directed towards the empirical naturalist's understanding of the *form* of moral motivation.

2.2

A familiar objection to any attempt to understand morality in terms of motives other than the motive of duty argues that there is only an accidental connection between the candidate motive and what common moral cognition takes to be right action. And Rousseau avails himself of this point. I will consider the two broad classes of motive available to the empirical naturalist: self-love or *sui generis* other regarding sorts, in turn.

Against the theory that self-love is the ultimate ground of moral motivation and evaluation, Rousseau advances some standard sentimentalist arguments. According to Rousseau, the self-love theory cannot explain why moral approval or disapproval attaches to actions or characters that have no relation to the appraiser's private interest: "it is surely of very little importance to us that a man was wicked or just two thousand years ago; nevertheless, we take an interest in ancient history just as if it all had taken place in our day" (E 288). Even more problematic, the *experimentum cruces* as Hume calls it in his discussion of the same problem (ECPM 42), is whether the self-love theory can plausibly explain how one might be motivated to do what could not possibly be seen to be in one's interest. Rousseau asks with Hume, "What is going to one's death for one's interest?" (E 287). The self-love theory, Rousseau decides, is "too abominable a philosophy—one which is embarrassed by virtuous actions, which could get around the difficulty only by fabricating base intentions and motives without virtue" (E 289).

The empirical naturalist regards the problem of the origin and foundation of morality as primarily a psychological problem. So, not surprisingly, the sentimen-

---

7 Translations of Kant's *Metaphysics of Morals* and *Groundwork for the Metaphysics of Morals* are Mary Gregor's, while page numbers refer to Vol. VI of the *Akademie-Ausgabe*.

talist response to the explanatory deficiencies of the self-love theory itself travels at the level of empirical psychology. It recommends an alteration in our understanding of the original materials of human concern and motivation. Usually this involves adding a sympathetic disposition—a "fellow-feeling or humanity," as Hume calls it, which is in all and directed towards all—as well as other more specific items, e.g., a parent's natural affection for their child (T 478). It seems likely that such a maneuver is sufficient for accommodating the above cases in which evaluation or action is seemingly distanced from a subject's own well-being. Indeed, Rousseau is friendly to the idea that man has an innate repugnance to see his kind suffer (DI 160)—going so far as to claim that "men would never have been anything but monsters if Nature had not given them pity in support of reason" (DI 161). He nevertheless does not regard the sentimentalist response as adequate. For Rousseau, sympathy—conceived as a basic and natural ability to feel and respond to the suffering of others on the basis of sense perception (DI 162) —is not a moral capacity and certainly not the central moral capacity. But why?

One reason for rejecting a morality of sympathy is that sympathy, like self-love, is only accidentally hooked up with right action. As Kant would later argue in the Preface to the *Groundwork*:

> in the case of what is morally good it is not enough that it conform with the moral law but it must also be done for the sake of the law; without this, that conformity is only very contingent and precarious, since a ground that is not moral will indeed now and then produce actions in conformity with the law, but it will also often produce actions contrary to the law (Kant, G 390).

Rousseau invokes this very contingency in opposition to the self-love theory when he tells us:

> he who keeps his promise only for profit is hardly more bound than if he had promised nothing, or, at most, he is in the position to violate it like the tennis players who put off using a bisque only in order to wait for the moment to use it most advantageously (Rousseau, E 101).

It is only an accident if a promiser who is guided by self-love has sufficient reason to do what he promised to do. And clearly there is a similar problem for a merely sympathetic agent since there are cases in which sympathy would have one break a promise when common moral cognition would have one keep it, or worse cases in which sympathy would have one kill one to save five.

To be sure, the ethical naturalist may be cognizant of the fact that action from self-love or, say, sympathy can be contrary to what we pre-theoretically regard as right. Such theorists have very often appealed to a convention or a practice to effect the appropriate, strict and general kind of connection between their favorite motive and right action. Pursuing the dialectic at this level, though, misses the deeper critique that Rousseau is aiming for. Appeal to a convention will not account for what is a plain fact for Rousseau—namely, that we have natural duties and rights—duties and rights the having of which does not depend on being hooked up to other agents through any particular convention or practice. For Rousseau, moral relations enter into all human relations; they do not presuppose that the agents enter into any particular conventional relations. To have knowledge of morality is "to have a sense of the true relations of man, with respect to the species" (Rousseau, E 219); it is to conceive of oneself as "an integral part of [one's] species" (Rousseau, E 220). The attempt to shore up a particular independent motive through an appeal to convention thereby demonstrates, in Rousseau's eyes, a fatal commitment to independence in our second sense, a failure to grasp the foundational place of relationality in our ethical life.

2.3

According to Rousseau, "No good action is morally good except when it is done because it is good" (E 104), and the empirical naturalist, as I have construed him, must disagree with this. It is a familiar objection to the self-love theory that it provides a morally repugnant account of moral motivation. We can see a further elaboration of Rousseau's attack on the independence of motives in his objection to the Humean account of the motive of duty.

Although Rousseau does not direct his substantive critique of modern moral life and society at sentimentalism, it is implicated in that critique just where it treats the motive of duty as secondary. In the hands of the sentimentalist, acting on the motive of duty is best understood as acting from the desire for approval from oneself or others. If it is thought that actions derive their moral status from our approval or disapproval of them, it seems that our motivation to act for the sake of that status would also be derived from a desire for approval. Consider Hume's view of the matter:

> But may not the sense of morality or duty produce an action, without any other motive? I answer, It may: But this is no objection to the present doctrine. When any virtuous motive or principle is common in human nature, a person, who feels his heart devoid of that principle, may hate himself upon that account, and may perform the action without the motive, from a certain sense of duty, in order to acquire by practice, that virtuous principle, or at least, to disguise to himself, as much as possible, his want of it (Hume, T 479).

For Rousseau, this account of doing something because it is right is no mere philosophical confusion—no innocent conception of moral motivation. Rather, it inextricably binds our moral lives to duplicity. At the beginning of the *Discourse on Arts and Sciences*, he writes,

> Today, when subtler inquiries and a more refined taste have reduced the Art of pleasing to principles, a vile and deceiving uniformity reigns in our morals, and all minds seem to have been cast in the same mold: constantly politeness demands, propriety commands; constantly one follows custom, never one's own genius. One no longer dares to appear what one is; and under this personal constraint, the men who make up the herd that is called society will, when placed in similar circumstances, all act in similar ways unless more powerful motives incline them differently (Rousseau, DAS 6).

The requirement that duty can only be a secondary motive entails a fundamental duplicity: so much the worse for our moral self-regard, a tough-minded thinker might respond. But Rousseau's criticism need not end here; without another way of understanding acting from a sense of duty, it will be impossible to treat morality and freedom as compatible. After all, the desire for mere approval is the source of our duplicity and is also, according to Rousseau, the source of slavish dependence,

> For one's own advantage one had to seem other than one in fact was. To be and to appear became two entirely different things, and from this distinction arose ostentatious display, deceitful cunning, and all the vices that follow in their train. Looked at in another way, man, who had previously been free and independent, is now so to speak subjugated by a multitude of new needs to the whole of Nature, and especially to those of his kind, whose slave he in a sense becomes even by becoming their master (Rousseau, DI 180)

But without being able to treat morality and freedom as compatible, Rousseau could argue that Hume also cannot treat morality and happiness as compatible —the aim of §9, Part II of his *Enquiry*.[8]

---

[8] What are Rousseau's grounds for dismissing the moral motive as a motive for self-approval? There is no problem with *self*-approval as such. After all, Rousseau understands the rewards and punishments of the afterlife in terms of "the pure delight born of satisfaction with oneself and the bitter regret at having debased oneself" (E 284). However, in Hume's case, the relevant self-approval requires self-deception; the agent acts from the motive of duty "at least, to disguise to himself, as much as possible, his want of it [the natural motive]" (T 479). Moreover, the motive which is thought to be lacking is thought to be so merely against the background of its presence in the motivational set had in common by most others.

2.4

For Rousseau, then, attempting to understand the motive of duty as derivative of the independent motive of other-approval leads Hume theoretically astray. But the situation turns out to be even worse for the empirical naturalist. The thoroughgoing insistence on independence turns out to leave him without a grasp on the conditions under which someone might be moved by such a passion in the first place.

This objection is developed via Rousseau's well-known criticism of Hobbes. But this criticism can prove significantly more slippery than many commentators appreciate. What exactly exercises Rousseau about the Hobbesian state of nature? Charity alone requires that we not regard Rousseau as merely complaining that Hobbes has given us an unacceptably nasty and brutish picture of man—such moralizing would be too obviously point-missing. We must also not accept a frequent classroom depiction of Rousseau's charge, according to which Hobbes mischaracterizes the state of nature so that "man is naturally intrepid and seeks only to attack and to fight" (Rousseau, DI 143), thereby permitting a construction of the state of nature as a state of war, and thereby setting the stage for a political philosophy which sees the individual's subjection to another as a necessary condition of her felicity. Putting the dispute in terms of the correct depiction of the state of nature prevents us from getting to the heart of the matter because "state of nature," rather than enjoying an independent existence that either theorist might succeed or fail in depicting correctly, functions as a technical term in their respective systems. For Hobbes, it picks out a condition in which "men live without a common power to keep them all in awe" (L, I. 13.8). It is life without the state. The sense that Rousseau attaches to the term is considerably more elusive; roughly, the state of nature is the condition in which none of man's developed capacities are traceable to "the faculty of perfecting oneself; a faculty which, with the aid of circumstances, successively develops all the others" (DI 149).

Rousseau's explicit complaint is that Hobbes "spoke of Savage man and depicted Civil man" (DI 139) when "he improperly included in Savage man's care for his preservation the need to satisfy a multitude of passions that are the product of Society" (DI 160). Famously, Rousseau's preoccupation is with glory. But why is it so clear that glory is a social motive? How are we to distinguish savage from social motives in the first place? And what prevents Hobbes from accommodating Rousseau's point without significant alteration to the rest of his theory? After all, are not competition and diffidence, in the absence of glory, sufficient to make the state of nature a state of war? If so, why accord Rousseau's charge the real significance he seems to think it deserves?

2.5

In "The Natural Goodness of Humanity," Joshua Cohen suggests that we see Rousseau concluding that the relevant Hobbesian motives are social on the basis of the following three claims: (i) "cognitively complex passions require 'enlightenment,'" (ii) "enlightenment is a result of social interdependence," and (iii) "the motivations relevant to Hobbes' account of human conflict are *cognitively complex*" (1997, 115). According to Cohen, Rousseau makes a distinction between natural motives and concept-dependent motives:

> By contrast with hunger or primitive sexual appetites or the desire for sleep, all other desires are concept- and belief-dependent. They depend in particular on opinions and judgments, and require that the subject be able to represent the particular object of desire as an individual with certain general properties (Cohen 1997, 113).

So, the appetites, more or less, are the natural motives; the naturalness of these consists in the fact that it is not a necessary condition of being moved by or having such a motive that an agent be able to employ concepts in the service of action. A creature might be moved by hunger even when it cannot, say, represent its hunger as "a reason for acting." As these motives frequently find expression in us—for example, in response to the question "Why are you A-ing?" one might say "because I'm hungry" or "because I like to A"—they are evolved from forms of expression where we have instead to do with something on the order of groans and moans. Concept-dependent motives, on the other hand, are those for which the ability so to employ concepts is a necessary condition. Here, the primary form of expression is linguistic—for example, in response to the question "Why are you A-ing?" one might say "in order to B." In order to explain oneself in this way and in order to have the concept-dependent motive of doing B, one must have the concept of B-ing, or grasp in thought what it is to do B—obviously, I cannot intentionally do B or intend to do B if I do not know what it is to do B.

Cohen's argument is that the conceptual capacities presupposed in motivation by a concept-dependent motive are essentially tied to facility with a language, and the existence of and facility with a language depends on the fact of coordinated interaction with others, i.e., social interdependence. If this is correct, reasons Cohen, then all concept-dependent motivation is "social."

There is undoubtedly an interesting and important distinction between natural and concept-dependent motivation. But if Cohen's reading of Rousseau's distinction between savage and social motives were the right one, Hobbes would have no problem accommodating the objection. Although not restricted by positive laws in their interactions with others, inhabitants of Hobbes' state of nature, whose practical rationality is perhaps captured by contemporary game theory, can nevertheless interact. But what could restrict Hobbes from holding that they can interact sufficiently often and with sufficient purpose so that various forms of coordinated behavior develop, e.g., linguistic practices? It does not follow from the fact that Hobbesian beings are such as to find themselves in prisoner's dilemmas in the state of nature that they cannot also find themselves in non-competitive game theoretic situations. Indeed, Hobbes seems to suggest that there are such when he considers the place of confederacies (L I. 13.1 and 3). Insofar as it is not unreasonable to understand a language as a practice whose origins can be modeled as a coordination problem, it is not unreasonable to hold that Hobbesian beings can be language users. Furthermore, I see no reason for thinking that Rousseau rejects the possibility of Hobbesian language users, and I even see some evidence that he already accepts it (DI, 172–173). So, Hobbes could claim that while inhabitants of the state of nature do not, for example, naturally have a concept-dependent motive to eat apples because they do not naturally or innately have, the concept "apple," they can develop this motive even while remaining guided by self-love and outside the structure of civil society. If so, agents in Hobbes' state of nature might be moved by social motives as these are understood by Cohen. This seems reason enough to seek a different account of Rousseau's distinction.

Granting inhabitants of Hobbes' state of nature a language and concept-dependent motives does not commit Rousseau to, as it were, granting unlimited scope to that language and those motives. For example, he need not admit that it has room for the concept of glory or that the speakers of it be capable of being moved in any way that *we* ought to describe as expressive of glory seeking. Consider the following cases of apple-involving action:

1. Young Kaspar Hauser is eating what is in fact an apple because he is hungry.
2. Helen is eating an apple in order to gain three pounds.
3. Helen is grabbing the apple because, as she says, she herself is "the fairest of them all."

Now, since Cohen identifies the set of savage motives with the set of natural (or concept-*in*dependent) motives, he would have us treat 1 as the only case of savage motivation and would have us treat both 2 and 3 as cases of social motivation. But this is too coarse. The distinction important to Rousseau is not that between 1 and (2 and 3)—a distinction between motives which do not have living *among others* in their causal past and those that do—but that between (1 and 2) and 3—a distinction between motives which do not have living *with each other* in their nature and those that do (E 235, n.).

Why does Cohen take the set of social motives to be as wide as the set of concept-dependent motives? One assumption that may lead him to lump cases 2 and 3 together is the thought that, if one has the capacity to be moved by some concept-dependent motive, then one has the capacity to be moved by any concept-dependent motive. Were this true, then we could infer that some creature has the capacity to be moved by considerations of glory and justice on the basis of its being moved by an intention to eat an apple. It is just a question of adding a few more concepts. What might lead someone to accept this thought? Let me venture a further hypothesis: if one sees every concept-dependent motive as completely described by a suitable substitution for φ in "I want to φ" (or p in "I want that p") then one will think that if one can have some substitution instance as a motive then one can have any substitution instance. All that is needed to meet the cognitive complexity requirement for having a motive is acquaintance with the relevant specification of φ. This, it seems, might be done in the most ordinary of ways. According to this view, we fully understand a motive when we understand what an agent aims at who has it at all; all differences between concept-dependent motives are differences in content or matter.

Such a view may seem simply to encapsulate common sense about concept attainment. But let us look more carefully at the case of glory. If having the motive of glory is nothing but a matter of grasping a particular content, what might that content be? Here is a plausible candidate: to have the glory motive is to want to bring it about that another grant that one is better in comparison. But if wanting this is what it is to have the glory motive, how are we to distinguish case 3 above from the following:

> 3a Private Haroldson races past his platoon in order to take out the well-fortified bunker in order to make the other privates think comparatively little of themselves so that they will collectively give him the only weekend pass.

That is, how do we distinguish someone who *really* acts from the motive of glory and someone who only aims at bringing about the relevant state of affairs as a means to some further end? After a few iterations of such maneuvers, one will probably be driven to say that glory is wanting that another think little of himself in comparison *in the right way*. But this is just a concession that there is no noncircular specification of the glory motive in terms of its content. As a result, there can be no guarantee that one, simply by virtue of general conceptual competence, enjoys the capacity for being moved by or attributing the motive. It may well be that only those embedded in a way of life within which the concept makes sense are susceptible to the glory motive.

Someone might object that a suitable specification can evade examples such as that of Private Haroldson: glory is wanting that another think comparatively little of himself as a final end or last end. But consider a parallel attempt to reduce a natural motive like hunger to wanting to eat as a final end. On this suggestion we are to distinguish being moved by hunger and being moved by an instrumental desire to eat (say to avoid being hungry later) according to whether the motive is final. However, someone might want to eat for no further reason, and if so then wanting to eat is last in a series—it explains why I intentionally extend my arm and lift the cashew off the counter—without being the same as hunger. So, we come upon the problem of distinguishing talk of "wanting to eat" when it expresses hunger and when it expresses something I want to do for no reason. Wanting to bring it about that another think little of himself in comparison when it is last or final need not be the glory motive: it might also be understood as *merely* wanting to do that, i.e., wanting to do it but for no reason.

On Cohen's view, the only interesting division among *forms* or *kinds* of motivation and agency is that between brutes and self-conscious concept exercising creatures like us. My suggestion is that just as Rousseau wants us to see a difference between the form or kind of willing, acting, and agency in play when Kaspar Hauser is eating because he is hungry and when Helen is eating in order to gain three pounds, so too does Rousseau want us to see a difference in the nature of the willing, acting, and agency in play when Helen is eating in order to gain three pounds and when she is grabbing for glory.

2.6

The way into the distinction between savage and social motives and the different forms of agency that underlie these is through Rousseau's distinction between *amour de soi* and *amour propre*. In Rousseau's system the power of desire or the generic capacity to act is oriented by either *amour de soi* or by *amour propre*; every motive, correspondingly, is grounded in either *amour de soi* or *amour propre*. Savage motives are based on *amour de soi:* "a natural sentiment which inclines every animal to attend to its self-preservation" (Rousseau, DI 226) and well-being, i.e., pleasure (Rousseau, DI 132). Social motives are based on *amour propre*, a sentiment that inclines every animal that has to rank itself in its own species (Rousseau, E 235, 278). The determinate expression of *amour de soi* will vary from species to species and also within some one species according to differences in surroundings and natural endowments (Rousseau, DI 171). What is less clear—or at least has been less clear to some interpreters of Rousseau—is that the expression of *amour propre* in human life can take a number of determinate shapes.

> The first glance he casts on his fellows leads him to compare himself with them. And the first sentiment aroused in him by this comparison is the desire to be in the first position. This is

the point where [*amour de soi*] turns into *amour propre* and where begin to arise all the passions which depend on this one. But to decide whether among these passions the dominant ones will be passions of beneficence and commiseration or of envy and covetousness, we must know what position he will feel he has among men, and what kinds of obstacles he may believe he has to overcome to reach the position he wants to occupy (Rousseau, E 235).

But what underlies these different shapes of *amour de soi* and *amour propre*? What are their common cores?

As they figure in developed humans, *amour de soi* and *amour propre* are kinds of rational self-concern. Rational self-concern is distinctive in that what one is concerned about is partly determined by one's conception of the kind of thing for which one has concern. So, by looking to Rousseau's characterization of the self-conceptions underlying *amour de soi* and *amour propre*, we are at the same time getting a glimpse of Rousseau's characterization of the different forms of agency, or orientations of will, involved in or underlying the savage and social motives. On the one hand, a human being guided by the absolute sentiment of *amour de soi* "views himself as the only Spectator to observe him, as the only being in the universe to take any interest in him, as the only judge of his own merit" (Rousseau, DI 226). On the other hand, a human being guided by the relative sentiment of *amour propre* views himself essentially in comparison with others; "as soon as *amour-propre* has developed, the relative I is constantly in play, and the young man never observes others without returning to himself and comparing himself with them" (Rousseau, E 243).

In denying that we can understand glory as merely a special content, of a sort that is in principle available to any being capable of concept use *überhaupt*, I am saying that Rousseau's idea is not simply that when *amour propre* comes on the scene the solitary-I of *amour de soi* comes to have an additional and strong interest, want preference, desire, or member of its subjective motivational set, in the way that it would were the solitary-I to develop a habitual longing for, say, sun bathing or eating gummy candy. Rousseau's idea is not that whereas the solitary-I does not care what others think about her, the relative-I does just happen to care about this. His idea is that with the development of *amour propre* agency itself takes on a radically different form. What was once a solitary-I is now a relative-I. A full account of the possibility and significance of this transformation lies beyond the scope of this paper. For our purposes, two lessons are paramount: first, the necessity for proposing such an alternate conception of agency, one according to which the availability of certain conceptual forms goes hand-in-hand with the possibility of certain forms of action and self-understanding, arises in part from the great difficulty of explaining action in pursuit of glory in terms of a possession of a desire with a certain special content; second, this unsatisfactory explanatory strategy is precisely what the empirical naturalist is committed to by virtue of his twin commitments to independence: the conceptual independence of motives according to which ethical motives must be replaceable by non-moral specifications, and the independence of subjects according to which the motivation of the moral subject must be in principle abstractable from larger contexts of sociality.

3 Resisting Rational Intuitionism: "The Entire Right of Nature Is Only a Chimera If It Is Not Founded on a Natural Need in the Human Heart" (E 235)

3.1

As I said above, the rational intuitionist gives up the motivational analysis of right action to protect the reality of obligations.[9] Laying out the threat of empirical naturalism, Price says,

> If no actions are, in themselves, either right or wrong, or any thing of a moral and obligatory nature, which can be an object to the understanding it follows, that, in themselves they are all indifferent ... But are we not conscious, that we perceive the contrary? (Price 1991, 147).

In order to accommodate our awareness that we give voice to necessary truths when we attribute rightness or wrongness to actions, Price asserts that right and wrong are "real *characters* of actions. They must immutably and necessarily belong to those actions of which they are *truly* affirmed" (1991, 148). Price then equips us with a rational "power *immediately* perceiving right and wrong" to explain how we know which actions are right and which wrong (1991, 142). Finally, to account for our intuition that judging right or wrong and being motivated are intimately connected, Price asserts that "when we are conscious that an action is *fit* to be done, or that it *ought* to be done, it is not conceivable that we can remain *uninfluenced*, or want a *motive* to action" (1991, 194). Price is thereby able to preserve both the reality of obligations and the purity of the motive of duty: the first is stipulated and when rightness is an intrinsic property of actions it is possible to act straightforwardly because of it.

---

[9] I will be taking Richard Price's *Review of the Principal Questions in Morals* as the model of such a view.

There are two pressures to interpret Rousseau as a kind of rational intuitionist. The first is philosophical and stems from recognition of his objectivism, while the second is textual, arising from a number of passages which appear to commit him to such a view. I will address the former in §3 and the latter in §4, and in each case, I will argue that we have not been given reason to accept such an interpretation.

3.2

Rousseau is perfectly clear about the absence of moral laws in the state of nature (DI 1313). His central complaint against those who include such laws stems from the thought that one ought not "to make a Philosopher of man before making a man of him" (Rousseau, DI 133 and E 290). What Hobbes saw when he "very clearly saw the defect of all modern definitions of Natural right" (Rousseau, DI 159) was that "the desires and other passions of man are in themselves no sin. No more are the actions that proceed from those passions, till they know a law that forbids them" (Hobbes, L I. 13.10). But if there is no law with moral content that can be grasped by savage man, then what he does is not a possible subject of moral evaluation. For a law "to be natural, it must speak immediately with the voice of Nature" (Rousseau, DI 132), but conscience, the moral voice, does not speak to savage man who is concerned only with his own well-being.[10] But this does not decisively refute the intuitionist reading of Rousseau: it might be that while Rousseau thinks that man is not obligated in the state of nature because "man can be punished only for the mistakes of his will, and…an invincible ignorance could not be imputed to crime" (E 258), he nevertheless thinks that moral laws are there, in some sense. Savage man would stand to those laws as, for example, my fish stand to the laws of the State of Massachusetts.

The intuitionist interpretation can seem attractive through attention to Rousseau's objectivism; the guiding thought would be that if the moral law is to be an objective measure of the operations of particular creatures, then its validity cannot depend on such creatures. It must stand over against them, and so Rousseau must

---

10 In my view, showing that moral laws are not part of Rousseau's state of nature is sufficient for demonstrating that Rousseau does not think that intuitionist "metaphysical principles" are *in* nature. But a full demonstration of this would require an appropriate account of why Rousseau uses a device such as the state of nature to consider the character of requirements on the will, moral or otherwise. I take the alternative tack through Rousseau's objectivism, in part because I believe it casts more light on both the attractiveness and the shortcomings of intuitionism, ultimately enabling a fuller appreciation of what makes Rousseau's notion of conscience distinctive.

locate the standards of action elsewhere, namely, in the nature of things. Now, it seems correct that the fundamental measure of right action does not depend on the existence and operations of any particular people; if tomorrow each of us— or if in 150 years each of them—signed on to the Calliclean program of how to live, it would still be true that an unjust man is a bad man, an act of injustice a bad act. But this thought of the independence of moral law from the particular creatures subject to it, or again from human *beings*, must be distinguished from the thought that the moral law is constitutively independent of human *being* simply, or again, what it is to be human. The one who assimilates Rousseau to Price simply on the basis of a commitment to the objectivity of moral requirement runs together these conceptions of the independence of moral standards and what it is a standard of, failing to see that the unproblematic independence of norm and individuals of a kind need not entail the far more fraught metaphysical independence of norm and the kind itself.

In order for Rousseau's objectivism to be sufficient for interpreting him as an intuitionist, it must be that there is no other way to account for this than by sticking moral requirements in nature. Now, Charles Taylor does think that there are other ways:

> It is quite possible to conceive that the best theory of the good, that which gives the best account of the worth of things and lives as they are open to us to discern, may be a thoroughly realist one—indeed, that is the view I want to defend, without wanting to make a claim about how things stand for the universe "in itself" or for a universe in which there were no human beings (Taylor 1989, 257).

But Taylor does not think Rousseau avails himself of such alternative possibilities. On Taylor's interpretation, Rousseau "ran his inner voice in tandem with the traditional way of understanding and recognizing universal good" (1989, 361). The Deist tradition to which Taylor refers locates the good within the order of nature as instituted by God: we know what is required by seeing which actions fit into the order as it is discerned by reason, and we want to do what is so recognized because of a natural love of what reason recognizes to be good, i.e., conscience. The picture is one in which the virtuous person has a faculty of desire that accords with knowledge of the universal good acquired through an entirely independent faculty.

Taylor contrasts Rousseau's position with what he takes to be its natural development in Kant : "the inner voice of my true sentiments *define* what is the good: since the élan of nature in me *is* the good, it is this which has to be consulted to discover it" (1989, 362). But this is precisely the position Rousseau occupies. It is one of his distinctive and fundamental ideas that morality is not to be understood by looking to nature *tout court*, but rather, to *our nature:*

> There is in the depths of souls…an innate principle of justice and virtue according to which, in spite of our own maxims, we judge our actions and those of others as good or bad. It is to this principle that I give the name conscience (Rousseau, E 289).

It is because he views moral requirements as rooted in our nature as expressed in conscience that Rousseau does not think that the fact that "the idea of right… and still more that of natural right, are manifestly ideas relative to the Nature of man" (DI 131) is a threat to the objectivity of moral requirement.

3.3

Perhaps we can explain Taylor's urge to treat Rousseau on the model of intuitionism by appeal to the fact that the intuitionist and Rousseau each endorse a picture of the moral agent as cognitively self-sufficient and naturally good. Like the intuitionist, Rousseau holds that we need not rely on another to apprehend moral truths, and that recognition of the rightness of an action can, in some sense, prompt performance. The first thought is exhibited in Rousseau's frequent charge that moral knowledge need not, indeed cannot, be esoteric: "We can be men without being scholars" (E 290); "Either he will learn these duties by himself, or he is excused from knowing them" (E 303). The second is implied by his claim treated above that "No good action is morally good except when it is done because it is good" (Rousseau, E 104).

But is this sort of independence and natural goodness sufficient to account for the connection Rousseau seems to draw between freedom and morality? Is this conception of moral self-sufficiency enough to explain Rousseau's thought that we most fully express our nature as "active and free" when acting from conscience (E 380–381) or that "the sentiment of my freedom is effaced in me only when I become depraved and finally prevent the voice of the soul from being raised against the law of the body" (E 380)? Taylor seems to think so. According to him, it is because conscience is within us and because it is sufficient to motivate that Rousseau identifies morality and freedom. He says, "The distinction of vice and virtue, of good and depraved will, has been aligned with the distinction between dependence on self and dependence on others. Goodness is identified with freedom, with finding the motives for one's actions within oneself" (Taylor 1989, 361). In order for the thought that one is free and virtuous in "finding the motives for one's actions within oneself," to be illuminating, we need to understand the significance of a motive's coming from *within* and of an *inner* source of motivation. When I want, for example, to coach the Boston Red Sox or to build a stadium for them, there is something "external to me determining me" (Rousseau, E 380). In order to have such ends I must have "acquired knowledge" of them (Rousseau, E 286) and done so through the senses, i.e., that which puts us in touch with the external world. It thus seems that being moved by such ends is quite different from being moved by that "faculty called instinct, which appears without any acquired knowledge to guide animals toward some end" (Rousseau, E 286). Of course, only animals, i.e., beings which sense, have instincts of this sort; nevertheless, these instincts are somehow already in them prior to the actual operation of the senses. Drawing on a traditional metaphor, Rousseau directs our attention to another sort of instinct, "divine instinct" or conscience, which he claims is "to the soul what [animal] instinct is to the body" (E 286). Rousseau seems to regard both natural needs, i.e., the appetites (DI 142), and conscience as inner sources of motivation. Yet, for Rousseau, it is not correct to say that one's freedom or true nature is expressed in the appetitive pursuit of food, water, sex or sleep, while it is correct to say this of someone who acts from one's conscience (E 380).

In other words, "coming from within" and "inner" cannot do the work Taylor wants them to do in characterizing Rousseau's views. What he needs to account for the connection between morality and freedom is a way of distinguishing natural needs from conscience as inner sources of motivation. Taylor might say that Rousseau identifies the real self with the soul, pointing to such passages as the following: "man lives only halfway during his life, and the life of the soul begins only with the death of the body" (Rousseau, E 283) and "I aspire to the moment when, after being delivered from the shackles of the body, I shall be me without contradiction or division" (Rousseau, E 293). And Taylor might then say that only motives that arise from the soul really originate within an agent and that conscience clearly is such a source; it is after all the voice of the soul. But in order to see whether Taylor is entitled to this move, we must consider what drives Rousseau to talk of a soul in this context. Only then will we be in a position to ask whether, why, and in what way Rousseau takes conscience to be a part of it.

3.4

In dividing body and soul, Rousseau is not expressing some primitive intuition that certain things are immaterial and others material. Rather, he is led to this divide in the first moments of the "Profession of Faith" with the question "Who am I?"[11] In

---

[11] Is it irresponsible to thus identify the Vicar's words with those of his author? In defense of doing so, note that Rousseau took the result of "the most ardent and sincere investigations ever conducted by any mortal" (R 54) to be "more or less what I have written down in my 'Profession

asking who he is, Rousseau does not aim at an account of his idiosyncrasies or a catalogue of the details of his life. Instead, this question initiates an inquiry into the nature of man, through a form of internal reflection; "I know will only by the sentiment of my own will, and understanding is no better known to me" (E 280). The will and conscience will concern us in §4; for the present purposes, the discussion of understanding is most salient.

Rousseau's inquiry into the understanding begins with reflection on its acts, on what it does, and not with something like an attempt to directly intuit its nature or to derive claims about that from metaphysical first principles. According to him, the primitive mental happening is sensing in which objects are presented "isolated, such as they are in nature." Rousseau then tells us that he compares the materials of sensation: "I superimpose them on one another in order to pronounce on their difference or their likeness and generally on all their relations" (Rousseau, E 270). Such comparing and pronouncing are really just judging (Rousseau, E 270). But judging and erring (which is simply the abuse of the capacity to judge) cannot according to Rousseau be accounted for by empiricist psychology as the effects of a "purely sensitive being":

> I seek in vain in the purely sensitive being for this intelligent force which superimposes and which then pronounces; I am not able to see it in its nature. This passive being will sense each object separately, or it will even sense the total object formed by the two; but, having not force to bend them back on one another, it will never compare them (Rousseau, E 270–271).

Not surprisingly, Rousseau goes on to claim that judging and misjudging are instead to be understood as the expression of an active force or power. The capacity to judge is "the distinctive faculty of the active or intelligent being," since to have the power of judgment "is to be able to give a sense to the word *is*" (Rousseau, E 270); it is to have the capacity to think about how things are. Rousseau then identifies himself or "the individual I" (Rousseau, E 279) with this capacity:

> Let this or that name be given to this force of my mind which brings together and compares my sensations; let it be called *attention, meditation, reflection*, or whatever one wishes. It is still true that it is in me and not in things, that it is I alone who produce it…I am not simply a sensitive and passive being but an active and intelligent being; and whatever philosophy may say about it, I shall dare pretend to the honor of thinking (Rousseau, E 271–272).

After asserting that he "need only know that matter is extended and divisible in order to be sure that it cannot think" (Rousseau, E 279), he claims that his active

---

of Faith of a Savoyard Priest'" (R 55), while making perfectly clear that he is the one who executed these "unparalleled" investigations.

and passive parts are immaterial and material respectively. Striking as that claim might be, the heavy metaphysical reading it invites obscures the real import of Rousseau's discussion. The important point is that in order for a certain kind of event to be an expression of an immaterial part, i.e., the soul, it must be *activity*, where this means an expression of "the power of comparing and judging" (Rousseau, E 280). Treating the soul as immaterial is simply a way of insisting on the primitiveness and irreducibility of the idea of activity and the active powers themselves; it is, I think, best not regarded as an insistence on substance dualism.

It is beyond doubt, Rousseau thinks, that empiricist psychology is unable to account for judgment and thought: whatever philosophy may say about these, it may *not* say that the purely sensitive being thinks.

> It seems to me that far from saying that rocks think, modern philosophy has discovered, on the contrary, that men do not think. It no longer recognizes anything but sensitive being in nature, and the whole difference it finds between a man and a stone is that man is a sensitive being with sensations while a stone is a sensitive being without them (Rousseau, E 279).

In so far as there is something left for philosophers to dispute, it is, perhaps, the claim that he thinks or that humans think. But if we grant Rousseau this starting point, he is confident that he has shown that we are active on the ground that such is a condition of the possibility of thought or judgment: "If I have just discovered successively these attributes of which I have no absolute idea, I have done so by compulsory inferences, by the good use of my reason" (E 286).

In the "Profession of Faith," then, Rousseau distinguishes between his soul and body, his active and passive parts, his interior and exterior, according to whether such exhibit or are responsible for thought and judgment. The basis for the distinction here is of the utmost importance. We do not make any progress towards understanding the soul by simple appeal to the concepts of activity, the inner, and immateriality. More generally, we do not make any progress towards understanding any of these by appeal to any of the others. All these notions and the distinctions associated with them—soul/body, activity/passivity, inner/outer, immateriality/materiality—are subtly interconnected; each is susceptible to deployment and specification in widely various ways, and the shading given to any one will systematically affect the understanding of the others. That these are concepts which admit of several determinations is not unrecognized by Rousseau. Indeed, one could argue that his use of metaphors of biological defect (Rousseau, E 37, 254) and his discussion of animal instinct (Rousseau, E 286) indicate that he thinks that there is a sense in which plants, brutes, as well as humans, have souls, natures, or inner sources of change. In the context of Rousseau's discussion of the understanding (which is the same context as his discussion of conscience), crucially, "soul" means *rational* soul, and "activity" means *rational* activity. When he identifies himself, or his real self, with the soul, his active nature, and what is in him, Rousseau's attention is on what we might call intelligent activity, the intelligent soul, and reason as a source of change.

Now we are in a position to ask whether Taylor is entitled to hold that the motives arising from the soul are those that *really* originate within an agent, and that conscience is such an inner source. One requirement, on Taylor's interpretation, is that it have a way to understand the connection Rousseau makes between morality and freedom. We have seen that Taylor's suggestion—one acts freely when one acts from motives which originate within oneself—will not do; "coming from within" is not sufficiently fine grained to capture the special character of motivation by conscience. On Taylor's behalf, I suggested that we might distinguish those motives which *really* originate within an agent according to whether they are to be regarded as an expression of the soul. But the course of our discussion has shown that talk of the soul by itself will get us no farther than talk of the inner. When we pay attention to the primary context in which Rousseau discusses the soul, though, we can see that he has something more determinate in mind: namely, the rational soul. Given the way that judgment is linked with this primary use of "soul," "activity," and "inner," it is not open to Taylor to say that conscience is part of the soul, while giving an account of it on which it is not an intelligent power—and on which it is merely a natural love of what reason anyway recognizes to be good, i.e., a mere passion.

4 Conscience: "It Is You Who Make the Excellence of His Nature and the Morality of His Actions" (E 290)

4.1

If Rousseau is to avoid the difficulties of rational intuitionism, and if he is to hold that being motivated by one's conscience is what it is to be "really free," then conscience must be something other than a passion sensitive to the judgments of reason and its particular expressions must be something other than mere feelings. His own appreciation of the active, rational character of conscience may be seen reflected in a key passage from *Emile:* "If one clearly understands that man is active in his judgments and that his understanding is only the power of comparing and judging, one will see that his freedom is only a similar power or one derived from the former. One chooses the good as he has judged the true." Yet, Rousseau sometimes calls conscience and its particular expressions "sentiments," and this has understandably led commentators to attribute a non-cognitivist theory of conscience to him. For someone aiming at such a reading, the following passages are the basic textual resources: "Reason alone teaches us to know the good and bad. Conscience, which makes us love the former and hate the latter, although independent of reason, cannot therefore be developed without it" (Rousseau, E 67); "The acts of conscience are not judgments but sentiments" (Rousseau, E 290); "As soon as his reason makes him know [the good], his conscience leads him to love it. It is this sentiment which is innate" (Rousseau, E 290); "To know the good is not to love it; man does not have innate knowledge of it, but as soon as his reason makes him know it, his conscience leads him to love it" (Rousseau, E 290); and "Did [God] not give me conscience for loving the good, reason for knowing it, and liberty for choosing it?" (Rousseau, E 294). Indeed, in his defense of a non-cognitivist interpretation of conscience as "a love of order" or "desire for the good," Jerome Schneewind cites most every one of these.[12] In order to find our way into a proper understanding of conscience, then, while doing justice to Rousseau's text, we must locate a sense of "sentiment" as something other than mere feeling, distinct from sensation, appetite, impulse and the like.[13] Against always hearing "sentiment" as "feeling," consider the following passage from the "Profession of Faith:" "I am not propounding to you the sentiment of another or my own as a rule. I am offering it to you for examination" (Rousseau, E 260). An implication of this is that a sentiment can be commanded, even if in this instance, as it happens, the sentiment is not offered in that way. Similarly, Rousseau's warning to "always remember that I am not teaching my sentiment; I am revealing it" (E 277) suggests that a sentiment is something that can be taught—what is clearly not the case with mere feeling. At the same time, a mere tendency or a brute inclination might be thought to be graspable in thought and teachable because it, unlike a particular feeling, appears to have a kind of generality and content. Supposing that this is true, we have not yet done anything to distinguish these from the hoped for sense of "sentiment." Rousseau's discussion of instinct proffers a potential key to this distinction.

For some, an instinct is simply an innate mere tendency to do A in C. Those suspicious that there is any such thing seem to be moved by a more general sus-

---

[12] See Schneewind (1998, 474–477).
[13] In defense of such an interpretative gesture, we might note Rousseau's own warning about the equivocal nature of his central theoretical terms: "I have a hundred times in writing made the reflection that it is impossible in a long work always to give the same meanings to the same words. There is no language rich enough to furnish as many terms, turns, and phrases as our ideas can have modifications" (E 108).

picion about innateness. They attempt to account for a pattern of behavior that is purportedly an expression of instinct by reconstructing the real origins of the habit: here an instinct is said to be merely "a habit without reflection which is, however, acquired by reflecting" (Rousseau, E 287). But notice that on this understanding of instinct each of the following mere tendencies, if innate or unlearned, counts as one: (i) the tendency of zebras to drown when in rough seas, (ii) the tendency of lemmings to jump off cliffs when afraid, and (iii) the tendency of humans to drink when thirsty. However, it flies in the face of common sense to understand (i) or (ii) as instincts. But why? For something to be an instinct it has to have a point: as Rousseau tells us an instinct "appears without any acquired knowledge to guide animals toward some end" (Rousseau, E 287). But not just any end: instinct guides creatures to do those things that are good for it—which are suitable to its nature.

The nature of a thing is itself determined by whether it has what we might think of as a master instinct, what Rousseau calls an "original disposition:" "they are what I call in us nature. It is, then, to these original dispositions that everything must be related" (E 39). Sometimes he calls these "instincts," sometimes "sentiments," and sometimes "principles." In addition, he calls their particular expressions "instincts" and "sentiments" as well. Of course, this can give rise to limitless confusion. To try to avoid that while motivating my cognitivist interpretation of conscience, I will examine the content of each of the three original dispositions described at E 39 with an eye to seeing how the sentiment, instinct, or principle of conscience is integrally bound up with the final one.

If we restrict our view to the merely animal world, self-preservation provides the standard according to which a pattern of behavior is determined to be natural (Rousseau, E 97). Of course, brutes do not have the concept of self-preservation. Still, nature has conveniently made it so that all of what living requires is pleasant to do, e.g., eating and sleeping; thereby a connection is formed between what is naturally good and what is pleasant. Indeed, Rousseau claims early on in Emile that our first nature—the first original disposition—is our being "disposed to seek or avoid the objects which produce sensations...according to whether they are pleasant or unpleasant to us" (E 39). The brute, like the child, does not reason: "restricted to pure sensations" (Rousseau, DI 171), each has only "the sentiment of its present existence" (Rousseau, DI 151). However, unlike mere animal life, childhood is "reason's sleep" (Rousseau, E 107). Waking up happens in stages, where each stage is governed by one of the forms of *rational* self-concern I considered earlier: *amour-de-soi* and *amour propre*. Where it is in the nature of animal life to do what sustains it in doing what is pleasant, it is in the nature of animal life modified by reason to be moved by the *ideas* of self-preservation and pleasure. Our first second nature, as it were, is a self-conscious version of our original animal nature modified by technical abilities and a "mechanical prudence" (Rousseau, DI 171).

> It is at this second stage that, strictly speaking, the life of the individual begins. It is then that he gains consciousness of himself. Memory extends the sentiment of identity to all the moments of his existence; he becomes truly one, the same, and consequently already capable of happiness or unhappiness (Rousseau, E 78).

Here, reason is in the service of immediate and particular pleasures—say figuring out how to get to an apple which hangs from a branch twenty feet up—as well as more long-term interests—say setting traps in summer for the autumn migration. Just as before, Rousseau articulates a standard or original disposition which governs this kind of life: "we are disposed to seek or avoid the objects which produce [sensations]…according to the conformity, or lack of it, that we find between us and these objects" (E 39), where our judgments of conformity are themselves governed by considerations of self-preservation and pleasure.

In a spirit similar to Kant's well known teleological argument in the *Groundwork* (Kant, G 395–396), Rousseau suggests that it would be contrary to "the order of nature" were the purpose of reason the preservation and pleasure of the creature which has it: "if it [nature] destined us to be healthy then, I almost dare assert, the state of reflection is a state against Nature, and the man who meditates a depraved animal" (Rousseau, DI 145).[14] If reason is part of our nature at all, Rousseau would have us expect to learn of another and higher purpose. It is here that we are introduced to the third original disposition; it is the capacity to act "according to the judgments we make about them [sensations] on the basis of the idea of happiness or of perfection given us by reason" (Rousseau, E 39). Our second nature, as it were, is the capacity to be moved by goods as good.

4.2

As Rousseau tells us, conscience "is to the soul what instinct is to the body" (E 286–287), and more specifically he tells us that it is "an innate principle of justice and virtue according to which, in spite of our own maxims, we judge our actions and those of others as *good or bad*" (E 289; emphasis added). Conscience is the principle or measure by which we are moved by normative considerations, the possession of

---

[14] These remarks are read rather differently by Cohen, who does not see that in this passage Rousseau is actually talking about health and not about something grander, like being well-ordered or being in accord with oneself (Cohen 1997, 117).

which is our ultimate original disposition. I propose to understand this principle in terms of its status as the principle of a being that acts "without anything external to me determining me," said with a very special emphasis (Rousseau, E 280). The fundamental point that will enable us to hear Rousseau's remarks on conscience in their proper register is this: *Rousseau thinks that acting and choosing are practical employments of the active power of reason.* Recall the passage quoted above: "if one clearly understands that man is active in his judgments, and that his understanding is only the power of comparing and judging, one will see that his freedom is only a similar power or one derived from the former. One chooses the good as he has judged the true" (Rousseau, E 380). In passages that purportedly support a non-cognitivist interpretation of conscience, e.g., "acts of conscience are not judgments but sentiments" (Rousseau, E 290)., I take Rousseau to be emphasizing that acts of conscience are not theoretical judgments in which what is already the case is represented, but practical judgments in which what would be good is realized.

But what is the power of choice or freedom? In warning us not to mistake "unbridled license for freedom" (Rousseau, DI 120), I take Rousseau to mean that judging and choosing are judging and choosing according to a rule or law. Indeed, Rousseau thinks that being free is having the capacity to make a judgment about what it is good to do "without anything external to me determining me" (E 280) and that he thinks this is the very same as the capacity to act and choose according to the moral law. We can find support for this reading in Rousseau's remarks about "pure spirits," what are, I take it, the equivalent of Kant's holy wills. Here is one: "Where our perishable needs end, where our senseless desires cease, our passions and our crimes ought also to cease. To what perversity would pure spirits be susceptible? Needing nothing, why would they be wicked? ... they would be able to will only the good" (Rousseau, E 284). Of course, we humans are not nearly this pure, and so in us the expression of this capacity takes the form of conscience; "Conscience, conscience! Divine instinct, immortal and celestial voice, certain guide of a being that is ignorant and limited but intelligent and free; infallible judge of good and bad which makes man like unto God" (Rousseau, E 290).

Rousseau's conception of conscience is then very much like Kant's—"conscience is practical reason holding the human being's duty before him for his acquittal or condemnation in every case that comes under a law" (Kant, MM 399). For both Kant and Rousseau, conscience is "the condition of all duties as such" (Kant, MM 407).

Rousseau, like his great successor, finds a conception of conscience that eludes both the Scylla of Humean naturalism and the Charybdis of rational intuitionism by insisting upon the essential unity of rationality as it is expressed in cognitive judgment and in practical action. But our reading thus far leaves room for a question about whether conscience is actually "the work of the prejudices" (Rousseau, E

267), about whether morality is "a chimerical idea without any truth" (Kant, G 445). Rousseau has two responses to this kind of skepticism. First, he says that the skeptic does not prove that conscience doesn't exist, offers some empirical evidence that "all mankind" does as a matter of fact share a fundamental moral code, and emphasizes the strength of the testimony of his heart. But these points, especially the last, do not have quite the same force after Nietzsche's expression of the testimony of his heart, his *a priori*, and his discourse on the origin of conscience, as it were. In the spirit of DI, I suggest that we set aside all the facts.

The second response, more compelling to us disenchanted moderns, is not to be found at any particular point in the text. But it can be reconstructed from Rousseau's explicit commitments through the whole of it. The argument, roughly, is as follows. Either we have *amour propre* or we do not. Suppose that we do not. Then, the whole range of social motives is not ours, something it would be hard for anyone to accept. On the assumption that we do have *amour propre*, we must ask whether any substantive determination is internal to it. *Amour propre* inclines every animal that has it to rank itself in its own species (Rousseau, E 235 and 278) and Rousseau thinks that this ordering can take one of two basic forms: "the good man orders himself in relation to the whole, and the wicked one orders the whole in relation to himself. The latter makes himself the center of all things; the former measures his radius and keeps to the circumference" (E 292). Rousseau argues that if our principle were inflamed *amour propre* (E 247), then we would be creatures who were destined to be unhappy—creatures which are "never content and never could be" (E 213). This is so because of the logic of competitive self-conceit: the sentiment of "preferring ourselves to others, also demands others to prefer us to themselves, which is impossible" (Rousseau, E 213–214).[15] In addition, on the hypothesis that *amour propre* is inflamed, instrumental irrationality would be ground into our nature because it "is forbidden to us by reason to want what we cannot obtain" (Rousseau, E 445). This intrinsic irrationality and our necessary unhappiness are each inconsistent with the hypothesis of the order of nature—a hypothesis that in some sense supplies the explanatory bedrock of *Emile*. Rousseau, after all, opens his "collection of reflections and observations" by claiming that "everything is good as it leaves the hands of the Author of things" (E 37). So, by elimination, conscience—the principle of the person who orders himself in relation to the whole—is the true shape of *amour propre*.

---

[15] I think that it is for exactly this reason that Kant says that someone who has *superbia*, "the inclination to be always on top," is a "conceited ass" (MM 465).

5 A Final Problem

5.1

Thus far, we have seen that Rousseau rejects the empirical naturalist analysis of morality because it fails to account for the content and the form of moral thought and motivation. As a result, Rousseau accepts that the primary moral motive is the motive of duty—that recognition of the rightness of an action is the proper reason for doing it. The point is not simply that the moral worth of an action depends on the intention with which an action is done—Hume agrees with this—but rather that the only time an action has moral worth is when it is done because it is right.

But this is not yet to say anything about how it is that right action is to be identified or defined. The intuitionist agrees with Rousseau that it is only when an action is done because it is right that an agent deserves our esteem.[16] But Rousseau's dismissal of intuitionist metaphysics brings with it the acceptance of a Humean style analysis of right action in terms of motives—an analysis of morality in terms of what goes on in human beings. In denying that the source of moral requirement is in nature, and affirming that it is in our nature in the form of conscience, Rousseau has in effect said that the way to understand what it is right to do is in terms of what conscience commands. This means that conscience must be able to independently identify which actions are right.

To hold these two theses, one about the proper motivation for right action and one about the proper analysis of which actions are right, is to do what Hume denied could be done. It is a rejection of Hume's dilemma and involves making a commitment to the centrality of the concept of self-determination or autonomy in one's moral theory. By rejecting the dilemma, one marks out moral thought as a wholly independent sphere of practical thought—it is independent of lower sources of motivation and of the all too sublime intuitionist metaphysics.[17] So, Rousseau's conception of morality commits him to a picture on which there is no moral good identifiable independently of the commands of conscience. But if conscience is to require us to do anything, then presumably Rousseau must be able to say how the standards of conscience specify particular actions as to be done.

Here is our problem: he does no such thing.

---

[16] Cf. Price (1991, 602).
[17] Note that this sense of independence is entirely separate from the conceptual and methodologically individualistic independence we saw as constraints on the empirical naturalist's account of motivation.

6 The Quietism of Emile: "Do Not Expect Lengthy Precepts of Morality from Me. I Have Only One Precept to Give to You, and It Comprehends All the Others. Be a Man" (E 445)

6.1

Rousseau offers no account of how the will is able to direct itself to action without depending on a principle which specifies the satisfaction of a motive as an end. This absence might be seen as decisive evidence against my interpretation of conscience; surely, Rousseau must hold a different view, one on which no such problem arises. But such a reaction, though understandable, is not obligatory. Instead, we ought to see the absence of such a discussion as a kind of quietism. Rousseau's silence is both philosophically and morally motivated. If this alternative reading of Rousseau's silence is tenable, it should serve as evidence, albeit indirect, for my interpretation of Rousseau's account of the nature of moral requirement. I will argue that the reason he halts his analysis of conscience where he does is that by his lights going further is ineffective and unnecessary in the course of an education, and so there is no reason we should expect to encounter such an extended account in a work such as *Emile*. More importantly, however, I will argue that Rousseau thinks that pursuing such an analysis could be nothing other than an expression of vanity.

Rousseau thinks that providing a criterion for duties and a list of such duties would not effectively contribute to Emile's moral development. We can get the uselessness of explicating conscience in view by looking at Rousseau's attitudes towards methods of education in which one reasons with children (E 89). When considering instruction in theoretical matters, Rousseau says that "to substitute books for [experience] is not to teach us to reason. It is to teach us to use the reason of others. It is to teach us to believe much and never to know anything" (E 125). Belief in this sense is sufficient for impressing one's companions at dinner parties, but the context of its usefulness is limited to unhealthy forms of social dependence. For example, the truth about planetary movements is very little a part of what is involved in saying that "the earth goes around the sun" at a dinner party in order to make a good impression on others. It only matters that there is agreement that the statement is true. This kind of agreement, however, is irrelevant when predicting astronomical events. Such a distance from the object of one's beliefs indicates that this sort of education does not facilitate one's practical attachments to the world; moreover, as we will see, Rousseau believes that it encourages a destructive separation from the world and one's freedom.

It should be unsurprising that the same criticism arises when Rousseau considers the method of teaching practical matters through rules or maxims; "put all the lessons of young people in actions rather than in speeches. Let them learn nothing in books which experience can teach them" (E 251). When direct experience is not the most suitable means for moral education, Rousseau recommends learning from detailed history or biography; but he is clear that this also does not involve setting out moral rules (E 248). Indeed, it is important that Rousseau thinks valuable moral learning can take place by reading history and biography, since it keeps alive the possibility that *Emile* and *Confessions* may be used in this capacity. Giving a set of rules to another merely as "the rules to follow" is to provide instructions without elucidating their goodness or point. The only incentive one has for following such rules grasped in this way is to receive the praise or avoid the punishment of the rule giver. In this sort of education, only an ability to imitate virtue develops but "all these virtues by imitation are the virtues of apes" (Rousseau, E 104).

For a moral education to be successful, the pupil must be taught to do what is right for the reason that it is right. In order for this to happen, the pupil must come to recognize the rightness of an action as a reason for doing it; only if we see the role of certain kinds of actions in the sphere of human purposes can we come to recognize doing what is right as good in-itself. "In doing good…one becomes good" (Rousseau, E 250), i.e., comes to do what is good to do because it is good. This is because practicing virtue is naturally enjoyable, and we most readily come to see this by experiencing this goodness for ourselves. Of course, Rousseau does not think that everyone actually enjoys doing what is right, but just as "it is not for Slaves to reason about freedom" (DI 187), so I suspect he would say that it is not for the vicious or weak to reason about virtue. Since moral knowledge is practical, without addressing the motivational features that are part of such knowledge, one can only come to learn what others regard as required of us; "cold arguments can determine our opinions, but not our actions. They make us believe and not act. They demonstrate what must be thought not what must be done" (Rousseau, E 323). What is wanted from a moral education is to make knowledge of the practically necessary practically significant.

Given Rousseau's views about the innateness of conscience and its implicit operations, specifying its content is unnecessary in the educational context. Let me begin with a nearly parallel case found in our theoretical lives. In order to teach a child to make good deductive inferences, one need not specify the rules that govern this activity. It is unnecessary, Rousseau would say because "reason is common to us" (Rousseau, E 266). I suspect that his claim would be that the situation is nearly the same with practical reason: goodness is common to us. However, just as it is necessary for a teacher to lead her pupil to make good inferences in order to successfully initiate the pupil into the rational order, so it is necessary for a teacher to lead her pupil to perform right acts in order to successfully initiate the pupil into the moral order. As Rousseau puts the point, "it is not by teaching the names of these virtues that one teaches them to children. It is by making the children taste them without knowing that they are" (E 131).

For Rousseau, a duty cannot be the kind of thing that must be learned from another. If he is right, then there is a moral argument for the claim that it is unnecessary to explicitly teach Emile what morality requires. In the "Profession of Faith" Rousseau says,

> I shall never be able to conceive that what every man is obliged to know is confined to books, and that someone who does not have access to these books, or to those who understand them, is punished for an ignorance which is involuntary. Always books! What a mania... Either he will learn these duties by himself, or he is excused from knowing them (Rousseau, E 303).

In modeling conscience on instinct, and developing a picture of the moral subject as autonomous, Rousseau restricts the role for moral education. It cannot be a matter of telling a person what they could not know by themselves. Still, it might be a matter of getting a person to become sensitive to features of a situation to which she might not otherwise have been sensitive. If there is a problem about the accessibility of conscience, it is not a problem about the accessibility of its content, so not a problem that can be addressed by being told what conscience says; one still would not have the ears for it. That is, moral education is best thought of as doing what is necessary to give the pupil a sensitivity to the promptings of conscience.

Furthermore, it would be morally wrong for the teacher to specify the rule governing the activity of conscience and the rules that conscience specifies as duties. As a result, Rousseau himself is constrained by conscience to abstain from such a thing. Before the age of reason, "appearing to preach virtue to children, one makes them love all the vices" (Rousseau, E 103). At this stage, when the moral sentiments and notions (Rousseau, E 219) are utterly foreign to one, being told "Do not lie" or "Be generous" encourages one to regard the demands of morality as interferences to one's happiness. It makes acting in accord with such commands unpleasant and encourages one to think that to violate those commands is to determine oneself. This is because at this early stage, practical reason is guided by *amour de soi* and must see moral restrictions as mere obstacles to what one's will prescribes. Apart from making something other than a virtuous person, this kind of education engenders unhappiness because a pupil's conscience eventually demands (Rousseau, E 212) that he do exactly those things he has come to see as incompatible with his happiness and "self-determination."

6.2

But what about when Emile has reached the age of reason, when the moral sentiments and notions are not so foreign? This case is more interesting to a reader of *Emile* because the reasons that Rousseau has for refraining from giving an analysis of conscience to Emile here will be reasons he has for refraining from addressing the reader in the same way.

We need to distinguish merely listing those actions specified as duties by conscience and giving an analysis of conscience itself. Simply to supply a list of duties, claiming that the truth of the list is supported by philosophical argument without providing the argument, would require the subjection of the recipient's reason to authority. The situation is the same when belief in revelation and miracles is required by the church: "a belief in all this on the faith of others, and a subjection of the authority of God, speaking to my reason, to the authority of men" (Rousseau, E 301). Providing a list would be providing a temptation, if not encouragement, to abandon one's responsibility for oneself; but "no one is exempt from the first duty of a man; no one has a right to rely on the judgment of others" (Rousseau, E 306). However, it seems that this difficulty can be resolved by supplying the missing argument, by showing how conscience specifies precisely those actions as duties. Besides, it is this analysis that is of real philosophical interest.

Here, I think, it is not silly to ask whether Emile might understand such complicated matters. Rousseau has doubts about the capacity of his own reason; "I knew, when I was pondering these things, that the human understanding, limited by the senses, could not fully comprehend them. I confined myself therefore to what was within my reach and did not attempt to understand what was beyond me" (R 59). Furthermore, the complexity would make it impossible to have the audience that he intends, namely, everyone; "O Man, whatever Land you may be from, whatever may be your opinions, listen" (Rousseau, DI 140). As long as Rousseau sees the sort of inquiry that I have been suggesting others have found necessary to give as unnecessary for his own conduct, he will regard its results as nothing other than one of "the ills caused by our vain curiosity" (DAS 7). So, we can see his silence on this matter, not as evidence for an alternative theoretical account of conscience, but as motivated by a duty to his reader and to himself: "I renounce idle questions which may agitate my *amour-propre* but are useless for my conduct and are beyond my reason" (Rousseau, E 277).

6.3

The points I have developed so far depend on construing Emile as a work with practical aims, in its own internal narrative and in its relation to its readership. But what about the "Profession of Faith," the most distinctively philosophical part of the book, a part set off from the rest in layout and narrative voice? Suppose that it is true that Rousseau intends *Emile* to affect the practical attitudes of his readers; is it not also true that parts of *Emile*, especially the "Profession of Faith," are devoted to the unearthing of speculative truth? If the "Profession of Faith is to be seen as simply pursuing answers to a set of philosophical questions, then the above pragmatically "moral" considerations are not reason enough for keeping quiet in that context. So, one might argue, the absence of an analysis of conscience there is evidence either that Rousseau does not have the moral theory I have suggested or that his account is a failure because he has not shown how self-determination is possible. But this line of objection hinges on a misinterpretation of the role of the "Profession of Faith" in *Emile*. Rather than taking the "Profession of Faith" to provide the philosophical underpinnings of *Emile*, my suggestion is that we see it as an example of the kind of education one should give to a person who has already been corrupted by the influence of philosophy.

That Emile does not hear the "Profession" shows that understanding it is not necessary for an education according to nature. Indeed, it is addressed to the reader with a directness unmatched in the body of *Emile*. The vicar says to Rousseau "if your sentiments were more stable, I would hesitate to expound mine to you. But in your present condition you will profit from thinking as I do," to which Rousseau adds the following footnote: "this is, I believe, what the good vicar could say to the public at present" (E 295). But what is our present condition? In the *Reveries*, Rousseau writes that instead of "removing my doubts and curing my uncertainties they [philosophers] had shaken all my most assured beliefs concerning the questions which were most important to me" (R 52). *Emile* confirms this: "in instructing him there about the religious controversy, they gave him doubts he had not had and taught him evils of which he had been ignorant. He heard new dogmas; he saw morals that were still newer to him. He saw them and almost became their victim" (Rousseau, E 260).

Rousseau is clear about the sort of address he wants the "Profession of Faith" to be both to its fictional recipient, who we later learn is Rousseau, and to the reader: "it is not my design here to enter into metaphysical discussions which are out of my reach and yours, and which, at bottom, lead to nothing. I have already told you that I wanted not to philosophize with you but to help you consult your heart" (E 289). This is why Rousseau requests that we permit him "to leave aside Emile, whose pure and healthy heart can no longer serve as a rule for anyone, and to seek in myself an example that is more evident and closer to the morals of the reader" (E 344). If I am right that the "Profession" is primarily addressed to the reader for the sake of dislodging morally dangerous philosophical prejudice, then the question of whether to include an analysis of conscience becomes a question about the degree to which such a discussion is necessary or sufficient for dislodging the relevant philosophical prejudices. It becomes a question of which philosophical thoughts are needed as "resources for living" (Rousseau, R 56).

For the most part, Rousseau takes writing philosophy to be what he is left with as a way of addressing the problem of modern man—that he is "born free and everywhere in chains" (SC 46). Describing his motivation to write *Emile*, he says, "Not in a condition to fulfill the most useful task, I will dare at least to attempt the easier one; following the example of so many others, I shall put my hand not to the work but to the pen; and instead of doing what is necessary, I shall endeavor to say it" (Rousseau, E 50). Similarly, in the *Social Contract*, he says, "if I were a prince or a legislator, I would not waste my time saying what has to be done. I would do it, or keep silent" (Rousseau, SC 46). However, philosophy itself becomes useful, and perhaps indispensable, when it is set to the task of correcting the corruptions of prior philosophical endeavors.

We see here, I think, a precursor of Kant's thought that philosophical reflection is easily, frequently, and secretly put in the service of the unrestrained pursuit of the satisfaction of inclination, and a precursor of his own attempt to justify doing practical philosophy on the ground that it is the only way to counter these seductions (Kant, G 390 and 405). However, while Kant thinks that when ordinary practical reason cultivates itself a natural dialectic ensues which "constrains it to seek help in philosophy" (Kant, G 405) and that it will find no rest "except in a complete critique of our reason" (Kant, G 405), Rousseau seems to think that the philosophical impulse is not a necessary or natural expression of reason in us, and that consequently something much less than a complete critique is required to squelch in someone the propensity "to put his hands over his ears and to argue with himself a little" (DI 162) for the sake of doing what he feels like doing. Rousseau can appeal to the difficulty of the analysis of conscience as evidence for its frivolousness, while citing his own experience as evidence for the usefulness, and perhaps sufficiency, of the content of the "Profession of Faith." Not only does Rousseau have moral reasons for not engaging in the sort of analysis Kant does; he makes no positive commitment to give such an analysis simply by having inquired about the nature of morality. This is because he sees philosophical inquiry as itself rooted in practical aims that would not be served by taking the "How possible?" question further than he has.

7 Conclusion: "Others Will Perhaps Demonstrate What I Only Indicate Here" (E 235)

7.1

I have argued for an interpretation of Rousseau's moral theory on which the problem of content arises; at the same time, I claim that Rousseau has moral reasons for not spelling out its possibility. This allows us to read him as offering a theory of the will and an account of the nature of moral requirement that is more than an inspiration for Kant. According to Taylor, Rousseau's role in the transition to Kant was as "the crucial hinge figure, because he provided the language, with an eloquence beyond compare, which could articulate this radical [Kantian] view." But Taylor goes on to say the Rousseau did not think that "the moral law is what comes from within" and that it cannot "be defined by any external order" (Taylor 1989, 364). In contrast to Taylor, I take Rousseau to have done more than provide Kant with the language to talk about the will as autonomous. We can understand him as advocating a conception of moral philosophy grounded on a conception of the will as practical reason. And we can understand him as having such a view even though no action guiding principles of practical reason are specified, and even though conscience does not receive the title of "reason." Once Rousseau's thought is seen in this light, we might take the moves made by Kant regarding the question of the content of conscience as the development of an idea Rousseau thought needed no further discussion. It is not simply that there is no skeptical question to be asked but that other considerations, namely, practical ones, demand that he not inquire. Rousseau is not worried about discovering something horrible —that there is no principle, and so no morality. He is concerned about what he would have to be like to want to investigate such things.

Abbreviations

Hobbes' Works

L   Hobbes, Thomas (1966): *Leviathan*. In: Hobbes, Thomas: *The English Works of Thomas Hobbes*. Vol. III. William Molesworth (Ed.). Aalen: Scientia. Cited by book, chapter, and section.

Hume's Works

T Hume, David (1978): *A Treatise of Human Nature*. Lewis Amherst Selby-Bigge and Peter Harold Nidditch (Eds.). Oxford: Oxford University Press.
ECPM Hume, David (1983): *An Enquiry Concerning the Principles of Morals*. Jerome Schneewind (Ed.). Indianapolis: Hackett.

Kant's Works

G *Groundwork for the Metaphysics of Morals.*
MM *The Metaphysics of Morals.*

I have consulted the text in the following volume: Kant, Immanuel (1996): Practical Philosophy. Mary J. Gregor (Ed. and Trans.). Cambridge: Cambridge University Press. Page references are to Vol. VI of the Akademie-Ausgabe.

Rousseau's Works

SC Rousseau, Jean-Jacques (1978): *On the Social Contract*. Roger Masters (Ed.). Judith Masters (Trans.). New York: St. Martin's Press.
E Rousseau, Jean-Jacques (1979a): *Emile*. Allan Bloom (Ed. and Trans.). New York: Basic Books.
R Rousseau, Jean-Jacques (1979b): *The Reveries of the Solitary Walker*. Peter France (Trans.). London: Penguin.
DAS Rousseau, Jean-Jacques (1986a): *The Discourse on the Arts and Sciences*. In: Rousseau, Jean-Jacques: *The First and Second Discourses together with the replies to critics and Essay on the Origin of Languages*. Victor Gourevitch (Ed. and Trans.). New York: Harper, 1–116.
DI Rousseau, Jean-Jacques (1986b): *The Discourse on the Origin of Inequality*. In: Rousseau, Jean-Jacques: *The First and Second Discourses together with the replies to critics and Essay on the Origin of Languages*. Victor Gourevitch (Ed. and Trans.). New York: Harper, 117–230.
EOL Rousseau, Jean-Jacques (1986c): *Essay on the Origin of Languages*. In: Rousseau, Jean-Jacques: *The First and Second Discourses together with the replies to critics and Essay on the Origin of Languages*. Victor Gourevitch (Ed. and Trans.). New York: Harper, 239–295.

RJJ   Rousseau, Jean-Jacques (1990): *Rousseau, Judge of Jean-Jacques.* Judith Bush, Christopher Kelly, and Roger Masters (Trans.). Hanover: Dartmouth College Press.

References

Cassirer, Ernst (1945): *Rousseau, Kant, Goethe: Two Essays.* James Gutmann, Paul Oskar Kristeller, and John Randall (Trans.). Princeton: Princeton University Press.
Cassirer, Ernst (1951): *The Philosophy of the Enlightenment.* Fritz Koelin and James Pettegrove (Trans.). Princeton: Princeton University Press.
Cassirer, Ernst (1989): *The Question of J.J. Rousseau.* Peter Gay (Trans.). New Haven: Yale University Press.
Cohen, Joshua (1997): "The Natural Goodness of Humanity." In: Herman, Barbara, Korsgaard, Christine, and Reath, Andrews (Eds.): *Reclaiming the History of Ethics: Essays in Honor of John Rawls.* Cambridge: Cambridge University Press, 102–139.
Korsgaard, Christine (1989): "Kant's Analysis of Obligation: The Argument of *Foundations I*." In: *The Monist* 72, 311–340.
Korsgaard, Christine (1996): *Creating the Kingdom of Ends.* Cambridge: Cambridge University Press.
Price, Richard (1991): "Review of the Principal Questions in Morals." In: Raphael, David Daiches (Ed.): *British Moralists.* Vol. II. Indianapolis: Hackett, 131–198.
Rawls, John (1971): *A Theory of Justice.* Cambridge.: Harvard University Press.
Rawls, John (1993): *Political Liberalism.* New York: Columbia University Press.
Schneewind, Jerome B. (1998): *The Invention of Autonomy: A History of Modern Moral Philosophy.* Cambridge: Cambridge University Press.
Taylor, Charles (1989): *Sources of the Self.* Cambridge: Harvard University Press.
Wood, Allen (1996): "General Introduction." In: Kant, Immanuel: *Practical Philosophy.* Mary J. Gregor (Ed.). Cambridge: Cambridge University Press, xiii-xxxiii.

Anastasia Berg
Kant and the Freedom to Do What We Want

Abstract: Even a morally good practical agent does not act solely from the recognition of the abstract demands of moral duty. Often, she acts to satisfy desires for particular ends that are not intrinsically moral. But if freedom, as Kant claims, consists in acting from universal principles one adopts from respect for the moral law, how can agents freely act to satisfy desires for particular ends? The standard answer to this question, the so-called Incorporation Thesis, is, I argue, unsatisfactory both as an interpretation of Kant and on philosophical grounds. I propose instead that, for Kant, the capacity to act freely for the sake of a particular, non-intrinsically moral end is not exhausted by the ability to step back, reflect and decide whether a desire is or can provide a reason to act. Rather, Kant shows, the place for the pursuit of particular ends is determined by practically rational agents' spontaneous constitution of their moral character, whereby they subordinate the pursuit of material, particular ends to the pursuit of formal, moral ones or vice versa.

1 Introduction

Let us begin with an apparently indisputable fact: a moral agent does not act solely from the recognition of her general moral duties. In performing a concrete action, she acts to realize particular ends, which may be given by, or traced to desires that are not intrinsically moral. In such cases, the explanation of the action will not be exhausted by the fact of the agent's recognition of her general moral duties. To get into view the kinds of case I have in mind, suppose I reach for a piece of cake. Such an act may be morally bad, as when I reach for someone else's piece of cake, having first made sure its rightful owners are distracted; it may also be morally permissible, as when I try a piece freely offered to me because I would like to find out what it tastes like; and it may even be morally worthy, as when I reach for the slice that seems best to me, among many, but only insofar as I recognize that, in addition to my hankering for some cake, it is my duty to sustain my life or offer support to my friend, the aspiring pastry chef. A moral theory ought to render the possibility of—as well as the differences between—these kinds of actions intelligible.

On the face of it, however, it is not obvious how the standard Kantian account of action could make sense of these ordinary intuitions, and in particular of the idea that agents may come to act freely in pursuit of particular ends given by their desires. For if, as Kant claims, acting rationally and so freely, consists in acting from the recognition of principles (not to mention moral principles), it is not immediately clear how moral agents can ever come to act freely on ends picked out by contingent desires or, as we would say, do something simply because they want to.

The standard way of tackling this problem in the literature has been by means of the so-called "Incorporation Thesis" (IT). According to the IT, we act on particular desires only insofar as we evaluate them and deem them reasons to act by "taking them up" or "incorporating them" into principles of action. The IT has not only been uncritically adopted by the vast majority of Kant interpreters,[1] but has also widely influenced Kantian strands of contemporary practical philosophy—particularly through the work of Christine Korsgaard.[2] It is a testament to the popularity of the thesis that it has become hard for us to so much as recognize the question I am posing here as a real challenge.

However, I will argue that according to Kant, the freedom to pursue particular desires does not fundamentally turn on an encounter with particular desires which we stand back from, evaluate, and endorse or reject. Instead, we shall see, the freedom to pursue particular desires is grounded in the agent's exercise of her agency in constituting her own moral character.

2 A Problem for the Kantian

Let us begin by bringing the problem into clearer focus. Human willing, according to Kant, is a capacity to be the cause of the reality of objects not just in accordance with principles (as is the case with respect to non-rational animal activity) but by means of the representation of principles. Consequently, if an action were per-

---

[1] With respect to Kant's practical philosophy, no single interpretative position—apart perhaps from John Rawls' "CI Procedure"—has enjoyed as much support as the IT. For examples of uses of the IT following its introduction by Allison (1991), see Wood (1999, 51–53), Hill (1991a, 86), Timmons (1994, 116–19), Johnson (1998), Morrisson (2005), Bojanowski (2007), Papish (2007, 129–130), Guyer (2008, 51–53 and 293–94), Schadow (2012, 112, n. 90, 180–186, and 291, n. 122), and Kang (2015, 96–101). Jens Timmermann (2003, 15) thinks Allison's IT account requires supplementation by a more detailed account of the role of maxims in Kant's theory of action and moral psychology but does not dispute the thesis itself. There are two notable exceptions: McCarty (2008) challenges the incorporation thesis on textual grounds and Dewitt (2018) flags Allison's approach as generally unsatisfactory on philosophical grounds. I will return to both dissenting views below.

[2] Korsgaard's account distinctly evokes the IT (see Korsgaard 1996b, 94; 2009, 105 and 115; and 1996a, 162 and 165). I will return to her account below.

formed not from the recognition of the validity of a principle, but simply and solely because someone felt like pursuing a certain end, it could not be an exercise of the will and would therefore not be free. Since freedom is necessary for the imputation of action, such actions—if they would be actions at all—could not be imputed to an agent. It thus seems to follow that acting on ordinary felt desires cannot be understood as an exercise of will and that therefore one cannot be held responsible for acting on one's desires.[3]

A Kantian account of the ability to act on desires must therefore explain how an agent can come to act on a contingent desire without relinquishing herself to the mercy of natural forces. This way of setting up the problem seems to call for the possibility of a transition from having an ordinary, contingent desire to having a principle that aims at that desire's satisfaction—a transition that would have to itself be an exercise of our freedom. Responding to the challenge, thus conceived, Henry Allison drew attention to a passage in Kant's late work, *Religion within the Bounds of Bare Reason*,[4] in which Allison took Kant to describe just such a transition from having a desire to freely adopting a principle of action. This transition guarantees, for Allison, that the agent's pursuit of that desire is itself an act of freedom. Here is the passage from Kant:

> The power of choice [*Willkür*] has the quite peculiar characteristic that it cannot be determined to an action by any incentive [*Triebfeder*] except *insofar as the human being has admitted the incentive* [*Triebfeder*] *into his maxim* [*nur sofern der Mensch sie in seine Maxime aufgenommen hat*] (has made this a universal rule for himself, according to which he wills to conduct himself) (Kant, *R* 6:23–24).

I shall designate this passage the "incorporation requirement" passage, and, following Allison, refer to his interpretation of it as the Incorporation Thesis (IT).

According to Allison, an agent's actions can be "genuine expressions of agency" and therefore "imputable" in cases where an agent acts on desires, as long as the actions are "thought to involve an act of spontaneity on the part of the agent,

---

3 It is important not to confuse the question just raised, which is the focus of this paper, with a different and distinct problem—namely, that Kant's equation of the will with practical reason leaves no room for the possibility of freely acting on a principle that opposes the moral law (the so-called Reinhold-Sidgwick objection). The question I address here is a different one: not how we can freely act on a non-moral principle, but how we can freely act to satisfy a desire.
4 Contemporary interest in the incorporation requirement passage dates to the early sixties and, in particular, to John R. Silber's "The Ethical Significance of Kant's Religion" (1960, lxxix–cxxxiv). Rawls refers to the incorporation thesis in his lectures on Kant (2000, 294). Gerold Prauss (1983, 93–94) initiated interest in it in the German-speaking literature in the early eighties. The label by which it is known today—namely, the "Incorporation Thesis"—was given to it by Allison (1991).

through which the inclination or desire is deemed to be an appropriate basis of action" (Allison 1991, 39). While an agent has no control over what she happens to desire or how intensely she desires it, she nevertheless exercises control over her actions insofar as she is never determined to act directly by a desire. According to Allison, for the agent to act on a desire she must step back from it and evaluate it in light of "objective (intersubjectively valid) rational norms," and can then accept or reject the desire "as sufficient reason for action" (Allison 1991, 39). A desire can be deemed a reason to act "only with reference to a rule or principle of action, which dictates that we ought to pursue the satisfaction of that inclination or desire" (Allison 1991, 40). On this account, when I have a desire, I consult the objective norms by which I determine myself to act, and then, as long as these norms do not preclude the pursuit of this desire, I find or articulate a principle according to which I *ought* to pursue the satisfaction of the desire. By virtue of adopting this principle I deem the desire a reason to act. If I happen to have a moral reason to pursue the end the desire specifies, all the better, but this is not necessary: that it is permissible to pursue the end the desire aims at is sufficient for the adoption of a principle according to which I ought to pursue it. For example, if I feel like having that slice of cake, I act freely insofar as I evaluate doing so in light of objective rational norms and, on the basis of these, deem my desire a reason for me to act by adopting a principle according to which I ought to pursue the desire in question.

The IT has become the canonical understanding of Kant's account of the relationship practically rational agents bear to their inclinations, desires, and natural impulses. Interpreters are in near unanimous agreement that Allison's reading of the passage captures a central Kantian commitment and that Kant was right to hold it—so much so that they rarely take the trouble to consider it in detail, instead often citing it in passing as a premise requiring no defense.[5] I will begin

---

5 See footnote 1 for examples of uncritical mentions and uses of the IT. Tamar Schapiro (2011) is an exception insofar as she defends Allison's interpretation of Kant in some detail and argues it is a valuable contribution to contemporary philosophy of action. While embracing the IT in general, Marcia Baron (1993a and 1993b) queries whether it can be reconciled with Kant's brief account of *Gebrehlichkeit*, the so-called Kantian version of weakness of the will. Iain Morrisson (2005) responds to Baron and dismisses the threat of conflict between the IT and Kant's account of weakness of the will. Importantly, both Baron and Morrisson endorse the IT. An exception is Richard McCarty (2008), who argues that the IT is not textually supported. While I agree with McCarty's general point that the incorporation requirement is concerned not with individual action but with moral character, I do not think, as McCarty does, that it has no application to the way we make everyday free choices. This is because I do not think that the free choice that the incorporation requirement is meant to apply to belongs to a separate noumenal world. Janelle Dewitt (2018,

my re-evaluation of the Kantian understanding of the relationship between practical reason and desire by demonstrating that the thesis is not textually supported and is philosophically unattractive.

3 Kant on the Principle of Incorporation

According to the IT, desire is incorporated into a maxim. This is Kant's term for a subjective principle of action, or the principle of action upon which an agent in fact acts.[6] Thus, when feeling a craving for some sweets I can act on this craving by reference to a principle like "when craving sweets, eat some." However, when we turn to Kant's own account of incorporation in the incorporation passage, we find that the kind of principle into which incorporation takes place is not an ordinary maxim, an ordinary principle of action, at all. Kant calls the maxim into which incorporation occurs the "supreme maxim" (Kant, *R* 6:36) and describes it as specifying not a particular course of action or even the requirement of the moral law but instead a kind of principle that constitutes the person's entire moral character, what Kant calls one's "*Gesinnung.*"[7] This supreme maxim is a single, unifying rule that the power of choice "makes for itself" and is the "first basis [...] for the adoption of good maxims or the adoption of evil (unlawful) ones" (Kant, *R* 6:21). It, Kant adds, "can only be one" and it "applies universally to the entire use of freedom" (Kant, *R* 6:25). By adopting this supreme maxim an agent adopts a governing principle for the exercise of their will in its entirety. It thereby constitutes the agent's moral character at the highest level of generality.[8]

---

68) flags Allison's approach as generally unsatisfactory, but as I shall argue below, I do not think her proposed alternative sufficiently forecloses the dualistic worries she insightfully raises.

6 I follow Stephen Engstrom's (2010) interpretation of "maxims" according to which a maxim, a subjective principle of action, is just the principle of action upon which we do in fact act, while an objective principle of action is a principle upon which we should act. Cf. *G* 4:420 and *KpV* 5:76. When we act morally well, our maxim—our subjective principle of action—is an objective principle of action, whose authority we recognize.

7 I follow Julia Peters (2018) in leaving the term *Gesinnung* untranslated. As she notes, rendering *Gesinnung* as "disposition" (as is the case in both George di Giovanni's translation in *The Cambridge Edition of the Works of Immanuel Kant* and the earlier translation by Theodore M. Greene and Hoyt H. Hudson) is misleading, insofar as "disposition" can also refer to a behavioral disposition or tendency, a connotation absent from the German *Gesinnung*. "Attitude," Werner Pluhar's preferred translation, is closer to the German meaning.

8 It is possible to ask here whether the maxim referred to in the incorporation passage and into which a *Triebfeder* is to be incorporated is indeed the *Gesinnung*-constituting maxim, the single, supreme maxim which the power of choice makes for itself to guide all its exercises. To see that it must be so, it is important to, first, note that the discussion of incorporation occurs as a

This may come as a surprise against the background of the *Groundwork* and the second *Critique*, where no such supreme maxim is discussed. But although Kant mentions the need for this single, unifying principle for the power of choice for the first time in the *Religion*, the idea is implicit in his earlier work and, in particular, in the central thesis that the moral worth of an action depends on the principle on which an agent acts. In the *Religion*, Kant merely makes explicit an implication of this idea; namely, that in order to determine the moral worth of an action we must consult not just any principle of action, but the highest principle from which it is derived: the moral law, in the case of morally worthy action, or the principle of one's happiness, in all other cases.

To this point, that an action's moral worth is determined by the highest principle from which it is derived, Kant adds the claim that in a mature moral agent, this principle is singular and constant across all actions. The argument for this latter claim, which constitutes Kant's "rigorism," is in brief as follows: because the moral law commands universally, properly recognizing its authority means recognizing its authority universally, i.e., over all of one's actions. It follows that an agent cannot act only occasionally from genuine recognition of the moral law, for to allow oneself to occasionally deviate from the commands of the moral law is simply to refuse its authority as universally binding, which is to refuse its authority *tout court*. For whatever set of exceptional circumstances in which an agent would not follow the moral law, the highest principle an agent would act on would be "follow the moral law, except in that special set of circumstances in which you may choose to do otherwise," and so the observance of the moral law, at any and all points, would not be absolute but conditioned on that set of circumstances not obtaining. An agent is thus either committed to the supremacy of moral considerations in all matters, or, in effect, in none.[9] In the *Religion*, Kant titles this overarching commitment the *Gesinnung* or the *Gesinnung*-constituting maxim.

---

part of the discussion of "rigorism"—the way of thinking according to which the human being is "either morally good or morally evil" (*R* 6:22). Kant defends rigorism by arguing that a commitment to the law, which amounts to the incorporation and prioritization of the moral *Triebfeder*, cannot be partial, and that, conversely, any admission of an exception to the moral *Triebfeder* in the form of an incorporation or admission and prioritization of a sensible *Triebfeder* as prior to the moral law is wholly corrupting. In other words, Kant disputes by this very argument the idea that incorporation of a *Triebfeder* can be a local affair and aims to show why any seemingly local deviation is wholly determining of the subject. Second, at *R* 6:36, Kant speaks explicitly of the incorporation or admission of *Triebfedern* as into an agent's "supreme maxim." I discuss the rationale for these claims in what follows.

9 The claim that maxims stand to one another in a hierarchical system has been defended in Beck (1996, 118), Korsgaard (1996a, 58), O'Neill (1989, 83–85), and Allison (1991, 91–94).

We can therefore conclude that the incorporation maxim introduced by Kant in the *Religion* is the not the kind of thing proponents of the IT purport to find there: it is not a principle that "dictates" that we "ought" to pursue a particular desire or which deems a particular desire "sufficient reason" to act. It is a principle that organizes our most fundamental practical priorities by determining whether we are committed to the moral law absolutely or only conditionally.

But if the text is straightforward on this matter, why have interpreters insisted that incorporation concerns the adoption of an ordinary principle of action in the pursuit of an ordinary desire? Perhaps this is because of the interpreters' conception of what *must* be the object of incorporation; namely, their conception of desire. This is the second way in which the IT interpretation deviates from Kant's account of incorporation and the topic to which I will now turn.

4 Kant and the Object of Incorporation

As we have seen, proponents of the IT claim that the object of incorporation is a particular desire, which the agent evaluates, and thereby either accepts or rejects as a reason to act. This claim traces to Allison, who saw the IT as a corollary to his well-known "two-aspect" reading of transcendental idealism. I shall consider his account first.

4.1 Allison's Conception of Desire

According to Allison, Kant's famous distinction in the first *Critique* between appearances and things in themselves should be understood as a distinction between two "aspects" of one and the same underlying reality. The IT is the application of the two-aspect reading to the case of human agency. On this interpretation, we need not attribute to Kant the claim that, to quote Allison, "free agency occurs in a distinct 'intelligible world'" or that "noumenal activities intervene in the causal order of the phenomenal world" (Allison 1991, 4). Instead, the contrast between freedom and nature is the contrast "between two 'points of view' or descriptions under which a single occurrence (a human action) can be considered" (Ibid.).

This framework justifies the attribution of a double character—both empirical and intelligible—to one and the same rational agent. The empirical perspective on human action conceives it as being causally determined according to natural laws. Here human action is to be explained in terms of the "familiar belief-desire" model, according to which "an agent's empirical character, understood as a set of relevant beliefs and desires, functions as the empirical cause of the action" (Allison 1991, 4). However, from the standpoint of the agent's intelligible character, the agent is not causally determined to act based on the set of their beliefs and desires but is "free," in the sense established by the IT; that is, from the standpoint of the agent's intelligible character the agent is free to adopt objective norms and in the light of those to incorporate their desires into principles of action—it is up to the agent to deem desires reasons to act.

Note, however, that while the intelligible and empirical characters are meant to provide two distinct perspectives on a single underlying reality, the term "desire" figures in both. In the empirical model, it is the sufficient cause of action: from the intelligible perspective, it is the thing that is evaluated and, on the basis of this evaluation, accepted or rejected as a reason to act. How are we to make sense of this double occurrence? To meet the criteria set by the two parts of the account, "desire" ought to mean something different in each, for otherwise what is the sufficient condition for action from one perspective is only a necessary one from the other. But if desire means something different on each side of the divide, it remains mysterious what it is that gets incorporated from the rational standpoint.

4.2 The Animal-Desire Conception of Desire

Implicitly addressing this worry, later interpreters sometimes characterize desire not as part of a simple causal explanation, but as the sort of thing that could play a part in an account of animal activity. Allen Wood, for instance, characterizes the faculty of desire in rational beings as the power to determine oneself to act on the basis of an "empirical impulse," where the account of this impulse "applies equally to rational beings and to brute animals" (Wood 1991, 51). Whereas for the mere brute the power of choice is determined by the sensuous, empirical impulse, rational beings are able to resist such impulses and only act on them if they decide to.

This animal-desire version of the IT, the version which characterizes human sensible desire with reference to the desire of brute animals, has been introduced into contemporary ethics. Its most well-known proponent is Christine Korsgaard, who attributes to Kant an account according to which desires are located outside of reason and must be approved of by reason if they are to be acted upon: "At the basis of every desire or inclination, no matter how articulately we can defend it, is a basic suitableness-to-us, that is a matter of nature and not of reason" (Korsgaard 2009, 122) or "the reflective mind must endorse the desire before it can act on it, it must say to itself that the desire is a reason. As Kant puts it, we must *make it our maxim* to act on the desire. Then although we may do what desire bids us, we do it freely" (Korsgaard 1996b, 94).[10]

In this account, human desire begins as a product of nature and only afterwards becomes distinctly rational, and thus, distinctly human: it is the reflective endorsement of human desire which distinguishes it from the desires of a non-rational animal.[11] Tamar Schapiro summarizes the point as follows: "When I have an inclination, the reflecting part of me is aware of the non-rational principle that shapes my inner animal's way of seeing and responding to the world" (Schapiro 2011, 165). Crucially, although these interpreters diverge from Allison's two-aspect reading of human action, they share in common with Allison the idea that desires are fundamentally extra-rational (it "is a matter of nature and not of reason," the reflecting part is aware of "the non-rational principle"), and must be reflectively endorsed in order to be freely acted upon.

There are two fundamental problems with this kind of account of desire.[12] The first is the more familiar. Proponents of the IT claim that the sort of thing which, without modification, could either causally determine movement or naturally determine an animal to act, and whose occurrence therefore does not itself involve the exercise of rational capacities, can supply something that can be evaluated and deemed as a *reason* by the rational subject. But if desire can find itself at home in the conceptual habitat of explanation through empirical laws or natural teleology, it is far from obvious that desires are something agents could, from their own perspective, intelligibly deem as *reasons* to act.[13] No doubt a rational agent can re-

---

10 The text in quotation marks is Korsgaard's interpretation, not a direct quotation. See also Korsgaard (1996a, 162 and 165 as well as 2009, 105 and 115).
11 While a non-rational animal's "perceptions are its beliefs and its desires are its will," in a human being perceptions and beliefs become the "objects of its attention," we can "think about them" and, therefore, "our capacity to turn our attention on to our own mental activities is also a capacity to distance ourselves from them, and to call them into question" (Korsgaard 1996b, 92–93). Likewise, she later writes, "The first result of the development of this form of self-consciousness is liberation from the control of instinct. Instincts still operate within us, in the sense that they are the sources of many of our incentives—in fact, arguably, though by various routes, of all of them. But instincts no longer *determine* how we respond to those incentives, what we do in the face of them" (1996b, 116).
12 For critique of the idea that Kant's account of moral deliberation is best understood on the model of "reflective endorsement," see Herman (2008). For criticism of reflective endorsement as inconsistent with a constitutivist reading of Kant's practical philosophy, see Bagnoli (2009).
13 This point echoes the one made by Warren Quinn in his influential essay "Putting Rationality in its Place" (1994). Quinn argued that we cannot conceive of desire merely as a brute impulse, or else we could never make sense of the way in which it rationalizes action. Desire, Quinn argues, must therefore be understood to involve more. Another way of making my point is that in Kant's

spond to a causal force (e.g., a push or pull) or a physical impulse (e.g., nausea) in various ways, but evaluating and responding rationally to a force or impulse, or even finding reason to resign oneself to it, address it, or resist it is not the same as deeming *it* a reason. An agent who finds herself, say, pushed by a crowd, can observe the crowd's movement, ask herself whether it promotes or hinders her interests, and evaluate the general trajectory with approval or disapproval. She can try to resist it or resign herself to it and she can do all this on rational grounds: she can decide resistance would be too costly, or that the pushing can be accommodated without undesired consequences. She can even decide that she has a reason to get to the other side and on that basis consider the push salutary. But no act of resistance or resignation would amount to deeming the push of the crowd itself *a reason to act*.[14] My reason to act cannot be that I have been pushed. The same goes for a bout of hiccups, or an itch: I might find that I have reason to try and hasten the hiccups bout's conclusion, or scratch the itch, but a hiccup attack is not making a rational recommendation that I act in this way or that.

Proponents of animal-desire may respond that my awareness of an extra-rational desire, or the operation of an extra-rational principle, need not operate analogously to the observation of a brute event. An animal's desire is not a mere event but is itself goal- or end-directed. All else being equal, an animal's particular desire belongs within a system of ends that jointly constitute the animal's self-preservation, as an individual and as a member of its species. As such, an animal's desire could be understood to make a suggestion or a "proposal"[15] concerning what it would take to, say, maintain the practical agent's preservation.[16]

I do not think this response is satisfactory. First, it cannot be assumed that a contingent, sensible desire could play the role of a proposal with respect to the agent's reason any more than a brute fact would. At first glance this may seem counterintuitive. Let us consider one of Schapiro's central examples: thirst.[17] Surely, we could justify drinking water by saying something like "I drank because I was thirsty." But while it is true that the feeling of thirst may indicate to us that we are in physical need of water, if when thirsty I proceed to obtain and drink water, it is not the physical indicator of that need that I deem a reason to act, it is rather my

---

system, as long as desire is located in nature, it can never be conceived along the lines that interpreters have wished it would—an evaluative perspective that can rationalize a particular action.
14 While some philosophers today are happy to admit of a sense of "rationalization" so thin that the very presence of a non-rational desire can rationalize acting on it, such a thought is antithetical to Kant.
15 See Schapiro (2009, 2014).
16 This is the strategy adopted by Schapiro (2009, 251).
17 See Schapiro (2009).

dependence on water for survival and the fact that I may have consumed an insufficient amount of it, of which thirst is usually reliable indicator. Likewise, my "pathological"—as opposed to practical—desire to check my e-mails points in the direction of a concrete action, but in the good case if I decide to check my e-mails it is not the pathological urge to revisit the inbox that I deem a reason to do so. To have a pathological urge just means to have an unreasoned, usually unproductive and potentially even destructive, inclination. This is why a pathological urge can be gratified, but not, standardly, rationalize action. I say "standardly" because there is of course a sense in which the itch and the pathological desire to check one's emails *can* be deemed as reasons to act: this is the case when I decide to succumb to the urge to scratch or scroll because I have no other way to alleviate the discomfort entailed by my failing to do so. But in such a case, the thirst or urge do not "recommend" the end in any way, i.e., they do not reveal anything of value about it, except as a means to alleviate pain, to make the nagging stop. This, however, is not what we standardly take our desires to mean to us and, subsequently, neither is it standardly what we take ourselves to do when we choose to act on them.

The animal-desire interpretation of the IT encounters a second challenge. It is not clear what would afford contingent desires the status of proposals. The intuitive answer, that, like thirst, desires indicate what is necessary for our survival, or wellbeing, is hard to sustain. This may be the case for actual non-rational animals, of course, as long as they are placed in their natural habitat. But ordinary practical agents' contingent desires are hardly restricted to those that can so much as purport to promote the agent's "animal wellbeing": contingent desires may be for ends that it would not make sense for sub-rational animals to have—for example, intellectual and artistic desires or the desire to check one's e-mails compulsively—and they could be for ends that downright contradict the ostensible aim of self-preservation—for example, a willingness to sacrifice one's material wellbeing for the sake of an abstract value. Here, the animal desire proponent may reply that while the desire may aim at ends that it would not make sense to attribute to animals, it nevertheless maintains the structure of or continues to function as animal desire. But if the ends of our contingent desires are in no way intrinsically linked to any intelligible notion of our wellbeing (material, physical, biological, etc.), if they are, in other words, from the standpoint of rationality *purely* contingent, it is hard to see why practical reason would acknowledge their authority to make so much as a suggestion concerning what should be done, let alone crown it a reason to do so. There is no reason, after all, empirical or otherwise, to assume the majority or even a large enough share of our contingent desires point to what is necessary for our survival, or even to what would in some way promote our objective well-being. Whether absolutely or in large part, contingent desires are so shaped by culture and society as to render their connection to our objective, rational good extremely tenuous.

4.3 The Pro-Tanto Reasons Conception of Desire

A similar problem arises for another proposal for how to conceive of contingent desire; namely, as the source of "pro-tanto reasons." According to this suggestion, the aim of the IT is to give an account of how different kinds of pro-tanto reasons are turned into all-things-considered reasons, that is, reasons on which we act. A desire gives rise to a pro tanto reason to act, but in order to act on it, I must first incorporate the pro-tanto reasons into a maxim. The advantage of this view over the animal desire view is that it apparently allows us to distinguish between desires that offer pro-tanto reasons and those that do not and that, according to it, no extra-rational reasons are turned into reasons for action. Rather, pro-tanto *reasons* for action are turned into all-things-considered reasons for action. As to modification of the incorporation thesis, the solution is wanting, for it would still leave it unclear how contingent desires, as such, can come to constitute pro-tanto reasons for us.[18] Alternatively, if desires are nothing but pro-tanto reasons, then we need an explanation of what justifies this equivalence between contingent desire and a pro-tanto reason, along the lines of our objections to the animal-desire model, and the idea that a sensible, contingent desire may be deemed, or, as in this case, just is a pro-tanto reason to act.

Importantly, however, none of this is to suggest that explanations of action that refer to "desires" are inappropriate in a Kantian framework. Rather, my aim is to show that the available interpretations of desire in the Kantian framework in general and in particular in the context of the IT readings cannot render such a practice intelligible. For on the IT understanding of what "desires" are, we could at best think of desires as proposing objects about which agents could ask themselves whether, *independently* of their desires, they have reasons to pursue them.[19]

---

18 See Engstrom (2009) for an account of this general shape.
19 The worry raised here echoes similar concerns that have been raised with regard to Kant's theoretical philosophy and in the philosophy of perception more broadly. John McDowell (2013, 256) argues against the idea that if the exercise of sensibility is understood as independent of the exercise of rational capacities, it cannot make objects available to cognition in a way that renders intelligible our capacity to make empirical judgments about the world based on our perceptual experience. If one is to attribute an epistemic role to sensory experience—one that attributes to experience the capacity to warrant or justify belief—one must therefore characterize it as a capacity whose exercises are *essentially* able to stand in rational relations. This specifically precludes the

4.4 The Problem of Psychic Alienation

A more general problem with the IT conceptions of desire is the kind of alienated relationship it posits between an agent's desires and her rational capacities. One interpreter who does criticize the IT, Janelle DeWitt, focuses on the psychic alienation that it implies. Referring to the assumptions underlying the IT, De Witt writes as follows:

> Though this "distinct natures" view is able to give an explanation for how reason can generate a form of agential control (via the incorporation thesis), it unfortunately seems to come at the high price of a unified psychology. Because the subject's two natures are *entirely* distinct, reason can *only* exercise control as an alien force external to his lower nature. The result of this, however, is a deep rupture between fundamental parts of the subject's psychology—of who and what he is—because he can identify with only one of his two natures at any given time (DeWitt 2018, 68).

Dewitt's dissent is rare and insightful: the IT proponents cannot avoid the threat of saddling Kant with a conceptually dubious and psychologically unattractive dualism.

Nevertheless, despite its merits, DeWitt's own solution does not, I think, fully take the measure of her own concerns. She proposes that we can avoid attributing to Kant "a fractured sense of what it is to be human," by showing how in his system a person is able to "take on the perspective of his rational *and* animal natures at the same time" (DeWitt 2018, 68). This, however, raises the question of how to characterize this third, "human" perspective, as DeWitt aptly names it, from which one is supposed to adopt both perspectives, of one's rational and animal natures, at the same time. If adopting both perspectives at one and the same time is a matter of having both sets of separate concerns simultaneously, we seem to get ourselves back to square one. Perhaps, then, it is a matter of adopting a third perspective—one that allows us to evaluate the two others. But what kind of perspective or stance is adequate to reflect upon and decide between the two original perspectives? If it is to genuinely constitute a different perspective, it cannot itself be either a rational perspective or an animal one. But then what perspective is it? And how does it allow the agent to adjudicate between the claims of reason and sensibility? To quote Korsgaard's objection to a similar model, "if the person identifies

---

possibility that experiences understood in merely causal terms can play any epistemic or justificatory role in our thinking. See also Boyle (2016) for related thoughts about the application of this form of worry about our perceptual capacities to the case of human desire and action.

neither with reason nor with passion, then how—on what principle—can she possibly choose between them?" (2009, 123). DeWitt leaves the question open.

Objections to Kant's practical philosophy along these lines are not new. Most interpreters have learned either to resign themselves or defend Kant's account as a prescient characterization of our cursed fate. However, there is another worrying consequence of this account of contingent desires, to which interpreters have not yet paid sufficient attention.

4.5 The Problem of Particular-Moral Ends

Every action, moral or not, aims at a particular, material end. For example, in order to generally "keep my promises," I must return particular debts at particular times. This was clear to Kant. In the second *Critique*, he writes that it is "undeniable that *every* volition must also have an object and hence a matter" (Kant, *KpV* 5:34).[20] The fact that an action aims at a particular end or has a matter does not make that action morally bad. The moral worth of an action depends on whether or not this matter is "the determining ground and condition" of the action (Kant, *KpV* 5:34). In other words, it is only if one's action is dedicated *solely* to securing some particular end—pursuing it as if it is worthy in itself—that it loses moral worth.

Kant moreover held that merely formal principles cannot provide matter for particular actions. The source of "matter"—for Kant, the source of particular ends—is sensible desire.[21] It follows that the choice of specific objects of pursuit, in *all* our actions, is determined by what we sensibly desire.[22] We have seen that most IT

---

20 See also Kant, *R* 6:4–5.
21 See Kant, *KpV* 5: 33–34, 109.
22 The assumption that sensible, extra-rational desire is necessary to provide objects for the will is ubiquitous. Even recent interpreters like Carla Bagnoli, Dewitt, and Jessica Tizzard, who explicitly claim to offer non-dualistic accounts of the interaction of our spontaneous and receptive practical capacities, still maintain this hallmark of the IT: the assumption that reason cannot supply the so-called matter of the will—particular possible ends to be pursued—and that extra-rational input is necessary for every action. Bagnoli writes, "Respect [...] explains how moral reasons drive us to action. It does so not by adding to the many incentives that rational agents review in deliberation, but by constraining and ranking such incentives" (2011, 76). In other words, reason does not provide its own ends to pursue but only limits and organizes hierarchically given extra-rational ends. Tizzard means to show how reason can structure sensibility through and through and to this end argues that moral respect is a form of practical sensibility analogous to the forms of intuition, space, and time. However, on her account the agent's orientation towards particular ends still requires the contribution of given, extra-rational sensible desires. Practical reason requires "sensible

proponents conceive of sensible desire as essentially having its source outside of reason, an object in the empirical world, a physical urge or something akin to animal desire. For this view, reason may constrain and structure such extra-rational matter, but the matter on which reason exerts its influence must come from outside it. However, taking these two points together yields a highly worrying consequence: namely, that even if an agent recognizes that her duty requires generally keeping her promises, for her to keep her particular promise by performing a particular task, that agent would have to experience, over and above her recognition of the formal demand to keep promises, an extra-rational sensible desire for the concrete ends that constitute a realization of that duty. In other words, if the matter of the will were extra-rational, concrete realizations, even of one's moral commitments, would essentially depend on a supply of extra-rational matter.

This saddles Kant with a claim that is deeply at odds with our moral self-understanding. When an agent recognizes their moral obligation, i.e., when they realize they *should* or *ought* to do something, they not only recognize what they should do in general terms—for example, that they should keep promises or help friends in need—they are also able to recognize specific concrete courses of action as the morally right thing to do. In particular, an agent can direct herself towards fulfilling a particular end in the course of performing her duty without needing to have, in addition to her capacity to recognize duties in their general form (keep promises or help friends), an extra-rational, *non-moral* desire for that particular end. I need not "feel like" transferring some money, independently of being aware of my duty to repay a debt, in order to do the morally right thing *in concreto*. As the Kantian ethicist would presumably want to put it: I should be able to do the right thing completely independently of whatever it is I anyway happen to feel like doing.

---

deliverances to identify and seek out particular objects" (Tizzard 2018, 632). DeWitt's account comes closest, certainly in its ambitions to the one proposed in this paper. She argues that it is the "extra-rational" conception of feeling and desire that is the source of the problem with the IT account and proposes an account of feelings and desires as partially constituted by reason in order to resolve the problem. However, on Dewitt's account, the performance of action depends on extra-rational matter. Actions, according to her, require "the adoption of an empirical object or state of affairs as the matter of my will," but the sort of feelings reason engenders, so-called "formal" feelings "cannot provide this type of matter." The higher formal feelings "can only motivate me to adopt general principles of good-willing, such as honesty, and this activity is confined to the will itself." For matter, "the lower feelings, as material feelings" must be consulted (Dewitt 2014, 55–56). This implies that in order for me to exercise my duties in concrete circumstances I must have non-rational feelings for the ends that might realize my formal ends. This is the element of her account that I worry belies her ambitions..

In fact, although it is often overlooked, the idea that a particular end can be pursued *from* recognition of one's duty features explicitly in Kant. In the Preface to the First Edition of the *Religion*, Kant writes,

> although morality does not on its own behalf need a presentation of a purpose which would have to precede determination of the will, yet it may well have a necessary reference to such a purpose, namely not as the basis of the maxims adopted in conformity with those laws but as these maxims' necessary consequences.—For without any reference to a purpose, no determination of the will can take place in a human being at all [...]. Without this purpose, a power of choice that, to a projected action, adds in thought no either subjective or objectively determined object (that it has or should have), [hence being] instructed indeed as to *how* it is to operate but not *toward what*, cannot be adequate to itself (Kant, R 6:4)

Crucial to note here is that Kant not only asserts that every action, moral or otherwise, must have a "necessary reference" to a particular purpose, but that the pursuit of material ends can itself come in one of two varieties: The material object of an action can be merely "subjectively" determined, as when an agent pursues an end only because it would contribute to their own satisfaction, but the particular, material end can also be "objectively" determined, as when that end is an effect of a morally required action. Crucially, ends that are both material and objective emerge as the adopted formal principles' "necessary consequences." In other words, we pursue them solely *because* they are the effects of those actions that constitute the concrete realization of our moral duties. They are not extra-rational but proceed from the agent's recognition of what her duties demand of her, right there and then. Thus, the IT's assumption that the object of desire is extra-rational is not only philosophically unattractive; it renders it impossible to find room for the central phenomenon Kant articulates here: that of pursuing particular ends through the recognition of duty.

5 Rethinking Incorporation

To get Kant's actual account of incorporation into view, we can begin by asking: if what gets incorporated is not or is not grounded in an extra-rational desire, what is it? The first thing to note is that in the original incorporation requirement passage Kant does not speak of *Begierde* or *Neigung*, i.e., what we standardly translate as "desire," or "inclination," respectively, at all; the object of incorporation is rather what he calls a *Triebfeder.* Here it is again, for reference:

> The power of choice [*Willkür*] has the quite peculiar characteristic that it cannot be determined to an action by any incentive [*Triebfeder*] except *insofar as the human being has admitted the incentive* [*Triebfeder*] *into his maxim* [*nur sofern der Mensch sie in seine Maxime auf-*

genommen hat] (has made this a universal rule for himself, according to which he wills to conduct himself) (Kant, *R* 6:23–24).

What is incorporated into the singular, most general *Gesinnung*-constituting maxim is a "*Triebfeder.*"[23] What is a *Triebfeder?* Kant defines it as the "subjective ground of desire" (Kant, *G* 4:427) or "subjective determining ground of the will" (Kant, *KpV* 5:72). But what is it that "determines the will"? *Triebfeder* is most commonly translated as "incentive." This is somewhat misleading, however, because, as other interpreters have noted, Kant does not have in mind an object or circumstance that incites the agent to act, like a tax incentive.[24]

Instead, interpreters have proposed that a *Triebfeder* is best thought of as something like "the dynamic or conative factor in willing" (Beck 1996, 216; cf. 90) or "the driving or propelling force from which action or effort springs" (Herrera 2000, 395), as opposed to the cognitive or representational factor. Nevertheless, this reading misses the implication of a key part of Kant's account in the second *Critique:* namely, the idea that when the agent acts from consciousness of the moral law, the moral law *itself* is the *Triebfeder* of the human will (Engstrom 2010, 93).[25] Thus, Stephen Engstrom writes, in order for the moral law to move you, the objective principle must become the subjective principle and thereby become itself *Triebfeder*. In other words, the *Triebfeder* is not a conative "something" that motivates the agent to adopt a certain cognitive principle, it is rather a principle of action—in the good case, the moral law—as *actually motivating* the agent (Engstrom 2010, 93). It is, in other words, the principle insofar as it is adopted as a maxim.

---

[23] This is not of course to suggest that Allison or his followers' error was one of translation. My aim is to draw attention to the fact that by attending to the original term we might find reason to deem its translation by the word "desire," something that perhaps was meant to align Kant's position with contemporary philosophical ones, inadequate. In other words, the question is not whether the object of incorporation is a desire or a *Triebfeder* but rather what a *Triebfeder* is.
[24] This is the sense in which Korsgaard, for example, interprets it: "An incentive is a motivationally loaded representation of an object" (2009, 104–5). Earlier, however, she claims more simply that "incentive" is just Kant's "own language" for "desire or impulse" (Korsgaard 2009, 72). The translation of *Triebfeder* by incentive is persuasively objected to by Larry Herrera (2000, 395, n. 1) and Engstrom (2010, 91–93). I leave the term untranslated.
[25] Indeed, while in the *Groundwork*, Kant uses the term *Triebfeder* exclusively with reference to non-moral activity (see Kant, *G* 4: 400, 404, 407, 411, 412, 419, 425, 427, 431, 439, 441, 444, 449, and 461), from the second *Critique* onward, he employs the notion also to express what it is for reason to be practical in a finite rational being: *the moral law itself* must serve as the will's *Triebfeder* (*KpV* 5:72).

Engstrom was only concerned with the moral *Triebfeder*, but I propose to extend the suggestion that the moral *Triebfeder* is the moral principle as adopted by the agent to the interpretation of the role of both kinds of *Triebfeder*. In so doing, we can interpret the distinction between the moral and non-moral *Triebfedern* against the background of Kant's distinction between moral and non-moral *principles* of action. Consequently, whereas proponents of the IT distinguish non-moral motivation from moral motivation by pointing to non-moral desires' extra-rational source, I suggest that we should understand the contrast between non-moral *Triebfedern* and moral *Triebfedern* as the contrast between acting on *material* (instrumental) principles and acting on *formal* (moral) ones. Accordingly, to admit non-moral *Triebfedern* into one's "supreme maxim" is to admit instrumental principles of action into one's will.

Thinking of moral and non-moral *Triebfedern* along the lines of the distinction between formal and material *principles* is consonant with an oft-neglected strand in Kant's writings prior to the *Religion*. Throughout his critical works, Kant contrasts the kind of action that is performed from consciousness of the laws of reason, or "formal" principles, not with action from empirical or animal causes or sources, but with the sort of action that is directed at particular ends in consciousness of instrumental or "material" *principles* (Kant, *G* 4:428).

In the opening section of the second *Critique*, Kant claims that the difference between the higher and lower faculties of desire is just the difference between the kinds of principle upon which a person can act: material or formal. What is more, Kant makes explicit that both material and formal principles and so both the higher (moral) and lower (sensible) faculties of desire are both "always a product of reason" (*KpV* 5:20). The difference lies in *how* they determine the agent to act: material principles specify what an agent must do to attain a particular effect. Formal, moral principles specify not the effect of an action, but its form, its suitability for the giving of universal law (see Kant, *KpV* 5:21). What is crucial is that whether the agent exercises the lower or higher faculties of desire—namely, whether she acts on a non-moral material principle or a moral-formal one—the agent is acting on a representation of principle and therefore exercising a *rational* capacity to act.

Further evidence for the claim that the contrast between the moral and non-moral action is not one between reason and nature but between formal and material ends and principles is provided by Kant's extensive list of possible non-moral ends an agent might pursue. Kant explicitly states that the representations of ends an agent can pursue in accordance with material principles can have their origin "in the understanding" or even in "reason" (Ibid.) and includes things like reading "an instructive book," enjoying "a fine speech" or "an intellectual conversation," experiencing the "joy" in benefitting "a poor man" (Ibid.) even the "consciousness of our strength of soul in overcoming obstacles opposed to our plans," or "cultivating our talents of spirit" (Ibid.) All of these make sense only as the ends of a rational being, and moreover, could, in principle, be pursued out of recognition of moral duty. But if pursued for their own sake, Kant says, as though they were good in themselves, the actions aiming at such ends would lack moral worth.

Kant's central point here is that *no* particular end is good or bad in itself. Therefore, even what starts as a commitment undertaken for moral reasons can ossify into an action performed simply for the sake of a particular end that is pursued merely for its own sake, in blindness to the requirements of duty. A singular focus on a particular purpose (e.g., scholarship) or the fetishizing of a particular kind of action for its own sake (e.g., political activism) may both be as opposed to the morally good conduct of an upright agent as would be the prioritization of the simplest forms of bodily pleasure.

But if having "sensible" desire is not a matter of having ends from a particular source (say, sensible nature) but is instead about the way an end motivates, i.e., about the sort of principle an agent may act upon, why call it "sensible"? Is the price of the interpretation proposed here ignoring the significance that Kant attributes to our being sensible beings? Not at all, though it does mean that we might want to modify our understanding of what "sensible," in sensible desire, really means. According to Kant, it is a condition of choosing immorally that we have a sensible nature. A will that is not "affected by needs and sensible motives," Kant says, would be a "holy will" that "would not be capable of any maxim conflicting with the moral law" (*KpV* 5:32). But we should be careful not to import our own ideas about what "sensibility" means into our interpretation of Kant. The form of human practical sensibility for Kant is feeling—in particular, pleasure and displeasure. Kant holds that pleasure and displeasure are forms of awareness of the agreement or disagreement of a representation with a power of the mind. In pleasure and displeasure, we sense whether the objects of our representation harm or benefit us qua possessors of different capacities. Some of these capacities are bodily, but not all of them are. Our fundamental mental capacities are rational: the capacity to reason theoretically and practically. A rational, sensible subject thus registers *sensibly*, i.e., through feeling, how objects around them stand to benefit or harm them *qua possessor of rational capacities*, no less than she registers how objects benefit or harm her qua possessor of physical powers and therefore insofar as she is not materially self-sufficient. Thus, for Kant, pleasure is to be had in anything that can benefit us, promote our goals, support our activity, and of which we can be aware. Kant's general account of feeling thus makes intelligible the claim that humans can take pleasure, as in Kant's examples, in distinctly rational ends like intellectual conversation or book reading or the cultivation of one's spiritual talents. Sensibility, in the practical realm, is therefore not a faculty whose principles are merely empirical causal laws or the laws of animal sentience and desire. Practical sensibility can reveal our attitude toward particular ends, whatever they may be. As a consequence, we see we must expand our conception of sensibility—what we are practically receptive to—so that we include the whole gamut of practical ends that practically rational beings plausibly pursue.[26]

According to the account I have presented here, what *morality* constrains, is thus not our extra-rational "nature," but the rational capacity to value—and so act for—*particular* ends. The most important consequence of this account is that it allows us to recognize that the primary locus of the opposition to morality is the capacity to act on principles which guide our action towards particular ends. In other words, the opposition to morality is *internal* to practical reason.

Having clarified the distinction between the two kinds of *Triebfedern* as the distinction between the sort of principles an agent may come to act upon, we can finally identify the proper object of incorporation in Kant's account. In light of the association of the sensible and moral *Triebfedern* with material-particular and formal-moral principles, respectively, we see that when Kant speaks of *Triebfedern* to be incorporated into the general maxim of one's will, we need not take him to mean the incorporation of extra-rational desires characterized by their non-rational form of motivation. Rather, we ought to recognize that claim as referring to the admission, into our highest maxim, of two possible kinds of principles upon which we might act: formal-moral principles and those aiming at particular concrete ends.

To see what all of this means we must consider another key element in Kant's account of the incorporation of *Triebfedern* into the *Gesinnung*-constituting maxim, a feature that finds little room in the interpretation given by the IT's proponents and one which our interpretation puts us in a unique position to understand. A few pages after the "incorporation requirement passage" Kant claims that human beings admit "both incentives [*Triebfedern*] for determining the will" into the supreme maxim, and that the distinction between good and evil character lies not in which *Triebfeder* is admitted but in the "subordination (in the maxim's form): which of the two he makes the condition of the other" (Kant, *R* 6:36). Thus, Kant claims that, without exception, *both* moral and non-moral *Triebfedern* are taken up into the *Gesinnung*-constituting maxim and are ordered by it.

On the standard reading, this could only mean that the agent is saddled with two sources of motivation, which are always in potential conflict with one another, with one source simply given priority over the other. In particular, it means that

---

26 Cf. Kant, *KpV* 5:9, n.; *MS* 6:211; *KU* 5:220, 204, 230–233, and 278; and *Anth* 7:321. For a good exposition of this aspect of Kant's account, see Newton (2017). I discuss Kant's faculty of feeling at greater length in Berg (2021).

the good agent commits herself to pursue her contingent, non-rational desires only as long as these do not conflict with her commitment to the moral law. She is psychologically divided, and her moral activity depends on extra-moral matter to be supplied to her by her desires. By contrast, by interpreting the distinction between *Triebfedern* as the distinction between practical *principles*, we can recognize an altogether different motivation for admitting both kinds of *Triebfedern:* both kinds of principles are admitted because both are necessary for practical agency. No action is merely formal; all action is always directed at a particular purpose, even moral action.

We can also recognize an altogether more attractive notion of subordination, one which points to the hierarchical organization of one's practical priorities: the moral agent always acts on both moral and non-moral principles. Morally good actions stem from a commitment to never let the pursuit of a particular purpose from which one expects gratification, even one that is derived from moral commitments, take priority over commitments to formal and unconditional principles of action; that is, over her commitment to the moral law. Morally bad actions trace to the agent's subordinating the commitment to act from consciousness of the moral law to particular, material goals. This need not involve a stable commitment to the satisfaction of one's every whim; it suffices that an agent makes their moral conduct dependent on the absence of particular circumstances that would, if they were to obtain, constitute a sufficient reason to excuse oneself from doing what she ought to. Thus, according to Kant's incorporation requirement, our freedom to act on desires is grounded not, in the first place, in our responsibility for the evaluation of concrete desires, but in our set of practical priorities: we are responsible for the way in which we organize our practical life as a whole.

Furthermore, this interpretation of the objects of incorporation, *Triebfedern*, as the capacities to act from the recognition of two different kinds of principle, makes room for the idea that particular ends can be pursued not merely insofar as they do not oppose the moral law but also from genuine recognition of one's moral obligations. As we have seen, the IT rendered problematic the possibility of a particular end being pursued from recognition of duty. Conceiving of incorporation in terms of the ordering of principles of action allows us to accommodate the intuition that acting to realize one's duty does not require matter to be supplied by an extra-rational sensible desire, and that an agent's recognition of what they should do can find expression *in concreto*. For according to the interpretation advanced, the revolution that rationality brings to our practical receptive faculties makes it intelligible that the agent could "sensibly desire" an end; that is, pursue an end according to an instrumental principle, which is objectively determined, and thus whose value is moral. An agent, in other words, can act for particular purposes that themselves reflect particular morally worthy ends to pursue.

This means reason can direct itself to particular purposes of its own accord. Reason's form can provide for its own matter: its own objectively determined ends.

6 The Freedom to Do What We Want

According to Kant, to freely do something because I want to do it, is not a matter of rationally evaluating a particular desire, with which I happen to find myself contingently saddled, and in light of such evaluation deeming it a reason to act. It is a matter, rather, of pursuing a particular end, in which I do or expect to find pleasure. In pursuing such a particular end, I exercise a will whose fundamental organizing principle and thus shape, its *Gesinnung*, I have determined and for which I can therefore be held responsible. In this self-organization I determine the priority relation between the pursuit of material ends according to instrumental principles and moral ends according to formal ones. It follows that in pursuing a particular end I may be pursuing an end derived from a formal, moral principle or I may pursue the satisfaction of a simple bodily need. In a sense, I may do either from the recognition of duty or simply for its own sake (for, as I have shown above, even a particular end derived from general moral principle can in turn be pursued as if it is good in itself). No transition from having the desire to the having of a principle is required since to have a particular desire is to have a particular end and a principle of instrumental action aiming at its realization. This principle does not specify that one ought to pursue it and therefore that one has reason to pursue it, it specifies rather how one would go about achieving it. Whatever the moral worth of the action, I am free in acting on such desires because, having admitted both kinds of *Triebfedern*, both kinds of principles or both kinds of action-determination, into my highest maxim, I have freely determined how to subordinate the one to the other.

This interpretation in turn leaves us with an important question, which has been obscured by the proponents of the IT: how should we understand the idea that agents freely determine their own practical priorities (i.e., their moral character)? It is clear that the freedom we exercise over the constitution of our character cannot be an instance of an ordinary exercise of agency—for it is not the result, at least not in any obvious way, of an ordinary act of the will—and therefore good moral character is not something we can simply decide to bring about. Our character, in other words, is not another thing that we can pursue. How, then, can we be held responsible for its structure? Whether Kant has the resources to answer *this* puzzle is an important and difficult question, one which I will have to take up elsewhere. I take it to be one of the major virtues of my account, however, that it allows us to see this puzzle clearly.

Abbreviations

Kant's Works

In the case of the *Critique of Pure Reason*, I follow the standard practice of referring to the 1781 (A) and 1787 (B) editions. For all other texts, citations are given as abbreviation, volume number, and page number as per the *Akademie Ausgabe* (AA), *Kants Gesammelte Schriften*, edited by the *Königlich Preussische Akademie der Wissenschaften* (29 Vols.; Berlin: de Gruyter, 1900–). Unless otherwise stated, all translations come from *The Cambridge Edition of the Works of Immanuel Kant*, edited by Paul Guyer and Allen Wood (Cambridge: Cambridge University Press, 1992–).

References

Allison, Henry E. (1991): *Kant's Theory of Freedom*. Cambridge: Cambridge University Press.
Bagnoli, Carla (2009): "Review of *The Constitution of Agency: Essays on Practical Rason and Moral Psychology*, by Christine M. Korsgaard". In: *Notre Dame Philosophical Reviews*.
Bagnoli, Carla (2011): "Emotions and the Categorical Authority of Moral Reason." In: Bagnoli, Carli (Ed.): *Morality and the Emotions*. Oxford: Oxford University Press, 62–81.
Baron, Marcia (1993a): "Freedom, Frailty, and Impurity." In: *Inquiry* 36. No. 4 (December 1), 431–441.
Baron, Marcia (1993b): "Henry Allison on Kant's Theory of Freedom." In: *Dialogue: Canadian Philosophical Review/Revue Canadienne de Philosophie* 32. No. 4, 775–781.
Beck, Lewis White (1996): *A Commentary on Kant's Critique of Practical Reason*. 2nd ed. Chicago: University of Chicago Press.
Berg, Anastasia (2021): "Kant on Moral Respect." In: *Archiv für Geschichte der Philosophie* 103. No. 4, 730–760.
Bojanowski, Jochen (2007): "Kant und das Problem der Zurechenbarkeit." In: *Zeitschrift Für Philosophische Forschung* 61. No. 2, 207–228.
Boyle, Matthew (2016): "Additive Theories of Rationality: A Critique." In: *European Journal of Philosophy* 24. No. 3, 527–555.
DeWitt, Janelle (2014): "Respect for the Moral Law: The Emotional Side of Reason." In: *Philosophy* 89. No. 1, 31–62.
DeWitt, Janelle (2018): "Feeling and Inclination: Rationalizing the Animal Within." In: Sorenson, Kelly and Williamson, Diane (Eds.): *Kant and the Faculty of Feeling*. Cambridge: Cambridge University Press, 67–87.
Engstrom, Stephen P. (2009): *The Form of Practical Knowledge: A Study of the Categorical Imperative*. Cambridge: Harvard University Press.
Engstrom, Stephen P. (2010): "The Triebfeder of Pure Practical Reason." In: Reath, Andrews and Timmermann, Jens (Eds.): *Kant's Critique of Practical Reason*. Cambridge: Cambridge University Press, 90–118.
Guyer, Paul (2008): *Kant on Freedom, Law, and Happiness*. Cambridge: Cambridge University Press.

Herman, Barbara (2008): *Moral Literacy*. Cambridge: Harvard University Press.
Herrera, Larry (2000): "Kant on the Moral Triebfeder." In: *Kant-Studien* 91. No. 4, 395–410.
Hill, Thomas E. (1991a): *Dignity and Practical Reason in Kant's Moral Theory*. Ithaca: Cornell University Press.
Hill, Thomas E. (1991b): "Kant's Argument for The Rationality of Moral Conduct." In: Hill, Thomas E.: *Dignity and Practical Reason in Kant's Moral Theory*. Ithaca: Cornell University Press, 77–122.
Johnson, Robert N. (1998): "Weakness Incorporated." In: *History of Philosophy Quarterly* 15. No. 3, 349–367.
Kang, Ji-Young (2015): *Die allgemeine Glückseligkeit: Zur systematischen Stellung und Funktionen der Glückseligkeit bei Kant*. Berlin: de Gruyter.
Korsgaard, Christine M. (1996a): *Creating the Kingdom of Ends*. Cambridge: Cambridge University Press.
Korsgaard, Christine M. (1996b): *The Sources of Normativity*. Cambridge: Cambridge University Press.
Korsgaard, Christine M. (2009): *Self-Constitution: Agency, Identity, and Integrity*. Oxford: Oxford University Press.
McCarty, Richard (2008): "Kant's Incorporation Requirement: Freedom and Character in the Empirical World." In: *Canadian Journal of Philosophy* 38. No. 3, 425–451.
McDowell, John (2013): "Avoiding the Myth of the Given." In: McDowell, John: *Having the World in View: Essays on Kant, Hegel, and Sellars*. Cambridge: Harvard University Press, 256–272.
Morrisson, Iain (2005): "On Kantian Maxims: A Reconciliation of the Incorporation Thesis and Weakness of the Will." In: *History of Philosophy Quarterly* 22. No. 1, 73–89.
Newton, Sasha (2017): "Kant on Animal and Human Pleasure." In: *Canadian Journal of Philosophy* 47. No. 4, 518–540.
O'Neill, Onora (1989): *Constructions of Reason: Explorations of Kant's Practical Philosophy*. Cambridge: Cambridge University Press.
Papish, Laura (2007): "The Cultivation of Sensibility in Kant's Moral Philosophy." In: *Kantian Review* 12. No. 2, 128–146.
Peters, Julia (2018): "Kant's Gesinnung." In: *Journal of the History of Philosophy* 56. No. 3, 497–518.
Prauss, Gerold (1983): *Kant Über Freiheit Als Autonomie*. Frankfurt am Main: Klostermann.
Quinn, Warren (1994): "Putting Rationality in Its Place." In: Quinn, Warren: *Morality and Action*. Cambridge: Cambridge University Press.
Rawls, John (2000): *Lectures on the History of Moral Philosophy*. Cambridge: Harvard University Press.
Schadow, Steffi (2012): *Achtung für das Gesetz: Moral und Motivation bei Kant*. 1st ed. Berlin: de Gruyter.
Schapiro, Tamar (2009): "The Nature of Inclination." In: *Ethics* 119. No. 2, 229–256.
Schapiro, Tamar (2011): "Foregrounding Desire: A Defense of Kant's Incorporation Thesis." In: *Journal of Ethics* 15. No. 3, 147–167.
Silber, John R. (1960): "The Ethical Significance of Kant's Religion." In: Kant, Immanuel: *Religion Within the Limits of Reason Alone*. Theodore M. Greene and Hoyt H. Hudson (Trans.). New York: Harper & Row, lxxix–cxxxiv.
Timmermann, Jens (2003): *Sittengesetz und Freiheit: Untersuchungen zu Immanuel Kants Theorie des freien Willens*. Berlin: de Gruyter.
Timmons, Mark (1994): "Evil and Imputation in Kant's Ethics." In: *Jahrbuch für Recht und Ethik* 2, 113–141.
Tizzard, Jessica (2018): "Kant on Space, Time, and Respect for the Moral Law as Analogous Formal Elements of Sensibility." In: *European Journal of Philosophy* 26, 630–646.

Wood, Allen W. (1999): *Kant's Ethical Thought*. Cambridge: Cambridge University Press.

Part III: **Political Philosophy**

Anton Ford and Benjamin Laurence
The Parts and Whole of Plato's Republic

Abstract: In the second book of Plato's *Republic*, Glaucon challenges Socrates to defend the thesis that justice is a benefit to its possessor. As every reader of the dialogue knows, Socrates thinks that the justice of a human being will best be understood after one has considered the justice of a city. But his reason for thinking this is far from obvious. Why should Socrates discuss the city first? Why, indeed, should he bother to discuss it at all? On a familiar interpretation of Socrates' method, what he offers Glaucon is an argument by analogy: the city serves him as an expository device. This interpretation faces many well-known difficulties, including the fact that it appears to leave Socrates without an answer to Glaucon's challenge. We will argue that Socrates begins with an account of the city and proceeds to an account of the soul, not primarily because he believes that a city and a soul are alike, but because he believes that a human being is *part* of a city *by nature* and because a city, as he conceives it, is a natural, functional whole.

1 Introduction

In the second book of Plato's *Republic*, Glaucon challenges Socrates to defend the thesis that justice is a benefit to its possessor. As every reader of the dialogue knows, Socrates thinks that the justice of a human being will best be understood after one has considered the justice of a city. But his reason for thinking this is far from obvious. Why should Socrates discuss the city first? Why, indeed, should he bother to discuss it at all?

Socrates compares the difficulty of answering Glaucon's challenge to the difficulty of reading small letters from a distance, letters that, for some reason, we believe are the same as some bigger ones elsewhere (368d). For his part, Socrates believes that the justice of a human soul is identical in form with the justice of a city (369a, cf. 434d, 435b, 435e): beginning with a just city is, he says, like beginning with the larger inscription. Now, when Socrates first compares the justice of a city to the bigger letters, it is natural to imagine these letters as large and as legible as the Hollywood sign. But a later methodological remark reveals that this is not what Socrates has in mind. After he has identified the justice of his *Kallipolis* but before turning to the individual human being, Socrates warns Glaucon that if justice should turn out to look different in the individual than it did in the city, the account of the city will have to be revised (434e–435a). This suggests that the justice of a city is fairly inscrutable in its own right: if the bigger letters were so big as for it to be obvious what they said, it would be ludicrous to suggest that we revise our interpretation of them on the basis of letters that are illegibly small. Though Socrates evidently believes that it is difficult to read *either* inscription in isolation, he nevertheless thinks we will see *both* of them aright if we examine them together (434e). Just as it requires two fire-sticks to make a fire, Socrates thinks he will need two accounts to illuminate justice (435a). "All will be well," he says, when the two accounts have finally been brought into line (434d).

These methodological remarks are commonly taken to announce an argument by analogy.[1] On any such interpretation, Socrates believes that the justice of a soul is *like* the justice of a city: this is what it means that the two inscriptions say the same thing. He also believes that the justice of a city is easier to apprehend: this is what it means that one inscription is bigger. So, the city will serve Socrates as an expository device. He will exploit the given similarity in order to illuminate the soul, which is the primary object of his interest.

The usual interpretation of Socrates' method, which is first encouraged by his methodological remarks, seems later to be confirmed by the results of his investigation.

For Socrates' accounts of the city and the soul are, in the end, obviously and intentionally parallel. According to him, a just soul, like a just city, is one each part of which performs its own function.[2]

However, the usual interpretation faces a number of formidable difficulties. In the first place, it is unclear why Socrates (or we) should expect that the justice of a city and the justice of a soul are, in any interesting way, alike.[3] Even supposing that they are, it is difficult to understand why Socrates should go on to devote the great-

---

[1] See, for example, Annas (1981,72–73) and (1999, 81–83), Cross and Woozley (1964, 75–78), Irwin (1971, 204, n. 29), Kraut (1997, 201), Murphy (1951, 68–86 and 89), Reeve (1998, 236–237), White (1979, 82–83), Grote (1998, 46), and Williams (1997, 49).

[2] See 435b.

[3] Annas (1981, 73) writes that "Plato does not even consider the possibility at the outset that justice in the case of cities, and collections of individuals, might be a very different matter from justice in the case of an individual." Concerning Socrates' remark that the word "justice" is predicated of cities and individuals alike, Vlastos (1971, 88) comments: "Had Plato seen...how absurd it would be to expect that a man, a complexion, a habitat, and a diet must be 'exactly alike' in the respect in which the predicate 'healthy' applies to each, he could scarcely have failed to see how little his [argument at 435a] would cover the case of a predicate like 'just.'" Cross and Woozley (1964, 77) look elsewhere in the text for an argument that a just city and a just soul are alike, and reach for the idea (at 435e) that the justice of a city *comes from*—and therefore resembles?—the justice of its citizens: "[Socrates'] argument at 435e may or may not be a good argument, but it is there." Williams (1997, 50) claims that, in fact, the argument at 435e induces a regress. Most commentators who attribute to Socrates an argument by analogy conclude, in the end, that he has not said enough to justify this method.

er part of the dialogue to his account of a just city—if, that is, this is merely an object of comparison, introduced for the sake of an analogy with the soul. What is more, Socrates discusses countless features of the city to which he never draws any psychic analogy.[4] How, then, are we to avoid the conclusion that much of the dialogue is a highly elaborate distraction, which fails to serve even the modest function of an expository device?

The most serious difficulty for the usual interpretation is that it appears to leave Socrates without an answer to Glaucon's challenge. Near the end of Book IV (444c–445b), Socrates argues that one cannot be happy unless each part of one's soul performs its proper function—that is, unless one possesses psychic justice. He appears to think that in giving this argument he has offered some form of answer to Glaucon's challenge, for at this point he and Glaucon agree that the challenge looks "ridiculous" (445b). However, David Sachs has rightly emphasized that Socrates' principal task in the *Republic* is to show, not that happiness depends on having a well-functioning soul, but that it depends on treating others fairly, on refraining from actions like murder and swindling, actions that are proscribed by the justice of a city.[5] But if the primary relation between what goes on in a well-functioning soul (psychic justice) and what goes on in a well-functioning city (civic justice) is *analogical*, then Socrates appears to need an additional argument to the effect that a well-functioning soul does not, in fact, issue in actions like murder and swindling. But no such argument is to be found in the text.

In view of these difficulties, there is reason to seek an alternative to the usual interpretation of Socrates' method.

If you ask someone to defend his judgment that such-and-such is health in a human hand, and if he begins his reply by explaining certain facts about the anatomy of the entire body, doing so on the grounds that you could not understand the answer to your question without appreciating these facts, he is *not* giving you an argument by analogy. Neither, we will argue, is Socrates. We will argue that Socrates begins with an account of the city and proceeds to an account of the soul, not primarily because he believes that a city and a soul are alike, but because he believes that a human being is *part* of a city *by nature*, and because a city, as he conceives it, is a natural, functional whole. This latter is to say, not only that a city is a natural whole, and that it has a function, but also that each of its parts has a func-

---

4 Socrates discusses the sort of story that should be told to children, and the equality of women, to choose two random examples. But now, to what features of a soul could these features of a city conceivably be analogous? Annas (1999, 83) mentions this as a problem for the extreme view that Socrates' discussion of the city is merely metaphorical, but she does not explain how it can be avoided by a proponent of the usual interpretation.

5 See Sachs (1963). We return to the problem raised by Sachs in §6 below.

tion, a function that serves simultaneously to further the work of the whole and to further the work of each of its other parts.[6]

It is no secret that Socrates thinks something of the sort. He is forever comparing a city to a body, a citizen to a bodily part, and the virtue of justice to health.[7] But the idea that there is a natural relation between an individual human being and some larger social whole is nowadays widely regarded with suspicion. Recent commentators have tended to play down this idea (without denying its presence in the dialogue), roughly to the extent that they have *defended* Plato's ethical and political teachings. The scholarly consensus is that Socrates is an individualist: he believes that the nature, virtue, and happiness of a human being can all be understood without reference to the *polis*, and that the *polis* is a conglomeration to which an individual belongs accidentally, rather than by nature. Much of our effort will be directed against that presumption.[8] For we think it prevents one from seeing even the rough shape of Socrates' argument. Our own interpretation is to be justified by the result that many problems now commonly thought to ruin the argument will immediately vanish. We count among these, not only the fallacy alleged by Sachs and the other difficulties mentioned above, but also the appearance that Socrates merely assumes that justice is a virtue in a city.[9] As we are concerned with the whole of Plato's republic and not the whole of his *Republic*, we will limit our discussion to Books I-IV.

In order to show that Socrates is arguing from whole to part and not from like to like, we need not deny that he thinks a city and a soul are alike or even that this thought plays a role in his argument. We need only to show that the salient resemblances are subordinate to a more encompassing structure, and that this structure

---

[6] We will elaborate the idea of a functional whole in §3.

[7] For some conspicuous examples in the *Republic*, see 357c–e, 420c–e, 444c–e, 462c–e, and 608e–610b. See also *Gorgias* 479a–c.

[8] Our proposal is in line with a tradition of reading the *Republic* that seems to have ended sometime during the Cold War. There is a casual acknowledgement of Plato's "organicism," as it is now disparagingly called, on every page of Barker (1906) and Foster (1931). And in an essay originally published in 1912, Cornford (1997) could begin with these words: "It is now generally recognized that Plato's whole theory of the Ideal State is based upon the principle that human society is 'natural' (φύσει). As against the antisocial doctrines of certain sophists, this proposition means, in the first place, a denial of the view that society originated in a primitive contract. But Plato does not merely reject this false opinion; he also sets up an alternative doctrine that the state is natural, in the sense that a human society constructed on ideal lines would be one that should reflect the structure of man's soul, and give full play to the legitimate functions of every part of his nature." What was once "generally recognized" to be Plato's view is no longer even acknowledged as an interpretative possibility. It is now presumed obvious that Plato holds the very "antisocial doctrines" that Cornford attributes to the sophists.

[9] The last point is discussed in §5 below.

is what explains and unifies Socrates' basic theses.[10] To this end, let us distinguish two claims that Socrates makes for an analogy between a city and a soul: first is the claim that a city and a soul are both functional entities composed of functional parts (with all that this entails about the harmonious relations of their parts); second is the claim that the parts of a city and the parts of a soul are equal in number and similar in function. Notice that the first claim is logically weaker: it is presupposed and elaborated by the second but by no means entails it. Now consider the following passage from Book V, where Socrates asks Glaucon *how* a city is like a human being:

> What is it about the city that is most like a single person? For example, when one of us hurts his finger, the entire organism that binds body and soul together into a single system under the ruling part within it is aware of this, and the whole feels the pain together with the part that suffers. That's why we say that the man has a pain in his finger. And the same can be said about any part of a man, with regard either to the pain it suffers or to the pleasure it experiences when it finds relief.—Certainly. And, as for your question, the city with the best government *is* most like such a person.—Then, whenever anything good or bad happens to a single one of its citizens, such a city above all others will say that the affected part is its own and will share in the pleasure or pain as a whole (462c–e).

This passage is particularly important for understanding Socrates' method because in it, he addresses both analogy and mereology at once. Socrates says that a good city and a human being are "most" alike inasmuch as they both have parts, and are related to their parts in similar ways: here we have the first point of analogy, upon which the second depends. But Socrates does not present a city and a human being as two entities, side-by-side, which happen both to have parts. For he says that the parts of a city are human beings! This means that the parts of a human being—body and soul, to begin with, and the parts of each of these—are themselves parts (or subparts) of a city, rather as the parts of an organ are parts of the organism to which the organ belongs. For our purposes, the important point is that any analogical relation there may be between a city and a soul is subordinate to a mereological relation.

The idea that a human being is naturally a part of a functional whole in fact fits very nicely with Socrates' methodological remarks. A functional whole is, in some fairly straightforward sense, "bigger" than its parts. Because the functions of the whole and its parts are internally related, it is necessary for someone

---

[10] Lear (1998, 220) too argues that the analogy between city and soul is embedded in a larger structure. We write in sympathy with his claim that, "*psyche*-analysis and *polis*-analysis are, for Plato, two aspects of a single discipline," and hope that our analysis of the *polis* might complement his analysis of the *psyche*.

who is interested in a part to investigate the whole; and if it is not quite necessary to *begin* with the whole, this is at least a perfectly reasonable way to proceed. Moreover, it is reasonable to revise one's account of the whole in light of one's account of a part, for the two accounts must ultimately harmonize. Now the claim that a just city and a just soul share the same form is put forward to legitimize Socrates' method, and it is connected with an observation about ordinary language (see again 369a, 434d, 435b, 435e). Socrates points out that both a city and a soul may be called just. Notice that it is likewise the case that both a body and a hand may be called healthy. A complete account of the health of the body *is* a complete account of the health of a hand, and vice versa: for the health of the hand and the health of the body are not two things, but one, and their account is one, as the body and hand are one. But of what there is one account, is there not also—one form?

Needless to say, an interpretation of Socrates' methodological remarks must stand or fall with an interpretation of the method he actually pursues. Our aim here is to sketch the argument of Books I-IV in the broadest possible strokes. In §2, we will argue that the accounts of justice put forward by Socrates' principal interlocutors are united by an underlying conception of human nature, according to which society unites human beings in something like the way that a contest unites its contestants. In §3, we turn to Socrates' account of a city: we will argue that he conceives of a city as a functional whole the members of which are "partners and helpers" (369c), rather than the adversaries that his interlocutors imagined. Next, we will draw out the implications of Socrates' account of a city, first for his conception of happiness in §4 and then for his conception of justice in §§5 and 6. Finally, in §7, we will attempt to distinguish the form of Socrates' account from its content, with a view to showing how much of its political and psychological content may be criticized, and rejected, even by one who is committed to an account of the same form.

2 Polemarchus, Thrasymachus and Glaucon

To see what Socrates is arguing in the *Republic*, one must first see, at least in outline, what he is arguing against. Our aim in this section is to show that Polemarchus, Thrasymachus and Glaucon are all moved by the same general conception of human nature. We will argue that their three accounts of justice are three increasingly sophisticated expressions of the idea that human beings are united in their life together as adversaries. This conception of human nature is, we think, the real object of Socrates' criticism. We offer the following abstract reflections about competition and cooperation as a simple framework within which to understand the dialogue's central dispute.

2.1 Competition and Cooperation

Some of the things we do we can only do together: playing checkers, for example, or felling a tree with a two-man crosscut saw. We might call these *collective activities* to mark that they essentially involve a plurality of agents, and to distinguish them from *solitary activities* such as hammering a nail or playing the card game solitaire.

Among collective activities, we can distinguish those that are *competitive* from those that are *cooperative* according as they unite their participants either as *adversaries* or as *partners*. Where the activity is competitive, doing is a matter of outdoing. It is built into the game of checkers, for example, not only that there should be two players, but that the two should be at odds: the end pursued by each player is precisely his own victory over the other. Note that the ends in question are *opposed*, and not merely distinct: far from being unconcerned with his opponent's doing well, each is positively set against it; indeed, the failure of his opponent is the *sole* concern of each inasmuch as this is identical with his own success. In a game of checkers, as in a duel, or in a wrestling or a tennis match, each participant attends to the moves of his adversary because getting the better of him requires divining his intentions and thwarting his efforts, discovering and exploiting his weaknesses and capitalizing on his mistakes. And since each knows this of the other, he employs what tricks he can to conceal his own plan of action, or else, if it is possible, he simply overpowers him. Hobbes rightly observed that "force and fraud are in war the two cardinal virtues."[11] But the remark applies as well to tennis as to war. For it is a feature of competitive activities as such that to be good at them—that is, to possess the salient intelligence and skill—is to be capable of getting and maintaining the upper hand over another by just such means as these.[12]

---

[11] Hobbes (1996, 85). Reginald E. Allen (1987) also sees competition and cooperation as being at the heart of the dispute between Socrates and his interlocutors and also draws the connection to Hobbes.

[12] The remarks of this paragraph have nothing to do with cheating or dirty play; they concern the internal dynamics of a competitive activity as such, and are intended to be uncontroversial. The point of these reflections is ultimately to illuminate the debate between Socrates and his interlocutors over justice, so we have emphasized the features of competitive and cooperative activities

In cooperative activities, agents are joined, not as adversaries, but as partners. Now, felling a tree with a crosscut saw is as much a job for two as checkers is a game for two. But whereas the adversaries in a competitive activity pursue ends that are distinct and opposed, the partners in a cooperative activity share a single end and pursue that end together. Because partners share an end, they also share success or failure. It follows that two partners, considered merely as such, never have a thought of outdoing one other, whereas two adversaries never think of anything else. And while each partner, like each adversary, attends to the actions of the other, this is in order to further his partners efforts and not to undermine them. Where the one partner is noticeably weak, struggling or in need of something, the other lends his strength, support, or aid. Neither sees his partner's inability as an opportunity to exploit; for his partner's inability is, in a sense, his own. This being so, partners tend to communicate, rather than to conceal, their intentions. Here force and fraud are out of place.

Now the internal structure of certain activities neatly combines competition and cooperation. Where the opponents in a contest are collective agents rather than individuals—as in a war, a soccer match or a game of bridge—there are teams or sides. But at the same time that opposing teams are related as adversaries, players are related within a team as partners: thus, the end shared by the members of one team—viz. their own victory over their opponents—is opposed to the end shared by the members of the other. With these observations in mind, let us turn to the text.

Polemarchus

The poet Simonides wrote that, "It is just to give to each what is owed to him" (331e). What he meant by this, Socrates claims, is that it is just to give a person what is *appropriate* or *fitting* for him (332c). Polemarchus accepts this interpretation and offers a substantive account of what it is to treat people appropriately: it is appropriate, he says, to benefit one's friends and to harm one's enemies (332b and 334b). Polemarchus' double-standard may appear too unpromising an account of justice to merit serious philosophical consideration. But in fact, it inaugurates the idea that will occupy Socrates for the remainder of the *Republic*—an idea that is helpfully expressed here in a crude and unguarded form. As the game of football collects the players on a field into opposing teams, Polemarchus imagines

---

that are relevant to that debate. Nothing we have said is meant to imply that there is anything morally objectionable about enjoying competitive games.

that social life collects human beings into relations that are essentially adversarial. Nothing could be more appropriate for a football player than to further the efforts of his teammates and to undermine those of his opponents. Likewise, Polemarchus thinks, it is appropriate for a human being to benefit his friends and to harm his enemies.[13]

Polemarchus' account of justice first comes to grief when he tries to specify the matters in which justice is useful. He tells Socrates that justice is concerned with guarding money for safe keeping (333c). The problem is that if justice is helping one's friends and harming one's enemies, it would seem that it is appropriate to *guard* money only when it has been deposited by a friend, and that when an enemy deposits the money, justice demands one to *steal* it. Thus, Polemarchus appears to be committed to the thesis that a just person is as much a thief as he is a guardian (334b). Though he concedes this must be false, Polemarchus boldly reaffirms his original claim. Socrates then confronts him with another of its apparent consequences: if Polemarchus' account is correct, then justice requires one to harm people who are good and innocent of any wrong-doing, so long as they happen to be one's enemies (334d). Of course, Polemarchus cannot bring himself to accept this, either. No one as conventionally-minded as he could maintain that justice requires thieving and harming the innocent: for justice is conventionally thought to exclude precisely these actions; and what is more, justice is thought to be a virtue, whereas these actions are thought to be vicious.

---

13 In fact, the theme of competition reappears throughout Socrates' discussion with Polemarchus, beginning with their very first exchange. When Polemarchus and his friends overtake Socrates and Glaucon, who are heading back to Athens, Polemarchus makes a joking threat that he and his companions will force Socrates to do what they want: "Do you see how many we are? [Y]ou must either prove stronger than we are, or you will have to stay here" (327c). Socrates questions whether they are right to conceive themselves as matched in a contest of strength, rather than as partners to a rational conversation: "Isn't there another alternative, namely, that we persuade you to let us go?" Later, when Socrates asks what field of activity stands to justice as healing stands to the art of medicine, Polemarchus' reply is "wars and alliances" (332e). Once he has been forced to admit that justice is also valuable in peacetime, Polemarchus says that what it is useful for is getting partnerships in money matters (333a). Now, Polemarchus was famously the son of a rich arms dealer, and it cannot have been lost on Plato's audience that nearly every word put into his mouth concerns either arms or deals. War is a paradigm of adversarial activity, where (if anywhere) stealth and force are obviously fitting. But in business, too, one's own advantage is always at odds with that of the competition.

Thrasymachus

These difficulties are resolved by Thrasymachus, who carries on the spirit of Polemarchus' account in a more coherent and radical form. The details of Thrasymachus' account of justice are notoriously difficult to pin down, and scholars debate whether all of the things he says are consistent with each other, much less expressions of a single idea.[14] But Plato marks a point in the dialogue where Thrasymachus' driving thought is finally articulated. At this point, Socrates says, chillingly: "We mustn't shrink from pursuing the argument and looking into this, just as long as I take you to be saying what you really think. And I believe that you aren't joking now, Thrasymachus, but are saying what you believe to be the truth" (349a). What Thrasymachus says, once he has stopped joking, is that true human excellence lies in injustice. To see how this resolves the difficulties that confounded Polemarchus, recall that Polemarchus tried to maintain: (1) the adversarial conception of human nature and society (implicit in his account of justice); (2) the conventional idea that justice rules out actions like stealing and harming the innocent; and (3) the equally conventional idea that justice is a virtue. Thrasymachus realizes that if the third idea is rejected, the first two can be coherently maintained. He therefore claims justice is a human vice: it is not a trivial defect of the body but an infirmity of the soul suffering from which one goes about one's entire life in the wrong way; it is a thing worthy of scorn, or perhaps pity, but certainly not the praise it commonly receives.

Though he thinks that justice is a vice, Thrasymachus has a fairly conventional conception of what is involved in being just. He is happy to say, for instance, that justice requires treating others fairly; that it involves being honest, peaceable and beneficial, not only in relation to friends but all around (343d–e); and that a just person is not the sort to try to get the better of his fellows (349b). Moreover, he is happy to say that injustice is characterized by the use of "stealth and force" in maintaining the upper hand over others (344a).[15] What Thrasymachus praises as the health and vigor of the human soul is *pleonexia*, the state of character that is, on all accounts, directly opposed to justice.

---

14 On the interpretation we are proposing, inconsistencies are to be expected: just as difficulties internal to Polemarchus' position are worked out by Thrasymachus, so difficulties internal to Thrasymachus' position will in turn be worked out by Glaucon. If the three accounts are indeed related in this way, then the salient problems with each of the first two accounts are indicated by the shape of the account that follows.

15 The importance of "stealth and force" in Plato's conception of injustice is signaled by Socrates, whose immediate response to Thrasymachus begins from the idea that injustice is exercised through "trickery or open warfare" (345a).

Pleonexia fits a human being to live well only on the assumption that our living together is the kind of activity in which doing well is outdoing. It is important to see that if this underlying conception of human nature is accurate, then Thrasymachus is right: justice is a vice. To bring this out, we may imagine a kind of sentimentalist about tennis, all of whose actions are guided by the concern that his opponent do well: from the fact that his opponent has a weak backhand, he infers that he ought to serve to the forehand; and when his opponent serves the ball, he lets it go by. He is wildly confused, for he thinks that this is how the game is played —not in special circumstances that call for something less than one's full effort, but normally and by its experts. Yet, as everyone knows, it is not for his having *such* thoughts or for his acting in *such* ways that someone is an excellent player. According to Thrasymachus, anyone who believes that justice is human excellence is a kind of sentimental idiot, radically mistaken about the kind of game we are playing.[16]

Glaucon

When Thrasymachus loses his composure, Glaucon takes over, giving the idea first introduced by Polemarchus its most sophisticated and persuasive expression. Glaucon famously prefaces his account with a three-fold division of goods (357b–d). He does so in order to argue that justice, like surgery, is onerous in itself and good only for the sake of what comes from it. He wants Socrates to argue against this and to prove that justice is instead like being healthy: something that is good not only for what it brings but for its own sake as well.

Glaucon's account of justice takes the form of a creation myth, but inasmuch as this is intended to be an articulation of the nature of justice (358c) and not an

---

[16] Let us make a brief suggestion about how all this might be related to Thrasymachus' earlier claim that justice is the advantage of the stronger (338c–339a). Much of what he says in that speech falls neatly into place if it is seen against his background conception of human nature. For if the members of a society are locked in a competition in which success is a matter of getting and maintaining the upper hand over everyone else, then a ruler is naturally seen as the reigning champion —one who has already used stealth and force to defeat his opponents, and who now constantly defends his title against challengers by means of laws that he manipulates to his advantage. Against that background, Thrasymachus appears to be right about what the art of ruling is. He also appears to be right in thinking that laws established in accordance with that art will dictate actions that benefit those in power. In saying this little, we admittedly pass over countless matters of detail. But our aim here is only to suggest the shape of an idea that promises to organize the various pronouncements of Thrasymachus and to place him in line with Polemarchus and Glaucon.

exercise in speculative anthropology, we may abstract from its historical trappings. The by now familiar line of thought is encapsulated in Glaucon's opening claim that "to do injustice is naturally good and to suffer it naturally bad" (358e). As Glaucon has it, we are by nature creatures who aim "to outdo others and to get more and more—this is what anyone's nature naturally pursues as good" (359c). Since human beings are each others' natural adversaries, human flourishing is a kind of supremacy, the capacity to win it is excellence, and the actions through which it is typically won are naturally good actions.

But Glaucon goes on to point out that a perpetrator of injustice often benefits significantly less than his victim is harmed (358e). Indeed, if nothing restrained the use of stealth and force in our struggle for supremacy—if people went around inflicting the greatest harm upon others for the slightest advantage to themselves—the typical person would live in constant peril. That is why it necessary for us to impose laws upon ourselves and why we praise those who curb their own *pleonexia*. It serves everyone (except the most powerful) to have the protections of law and reputation in place (359a). Still, the whole business of justice is properly understood as an artifice designed to inhibit our true nature. That we treat it with respect is a kind of "perversion" (359c).

The fact that we have the protections of law and reputation does nothing to alter our fundamental antagonism—a fight in padded gloves is nonetheless a fight—but it does make winning the advantage more complicated than it would otherwise be. For as things stand, to break the law is risky business. And no one will get ahead in life who is known to employ stealth and force. Since we often need the help of others to get what we need, we are forced to win their trust; and this requires that we at least *appear* to be trustworthy. On Glaucon's account, there is nothing wrong with injustice except that, if it is discovered, it tends to incur harsh punishments and to undermine our success in a subtle contest. It is thus good and wise and to any individual's advantage to throw off the gloves, when he can do so without getting caught. Anyone who is not "wretched and stupid" will do just this when the occasion arises (360d). For a person whose "way of life is based on the truth about things" (362a) sees that justice is a burden and practices it only unwillingly (359b).

Thus understood, Glaucon's account of justice is a notable improvement over that of Thrasymachus. In the first place, Glaucon points out that violence, deceit and unlawfulness are apt to cause one trouble in life; and that many social and financial advantages accrue to a person who has a reputation for justice. This went totally unacknowledged by Thrasymachus, who refused to count justice as a good even of the lowest sort. Glaucon also insists that life would be impossible for most of us without the impositions of law and reputation. This means that justice is an advantage, not only for rulers, as Thrasymachus claimed, but for the ruled as well. It is no doubt common sense thoughts like these that lead Polemarchus to say that justice is a benefit to its possessor. Glaucon shows that this conventional belief is not as wildly confused about human life as Thrasymachus would have had us believe.

Perhaps Thrasymachus would have embraced Glaucon's account. Doing so would have enabled him to recuperate the common sense moving Polemarchus while maintaining his own driving thought. For although, on Glaucon's account, justice inhibits the exercise of our natural *pleonexia*, still, pleonectic satisfaction remains the standard of human well-being. So, justice is at once a natural vice and a pantomime virtue.

In his closing remarks, Glaucon offers a final description of the unjust man that neatly ties the three accounts together:

> He rules his city because of his reputation for justice; he marries into any family he wishes; he gives his children in marriage to anyone he wishes; he has contracts and partnerships with anyone he wants; and besides benefiting himself in all these ways, he profits because he has no scruples about doing injustice. *In any contest, public or private, he's the winner and outdoes his enemies.* And by outdoing them, he becomes wealthy, benefiting his friends and harming his enemies…That's what they say, Socrates, that gods and humans provide a better life for unjust people than for just ones (362b–c).

Glaucon invokes Thrasymachus with his allusion to a ruler who profits himself by injustice; and his reference to contracts and partnerships recalls Polemarchus, whose definition of justice is then explicitly quoted. Glaucon thus presents his own account as the culmination of the two that preceded it. He suggests that at the center of it all has been a picture of human life as a contest, a contest that injustice fits one to win. If Socrates is to show that justice belongs in the highest class of goods, he will have to explain what is wrong with this conception of human life.

3 The Nature of a City and a Citizen

As he indicated that he would in his methodological remarks, Socrates begins his reply to Glaucon with an account of the city:

> I think a city comes to be because none of us is self-sufficient (αὐτάρκης), but all need many things. Do you think that a city is founded on any other principle?—No.—And because people need many things, and because one person calls on a second out of one need and on a third out of a different need, many people gather in a single place to live together as partners and helpers. And such a settlement is called a city (369b–c).

What Socrates describes here is the genesis of a city.¹⁷ But as the genesis of a thing may be natural or artificial, the question arises which sort of genesis Socrates has in mind. Is he thinking that a city is a natural growth, to which a human being belongs by nature? Or is he rather thinking it is an artifact, a conglomeration of naturally independent individuals, who for some reason find it expedient to join their disparate forces? Much depends on the answer to this question. For if a human being is naturally a citizen, then human virtue and happiness cannot be understood in abstraction from civic life. Whereas they must be so understood if a human being is not by nature part of such a whole.

Commentators today seldom pause to consider the question. They proceed as though it were obvious that Socrates holds the latter, individualistic conception of human nature.¹⁸ This, however, was not obvious to Aristotle, who rejected individualism himself, and who did so in the apparent belief that this was a point on which he and Socrates could agree. Aristotle criticizes Socrates throughout the *Politics*, perhaps even exaggerating their differences on occasion, but he never complains that Socrates denied or even that he failed to affirm the fundamental thesis of Aristotle's own theory: that a city is a natural creation and man by nature a civic creature.¹⁹ On the contrary, Aristotle defends this thesis in terms that he borrows directly from Socrates himself:

> The proof that the polis is a creation of nature and prior to the individual is that the individual, when isolated, *is not self-sufficient* (αὐτάρκης); and therefore he is like a part in relation

---

17 Here and throughout this paper, we are using the word "city" as a technical term, as Socrates uses the word "polis" (369c). The entities in question need not resemble Paris, much less France. Vlastos (1995a, 78, n. 40) rightly emphasizes that Socrates' account here "abstracts rigorously from all political institutions (no mention of government, laws, courts, army and the like)."

18 Thus, Cross and Woozley (1964, 80) write: "It should be realized not only that Plato supposes men induced to cooperate by their *economic* needs, but also that he maintains that they do so entirely selfishly. The first city is no high-minded community, fired by ideals of brotherly love. It is a group of men, each still out for his own interest as much as if he were living in a state of nature, but now realizing that enlightened self-interest is better served by a degree of cooperation. [...] It is straightforward capitalism: 'to each what by economic exchange he can get.' The attitude which Socrates ascribes to each of his imaginary citizens is that of putting into the common stock, or on the market, whatever he must in order to get out of it what he wants." That Cross and Woozley take the individualistic conception of human nature for granted (and so beg the question we have raised) is clear from their sense of the possibilities: the cooperation Socrates describes must be understood *either* as egoism *or* as altruism. They do not recognize the possibility that human beings might have a shared interest. This theme will recur in §5.

19 See Aristotle (1984), 1253a2–3.

to the whole. But he who is unable to live in society, *or who has no need because he is sufficient for himself,* must be either a beast or a god (1253a25–28).[20]

This appears to be an allusion precisely to *Republic* 369b.

Quite apart from what Aristotle thought, the individualistic interpretation of 369b is implausible. Socrates' claim that "none of us is self-sufficient" is *on the face of it* a claim about our nature. Notice, first, that it is categorical, much like the claim that we have speech but not telepathy, and thumbs but not wings. Moreover, the claim is conspicuously presented as the starting point of Socrates' argument that justice is a genuine human virtue. But the virtue of a living thing is nothing but a perfection of its nature. So, it would be very strange for Socrates to argue from our lack of self-sufficiency if he supposed this were an accidental feature of human life. Nor is there any sign, here or elsewhere, that he *does* think it is accidental.[21]

But if it is by nature that we lack self-sufficiency, then by nature we possess the "partners and helpers" who answer to our lack. For it is in general the case that a living thing has by nature, not only its need, but also the goods by which that need is satisfied and the means by which such goods are obtained. Along with its characteristic hunger, the spider has both its fly and its web. Now the spider is a solitary creature in the sense that *its* way of providing for itself does not involve others of its kind. But very young children know that not all creatures are like this—that a honeybee, for instance, obtains what it needs largely through the activity of other bees, together with whom it forms a hive. The point here is not that it is impossible for a honeybee to survive alone, but only that, if one were somehow to do so, *this* would be an accident, alien to its nature. We might express this homely truth by saying that, though the spider is, the honeybee is not self-sufficient. The corresponding truth about human beings is equally plain: we do not get what we need by ourselves; this is not our way. Socrates calls a city whatever

---

20 When Aristotle says that a city is a whole, what he has in mind is a functional whole, comparable to a body. The quoted sentence is preceded by this: "the city is by nature clearly prior to the family and to the individual, since the whole is of necessity prior to the part; for example, if the whole body be destroyed, there will be no foot or hand, except homonymously" (1253a19–21).
21 Vlastos (1995b) is representative of the interpretation we are opposing here. Vlastos (1995b, 106) says of the city introduced at 369b: "Its people had to choose between two options: on one hand, self-sufficiency, every man working only for himself, relying on his own labor to meet all of his needs; on the other, interdependence, every man working for himself *and* for each of his neighbors..." Vlastos appears to understand Socrates' claim that "none of us is self-sufficient" to mean that each of us is self-sufficient: for otherwise how could there be a choice between self-sufficiency and interdependence? The idea that we "choose" to be part of a city is nowhere in the text.

stands to human need as a hive stands to the honeybee's. Need is the principle of its unity, and our place in it is every bit as natural as our need.

This interpretation of 369b is confirmed by the subsequent development of Socrates' account. He begins with our need for food, shelter, and clothing (369d). But because the availability of such goods depends on their having already been produced by human beings, he straightaway introduces the farmer, the builder, and the weaver (369d). Socrates then reminds us that no productive activity is self-sufficient, but each needs many things: farming, building and weaving each depend for their possibility on the antecedent production of their tools and materials, as in turn do the productive activities responsible for these (370d). The idea is familiar from the opening lines of Aristotle's *Nicomachean Ethics*. When its implications are drawn out, the result is a system of mutually dependent productive activities related to one another as parts of a whole. Out of this whole, there arises: an olive, a house, a pair of shoes—whatever it may be that satisfies the day-to-day needs of an individual human being.

Socrates says that the members of a city "share things with one another, giving and taking" (369c). The meaning of this claim is best understood in connection with the system of activities we have just described. Notice that Socrates' construction of the city proceeds in two clearly marked phases. He first asks Glaucon how the necessary productive activities should be distributed amongst the members of the city (369d). Once this question has been answered, Socrates turns to the distribution of goods: "And how will those in the city itself share the things that each produces?" (371b). With an answer to the second question, the city is said to be complete (371e). The two questions that frame Socrates' construction of the city are on the face of it questions of policy, and we will eventually need to say a word about the specific policies that Socrates endorses.[22] But the tasks that these (or some other) policies are needed to address have been set for Socrates by a prior conception of the nature of a city. In asking *how* the city's work and goods are to be shared, he has already presupposed *that* they are to be shared. We discern, then, behind his pair of questions, the following two defining features of a city: (1) what a city does is done by its citizens, each of them doing a share, and (2) what a city has is had by its citizens, each of them having a share. The share that each individual citizen does is his contribution to the sum total of activity performed by the city as a whole, upon which sum total of activity depends, not only the share that he himself has, and so not only his own life and well-being but also that of each of his fellow citizens.

---

22 See §5.

Socrates develops his account of a city by focusing on material need. But of course, our need is not only material, and our mutual dependence is not only economic. Since Socrates introduces the members of a city as responding to one another's need quite generally (369b–c), we should expect him to have other aspects of human life in view, even at the earliest stage of his account. And indeed he does: we find the members of his rustic village sharing meals together, enjoying sex and singing hymns to the gods. These activities reflect a many-sided need and a many-sided dependence on others of our kind. As Socrates' account of the city develops, other, more exalted aspects of human life will enter the scene: e.g., education, art, medicine, law and philosophy. In all of these ways and more, partners and helpers answer to our lack of self-sufficiency.

To understand the significance of Socrates' account of a city in Book II, it is helpful to consider how it fits with his earlier claim that a city belongs under a common genus with an army and a band of robbers (351c–352c). He calls each of these groups a "tribe". If we allow ourselves momentarily to abstract from the differences between a city and these other tribes, so that we may consider the lot generically, the first thing we will notice is a common teleological structure. A tribe is a functional whole: each of its parts has a function, and the function of each part is such as to harmonize both with that of the other parts, and with that of the whole. This much can also be said of an artifact or a living organism. In each case, the salient harmony of part with part and of part with whole is made possible by the structure of the activity that it is the function of the whole to perform. Notice that in each case, the activity of the whole can be analyzed into teleologically ordered parts: a clock keeps time, but this involves various movements of gears, springs and hands; a hummingbird lives, but its life-activity includes seeing, flying, eating, and laying eggs; a band robs, but this involves, say, casing a bank, cracking a safe, collecting the loot and driving a getaway car away. The complex activity of the whole is in each case divided amongst its parts, so that the whole does what it does by way of its parts doing parts precisely of this.

What appears to distinguish a tribe from other functional wholes is the fact that its parts are *agents*. Thus, an army, a band, and a city are composed, respectively, of soldiers, robbers and citizens. It is among these that the activity of each is divided. This means that a division of productive labor, such as Socrates describes in the city, is but a special determination of something we find in all tribes. So, too, is the "partnership" of citizens. Socrates says that, whatever the end of a tribe may be, its success depends on a certain "friendship" (351d) holding amongst its members. Insofar as the members of a tribe are "enemies" or "at odds" (351e), he says, they are incapable of acting "as a unit" (352a) and so incapable of achieving their "common purpose" (351e).²³ The point of Socrates' talk about "friends" and "enemies" may be expressed less prosaically by saying that each member of a tribe must act so as positively to further the activity of his fellows, or else undermine the success of the tribe as a whole, and fail to perform his own function. The relationship between agents who act in this way is "friendship" or, as he says in the case of a city, "partnership."

The significance of the fact that a city is a tribe will become clear later on (in §§5 and 6) when we consider a generic feature of a well-functioning tribe about which we have so far remained silent: namely, that it has *justice* in it. But we should at no point lose sight of the great difference between a city and the other tribes that Socrates mentions. The fact that we belong to a city by nature, as we do not belong to an army or a band of robbers, means that a city stands in a special relation to human life and well-being and also that it has a special kind of unity.

Because that for the sake of which a city works is the well-being of its members, the benefit of a city's members is internal to its end. This is not true of an army or a band of robbers. To see why, it is helpful first to consider the work of a solitary agent, such as a fisherman. Insofar as he is what we call him, a fisherman aims only to catch fish: he does not aim to eat them, or to sell them, or to enjoy sea air and sunshine. Someone who is a fisherman might, of course, benefit from fishing in these and many other ways, but such benefits to himself do not figure into the description of his end *qua* fisherman (346b).²⁴ The same is true of a band of robbers and of an army. Whereas the end of a fisherman is caught fish, the end of a band is stolen loot and that of an army is victory won in battle. Notice that in describing the ends of *such* tribes we make no mention of any benefits accruing to the members thereof. Nor need there be any: a modern band of Merry Men might all have day-jobs and perform their moonlight theft for the poor,²⁵ just as an army of mercenaries might fight on behalf of a foreign nation. Even when benefits do accrue to someone who is part of such a tribe, they do not accrue to him *qua* member of it. The man who defends his country in war

---

23 Socrates accordingly speaks of "faction" or "civil war" as a liability, not specifically of social or political associations, but of tribes in general (351d).
24 This point is made repeatedly and at length by Socrates in Book I. See, for instance, 342c–e and 346e–347a.
25 See Plato's *Sophist* (219c–222d), where the fisherman and the pirate are both classified as hunters (cf. Aristotle's (1984) classification ,in the *Politics* at 1256a35–39 of the brigand). If what we said about the solitary fisherman is true—viz. that no benefit to himself is properly mentioned in a description of his end—then the same should apply, e. g., to a team of whale hunters. And if it applies to them, it should also apply to a band of thieves.

may thereby secure his own well-being, but this is because he wears the hat of a citizen as well as that of a soldier: it is *qua* citizen, and not *qua* soldier, that he is benefited by the army's success. A city differs from such tribes inasmuch as it is necessary to mention the good of its members in order to describe its work. Unlike an army or a band of robbers, a city aims to benefit its members *qua* members of it, and thereby to benefit itself. Recall in this connection that we identified *two* essential features of a city: a citizen both *does* part of what the city does and *has* part of what the city has. Yet only the former could figure into our general account of tribes. The reason for this should now be clear: there is nothing corresponding to the latter in an army or a band of robbers.

This points to a deep ontological distinction between a city and these other tribes. A city is a self-maintaining system: it is, as Kant might say, both the cause and effect of itself and therefore the cause and effect of its parts; meanwhile, its parts are reciprocally the causes and effects of each other.[26] For a city exists at one time only because the activity it performed at a previous time has sustained it in the interim. And since the parts of a city are citizens, these, too, owe their present existence—i.e., their lives—to the past work of the city. But the past work of the city was performed precisely by its citizens. Each citizen is thus partially responsible for the present existence of, at once, his city, his fellow-citizens and himself. A city is in this respect like a living organism, whose organs each reciprocally maintain both one another and the whole. But these natural wholes have a different kind of unity than we find in a clock and a band of robbers. It is true that the parts of a clock each serve to further the work of the others, and even that they exist in order to do this; but a clock does not make or maintain its gears, nor its gears the clock, nor its gears its springs. Part and whole alike owe their existence to an agency that is external to the system: namely, to a smith or clockmaker. The same is true of a band of robbers, which, because it aims to rob, aims at something quite other than its own existence.

Though we have cast this last point in a Kantian idiom, its true origin is Platonic. The idea that a city maintains itself, day by day, and generation by generation, is, in fact, a broad organizing principle of the *Republic*. Among other things, it explains Socrates' conspicuous concern with production (in Book II), education (in

---

26 See Kant (1952, 199–201). Though Kant is primarily concerned in these pages with living organisms, he remarks that it is fitting to apply the cognate "organization" in a context that is distinctly social. He says that: "In a whole of this kind [sc. a body politic] certainly no member should be a mere means, but should also be an end, and, seeing that he contributes to the possibility of the entire body, should have his position and function in turn defined by the idea of the whole" (Kant 1952, 203).

Book III),[27] and reproduction (in Book V). Socrates himself draws attention to the fact that a city's growth is cyclical:

> Once our city gets a good start, it will go on growing in a cycle. Good education and upbringing, when they are preserved, produce good natures, and useful natures, who are in turn well educated, grow up even better than their predecessors, both in their offspring and in other respects, just like other animals (424a).

This perpetual self-maintenance is characteristic of other animals, both solitary and gregarious, and of living nature in general. In it, we see the substance of the claim that a city is a natural growth.

This natural association of partners and helpers contrasts starkly with the conception of a city we found implicit in the accounts of Polemarchus, Thrasymachus, and Glaucon. We will now see how it guides Socrates in Book IV, where he turns his attention to happiness and justice.

4 The Happiness of a City and a Citizen

The mature city that Socrates names the *Kallipolis* is notoriously composed of three distinct classes: there are the producers, who perform the city's manual labor; the auxiliaries, who are soldier-police; and the guardians, who see to the affairs of state. In addition to performing three different functions in the life of the city, the members of these classes themselves lead three very different kinds of lives. The guardians, for instance, are forbidden to possess private property (416d–417b). When Book IV opens, Adeimantus is objecting to the *Kallipolis* on their behalf:

> How would you defend yourself, Socrates, if someone told you that you aren't making these men very happy and it's their own fault? The city really belongs to them, yet they derive no good from it (419a).

Adeimantus thinks, quite reasonably, that the guardians ought to benefit from their membership in the *Kallipolis*, but it seems to him that in fact they do not. For as Socrates has arranged things, the guardians are without "gold and silver and all the things that are thought to belong to people who are blessedly happy" (419a).

---

[27] Education belongs on the list because "the final outcome of education is a single newly finished person" (425c).

Socrates begins his reply to Adeimantus with an allusion to the method he has pursued thus far:

> I think we'll discover what to say if we follow the same path as before. We'll say that it wouldn't be surprising if these people were happiest just as they are, but that, in establishing our city, we aren't aiming to make any one group outstandingly happy but to make the whole city so, as far as possible (420b).

When Adeimantus objects that a part of the city is unhappy, Socrates diverts his attention to the happiness of the whole. But why does Socrates do this? And how is the maneuver continuous with the "path" he was following before?

Two things are reasonably clear. First, it is clear that Socrates believes that the *Kallipolis* as a whole is happy. As far as he is concerned, he has achieved his professed aim: the city is very close to being as happy as a city can be (see 427e and 434d–e).

It is also clear that Socrates believes there is an intimate relation between the happiness of a city and the happiness of its citizens.[28] Simply recall the passage from Book V, where he compares a city to a human body and a citizen to a bodily part (462c–e, quoted in our introduction). Socrates remarks that when a person's finger suffers either pleasure or pain, *he* suffers it: that is, the *whole person* suffers whatever is suffered by any of his parts. Likewise, he says, a city as a whole shares in anything good or bad that befalls its members. It must therefore detract from the happiness of a city if even one of its members is unhappy.

But what is not clear, and what we must understand in order to interpret Socrates' reply to Adeimantus' objection, is how, exactly, the happiness of a city supposed to be related to the happiness of its members. This question concerns the general shape of Socrates' political theory. One may find two contending interpretations of that theory in the literature, and 420b is at the center of the controversy. Some commentators claim that, for Socrates, the happiness of a city's parts is derivative of the happiness of the whole. Other commentators reverse the priority, claiming that the happiness of the city as a whole is derivative of the happiness of its parts. Let us consider these in turn.

---

28 This is a point on which most commentators agree. One notable exception is Grote (1998), who denies there is any significant relation between the happiness of a city and that of its members. Grote (1998, 139) reads 420b as a declaration that Socrates is concerned with "happiness for the abstract unity called the City, supposed to be capable of happiness or misery, apart from the individuals, many or few, composing it." See Vlastos (1995a, 80–84) for a decisive refutation of this interpretation.

Karl Popper is the most famous proponent of the first interpretation, which attributes to Socrates a certain methodological totalitarianism. According to Popper, Socrates begins from a conception of a city's well-being—one that makes no essential reference to the well-being of a citizen[29]—and proceeds to define a citizen's well-being as whatever conduces to the well-being of a city. Popper offers the following derisive summary of Socrates' position: "the criterion of morality is the interest of the state... the individual is nothing but a cog... ethics is nothing but the study of how to fit him into the whole" (Popper 1962, 108).

This, however, is certainly wrong. Socrates says explicitly that a city exists for the sake of satisfying the needs of its members (369b–c and 419e). But there is no conception of a thing's need apart from a conception of its benefit, nor of its benefit apart from its well-being. In that case, the function of a city cannot be understood prior to the well-being of its citizens. And if a city's function is not understood, then neither is its happiness: for its happiness lies in the performance of its function. Therefore, Socrates cannot think that the happiness of a citizen is a derivative phenomenon.

Commentators like Christopher Taylor reject Popper's interpretation, and instead attribute to Socrates a methodological individualism. According to them, Socrates begins from a conception of the well-being of an individual human being—one that makes no essential reference to the well-being of a city—and proceeds to define the well-being of a city as whatever conduces to the well-being of the individuals who belong to it. Taylor writes that, for Socrates, "the function and aim of the state is simply to promote the welfare of its citizens, that welfare being defined independently in terms of such individual goods as knowledge, health, and happiness" (Taylor 1997, 34).[30]

Proponents of the second interpretation claim to find in the text the very idea that Popper is enraged to find missing. But this too is difficult to reconcile with Socrates' account of the city. As we have understood that account, a human being is part of a city by nature. In that case, Socrates cannot think that the happiness of a city is a derivative phenomenon. For if we cannot understand human nature in abstraction from the nature of a city, then neither can we understand human happiness in abstraction from the happiness of a city.

A third interpretation is possible, though it has received little attention from recent commentators.[31] Socrates may think that the happiness of a city is related to the happiness of a citizen in such a way that neither can be understood prior to,

---

29 Popper (1962, 106) claims that according to Plato the well-being of a city consists in political stability and might.
30 Cf. Taylor (1997, 42). For a similar view, see Levinson (1953, 530).
31 This view seems to be implicit in Allen (1987).

or independently of the other. This is, in fact, what he must think if he thinks that a human being is by nature a civic creature: what it is to be a (happy) human being must both determine and be determined by what it is to be a (happy) city. Moreover, this is precisely what his comparison of a city to a living body suggests (see again 462c–e): for what it is to be a (flourishing) body of a certain kind both determines, and is determined by what it is to be a (flourishing) organ of such a body.[32] The comparison between a city and a body is significant for our present purposes because Socrates first introduces it in the course of his reply to Adeimantus' objection (420c–d; see below).

Now, if it is read in isolation, Socrates' remark at 420b appears to be consistent with any of the three interpretations. But that remark is only the preface of his reply to Adeimantus' objection, and we will argue in a moment that the substance of his reply speaks decisively in favor of the third. Unlike the arguments we have given so far, that argument will not depend on our interpretation of Socrates' account of a city (see §3); on the contrary, it will provide independent textual support for that interpretation and for our broad claim that Socrates is not an individualist.

Before coming to this, however, we must mention one point on which commentators tend to agree, whether they favor the totalitarian or the individualist interpretation. Socrates says at 420b that "we weren't aiming to make any one group outstandingly happy but to make the whole city so." It is characteristic of commentators on both sides to suppose that with these words Socrates is conceding to Adeimantus that the guardians have *not* been made "outstandingly" happy: Socrates too believes that the guardians would be happier if he had given them riches, but he has found it necessary to subordinate their interests to "the greater good," understood in either totalitarian or individualistic terms.[33] This consensus is surprising for several reasons. First, on the most literal and straightforward interpretation of the claim, it has no such implication: from the fact Socrates was aiming at Φ rather than at φ, it does not follow that φ was undesired or unachieved; Socrates may think that the best way to achieve φ is precisely to aim at Φ. Second, in the preceding clause of the very same sentence, Socrates says, "it wouldn't be surprising if these people were *happiest just as they are.*" Third, it would be extremely uncharacteristic of Socrates to think that riches contribute anything much to happiness, and he will later claim to have been "shocked" by Adeimantus' suggestion (465e). Finally, the guardians are the happiest people in

---

32 Our claim here is not that it is impossible for a flourishing organ to exist outside a flourishing body—for instance, in a sick body. We do not take a position on that question, or on the question whether a human being can be happy outside a happy city—for instance, in ours.
33 See, for example, Vlastos (1995a, 85–86) and Williams (1973, 50).

the *Republic:* they are happier than Olympian victors (466a), happier than Socrates, and happier, presumably, than any human being on earth. So, it is remarkable that commentators often come away from 420b with the distinct impression that Socrates is knowingly limiting their happiness. We will return to this point shortly: as we said, 420b should be interpreted in the light of what follows it.

The substance of Socrates' reply to Adeimantus takes the form of an analogy. He compares Adeimantus' objection to a certain wrongheaded criticism of a statue:

> Suppose that someone came up to us while we were painting a statue and objected that, because we had painted the eyes (which are the most beautiful part) black rather than purple, we had not applied the most beautiful colors to the most beautiful parts of the statue (420c).

The imagined critic begins from the idea that one ought to paint the most beautiful part of the body—in this critic's opinion, the eyes—more beautifully than the other parts. This is already rather odd, but let it pass. More bizarre is his idea that there is an answer to the question, "What is the most beautiful color?" asked just like that. Perhaps he has settled on purple because he associates it with a childhood memory, or with royalty, or with plums; perhaps it is because of the price of ultramarine. In any case, he thinks that, if one aims to make a part of a statue beautiful, purple is the color to paint it. And it would seem to follow that, if (contrary to the critic's advice) one aims to make the whole statue perfectly beautiful, one should paint it purple from head to toe. The result, of course, would look nothing like a beautiful body, and nothing like an ugly one, either.

In the face of such a criticism, Socrates imagines giving the following defense:

> You mustn't expect us to paint the eyes so beautifully that they no longer appear to be eyes at all, and the same with the other parts. Rather you must look to see whether by dealing with each part appropriately, we are making the whole statue beautiful (420d).

Socrates believes that if he paints the eyes "so beautifully" that they do not resemble eyes, they will not be beautiful *at all:* an eye has its beauty as a part of a beautiful body, and a plastic representation should reflect this. But the statue is analogous to Socrates' own discursive representation of a city. So, he is comparing happiness to beauty, a city to a body and a citizen to a bodily part.

What is significant here is Socrates' diagnosis of the art critic's error. The critic has tried to conceive the beauty of an eye in abstraction from the beauty of a body: he has treated the eye as though it were self-sufficient; he is, as we might say, an aesthetic individualist. Socrates diverts the critic's attention from the part to the whole because he thinks it is in this context alone that the beauty of the part can be seen. The point of the analogy is that Adeimantus has made a corresponding error. He has tried to conceive the happiness of a human being in abstraction from the happiness of a city.

As a result, Socrates thinks, Adeimantus has a ridiculous conception of both a happy human being and a happy city. Recalling the eyes of the statue, Socrates suggests that we might "clothe the farmers in purple robes," and "settle our potters on couches by the fire, feasting and passing the wine around," each with a pottery-wheel beside him in case he should tire of reveling: "And we can make all the others happy in the same way, so that the whole city is happy" (420d–e). Socrates will later call this conception of happiness "silly" and "adolescent" (466b). But his point is really that it is empty. Socrates diagnoses Adeimantus' error by saying that he "isn't thinking about a city at all" (421b): he is thinking instead about a festival. In that case, he is thinking about a merrymaker's merrymaking and not about a human being's life.

With this in mind, let us return to 420b. In the imagined scenario, Socrates has aimed to make the whole statue as beautiful as possible; the result (supposing that he achieved his aim) is that its parts are as beautiful as possible; and what explains this result is the fact that the beauty of a part is internally related to beauty of the whole, neither being prior to the other. This is how to understand his claim that, "in establishing our city, we aren't aiming to make any one group outstandingly happy, but to make the whole city so, as far as possible."[34] Things have turned out precisely as Socrates expected: the guardians are "happiest just as they are" (420b).[35]

---

34 We have argued that our proposal is consistent with most literal interpretation of Socrates' words: though he was aiming at Φ rather than at φ, nevertheless, he achieved φ, as intended, and he did so in the only appropriate manner, by aiming at Φ. "Still," someone might object, "doesn't Socrates *suggest* that he has *not* made the guardians 'outstandingly' happy? For instance, mustn't Adeimantus have heard the claim, not as you have interpreted it, but precisely as commentators usually do?" The answer is that there is some such suggestion, but it is ironic. Socrates suggests that, if he followed Adeimantus' advice, he would make the guardians supremely happy. He also suggests that, if he followed the critic's advice, he would make the eyes supremely beautiful— "so beautiful that they [would] no longer appear to be eyes." The irony of the latter suggestion should be obvious, and the two suggestions are presented as analogues. This irony may have been lost on Adeimantus at first, but it cannot have been long before even he realized that he was being ridiculed: Socrates' discourse on the statue and the farmers' purple robes is burlesque comedy.

35 Then why do commentators suppose that 420b implies a subordination of individual interests? Perhaps it is because they operate on the premise that individualism is true. Those, like Popper, who attack Socrates do so by arguing that he is *not* an individualist, and those, like Taylor, who defend Socrates do so by arguing that he *is* an individualist: all parties appear to agree that he should be. Cross and Woozley (1964, 97) cannot decide which of these two sides they are on, but they are sure about Socrates' claim at 420b: "at least it entails the idea of mutual-cooperation,

The story of the statue is an allegory by means of which Socrates explains why he must proceed the way he does in the *Republic*—why, that is, he must depict a happy city if he is to paint for us the visage of a happy human being. It is true that in his earliest remarks about happiness, at the end of Book I, Socrates was silent about the relationship between the happiness of an individual human being and the happiness of a city. What he said there was that the *ergon* of a human soul—its characteristic function or work—is "living" and that to live well is to be happy (353d–354a). But as his account has unfolded, in Books II and III, Socrates has revealed the context in which alone he thinks the function and happiness of a human being can be understood. No less than an eye, a human being is naturally a part of a larger whole.

Socrates continues to maintain that it is part of a human being's function to do a share of the city's labor. The importance of this contribution is not to be underestimated. Socrates goes so far as to claim that a person's life "is of no profit to him if he does not perform his work" (407a). This comes out in the course of his saying that a reasonable carpenter would refuse any lengthy medical treatment that required him to neglect his carpentry: "he'd bid good-bye to his doctor, resume his usual way of life, and either recover his health or, if his body couldn't withstand the illness, he'd die and escape his troubles" (406e). The same goes for every other member of the city (407e).

But the share of activity that a citizen *does* is related to the share of goods that a citizen *has*. On Socrates' view, there is such a thing as having too little or too much of something for one's own good. Because happiness depends on doing one's share, it is necessary to have everything that makes doing one's share possible, and nothing that makes it impossible. Socrates argued in Book III that private property would make the guardians unable to perform their function, and that is why he thinks it is incompatible with their happiness. Referring back to his exchange with Adeimantus, he will later invoke Hesiod's saying that "the half is worth more than the whole" (466c).

As we have understood it, Socrates' reply to Adeimantus proceeds on two assumptions. The first assumption is that the happiness of a city both determines and is determined by the happiness of a human being. The second is that the *Kallipolis* is a happy city. Now, the first of these claims may be true though the second is false: it is one thing to know that the flourishing of a human body stands in a certain formal relation to the flourishing of its organs and quite another thing to have

---

of a man being expected to subordinate his own interests to those of others." Vlastos (1995a, 82, n. 53) calls this an "excellent gloss." The idea of a shared interest is, evidently, so foreign to their way of thinking that it appears to them that "mutual-cooperation" *must* involve the subordination of an individual's interest. For a different view, see Allen (1987).

a correct anatomy.³⁶ We have thus far bracketed Socrates' substantive conception of a happy city, and we will not address this until the final section of the paper. Our aim here has only been to establish his commitment to the first claim, and to show how that is continuous with the "path" he was following before (420b). In the next two sections, we will explain what this has to do with justice.

5 Civic Justice

We have argued that the happiness of a city lies in the performance of its function, and that the function of a city is to provide for the happiness of its members. We will now argue that a city can perform this function only if it is just—that is, only if its members tend to act justly. But in order to do so, we must first gain a clear view of what civic justice is. That requires us to disentangle justice from Socrates' substantive conception of a happy city, a task that will occupy us for most of the present section. Once this disentangling is accomplished, however, we will see that the relation between a city's justice and its happiness is a simple consequence of Socrates' conception of the nature of a city. At that point, we will also see the ground of several other important Socratic theses.

Socrates presents his official account of civic justice in this well-known passage from Book IV:

> Justice, I think, is exactly what we said must be established throughout the city when we were founding it. It's either that or some form of it. We stated, and often repeated, if you remember, that everyone must practice one of the social services, the one for which he is naturally best suited.—Yes, we did keep saying that.—Moreover, we've heard many people say and have often said ourselves that justice is doing one's own and not meddling with what isn't one's own.—Yes, we have.—Then, it turns out that this doing one's own, provided it is understood in a certain way, is justice (433a–b).

According to Socrates, justice is "doing one's own." He appears confident both that there was some form of justice in the original city, and that it can be found in the

---

36 There are, of course, many different analogies one might draw between a city and body, and such analogies can be used for the most nefarious purposes: for instance, one might try to justify harming a minority by comparing it to a gangrenous limb that must be cut off. But the analogy that we have attributed to Socrates does not imply that such a thing is ever permissible. The point of our analogy is that what flourishing *is* for a human being stands in a certain formal relation to what flourishing *is* for a city. This abstract metaphysical claim gives us no indication of what should be done in this or that particular circumstance. The answer to any question of policy depends on some substantive conception of human happiness. See §7 below.

mature city as well. We will eventually identify the basis of this confidence. But first we must determine what it is to do one's own—for as Socrates says, this formula must be "understood in a certain way."

By this point in the dialogue, Socrates has offered a very detailed description of a happy city. He has argued that each member of a happy city ought to spend his entire life performing that work, and that work alone, for which he is naturally best suited. Socrates reminds us of this thesis in the passage quoted above: let us call it the *Principle of Specialization*. Shortly after the quoted passage, Socrates reminds us of another idea that has come to light since the city was founded. According to him, the members of a fully-fledged city collectively perform three fundamentally different kinds of work: they provide themselves with their material sustenance; they protect themselves from internal and external threats to the order of their city; and, finally, they impose that order, managing their life together in accordance with reason.[37] When this idea is combined with the Principle of Specialization, the product is a very determinate conception of what it is one's own to do in a happy city: a citizen belongs to one of three functionally distinct classes, and spends his entire life performing the work thereof. Call this the *Principle of Classification*. It is his commitment to this latter principle that leads Socrates to claim that the grossest form of injustice consists in a citizen's taking up the "tools and honors" of a class other than his own (434a–c).

Socrates does not himself call attention to the different strata of his account. On the contrary, he moves smoothly between the general claim that justice is "doing one's own" and his more determinate theses about what it is one's own to do. As a result, commentators frequently identify civic justice either with the Principle of Classification[38] or with the Principle of Specialization.[39] But Socrates has a conception of justice that is more basic than either of these principles, and that is presupposed by them both. There are two independent ways of arriving at this conclusion: one is to reflect on Socrates' claim, back in Book I, that a city is a tribe (see §3, above); the other is to consider the role that these principles play in Socrates' construction of a city.

In his early discussion with Thrasymachus, Socrates claims, not only that a city is a tribe, but also that *any* well-functioning tribe must have justice in it (351c). So, whatever Socrates thinks justice is, it must apply to tribes generically. But it is surely not *necessary* that the members of an effective tribe each perform one, and only

---

[37] Note that one might maintain this thesis and reject the *Principle of Specialization*. See Foster (1965, 1–38) for an illuminating discussion.
[38] See Reeve (1998, 242–243), Shorey (1933, 222–223), Cross and Woozley (1964, 110–111), and Annas (1981, 118–119).
[39] See, e. g., Vlastos (1995a, 78–79).

one clearly-defined task: a tribe of cooks *might* prepare a meal together by one of them chopping, one stirring, one seasoning, etc.; but they *might* each do a little of several things, or even a little of everything, and yet still do very well. In the latter case, they must still be acting justly. But then, the sort of rigid specialization that we find in Socrates' city cannot be essential to justice. *A fortiori*, it cannot be essential to justice that the members of a tribe perform specialized tasks that fall into three (or any number of) functionally distinct classes. Neither specialization nor classification belongs to well-functioning tribes as such.

If we are to speak of tribes generically, we must have a very general notion of what it belongs to a member of a tribe to do. The most definite thing we can say is that the activity of a tribe as a whole must be distributed *somehow or other* amongst its members: what, exactly, it is a member's part to do will depend on the principle of distribution that is in place. But whatever this principle might be, it will hold both that each member will have a part to do, which will be *his* part, and that the proper functioning of the tribe as a whole will depend on each member's being disposed to do his part. For the member of a tribe to act justly is simply to act in accordance with that disposition. So, we can say of tribes generically that the whole can do its work only insofar as its parts do theirs. We can also say that the success of a tribe—its doing well, or thriving—depends upon its members acting justly. For justice is the virtue of a partner *qua* partner.

Now, since a city is a tribe whose function is to provide for the happiness of its members, the actions of a just citizen must contribute to this end. Where such conditions prevail in a city—i.e., where each is disposed to do his part—there we have civic justice. This idea does not depend on specialization or classification.

We reach the same conclusion by a different route if we consider how Socrates develops his city. In the passage quoted above, where he says that justice is "doing one's own," Socrates suggests that his city has been just from the beginning (433a–b; see also 342d–e, 372a, and 443b–c). But, of course, there were no classes in the original polis: the members of that city all did the same kind of work (viz. production), and they themselves were all the same kind of citizen (viz. producers). Nevertheless, each did what it was his own to do. So, whatever civic justice is, it must be something more abstract than we find expressed in the Principle of Classification.

One might still think that specialization is essential to justice since each member of the original city did perform a single life-long task. Recall, though, that Socrates' construction of the original city proceeds in two discreet phases (see §3): first he answers the question how it is best to distribute the shares of what a city does; then he answers the question how it is best to distribute the shares of what the city has. As we remarked in §3, these questions *presuppose* that what a city does and has is to be distributed—somehow or other—amongst its members. So, the idea of a person's doing and having a share is already built into Socrates' conception of the nature of a city: it is this prior idea that forces him to address his two questions of distributive policy.

What it is important to see, in the present context, is that there is a step between Socrates' basic idea of doing and having a share and the distributive policies that he champions. The Principle of Specialization is his answer to the first question of distribution: each citizen should do *what he is predisposed to do*. In answer to the second question, Socrates initially says that each citizen should have *what he can get through buying and selling* (371b): call this latter the *Principle of Market Exchange*. It obviously requires an independent argument to show that either policy is any good, let alone better than the innumerable alternatives. Socrates recognizes the need for an argument: he provides an argument for the Principle of Specialization at 370a–d, and he provisionally accepts the Principle of Market Exchange from Adeimantus as a plausible default plan (371b). The first thing to notice is that these two principles occupy corresponding positions in Socrates' account: they are, as it were, on a level with one another. The second thing to notice is that Socrates revises the Principle of Market Exchange: by the time the mature city is complete, the scope of this principle has been limited to the producing class. Notice, finally, that the idea of having a share survives this revision. It survives, because it is a more abstract idea that attaches to the nature of a city quite apart from any substantive conception of what a flourishing city looks like. But so is the idea of doing a share. It is true, of course, that Socrates never revises the Principle of Specialization. This principle stands, from early on until the very end, on the strength of his argument at 370d–e. But the fact that Socrates is more committed to this principle does not alter its status; it remains his own best solution to one of the two distributive problems raised for him by the nature of a city. When we abstract from the concrete proposal embodied in this principle, we are left with the idea that it belongs to a citizen to do a *so-far-undetermined* share, portion, or part of the activity performed by the city as a whole. Doing this is "doing one's own."

That is by no means a trivial thesis. It entails that good human action is to be judged such in view of its place in an enterprise undertaken by one human being in cooperation with others, an enterprise whose aim is nothing but the happiness of the agents of this common activity. For civic justice is the virtue that fits a human being to be partner in a happy city.[40]

---

[40] We say in a happy city because justice should not be thought of as a disposition that greases the wheels for the operation of any random, rotten system. What justice *is* determines, and is determined by what a happy city *is*. One can, of course, be just in an *unhappy* city. But justice under

Let us sum up. Socrates believes that a happy city should divide into three functionally distinct classes, and that every citizen should perform a single lifelong occupation. Neither of these claims is undefended by Socrates: he presents a separate argument for each of them, so that each may be judged on its merits. But neither claim should be identified with his basic conception of civic justice. Having disentangled this latter, we can now address the question how the justice of a city is related to its happiness.

In explanation of his method in the *Republic*, Socrates says that he aims to construct a happy city because he wants to investigate justice, and because he is confident that a happy city will have justice in it (420b, 434d–e). But whence this confidence that a happy city is just? Or again, why think that justice is a civic virtue?[41] To many commentators, the claim has appeared unfounded.[42] For Socrates inaugurates his investigation of civic justice with an assertion: "I think our city, if indeed it has been correctly founded, is completely good... Clearly then, it is wise, courageous, moderate and *just*" (427e). So, he appears baldly to assume that justice is a civic virtue. If so, then his method is badly flawed. Things look especially bad on the interpretative hypothesis that Socrates' reply to Glaucon's challenge is an argument by analogy: for then Socrates will seem to move from the unsupported claim that justice is a civic virtue to the analogous claim that justice is a human virtue.

It should be clear by now that Socrates does not *assume* that justice is a civic virtue. It is true that his explanation for the thesis is not to be found at 427e, but this is not the place to look for an explanation. Since the virtue of a thing is a perfection of its nature, if we want to see why justice is a civic virtue, we must look to the nature of a city. A happy city is just because a city is a tribe, a functional whole whose parts are agents. Like anything with a function, a city does well only insofar as it performs its function. Like any tribe, a city is able to perform its function only insofar as its members each do what it is his own to do—that is, only insofar as its members are just. Thus, it follows from the nature of a city that a happy city has justice in it.

---

such conditions will manifest itself differently than it does in a happy city. In a happy city, the just engage in politics. But in a city as imperfect as Athens, Socrates says, the just person who engages in politics will perish before he benefits the city or anyone else (469d, cf. *Apology* 31d–32a). In Athens, the just person leads a quiet life, and practices philosophy—the true political art (cf. *Gorgias* 521d)—in a sadly private way: "like someone who takes refuge under a little wall from a storm of dust..." (496d).

41 The question we are addressing here is "Why is a happy city just?" and *not* "What is civic justice?" The so-called "elimination argument" that follows 427e takes it for granted that a happy city *is* just and proceeds to a discussion of what civic justice is.

42 See Stokes (1987, 69–74), Inwood (1987, 101), Irwin (1977, 206, n. 30), Annas (1981, 110–111), and Cross and Woozley (1964, 104–105).

We are now in position to draw three further implications. The first implication is that the happiness of an individual human being depends on his acting in accordance with civic justice. We argued in §4 that since a human being is by nature a partner in a city, and since happiness depends on the performance of one's function, happiness depends on one's doing one's part in a city. It has come out in the present section that doing one's part is "doing one's own"—i.e., acting in accordance with civic justice. In that case, happiness depends on acting justly.

The second implication is that acting in accordance with civic justice is furthering the happiness of one's partners. It furthers their happiness in two ways. On the one hand, doing one's own contributes to the work of the city as a whole, the aim of which work is precisely to secure the happiness of one's partners. But acting in accordance with civic justice also makes a more immediate contribution to the happiness of one's fellows. For the functions of partners are essentially complimentary: the work of one is always such as to further the work of the others. So, to do one's part is to help one's partner to do his part. But this is the same as helping him to perform his function (as we argued in the previous paragraph). It is therefore to further his happiness.

The third implication follows immediately from the first two: an individual human being is happy only if he lives in such a way as to further the happiness of his fellows.

These considerations explain the characteristically Socratic thesis that justice aims both at one's own good and at the good of another. It is worth pausing over this thesis, because it might be taken to suggest that justice is the sum of prudence and charity. But prudence aims at one's own good as distinct from that of another, and charity aims at the good of another as distinct from one's own. These virtues are specially suited to modern individualism: given the premise that a human being's nature is to be understood individually, one naturally interprets ethical and political phenomena in terms of selfishness and selflessness, egoism and altruism, greed and "brotherly love." But this whole way of thinking is alien to Socrates. The good at which justice aims is essentially a shared good, as the end of cooperative activity is essentially a shared end.[43] If we are the partners and helpers that Socrates describes, then the good of each of us is inseparable from the good of the others: this principle of cooperative activity is, he thinks, a principle of our nature.

---

43 Allen (1987, 58) is clear on this point.

6 Psychic Justice

As the happiness of a city depends on civic justice, the happiness of a human being depends on psychic justice. We will first explain why a just soul, like a just city, is one each part of which does its own. We will then argue that psychic justice *is* civic justice.

In order to see the relation between the happiness of a city and its justice, in §5, it was necessary to abstract from certain of Socrates' substantive (political-economic) theses regarding the constitution of a well-functioning city. Similarly, we must now abstract from his substantive (moral-psychological) theses regarding the constitution of a well-functioning soul. This, however, is easily done. As we have already said, the function of the human soul is living, and living well is being happy, so a human being is happy only insofar as his soul performs its function well. Now if, as Socrates believes, the soul has parts, then we may reapply to the soul the same general principle that we earlier applied to the city: the whole can do its work only insofar as its parts do theirs. According to Socrates, a soul each part of which does its work is just (441d–e). Thus, it is only insofar as he is psychically just that a human being lives well, and is happy. Notice that this thesis holds whatever exactly the parts of the soul may be, and however many.

Given what psychic justice is, it is no wonder that Socrates compares it to bodily health (444c). For as health is the good condition of the body, psychic justice is the good condition of the soul. In either case, the whole that is in good condition functions as it ought because its parts function as they ought: if justice is the health of the soul, then health is likewise the justice of the body. Now recall that when he first challenged Socrates to show that justice ranks among the highest class of goods, back in Book II, Glaucon offered health as a paradigm. Having shown psychic justice to be like health, Socrates believes he has given an (at least preliminary) answer to the challenge. And Glaucon, for his part, is convinced (445a–b).

David Sachs, whom we first mentioned in the introduction to this paper, has famously argued that Socrates' account of psychic justice is, in fact, "irrelevant" to Glaucon's challenge. The putative problem, recall, is that while Socrates has been charged to establish that happiness depends on acting in a certain manner in relation to other people, what he actually argues at the end of Book IV is that happiness depends on the parts of one's soul acting in a certain manner in relation to one another. It may be admitted that a happy human being has a just and well-functioning soul, but what fixes it that such a soul does not give rise to actions that are prohibited by the justice of a city? For all Socrates has said, might it not be that a happy human being is precisely one who is disposed to perpetrate murder, swindling, kidnapping, promise-breaking, and other characteristically unjust actions?

That is what Thrasymachus claimed, and what Glaucon asked Socrates to refute.[44] According to Sachs, Socrates has left a gap between the harmony of the parts of a soul and the harmony of souls: he merely *assumes* that they are connected; and in so doing, he begs the central question of the *Republic*.

The gap that Sachs believes Plato left gaping and that others have since tried to close[45] is one that on our account never opened up to begin with. If the question is why actions like murder and swindling are proscribed by civic justice, the answer is that such actions essentially involve *harming* others, whereas civic justice requires one always only benefit them (see §5). If the question is why human happiness depends on acting in accordance with civic justice, the answer is that a human being is by nature a part of a city, and a functional part does well only insofar as it contributes to the end of that of which it is a part. If the question is why the parts of a person's soul must act in accordance with psychic justice, the answer is that a person cannot perform his function unless his parts perform theirs. But it is senseless to go on from here to ask what the relations between parts of the human soul have to do with the relations between human beings. This is like asking what the relations between the parts of a certain organ have to do with the relations between this organ and the other organs of the same body. The latter question could only be asked by someone who did not know what an organ was, or who did not appreciate that the object in question was an organ. The former question gets asked because commentators have in general failed to appreciate that Socrates conceives the virtue of a human being as the virtue of a part of a city.

To say, as we ordinarily do, that a bodily organ is healthy is to say *both* that its parts interact harmoniously *and* that the organ itself interacts harmoniously with the other organs of the body. But this is not an equivocation: we do not have here two different conceptions, or principles, of an organ's health; nor do we use the word "health" in two different senses. For the harmony of parts of an organ and the harmony of organs are not two harmonies, but one. Now if a human being is by nature a citizen, then to say that a human being is just is to say

---

[44] See 348d for the characteristic acts of injustice mentioned by Thrasymachus, and see Glaucon's myth of Gyges (359d–360d) for a host of others. Socrates acknowledges that such actions are in dispute in Book IV, where he applies "vulgar tests" to his account of justice (442d–443b).

[45] Some commentators have argued that an answer to Sachs' problem appears later in the *Republic:* Dahl (1999), Demos (1964), and Weingartner (1964) find it in the theory of forms; Kraut (1997) and Cooper (1997) look to the account of the philosopher king; and Vlastos (1971) draws on Socrates' description of degenerate cities. The attempt to link Socrates' early account of justice with later parts of the dialogue is fruitful and necessary work. What we oppose is only the idea that there is a gaping hole in the argument of Books I–IV, which threatens, if unfilled, to ruin the dialogue.

both that the parts of his soul interact harmoniously *and* that he interacts harmoniously with the other members of his city. So, what we have thus far artificially called "psychic justice" and "civic justice" are not two similar, isomorphic, or analogous phenomena: they are, rather, two aspects of a single phenomenon. The unity of civic and psychic justice is the unity of a city and its citizens.

7 The Form and Content of Socrates' Account

Thus far, we have tried to articulate the bare form of the account that Socrates gives in answer to Glaucon's challenge. At each stage, we have set aside his substantive theses regarding the constitution of a city and a soul. Our aim in this final section is to explain how the form of Socrates' account interacts with its content.

A model may clarify the distinction between form and content that we will employ. Suppose that someone asked for an account of the excellence of a crosscut sawyer. Such an account would seem to presuppose a conception of a sawyer sawing well, for it is an account of the disposition in virtue of which a sawyer does precisely that. Meanwhile, a conception of a single sawyer sawing well would seem to presuppose a conception of two sawyers sawing well together, since (one might think) the former conception is simply the result of an abstraction performed on the latter. On these grounds, it is natural to say that an account of the sawyer's excellence must have a certain form: it must hold itself responsible to a conception of the partnered activity, such that it will count nothing as the excellence of a sawyer that does not fit with a sawyer sawing well, and it will count nothing as a sawyer's sawing well that does not fit with two sawyers sawing well together. Notice that it is because the sawyer's excellence has the place it does within a partnered activity that these formal strictures seem appropriate. But now, having a conception of the partnered activity *to which* one might hold oneself responsible involves having answers to specific questions like these: "With what cadence does the saw pull back and forth?" "Does one partner lead, as in dancing?" "What do they do when they hit a knot?" The answers to such questions will impinge in various ways on an account of the sawyer's excellence. But each answer requires a separate justification, and each justification may be disputed. Such disputes concern the content of the account. Two people may disagree about the content of an account, and yet be agreed as to the form that such an account must take.

Socrates has been asked to speak about human excellence, and this, he thinks, is the excellence of a partner in a city. It belongs to the form of Socrates' account that what an individual human being has and does is to be conceived as a share, portion, or part of what a city has and does. A city and its citizens are related to one another such that in a happy city every citizen is as happy as possible, every citizen benefits as much as possible, every citizen has what he needs, and every citizen is just. These are formal claims inasmuch as they fix the relation between the concepts, "happiness," "benefit," "need" and "justice" in their application to human beings and to cities. These concepts have the kind of fixedness with respect to one another that "flourishing," "benefit," "need" and "health" have in their application to organs and to organisms. We have argued that, by "justice," Socrates understands the disposition that fits a human being to be a partner in a happy city. So, several of Socrates' most characteristic theses also belong to the form of his account: that justice requires one to further the happiness of one's fellows[46] —that it requires one always to benefit them, and never to do them harm[47]— and that one's own happiness depends on acting justly.

The *Republic* contains theories of law, political economy, education, art, ethics and moral psychology. That it does is a consequence of the form of Socrates' account, but the theories themselves belong to the content. Socrates believes that an account of virtue is responsible to a conception of the whole of human social life. To articulate and defend such a conception requires one to speak about whatever it may be that human social life essentially involves. And this Socrates does. But what he says when he speaks on these topics is not dictated by the form of his account: that the shares of what a city has and does should be distributed according to the principles that Socrates adduces, that the city should have classes, that education and family life should be thus and so, that certain poetry should not be allowed, etc., etc.—for each of these claims, Socrates must offer a discreet argument. And this he does. Taken together, these arguments constitute a defense of his conception of a happy life in a happy city.

To say this is not to defend his arguments. It is, however, to insist that the arguments are there—everywhere—in the text, and so to defend Socrates against the charge that he has begged the question against Thrasymachus.[48] It is also to urge, against those who would attribute to Socrates an argument by analogy and who

---

[46] Plato's conception of justice is grounded in a shared community; and as he envisions this community, it does not include all rational beings, or even all human beings. In order to extend the account so that every human (or rational) being is a "fellow citizen," we should need an exceedingly abstract interpretation of the Platonic "city". Interestingly, the Stoics *did* extend the account in this way. For a fascinating discussion of the Stoic conception of a city, see Schofield (1991, 93–103).

[47] There is a special case of this in the Socratic thesis that the proper aim of punishment is the benefit of the punished (*Gorgias* 477a).

[48] See once again Sachs et al.

would therefore suppose that a complete account of the soul could *in principle* be given without mention of the city,[49] that, in fact, no detail of Socrates' description and defense of the city is superfluous. In that case, the dialogue is the unified discussion of justice that it purports to be.

Once the form of Socrates' account is distinguished from its content, we see that it is possible to hold onto the form, and with it the characteristically Socratic theses, while rejecting any feature of its content that is objectionable. For any account that takes this form is *by its own lights* susceptible to a number of different kinds of criticism.

First, one might criticize a conception of a happy city on the grounds that some or all of its members lack something that a human being needs, whether that thing be material, psychological, intellectual, or political. To show that a city is unwell, it is sufficient to show that someone in it is exploited or otherwise systematically harmed. So, one might deny Socrates' claim that the *Kallipolis* is a happy city by defending a conception of individual human happiness according to which, for example, a human being has a significant hand in shaping his own government.[50] One might then argue as follows: (1) since the producers have no such hand in their government, they are unhappy; in that case, (2) the *Kallipolis*, which requires most of its citizens to be producers, fails to perform its function, which is to secure the happiness of its citizens. Such a criticism depends for its force on the considerations that favor one's substantive conception of a happy human life. That such a criticism is forever available shows that the form of Socrates' account involves no commitment to the totalitarianism that many now associate with an "organic conception of the state."

Nevertheless, a conception of individual human happiness may be trite, adolescent or fantastic, and it may be shown to be such by an argument that proceeds from a substantive conception of a happy city. The form of Socrates' account fixes it that a life that is incompatible with the happiness of a city is not a happy human

---

49 This idea is explicitly embraced by Annas (1999). Annas (1999, 82) urges us to treat the account of the city as dispensable (as far as the ethics is concerned) on the grounds that, "The political suggestions [of the *Republic*] are absurd if taken literally." Annas discusses the even more radical view of Robin Waterfield (1993, xvi), who invites one "to read the book as a predominantly individualist approach to the issues, with the traditional political terminology of the debate suborned and largely turned over to metaphorical purposes, to describe the inner state of the individual." (What Annas objects to, incidentally, is *not* the suggestion that the *Republic* takes and "individualist approach" to ethics but the suggestion that the political dimension of the dialogue should be read as a metaphor, rather than an analogy.)

50 How is this different from Adeimantus' objection at the beginning of Book IV? Adeimantus did not *argue* that individual happiness depends on the possession of riches; he simply asserted a vulgar commonplace.

life. Socrates exploited this formal stricture in his reply to Adeimantus' objection at the beginning of Book IV (see §4), for he supposed that he had established the happiness of the *Kallipolis*. It is a legitimate form of criticism; but again, any actual criticism that takes this form will be as weak or as strong as the arguments put forward to justify one's substantive conception of a happy city.

These two forms of criticism are of equal force, neither having any special advantage over the other. The requirement is simply that a conception of a happy life and a conception of a happy city must harmonize. But now, whatever exactly a happy life may be—whatever specific activities it may include—it is the effluence of a healthy human soul. An acceptable moral psychology must, therefore, reveal the soul to be the source of such a life. In that case, criticism may run both ways between conceptions of a city and a human being, a human being and a soul, and a city and a soul. That none of these has absolute authority over the others is no reason to despair that disputes are unresolvable: anatomies of the body, of the hand, and of the thumb are responsible to one another in a similar way, but this has never prevented their fruitful study.

In this paper, we have attempted to liberate the form of Socrates' account from its often very objectionable content. But it may seem that if we are left with only this abstract schema we are left with little or nothing. Notice, though, that the schema is sufficient to rule out the claims of Polemarchus, Thrasymachus and Glaucon that a happy human life involves us harming our enemies, or anyone in our way, or anyone we can get away with harming. For it rules out that it is *ever* appropriate to do harm.

The suspicion may persist that lives substantially like the ones championed by Socrates' interlocutors could be fitted into his schema with a simple modification of rhetoric. It may seem that Thrasymachus, for example, could maintain his conception of an ideal human life, if he were only willing to stop *describing* his ideal man as crushing those around him: with a little more savvy, might he not weave a tale according to which such a man *benefits* his fellows? This, however, is not as easy as it may seem. Not just anything can plausibly be said to benefit a human being: concepts like "benefit" and "need" are tied to many goods that are beyond dispute, such as food, clothing and shelter, and the development of one's capacities. Nor would it be easy to square the life of Thrasymachus' ideal man with a plausible conception of a healthy community: simply imagine what a city of Thrasymachus' ideal men would look like. The fact is that in giving their accounts of human virtue, Socrates' interlocutors did not see themselves as responsible to *any* conception of civic happiness *whatsoever*. The very responsibility to *some such conception* prohibits one from entertaining many ideas about the virtue and happiness of a human being that might otherwise strike one as plausible.

We may be confident that the form of Socrates' account is not an empty abstraction, if only because so many people will find it controversial. Resistance will come from those who hold that the good of a political community is entirely derivative from the good of individuals, which is intelligible in advance. It will come as well from those who think that an account of justice should remain neutral on metaphysical views about human nature and the good life. Meanwhile, in ethics, the question that occupies Socrates in the *Republic*, whether justice is a *benefit* to its possessor, whether it *profits* one, is in one's *interest*, or to one's *advantage* —the question, that is, whether justice is a genuine human virtue—this question is thought to require an answer that proceeds from a conception of individual happiness, benefit, advantage etc. that is available in advance of any thought about the actions of the members of a happy community. One claims to know from the start what is good for a human being, and demands a proof that justice will bring one *this*. That is, one demands to be shown that justice pays in a coin that does not already bear its stamp.

If we have understood him, Socrates denies that such a demonstration is possible. For he denies that there is any meaningful conception of a happy human being that is not simultaneously a conception of a happy community, or any conception of a happy community that is not a conception of just human beings. In that case, justice and happiness, both individual and communal, enter the scene at once, or else do not enter at all. There is a great distance between Socrates' position and currently prevalent ways of thinking. Perhaps this explains why his method should so often appear so hopeless, his characteristic theses so improbable, and he himself so strange.

Plato's Works

References to Plato's works are given by title and Stephanus pagination. All English quotations are from the editions found in the bibliography below.

References

Allen, Reginald E. (1987): "The Speech of Glaucon: On Contract and the Common Good." In: Panagiotou, Spiro (Ed.): *Justice, Law and Method in Plato and Aristotle*. Edmonton: Academic Printing & Publishing, 51–62.
Annas, Julia (1981): *Introduction to Plato's Republic*. New York: Oxford University Press.
Annas, Julia (1999): "The Inner City: Ethics Without Politics in the *Republic*." In: Annas, Julia: *Platonic Ethics Old and New*. Ithaca: Cornell University Press, 72–95.

Aristotle (1984): *Politics.* Benjamin Jowett (Trans.). In: Aristotle: *The Complete Works of Aristotle.* Vol. II. Jonathan Barnes (Ed.). Princeton: Princeton University Press.
Barker, Ernest (1959): *The Political Thought of Plato and Aristotle.* New York: Dover Publications.
Cooper, John (1997): "The Psychology of Justice in Plato." In: Kraut, Richard (Ed.): *Plato's Republic: Critical Essays.* Oxford: Rowman & Littlefield Publishers, 17–30.
Cornford, Francis M. (1997): "Psychology and Social Structure in the *Republic* of Plato." In: Dunn, John and Harris, Ian (Eds.): *Great Political Thinkers: Plato.* Vol. I. Lyme: Edward Elgar Publishing, 7–26.
Cross, Robert C. and Woozley, Anthony D. (1964): *Plato's Republic: A Philosophical Commentary.* New York: St. Martin's Press.
Dahl, Norman O. (1999): "Plato's Defense of Justice." In: Fine, Gail (Ed.): *Plato 2: Ethics, Politics, Religion and the Soul.* Oxford: Oxford University Press, 207–234.
Demos, Raphael (1964): "A Fallacy in Plato's *Republic?*" In: *The Philosophical Review* 73. No. 3 (July), 395–398.
Foster, Michael B. (1965): *The Political Philosophies of Plato and Hegel.* New York: Russell & Russell.
Grote, George (1998): *Plato and The Other Companions of Sokrates.* Vol. IV. Dulles: Thoemmes Press.
Hobbes, Thomas (1996): *Leviathan.* John C. A. Gaskin (Ed.). New York: Oxford University Press.
Inwood, Brad (1987): "Professor Stokes on Adeimantus in the *Republic.*" In: Panagiotou, Spiro (Ed.): *Justice, Law and Method in Plato and Aristotle.* Edmonton: Academic Printing and Publishing, 97–104.
Irwin, Terrence (1977): *Plato's Moral Theory.* Oxford: Clarendon Press.
Irwin, Terrence (1995): *Plato's Ethics.* New York: Oxford University Press.
Kahn, Charles (1972): "The Meaning of 'Justice' and the Theory of Forms." In: *The Journal of Philosophy* 69. No. 18 (Oct. 5), 567–579.
Kant, Immanuel (1952): *The Critique of Judgement.* James Creed Meredith (Trans.). Oxford: Clarendon Press.
Kraut, Richard (1997): "The Defense of Justice in Plato's *Republic.*" In: *Plato's Republic: Critical Essays.* Lanham: Rowman & Littlefield Publishers, 197–221.
Lear, Jonathan (1998): "Inside and Outside the *Republic.*" In: Lear, Jonathan: *Open Minded: Working out the Logic of the Soul.* Cambridge: Harvard University Press, 219–246.
Levinson, Ronald B. (1953): *In Defense of Plato.* Cambridge: Harvard University Press.
Murphy, Neville R. (1951): *The Interpretation of Plato's Republic.* Oxford: Clarendon Press.
Plato (1992): *Republic.* George M. A. Grube, revised by C. D. C. Reeve (Trans.). Indianapolis: Hackett Publishing Company.
Plato (1997a): *Apology.* George M. A. Grube (Trans.). In: Plato: *The Complete Works of Plato.* John Cooper (Ed.). Indianapolis: Hackett Publishing Company, 17–36.
Plato (1997b): *Gorgias.* Donald J. Zeyl (Trans.). In: Plato: *The Complete Works of Plato.* John Cooper (Ed.). Indianapolis: Hackett Publishing Company, 791–870.
Plato (1997c): *Sophist.* Nicholas White (Trans.). In: Plato: *The Complete Works of Plato.* John Cooper (Ed.). Indianapolis: Hackett Publishing Company, 235–294.
Popper, Karl R. (1962): *The Open Society and Its Enemies.* Vol. I. Princeton: Princeton University Press.
Reeve, C. D. C. (1998): *Philosopher-Kings.* Princeton: Princeton University Press.
Sachs, David (1963): "A Fallacy in Plato's *Republic.*" In: *The Philosophical Review* 72. No. 2 (April), 141–158.
Schofield, Malcolm (1991): *The Stoic Idea of the City.* Chicago: University of Chicago Press.
Shorey, Paul (1933): *What Plato Said.* Chicago: University of Chicago Press.

Stokes, Michael (1987): "Adeimantus in the *Republic.*" In: Panagiotou, Spiro (Ed.): *Justice, Law and Method in Plato and Aristotle.* Edmonton: Academic Printing and Publishing, 67–96.

Taylor, Christopher C. W. (1997): "Plato's Totalitarianism." In: Kraut, Richard (Ed.): *Plato's Republic: Critical Essays.* New York: Rowman and Littlefield Publishers, 31–49.

Vlastos, Gregory (1971): "Justice and Happiness in the *Republic.*" In: Vlastos, Gregory (Ed.): *Plato II: A Collection of Critical Essays; Ethics, Politics and Philosophy of Art and Wisdom.* Notre Dame: University of Notre Dame Press, 66–95.

Vlastos, Gregory (1995a): "The Theory of Social Justice in the *Polis* in Plato's *Republic.*" In: Graham, Daniel W. (Ed.): *Studies in Greek Philosophy: Volume II: Socrates, Plato and Their Tradition.* Princeton: Princeton University Press, 69–103.

Vlastos, Gregory (1995b): "The Rights of Persons in Plato's Conception of the Foundations of Justice." In: Graham, Daniel W. (Ed.): *Studies in Greek Philosophy: Volume II: Socrates, Plato and Their Tradition.* Princeton: Princeton University Press, 104–125.

Weingartner, Rudolph H. (1964): "Vulgar Justice and Platonic Justice." In: *Philosophy and Phenomenological Research* 25. No. 2 (December.), 248–252.

White, Nicholas P. (1979): *Companion to Plato's Republic.* Indianapolis: Hackett Publishing Company.

Williams, Bernard (1997): "The Analogy of City and Soul in Plato's *Republic.*" In: Kraut, Richard (Ed.): *Plato's Republic: Critical Essays.* Lanham: Rowman & Littlefield, 49–60.

Wolfram Gobsch
Philosophizing as Dying: Self-Knowledge and Reconciliation in Hegel

Abstract: How does philosophy relate to life: to our life under ethical norms? The aim of the paper is to reconstruct Hegel's answer to this question by sketching the outlines of an argument that would reveal it to be true. Initially, Hegel's conception of philosophy's relation to ethical life is puzzling. On the one hand he claims that philosophy has "the *truth* for its object and, indeed, in the highest sense – in that *God* is and is *alone* the truth." On the other hand, he holds that to philosophize is to articulate one's "self-knowledge" as a participant of the ethical life of one's time, wherefore philosophy always "belongs to its time and is implicated in its confinedness". And yet, he remains uncompromising in his opposition to "making finitude into an absolute." The key to dissolving the puzzle of how Hegel takes these claims to be compatible with each other lies in his conception of the history of philosophy both as identical with philosophy itself and as bound up with world history, i.e., with the rise of and fall of forms of ethical life. "[T]he owl of Minerva begins its flight only with the onset of dusk": to philosophize is to comprehend as unconditionally necessary both the rise of the shape of one's own ethical life and its demise, it is to "recognize Reason […] in the cross of the present". In this sense, philosophizing is dying for Hegel: philosophy neither justifies the spirit of the age as rational in a sense that would reveal it to be exempt from demise, nor does it enable us to counteract the demise we philosophically know to be unconditionally necessary, nor does the reconciliation that it offers in the form of this knowledge avail a life that tolerates the demise. In the paper I develop the Hegelian conception of philosophy's relation to life in a series of argumentative steps from an initially abstract conception of what it is to philosophize, a conception most philosophers should be able to agree with.

1 Introduction

What is philosophy for Hegel? If we take Hegel at his word and survey what his work offers on the subject, we are confronted with the contours of an answer that we, as children of our time, must initially call outrageous.

Philosophy, Hegel says, has "the *truth* for: its object and, indeed, in the highest sense—in that *God* is and is *alone* the truth" (*Werke* 8:41).[12] Yet Hegel equally says that philosophy is "self-knowledge [*Selbsterkenntnis*]" (*Werke* 10:9, §377). As such, philosophy is essentially knowledge of the activity of philosophizing and of its subjects. In this respect, philosophy is, as Hegel puts it, "its own time comprehended in thought" (*Werke* 7:26). Philosophy "belongs to its time and is implicated [*befangen*] in its confinedness" (Hegel *Werke* 18:65). Taken together, this means that philosophy, for Hegel, is *at once* knowledge of the absolute and self-knowledge of the finite spirit of its age.

Yet this is not supposed to "make finitude into an absolute." For this is precisely the offense for which Hegel reproaches—early and with great vehemence—"Eudaimonism and false Enlightenment, as well as Kantian, Jacobian, and Fichtean philosophy" (*Werke* 2:301). Hegel's characterization of philosophy as, at once, knowledge of the absolute and self-knowledge of the finite spirit of its time is supposed to also respect the difference between the absolute and the finite. On Hegel's initial and quite abstract formulation of this distinction, "the finite" "*passes away* [*vergeht*], and it is not merely possible that it passes away," which is why one can say of the finite things "that [...] non-being [...] constitutes their being" (Hegel, *GW* 21:116). But, as Hegel continues, it is precisely in its passing away that the finite as such is *internally* related to the infinite as such and vice versa. Accordingly, it must equally be said of the finite that it is "its infinity to sublate itself" (Hegel, *GW* 21:133). Conversely, the absolute—as the truly infinite which, as such, cannot be merely different from the finite and thus bounded by it—must be said to be "*there*, present, attendant" precisely in the self-sublating finite (Hegel, *GW* 21:136).

That philosophy is at once knowledge of the absolute and self-knowledge of the finite spirit of its age therefore signifies for Hegel that it knows this finite spirit—precisely in its passing away—as the presence of the absolute and, hence, as un-

---

1 All translations of Hegel are my own. I have consulted and relied on the following standard translations: Hugh B. Nisbet's translation of *Elements of the Philosophy of Right* (Hegel 1991), Arnold V. Miller's translation of *Phenomenology of Spirit* (Hegel 1997), and Wallace and Miller's *Hegel's Philosophy of Mind* (Hegel 2007). All emphases in the quotations are from Hegel unless otherwise noted. I have also consulted Barbara E. Galli's translation of Franz Rosenzweig's *Star of Redemption* (Rosenzweig 2005) and Elizabeth Anscombe's translation of Ludwig Wittgenstein's *Philosophical Investigations* (Wittgenstein 1953).
2 A brief note on abbreviations: Citations of Hegel quotations from the *Theorie-Werkausgabe* (Frankfurt a/M: Suhrkamp (1986)) will be abbreviated as "*Werke* Volume: Page." Citations from Hegel's *Gesammelte Werke* (Hamburg: Meiner (1984)) will be abbreviated as "*GW* Volume: Page." Paragraph numbers are occasionally added for the reader's convenience. A list of the works from these editions which have been consulted can be found at the end of this paper.

conditionally necessary. Thus, he can say that philosophy is "the reconciliation of corruption [*Verderben*]" (*Werke*, 10:379, §573).

But since philosophy, as knowledge of the absolute necessity of this corruption, can only let it take its course, it is "reconciliation not in actuality [*Wirklichkeit*] but in the ideal world" (Hegel, *Werke* 18:71f.). True, the "dialectic" that is brought to completion in the passing away of the finite does indeed have "a *positive* result" (*Werke*, 8:176, §82). But to grasp this result "positive-rationally" or "speculatively" (*Werke*, 8:176, §82) can ultimately only mean "to recognize [*erkennen*] Reason [...] in the cross of the present" (*Werke*, 7:26). For Hegel, it is precisely as this sort of reconciliation that philosophy is self-knowledge.

Yet it is therefore impossible to gain a *practical* orientation this way, to lay down this "cross," to reduce its burden, or to counteract the demise of the finite spirit of one's age. And it is precisely as this sort of reconciliation that philosophy is *self*-knowledge, for Hegel. In philosophically knowing that demise as the presence of the absolute, the philosopher, in her particularity, cannot only not stave off this death. On the contrary, to philosophize is to take part in that dying, this self-yielding, of the finite spirit in which philosophy has its age and the philosopher her life: *philosophizing is this dying as its justification—and thus as its deepening.*

Philosophy comes from life and life leads to philosophy. But philosophy, for itself, does not lead back into life. As such, and only as such, philosophy is at once knowledge of the absolute and self-knowledge of the spirit of its age. *Thus, on the Hegelian conception, philosophy neither justifies the spirit of the age as rational in a sense that would reveal it to be exempt from demise; nor does it enable us to counteract the demise that it knows to be unconditionally necessary; nor does the reconciliation that it offers in the form of this knowledge avail us of a life that tolerates this demise.*

In philosophy, as Hegel understands it, "thinking spirit" does achieve "knowledge [*Wissen*] of absolute spirit as the eternally actual truth" (*Werke*, 10:353, §553). But this knowledge, Hegel thinks, is possible only as the speculative result of an effort in which thinking spirit "casts off its own worldliness" (*Werke*, 10:353, §553)—only as the result of an attempt to attain a "standpoint [...] where the I in this singularity relinquishes itself in deed and in actuality" (*Werke*, 16:186). This means that philosophy (unlike, perhaps, art or religion) is not an activity whose characteristic point could reside in life, in the good: *the modality of philosophical insight is ultimately not a modality of practical knowledge.*[3]

---

[3] Understanding this means observing, for example, that it must be impossible to interpret Hegel as a *practical-cum-political* apologist of a particular—outdated—praxis. I leave the elaboration of this consequence for another occasion.

That is the meaning of "absolute idealism" in Hegel. And therein lies, for us, the outrageousness of Hegelian thought. Hegel's conception of philosophy (though the proof of this general yet hopefully not all-too-audacious claim can here only remain a promissory note) contradicts the self-understanding of contemporary philosophy in all its mainstream forms: the self-understanding of thought not only in the tradition of figures such as Marx, Adorno, and Horkheimer or Peirce and James but also of Aristotle and Kant, Fichte and Schelling, Kierkegaard and Nietzsche, or Heidegger and Wittgenstein. For what these traditions seem to share, despite all their differences, is what Hegel calls the "standpoint of reflection": the standpoint "where finitude lies in the fully completed abstraction of pure thinking that does not actually grasp itself as universal but rather remains as I, as This One" (Hegel, *Werke* 16:186). Philosophizing from this standpoint—i.e., philosophizing that remains anchored in the concrete, individual self (the "I, as This One")—must conceive its characteristic significance to reside in life, in the good, and must therefore reject the Hegelian conception of philosophy in the sense just sketched as outrageous.[4]

This is probably also the source of the strong interpretative tendency to overlook or omit, in one manner or another, this seemingly outrageous feature of Hegelian thought. I am thinking here, in part, of attempts to resolve the tension that seems to lie in the Hegelian conception of philosophy's thinking, in one act, the identity and non-identity of the absolute and the finite, of God and the present. These are attempts which locate the true principle of this thinking either in a one-sided form of "ordinary language philosophy" or in a strictly ahistorical form of metaphysics or transcendental philosophy.[5] I am also thinking, in part, of attempts to construe Hegel's thought as a kind of Quietism: attempts that try to prevent this tension from arising in the first place by admitting that the absolute and the present—unconditioned form and finite content—are internally related while also declaring it nonsensical to regard any sort of content—and any spirit that has an age—as the presence of the absolute.[6]

---

[4] This holds true, as we shall see, even when this anchoring is conceived as an anchoring in ethical life (in *Sittlichkeit*).

[5] Think, for example, of Charles Taylor, Terry Pinkard, and Robert Pippin, on the one side, and Dieter Henrich, James Kreines, or Robert Stern on the other. As a rule, these contrasting interpretive strategies are correlated with opposing views of the relative priority of the *Science of Logic*, on the one hand, and the *Realphilosophie* texts in Hegel's corpus, on the other, especially the *Phenomenology of Spirit* and the *Philosophy of Right*.

[6] John McDowell, for example, pursues this sort of interpretive strategy in "Hegel's Idealism as Radicalization of Kant" (McDowell 2009c, 89) when he portrays Hegelian idealism as an elaborated form of the Wittgensteinian position he advances in *Mind and World*. An even more resolute quiet-

It seems clear that none of these interpretations, tendentious in the ways just described, can do justice to Hegel's mature work as a whole.⁷ Are we then to conclude that philosophizing as Hegel understands it is on the wrong track? To do so would be too hasty. Perhaps Hegel is right. Perhaps philosophy is really, at once, knowledge of the absolute and self-knowledge of the finite spirit of its time. Perhaps, because philosophizing would then be self-knowledge of what passes away —and, as a consequence, must be dying itself—it is impossible for philosophy to have life and the good as its ultimate aim.

If that is the case, then it should be possible for us to independently develop this Hegelian conception of philosophy, in its unmitigated radicality, as a plausible one. That is, it should be possible to arrive at such a conception from our own resources, through a series of comprehensible steps, departing from an abstract characterization of the activity of philosophizing that is shared by both Hegel and contemporary philosophy alike. If we wish to avoid the merely dogmatic rejection of Hegel's conception of philosophy, we should at least be able to admit the *prima facie* possibility of this sort of argument. It is in this spirit that I undertake the following deduction. I depart from the relatively uncontroversial concept of philosophizing as the pursuit of a particular form of clarity about oneself.

I must confess at the outset that the ground of my deduction and an explanation of its results properly warrant the kind of extensive treatment that only a book can provide. The present text will thus serve as a preliminary sketch—as preparation—for an interpretation of Hegel's conception of philosophy from the point of departure indicated. It will attempt to assemble its essential moments and render its most important stages transparent. I do not aim to achieve more than a first approximation of Hegel's conception of philosophy here. But I hope that this text nevertheless—or for this reason—goes some way towards answering the question of its truth.

2 The Life of Those Who Philosophize

What is philosophy? Philosophizing has to do with gaining a particular form of clarity about oneself. To philosophize means is to ask, "Who am I?" not in the

---

ism appears in the radical variant on McDowell's position that Adrian Haddock identifies with Hegel's absolute idealism (Haddock 2017, 208).

7 I believe that Hegel's explanation of his encyclopedic system as a *threefold syllogism* (*Werke* 10, 393 f., §§575–577) precludes both a one-sided prioritization of either the *Science of Logic* or *Realphilosophie and* a quietistic abstention from the *explanation* of their relation. §3.2 makes plain both the grounds and meaning of this supposition.

sense of "What distinguishes me from you, from others, and in what ways are we similar?" but rather in the sense of "Who am I, insofar as I am capable of asking who I am in the first place?"

That philosophy is an activity that is concerned with the kind of clarity about oneself that this question raises means that it must also essentially concern philosophizing itself. By the same token, the question "What is philosophy?" is only possible as a philosophical question. No other rational activity exhibits this form of self-reference. While every rational activity is inherently self-referential, the treatment of questions such as *what* physics or sociology or music *is* cannot lie exclusively within the proper domains of physics, sociology, or music themselves. In each of these cases, the "what is" question employs—but also exceeds—the specific approaches and methods of the respective activities.

Philosophy, as we are familiar with it from its canon, is about many things other than philosophizing and those who philosophize. But these things first become intelligible as objects with which philosophy engages in a non-accidental way, by revealing their internal relation to the question that the philosophizer asks about her own philosophizing. "Who am I, insofar as I am capable of asking who I am?" can thus be singled out as *the philosophical question*.

In accordance with the characterization of philosophizing as the effort concentrated in this question, Hegel demarcates philosophy from any particular self-knowledge—that is, from any knowledge regarding oneself in one's personal peculiarity. But he also goes further—as is clear, for example, in the introduction to his *Philosophy of Spirit:*

> *Know thyself.* This absolute command does not only mean—either in itself or in its historical articulation—*self-knowledge* according to the *particular* abilities, characteristics, inclinations, and failings of the individual. It is concerned with knowledge of what the human being truly is, of what truly is in and of itself,—with *Being* [*Wesen*] itself as spirit (Hegel, *Werke* 10:9, §377).

Why is Hegel not satisfied with distinguishing philosophy from particular self-knowledge? Why does he characterize philosophical clarity about oneself as knowledge at all? Why does he go on to crown philosophical clarity as knowledge of what the human being truly is, even as knowledge of what truly is in and of itself? And what does this mean?

I will try to answer these questions by developing a step-by-step account of Hegel's conception of philosophy through a reflection on the philosophical question just sketched. While this analysis will take up central Hegelian motifs along the way (and rendering them identifiable as such), it is not meant as an exact reconstruction of any line of argumentation that we might find in Hegel's work. It is not my primary aim to provide an interpretation of Hegelian texts but instead to offer an approach that, starting from the question I sketched above, helps makes sense of the Hegelian concept of philosophy, in its unmitigated radicality, for the philosophical present.

2.1 Subjective Spirit

Philosophizing is an attempt to become clear about ourselves. It is not, however, about answering the question, "What distinguishes me from you, from others, and in what ways are we similar?" Nevertheless, as I will show in what follows, philosophizing is internally related to these other questions—to begin with, simply because philosophizing is the asking of a question and is thus, due to its peculiar self-referentiality, internally concerned with what it is to ask a question at all.

That philosophizing is the asking of a question means that it is the effort to attain a clarity that is not yet attained at the outset of the effort. The clarity that is not yet attained in asking a question is achieved when what is asked is no longer in doubt. Paradigmatically, this will be the case when the question is answered. Sometimes, however, the clarity to be achieved will reside only in the questioner's understanding that she is incapable of answering the question or that she has asked a mere pseudo-question. What sort of questioning philosophical inquiry is—whether or not the kind of clarity to which philosophizing aspires takes the form of an answer, and thus the form of knowledge—is what we shall determine.

In any event, philosophizing is the struggle to attain a clarity that is not yet already attained in this effort. The name "philosophy" itself makes reference to this. As the "love of wisdom," it is the desire for a kind of lucidity that has not simply been achieved already in the desire itself. Sometimes, however, the name is associated with the additional assertion that this lucidity is fundamentally unattainable (for us). Hegel toys with this association when he declares that his philosophic program has the aim "to be able to reject the name of *love* of *knowledge* and to be *actual knowledge*" (*Werke,* 3:14). Despite rejecting the assertion that we cannot attain complete lucidity, Hegel does view philosophizing as work. He sees it as a striving towards a goal that, while attainable, is initially still outstanding.[8] And as we

---

8 In Hegel's Inaugural Address, delivered at the University of Berlin, he put this as follows: *"The resolution to practice philosophy launches itself into thought* [...],—it throws itself *as if into a boundless sea;* all the bright colors, all outposts disappear, all other familiar lights are extinguished. [...] [W]e don't yet know what we're aiming at, where we will come out. [...] [But] [philosophy] [...] will *return all* that is true in the representations that were first generated by the instinct of Reason" (Hegel *Werke* 10:415f.). The drama of this description of the incompleteness of the clarity philosophizing seeks along with the meaning of "true" here will be clarified later on in §3.3.

will see more clearly later on, even if Wittgenstein (for example) thinks of the aim of this effort specifically not as knowledge of any form, he still agrees with Hegel in regard to its character as a striving.[9]

We will proceed on the assumption that philosophizing is a struggle, that it is work. And we will likewise assume, at this initial juncture, that the question raised above—namely, whether philosophizing can attain the clarity it seeks—has already been answered to the following extent: in its character as an essentially self-conscious striving, philosophizing—and with it the concept of philosophizing—must evidently contain at least the presumption of the possibility of its own success.[10]

Philosophizing, as the attempt to achieve a clarity that has not always already been achieved, is only possible if the being [*Sein*] of the philosopher is invested in this effort but not exhausted by it. This means, in a first step, that the philosophic inquirer is the subject of determinations that keep her from the clarity to be achieved, but which she must nevertheless be able to cast aside, since she is to be regarded as at least *prima facie* capable of achieving the clarity for which she strives. Since these are thus determinations that we must be able to detach from the philosopher as well as ascribe to her, they are determinations that are *necessarily possible* but not *necessary* to ascribe to her. This means they are *contingent determinations*. And since the negation of a contingent determination must likewise be contingent, the philosopher will still be contingently determined after having cast aside the determinations that impede the clarity for which she strives. Generally speaking, this means that the being [*Sein*] of the philosopher is the being [*Sein*] of a *subject of contingent determinations, too.* A Being [*Wesen*] whose being [*Sein*] exhausts itself in philosophical clarity is, as a consequence, impossible.[11]

---

[9] "[T]he clarity that we are aiming at is indeed *complete* clarity. But this simply means that the philosophical problems should *completely* disappear" (Wittgenstein 2001, §133).

[10] This is not to say that the idea of an essential incapacity for philosophical clarity should be excluded upfront. It is only to say that the idea is only possible, at any rate, as the assertion of the antinomial character of the activity of philosophizing itself.

[11] This is not yet an assertion of the impossibility of a Being [*Wesen*] whose being [*Sein*] exhausts itself in a sort of clarity that is closely related to philosophical clarity—an unquestioning, effortless knowledge that knows itself to be knowledge which has always already been achieved. In the *Metaphysics* $\Lambda.7$, Aristotle provides an account of such non-philosophical, pure self-knowledge. Hegel's system, in contrast, is designed to make clear that knowledge that knows itself to be knowledge can only be acquired by philosophizing, i.e., by contingently determined Beings. It is for this reason that he chooses to conclude the *Philosophy of Spirit* (which ends with a discussion of philosophizing itself) with a lengthy citation from *Metaphysics* $\Lambda.7$. This also follows from his definition of philosophical clarity about oneself as "knowledge of what is true about man and what is true in of for itself," which I aim to have made plausible by the end of this essay.

Philosophizing is always also about philosophizing itself, and thus, among other things, about its character as the asking of a question. Hence, as we are now in a position to state, it is about the being [*Sein*] of the philosopher as the subject of contingent determinations. Therefore, in her philosophizing, the philosopher must be able to become conscious of her being [*Sein*] as this sort of subject and to determine which of her contingent determinations keep her from the philosophical clarity she seeks. The philosopher's *self*, in other words, must be the *self* of contingent determinations as well.

Because these contingent determinations *oppose* the clarity she strives for as philosopher—they oppose her being *as* philosopher—they therefore pertain to an *actuality* that exceeds her subjectivity *as* philosophical striver. And in this respect, the question that she must pose in the course of her philosophizing—"Which contingent determinations are ascribed to me?"—must be, initially and *regardless of the epistemological status of the striven-for philosophical clarity itself*, an expression of her own striving for *knowledge*.[12] Taken together, this means that the self of the philosopher must also be the self of *contingent self-knowledge*.

Within the framework of his *Encyclopedia*, Hegel first addresses this concrete self, and thus philosophy, not in the *Logic* but in the *Philosophy of Spirit*—whose topic differs from that of the *Logic* in that it presupposes nature.[13] The philosopher is *also* a subject of non-philosophical—and initially *contra*-philosophical—contingent self-knowledge. This "*also*," which is required to think a concrete self like the philosopher's, contains the idea of an *obstruction* [*Behinderung*] to philosophical clarity. According to Hegel, logic is capable of describing obstruction in general. But obstruction is only grasped in its real possibility when we have recourse to what we call *nature*, and not by logic alone.[14] The concept of the *absolute idea* that Hegel develops at the end of the *Logic*—an abstract concept of pure clarity about oneself—is therefore not to be confused with his concept of philosophy. The concept of philosophy is a concept of *Realphilosophie* rather than a logical

---

12 Knowledge is what enables us to answer the question of the actuality of a determination. In §2.2, it will become clear that although "actuality," in this sense, cannot be immediately identified with "objectivity," the actuality of the object of *self*-knowledge is ultimately possible only as objectivity.
13 We humans are bearers of spirit in the Hegelian sense—beings whose existence is oriented toward philosophical clarity without being exhausted in it; beings who initially owe their contingent determinacy to their origin "in nature" (Hegel *Werke* 10:17, §377, Addition).
14 See Hegel (*Werke* 9:27f., §248).

one. For philosophy, qua clarity about the inquiring character of philosophizing itself, must amount to more than logic.[15]

So, the self of the philosopher is also the self of contingent self-knowledge. Self-knowledge is knowledge to whose form as knowledge it belongs that the subject who thus knows herself is identical to the subject of the content that is thus known. Discovering with a glance in the mirror that my hair is turning gray, for example, is therefore just as little self-knowledge in this (proper) sense as is the observation I make by glancing out the window (perhaps also with the help of a mirror) that the gorse is blooming. The two observations share the same epistemological form. For the identity between knowing subject and known object is, in the former case, just as extrinsic to the relevant form of *theoretical knowledge* as it is in the latter.

Self-knowledge in its primary sense, in other words, cannot be theoretical knowledge. "I," the first-person singular pronoun, is employed in the grammatical expression of self-knowledge. And it is self-knowledge to which "I" owes its particular sense. So if, as in the example, "I am going gray" (as opposed to "This one here is going gray") is an expression of self-knowledge, then this cannot be explained, in any case, by its form as theoretical knowledge alone.

Let the statement "I know that I am Φ" (where "Φ" stands for a negatable determination of myself, the philosopher) be the expression of an act of contingent self-knowledge. Now, the form of the declarative sentence as such is (I shall assume here) the form of articulated knowledge claims. Therefore, the verb "to know" in this sentence does not initially belong to the expression of its content. And because this sentence is an expression of an act of self-knowledge—to whose form as knowledge it belongs that the subject who thus knows herself is identical to the subject of the content thus known—we must also, in order to give only its content, "cancel" the "I"s we find to the left and right of the "that" which separates the act from its content. The content of this sentence is therefore initially to be given thus: "Φ."

Self-knowledge whose content is given in this way is evidently only possible, however, if the "self" in "self-knowledge" characterizes at once the form in which the contingent determination Φ is known and the form of its being [*Sein*] as a (known) determination. In other words, this kind of self-knowledge is only possible if it is at the same time an act of self-*determination*. And because an act is only *knowledge* if it refers to a content that *actually* exists, such an act of

---

[15] Hegel's reasons for distinguishing the *Logic* from the *Philosophy of Spirit* in this way—namely, by way of the concept of *nature* as the concept of the "fall [*Abfall*] of the idea from itself" (Hegel *Werke* 9:28, §248)—will become evident in §3.2.

self-determination must further be knowledge that is *the cause of* the actuality [*Wirklichkeit*] of *what it knows.* Thus, it must be what we might call (loosely following G. E. M. Anscombe) *practical knowledge*—or, more simply, *action.*[16]

As the expression of the struggle to achieve self-knowledge that it must be, the question, "Which contingent determinations are ascribed to me?" is identical with the *simple practical question,* "What is to be done?" in which the verb "done" merely denotes the form of contingent self-determination. With this, our provisional answer to the philosophical question has become more concrete: Philosophizing is the activity of a subject who is also an agent.

The content of an answer to the simple practical question ("What is to be done?") initially amounts to nothing more than the contingent determination Φ that is generated through action. This, however, means that practical knowledge initially has a content that would make it impossible for the acting subject to ask: "What distinguishes me from you, from others, and how are we similar?" We might say, therefore, that Nietzsche's description of the ideal of the "noble way of valuing"—"there is no 'being' [*Sein*] behind doing, effecting, becoming; 'the doer' is merely a fiction added to the deed—the deed is everything" (Nietzsche 1988, 279)—is an accurate description of the acting subject's self-understanding. The following considerations, however, show why we cannot simply leave it at that.

The subject of action, according to the way we introduced it above, is a philosopher. As such, she is conscious in her actions of these actions as self-determinations that are contingent—and, because contingent, distinct from her philosophizing. In light of what we have just said, this can initially only mean that the active subject conceives of her actions as an activity of contingent determination whose only ground and source is a principle which, due to its form, is utterly universal, hence completely empty and unconditional. In other words, they must have their ground and source in the *practical law,* as I shall call it. We can think of this practical law as the principle of non-contradiction (which articulates the form of knowable contingent determinations in general), but conceived here as itself the ground and source of such determinations.

That Φ is a contingent determination of the active subject means, however, that possibility—i.e., the capacity of this subject to do Φ—should be distinguished here from the corresponding actuality—i.e., from her act itself. Now action, as self-determination, cannot have its source outside the acting subject itself. For this reason, her capacity to do Φ, which constitutes her as an active subject, is to be conceived at the same time as her *desire* to do Φ. And this would be fully unintelligible if this capacity were not also constituted by the negation of Φ or of an essential

---

[16] See Anscombe (1957, 87). The point here is the formula itself, not Anscombe's own take on it.

moment of Φ.[17] The negation of a contingent determination (or of a moment of the same) will be, to be sure, also contingent. Thus, the capacity of the active subject to do Φ—a capacity that is co-constituted by the negation in question—will itself be contingent and, as a consequence, *determinate*, i.e., particular.[18] Because action is knowledge that is itself the cause of what it known, and thus can only have its source in the subject itself, it must be the case that these particular capacities and desires constitute this subject as a *particular subject* to be distinguished from each of her individual actions—i.e., as a *person*. It is therefore no accident that the word "I," in fact, always stands for a *determinate* subject.

The active subject must be aware, in her actions, of those actions as contingent self-knowledge. Because of this, action—i.e., this contingent self-knowledge itself—must amount to something more than the answer to the simple practical question. It is ultimately impossible for an agent to understand herself merely as a "noble valuer" in the Nietzschean sense or as actualizing the empty practical law alone. Instead, in her action itself, she must distinguish herself as a particular subject (as a person) from any of her respective actions.

That she must, in her actions, distinguish herself as a particular subject from her actions means, in the first instance, that these actions have the character of preserving the active subject in her particularity; that is, they have the character of *vital activities*. But since, in the agent's self-understanding, her actions amount to an activity whose ground and source as self-determination lies solely in empty practical law, the character of action as vital activity cannot, for the agent herself, have the form of preserving a pre-determined Being [*Wesen*] of hers. Instead, action must be *free self-constitution*. In other words, the active subject's constitution —i.e., the capacities and desires which together make her the particular subject who differs from each of her respective actions—must be the subject's own work. It must be the work of the subject's actions, which are, ultimately, to be traced back to the empty practical law.

We can thus further specify our provisional answer to the philosophical question above as follows: Philosophizing is the activity of a subject who actively constitutes her *practical identity* herself, where *practical identity* consists in what, for her, is to be realized in action, i.e., in the *good*. Philosophizing is the activity of an

---

[17] The "or" in this sentence conceals a question about the relationship of the *action-theoretical determination* of action, of Φ-ing, as a form of κινησις, and the *praxis-theoretical* or *moral-philosophical determination* of the same, as a form of ενεργεια, which I will not address at the present time—trusting that a correct response to this question would not significantly alter the course of my argument.

[18] From this, it follows that not every arbitrary contingent determination can be produced by action but—as is actually the case—only those that the agents are *actually* capable of producing.

autonomous subject.[19] It follows from this that an action can no longer simply be thought of as a contingent determination of the subject. Instead, action—as the creation of one's own Being [*Wesen*] through practical self-determination—is to be conceived as sublating [*aufheben*] the dichotomy between the contingent and the essential. Thus, it is to be conceived as *activity* or *process*.[20]

That the agent constitutes herself as a person by acting has the further meaning that, in acting as the self-constituted source of her actions, she distinguishes herself from that empty practical law which she must nevertheless also think practically (in fact, first and foremost) as the ground and source of her actions. The first step toward resolving the contradiction that threatens here consists in conceiving the relationship of the empty practical law to those actions (and thus, to the particular practical identity of the subject who is to be constituted in them) as *normative*. Accordingly, the law (and likewise her practical identity) is to be understood as the *origin* of action in the sense that it *necessitates* it—that is, it provides motivation against inner resistance.[21]

This is how it must be. But how is that possible? How is it possible for a subject, proceeding from the formality of the "I" (which is necessary for action as self-determination) and the concomitant emptiness of the practical law, to think of herself as a particular person—and, as such, as compelled from this innermost point

---

19 See Korsgaard: "[I]n the relevant sense there is no *you* prior to your choices and actions because your identity is in a quite literal way *constituted* by your choices and actions" (Korsgaard 2009, 19). Korsgaard herself, however, strictly distinguishes between a person's practical identity and what the good consists in for that person: "[We must] maintain our personal or practical identity […] in order to maintain our agency itself. And the person who succeeds in that is good—not because he is striving to be good, but because he is striving to be unified, to be whole" (Korsgaard 2009, 26). The exclusion of the *adjectival* use of "good" here and its limitation to *adverbial* phrases is supposed to preempt a particular criticism (inspired by Hegel, among others) of the Kantian conception of the highest good as eternally eluding realization, I take it. In my view, however, this could be nothing more than an artificial, merely verbal dialectical maneuver. For how can a striving be good or be found to be good if this is not equally the case for what is being striven for? §2.3 brings out the systematic foundations of these doubts about Korsgaard's distinction.
20 Korsgaard's formulation is particularly apt: "Making the contingent necessary is one of the tasks of human life" (Korsgaard 2008, 23). And she sees the consequence clearly: "[S]elf-constitution is not a state that we achieve and from which action then issues […], it is action itself" (Korsgaard 2008, 44).
21 See Kant (1990b, 82) and Korsgaard (2009, 7 and 26). It would be a misunderstanding to see Hegel's well-known criticism of Kant's deontological ethics as a rejection of the idea of the ought itself. Hegel's own theory of ethical life—about the standpoint of which, he says that Kantian ethic "annihilates and scandalizes" the very idea (Hegel *Werke* 7:88, §33)—should also be understood, according to him, as itself a "deontology" (Hegel *Werke* 7:297, §148). In §2.2, I discuss the true core of the Hegelian criticism of Kant.

of departure? And how is it possible to then think of the determinacy she gives herself in her actions as initially contingent, and, as a consequence, to think of her actions as self-constitution?

The necessity of departing from the empty and the formal implies that this question cannot be answered by referring to an awareness of some sort of mere possibility. And it implies *that this question is therefore posed with necessity*. Accordingly, what is sought here is an actuality, which, when confronted, prompts the agent to move beyond her necessary, incipient awareness of determinations which are in themselves contingent (albeit not yet for her) and thus for the first time to place before herself her own character as a person with particular capacities and desires, her own inherent vitality [*Lebendigkeit*]. This has to be an actuality that is opposed to the agent's own life—one that is different from the agent herself. The same unconditional intractability which attaches to the agent's self-preservation of a practical identity—a practical identity that, as such, takes itself to spring from the unconditional ground and source of a practical law conceived as empty—must likewise pertain to it. The requisite actuality, in other words, can only be *another active subject*. And because, for an agent, self-consciousness is originally self-constitution (and therefore action), the confrontation with this actuality must, at least initially, consist in an activity in which both subjects seek the other's life in such a way as to therein become conscious of the fact that this is what they do.

The self-knowledge internal to action, in other words, must lie in a self-consciousness that consists in the active *recognition* of another agent as a person who is self-conscious in the same sense and in the same activity—a person in this very same struggle. With this, however, it is immediately clear that the confrontation with the other, although the life of both must be at stake in it, ought not to end with the other's death. And this consideration is, evidently, equally valid for both sides in the confrontation: Recognition is essentially mutual. It is equally evident that, precisely because the death of the other would make it impossible, this recognition cannot be some merely perspectival act. The reciprocity of recognition cannot consist in mutual one-sidedness. In other words, recognition —and thus the personality of the agents who are recognized as recognizing and, as such, are also the recognizing recognized—consists primarily in the real interaction of the two agents. Recognition consists in the reality of a shared practical life. Personality is practical relationality.[22]

---

[22] This conclusion accords with—to take one example—the basic argument of Robert Pippin's interpretation of Hegel's practical philosophy: "[It is] only qua participant that I can be said to have practical reasons at all" (Pippin 2008a, 247). The derivation I have sketched here, however, has con-

These are the outlines of a systematic answer to the question of the *how* of self-consciousness, which Hegel develops within the framework of his *Philosophy of Spirit* under the heading of "Phenomenology of Spirit." It follows from this answer that a person is inherently capable of asking: "What distinguishes me from you, from others, and how are we similar?" And because the philosopher's personality has proven to be a condition of the possibility of her philosophizing, what has been shown is that philosophizing actually is internally related to this other question—to start with, simply because it is itself the asking of a question and hence has, among other things, the asking of question as its content.

2.2 Objective Spirit

Our provisional answer to the philosophical question has, to the following degree, become more concrete: Philosophizing is the activity of a subject who participates in a shared practical life. That means that a person's self-constitution and self-preservation in action is only possible within the self-constitution and self-preservation of a community of persons. Because action, or practical self-knowledge, is the an-

---

sequences that go significantly beyond this interpretation, as will be seen especially in §§2.2 and 2.3. Christine Korsgaard fails to pose the question of the grounds for the possibility of self-consciousness that lie in necessitation. For her, necessitation—and thereby self-consciousness, and thus action itself—is simply our lot as human beings: "our *plight:* the simple inexorable fact of the human condition" (Korsgaard 2009, 2; see also 23 and 26). It is thus the case that, for Korsgaard, interaction with others cannot have a primary constitutive significance for action as such. Her attempt to explain interactions with others on the basis of the "interaction with oneself" that is—she thinks—already included in the idea of necessitation (Korsgaard 2009, 202 ff.) reveals this fact. (See also Haase 2014, 128 f.) It is obvious that this sort of explanation cannot account for the actuality or aliveness of the other; it must simply assume it. Korsgaard's philosophical conception of personal relationships—I am grateful to Sasha Newton for this reference—has its psychological corollary in Novalis' stylization of his love for his dead bride, Sophie, as the most intimate form of love in general: both are equally desperate. (Kant himself (Korsgaard's philosophical star witness) knows, on the contrary, that this sort of reductive explanation is impossible. His understanding of the difference between actual interactions with others and the necessitation that is already inherent in the categorical imperative is evident in the way he distinguishes the *Groundwork for a Metaphysics of Morals* and the *Critique of Practical Reason* from the *Metaphysics of Morals*, especially the *Doctrine of Right*, and *Religion Within the Boundaries of Mere Reason*, in particular the third main section. (For more on this, see Gobsch 2014, 185 ff.).) Because Korsgaard, as sketched above, fails to recognize the central significance for action of the confrontation with the other, she also does not recognize the significance of the unity of an agent's personality with her aliveness. Thus, she thinks of this unity as the mere unity of two actualities, in which one (the personality) "supervenes" on the other (animality). (Korsgaard 2009, 19; see also 42, 49, and 127). In effect, therefore, she promotes a certain type of *dualism* (on "dualism" in this sense, see Gobsch 2017, 125 f.).

swer to a question and thus an act of thinking, while the form of community in thinking is language, one of the pivotal claims of Wittgenstein's *Philosophical Investigations* follows from this provisional answer to the philosophical question: "If language is to be a means of communication there must be agreement not only in definitions but also [...] in judgments" (Wittgenstein 1953, §242).

Now, on the one hand, such agreement in judgments can only be conceived as the expression of a communal practical *life* (which this agreement must be) if the practical identity of the community in question—i.e., the communal good that manifests itself in this agreement—is thought of as essentially actualized and not as something which merely ought to be (and thus as an empty law whose actualization perpetually recedes). On the other hand, such agreement can only be conceived as the expression of a communal *practical* life (which it must equally be) if this good is constituted in such a way for it to be possible to ascribe the accordant judgments it manifests to the absolute which is initially conceived in the empty practical law, and in which action, as such, ought to have its ground and source. And this is evidently only possible if there is more to the actual good than the mere unity of goods that the actual members of the community in question actively realize at any given time as their personal identities. It is only possible, in other words, if this good is not conceived by the agents as the actual good of *their* community alone—i.e., as a merely *(inter)subjective* good.[23] This is the truth of contemporary Wittgensteinians' critique of what Wittgenstein calls the "sideways-on view."[24]

This community—understood as having emerged from an initial confrontation—must be a community of persons who, as its members, distinguish themselves from one another in a self-conscious way. As a consequence, the truth behind

---

[23] This means, among other things, that a community of agents cannot be created originally by contract, and that it cannot essentially belong to a community that is oriented toward the good to be limited to particular members or to a particular number of members. And it also means, conversely, that a person inherently is not only necessarily capable of asking: "What distinguishes me from you, from others, and how are we similar?" but also: "Who am I in comparison with *all possible* others?" It means that a person must necessarily have the capacity for *objective-particular*—or, if we want to put it this way, *psychological*—self-knowledge.

[24] McDowell, for example, formulates the underlying thought behind this criticism as follows: "We find ourselves always already engaging with the world in conceptual activity within [...] a dynamic system. Any understanding of this condition that it makes sense to hope for must be from within the system. It cannot be a matter of picturing the system's adjustments to the world from sideways on: that is, with the system circumscribed within a boundary, and the world outside it" (McDowell 1996, 34). See Hegel (*Werke* 7:296, §147, Addition). McDowell's own "minimal empiricism," however, cannot do justice to the truth of the criticism of the "sideways-on view," as I have tried to show in Gobsch (2017, 149 ff.).

the rejection of subjectivism cannot be—even in the best case involving the highest virtue—that the subjectivity of persons is simply transparent to the good of the community.[25] This means, on the one hand, that the individual person, in her actions, must understand the good as something that is only conceivable from the point of view of the unconditionality [*Unbedingtheit*] of her freedom—and thus as something essentially *spiritual* [*geistig*]. On the other hand, however, she must understand the good as an actuality that infinitely transcends her subjectivity as an agent. Taken together, this means that the good is to be understood as *spiritual objectivity*, as *objective spirit*.[26] As will be seen even more clearly in what follows, this means, among other things, that the relation of individual persons to the good in the ethical community cannot possibly be merely practical. On the contrary, it must contain a theoretical moment too.

Because the good that is thought as objective spirit constitutes the actuality of *freedom*, this good entails what Hegel calls the "right of the subjective will":

> The *right of the subjective will* is that whatever it shall acknowledge [*anerkennen*] as valid is known [*eingesehen*] by it *as good*, and that an action, as it enters upon external objectivity, is classified as just or unjust, good or evil, lawful or unlawful, in accordance with its *cognizance* [*Kenntnis*] of the value it has in this objectivity (Hegel, *Werke* 7:245, §132).

As the right to *know* the good, this right is just as unconditional as the "I" of self-knowledge is formal and the practical law is, correspondingly, empty. But as a person's right to know the *good*—i.e., that which is to be realized by her *in action*—it is the right to acknowledge the particularity of her person along with the concomitant limitations of her capacities and cognizance of all that belongs to the objectivity of the good. Hence, conceived of as the unity of absoluteness and particularity, the right of the subjective will (which is grounded in the idea of the good itself) contains—*a priori* and necessarily—the "potential [...] to elevate one's own *choices*, one's *own particularity*, above the universal to the status of the highest principle and realizing it through action—i.e., the potential to be *evil*" (Hegel, *Werke* 7:261, §139).

And that is not all. In light of this characterization of evil as the declaration of individual particularity as the highest law, the struggle at the origins of community

---

[25] This means that even in the best-case scenario, we must be able to think of the law of the good as *necessitating*. The grounds for action that lie in this good cannot possibly be understood primarily as, for example, McDowell describes them in the case of highest virtue: "not as outweighing or overriding any reasons for acting in other ways, [...] but as silencing them" (McDowell 1998, 55f.).
[26] See especially Hegel (*Werke* 7:295, §147). Conversely, and in view of the difference between the *Philosophy of Spirit* and the *Science of Logic*, this thought can also be expressed as follows: Objectivity, conceived as *Realphilosophie* is to conceive of it, *is* nothing other than objective spirit.

that is necessary for practical self-consciousness turns out to be, in retrospect, itself a figure of evil. And, conversely, in light of the necessity of this very confrontation, evil proves to be not only necessarily possible, but necessarily actual.[27]

The contradiction [*Widerspruch*] that hereby threatens both the good itself and the subjectivity that realizes the good cannot be resolved by abandoning either the objectivity of the good or the right of the subjective will.[28] Instead, the good is to be conceived as something *concrete* in which universality is "brought into harmony [*ausgeglichen*]" with the individual agent's particularity.[29] Conversely, we

---

27 See Hegel (*Werke* 7:262, §139). The sense in which the struggle for recognition is already a figure of evil is admittedly more complicated than I am able to go into here. For initially, precisely because it does not yet distinguish its own particularity from the universality of the true good, this struggle is to be thought of as entirely innocent. It is only with the retrospective insight that their struggle can neither end in death nor in a one-sided hegemony do those doing battle recognize it, in its relentlessness, as evil. Their recognition is apparent since, in their practical ideas about leading a *shared* life, they *retract* this relentlessness as precisely *what is to be overcome*. Disregarding the fact that Kant does not think of moral evil as a constitutively *social* act—and for that reason, ultimately misguided, he does get to the root of the matter when he explains in *Religion Within the Boundaries of Mere Reason*: "For no matter how far back we direct our attention to our moral state, we find that this state is no longer *res integra*, and that we must rather start by dislodging from its possession the evil which has already taken up position there (as it could not have done, however, if it had not been incorporated by us into our maxims). That is, the first really good thing that a human being can do is to extricate himself from an evil which is to be sought not in his inclinations but in his perverted maxims, and hence in freedom itself" (Kant 1900b, 56) Hegel confirms the difficulty to be found in this *retrospective self-recrimination* as necessary in a description that is similar to Kant's: "The *origin of evil* in general is to be found in the enigma of freedom—i.e., in its speculative aspect, in its need to depart from the *naturalness* [*Natürlichkeit*] of the will and to be *inward* in contrast to it. [...] Man is therefore evil both *in himself* or *by nature* and owing to his *reflection in itself*; and therefore neither nature as such—unless it is [conceived as] the naturalness of the will that sticks to particular natural contents—nor reflection that *turns inward* [*die in sich gehende Reflexion*], or cognition [*Erkennen*] in general—unless it were to hold itself in opposition [to the universal]—is evil in its own right [*für sich*]. [...] The individual *subject* as such, therefore, is entirely *to blame for evil*" (*Werke* 7:261, §139). On the Kantian origins of this thought and its significance for Hegel's theory of ethical life, see Gobsch (2014, 188–190).

28 "Conjoined in just as absolute a manner with this aspect of *the necessity of evil* is the fact that this same evil is determined as that which necessarily *ought not to be*—i.e., it ought to be sublated [*aufgehoben*]. It is *not* that the standpoint of separation [*Entzweiung*] ought never to appear [...], but the point is that things should not come to a standstill there, particularity should not be clung to as if it, instead of the universal, were the essential thing, and this standpoint should be overcome as null and void [*nichtig*]" (Hegel *Werke* 7:262, §139).

29 "[T]he concrete and the true (everything true is concrete)," as Hegel formulates one of his principles, is "the universality that has its antithesis in the particular, which, however, through reflection in itself is brought into harmony [*ausgeglichen*] with the universal" (*Werke* 7:55, §7).

can no longer understand the right of the subjective will as merely the subject's *right* to recognize the good. We must understand it as a *duty* or *task* as well. And since this duty's ground can only be located in her personality as such, the duty further implies that the individual person inherently must have a principal *interest* in her theoretical-practical *education [Bildung]*.[30] In this way—and only in this way—the good is no *stranger* to the subject. It is instead "its own Being [*Wesen*] [...] in which it has its *feeling of self*" (Hegel, *Werke* 7:295, §147). Therefore, communal life that is oriented toward the good, when the good is understood in this way, is precisely what Hegel calls *ethical life [Sittlichkeit]*.[31] Our provisional answer to the philosophical question can thus be specified still further: philosophizing is the activity of an ethical Being.

2.3 Ethical Life as Presence of the Absolute

Ethical life [*Sittlichkeit*] is *objectivity* that is known in action, i.e., in *self*-knowledge. As ethical knowledge—and in none of the forms discussed before—self-knowledge is knowledge in the *full* sense. The idea of self-*knowledge*, which subsequently emerged as the idea of action, was introduced in §2.1 to account for the actuality that must belong to the philosopher's internally accessible determinations, which keep her from the clarity that defines her striving and being as philosopher. There, it could still have seemed as if the acting subject were onto a reality that, while it exceeded her subjectivity as acting subject, was still ultimately grounded in this subjectivity. It could still have seemed, as we might put it, as if this reality were *appearance [Erscheinung]*.

---

30 See Hegel (*Werke* 7:345, §187).
31 In the *Encyclopedia Logic*, Hegel elucidates his concept of the object as a threefold syllogism using the state as a paradigm—an elucidation which we, conversely, can call on for a preliminary illumination of the concept of ethical life: "In the practical sphere, for instance, the State is a system of three syllogisms just like the solar system. (1) The *individual [Einzelne]* (the person) conjoins itself through his *particularity* (the physical and spiritual needs which, when further developed on their own account, give rise to civil society) with the *universal* (society, right, law, government). (2) The will, or individuals' activity, is the mediating [term] that satisfies these needs in the context of society, right, etc., and provides fulfillment and actualization to society, right, etc. (3) But it is the universal (State, government, right) that is the substantial middle term within which individuals and their satisfaction have and preserve their full reality, mediation, and subsistence. Each of these determinations, because this mediation conjoins them with the other extreme, conjoins itself with itself therein, produces itself; and this production is its self-preservation" (Hegel *Werke* 8:356, §198).

It could still have seemed, in other words, as if we could do justice to the idea of practical self-knowledge by describing the reality in which we act as Korsgaard does: "[W]e conceptualize the world in a way that makes it possible for us to act in it." Accordingly, we could seemingly do justice to our subjectivity as active Beings in saying, "The necessity of choosing and acting is [...] our *plight:* the simple inexorable fact of the human condition" (Korsgaard 2009, 89, 2).

It could still have seemed as if we could keep these two descriptions together, while preempting the objection that their conjunction, which grounds the idea of the world in a merely contingent fact, runs the risk of being misunderstood as expressing a merely *subjective-idealistic* "sideways-on view," by adding a variation of proposition 5.62 from Wittgenstein's *Tractatus* to the quotation above:

> In fact what our idealism *means*, is quite correct, only it cannot be *said*, but it shows itself. That the world is *our* world, shows itself in the fact that the limits of *the* language (the language which only we understand) mean the limits of *our* world.[32]

But in fact, the appearance of the possibility of a *transcendental Idealism* or *Quietism of practical or ethical reason* (as we might label this position) has by this stage vanished. Action had to deepen into ethical action. And as such, it is objective self-knowledge: *As clarity about oneself* it is *objective knowledge* and *as objective knowledge*, it is *clarity about oneself.* It therefore cannot have its ultimate ground in the agent's subjectivity alone—quite independent of whether this subjectivity is thought of in the singular or the plural, as monadic or relational; and quite independent of whether subjectivity is stated as this ground or merely shows in some way or accompanies our thoughts. And that means that we can no longer simply attribute the emptiness of the practical law—in which the truth of the critique of the "sideways-on view" of practical self-knowledge is grounded—to the formality of the "I." Instead, we must attribute the formality of the "I" itself, along with the emptiness of the practical law, to an unconditional ground and source. And then, at any rate, it must be true to say that this ground and source infinitely transcends and supports the "I"—and with this, the "we"—of practical knowledge's subjectivity. It is from the standpoint of this absolute that Hegel thinks the ethical good when he characterizes it as the *"absolute final end of the world"* (*Werke*, 7:243, §129).[33]

---

[32] Wittgenstein's original reads: "In fact what solipsism *means*, is quite correct, only in cannot be *said*, but it shows itself. That the world is *my* world, shows itself in the fact that the limits of *the* language (the language that only we understand) mean the limits of *my* world" (Wittgenstein 1922).
[33] Therefore, the most common explanation of the good today—in Christoph Menke's words, for example: "to be something good means to have a determinate role or a determinate "status" in a

Precisely as such, however, the ethical good is also *"realized freedom"* (Hegel, *Werke* 7:243, §129).³⁴ And this has consequences for the concept of freedom itself. Korsgaard understands autonomy proper to reside merely in our freedom to determine in our actions what acting as such (which she thinks of as our plight) amounts to for us. She thus understands our autonomy simply as the freedom to determine a particular practical identity. By contrast, she understands our relation to the practical law as such not as free in the proper sense of the word but as autonomous only in the sense that this law, which we actualize in acting, constitutes us—as our plight.³⁵ And the transcendental philosopher or quietist who is aware of the Wittgensteinian reproach of the "sideways-on view" grasps this understanding of freedom as an understanding that merely shows itself in our willing and speaking without constituting its content. In truth, however, the freedom with which we act must essentially also extend to *acting as such* itself. Hegel thus declares:

> The *Being* [*Wesen*] of spirit is, [...] formally, *freedom* [...]. On account of this formal determination, spirit *can* abstract from all that is external and even from its own externality, from its existence [*Dasein*] itself. It can endure the infinite *pain* of the negation of its individual immediacy (Hegel, *Werke* 10:25 f., §382).³⁶

Freedom, as the Being we realize and preserve in action, is *defined* as the capacity to also negate our existence [*Dasein*] as agents.³⁷ But the existence [*Dasein*] of free-

---

praxis" (Menke 2017, 680; see also Pippin 2008a, 97 ff.)—cannot be more than half the story about the ethical good.

34 Compare: "[E]thical life is the concept of freedom that became the existing world and the nature of self-consciousness" (Hegel *Werke* 7:292, §142).

35 "So we choose the principles of our own causality, and in doing so we constitute our identities as individual human agents. This doesn't mean, of course, that we choose the hypothetical and categorical imperatives themselves. The Kantian imperatives are principles that instruct us in how to formulate our maxims; autonomy and efficacy set standards for the form of our maxims. It is because for us constructing the will is in this way a *task*, that for us the standards of efficacy and autonomy take imperative form"(Korsgaard 2009, 131). This *constitutivism* or *expressionism* is frequently incorrectly ascribed to Hegel and the other German Idealists. See, for example, Taylor (1978, 28 f.) and Pinkard (2007, 210); see also Rödl (2007, 117 f.).

36 It is only from *here*, then, that Hegel's *positive* determination of free will is to be understood: "The abstract concept of the idea of the will is *the free will that wills the free will.*" (*Werke* 7:79, §27).

37 One might object that a constitutivist like Korsgaard is also able to account for the fact that the freedom of human self-constitution contains the possibility of suicide. This is true. What matters, however, is that as a constitutivist she cannot admit that we preserve freedom in self-constitutive action essentially *as* this possibility. In other words, she can only think the possibility of suicide as the capacity for types of action which, as causes, are *extrinsically* related to the effect of one's own

dom consists in our subsistence as ethical Beings. Ethical life is, as such, the condition of possibility for action, and hence for freedom. For this reason, this existence [*Dasein*] cannot be indifferent to the Being of spirit, or freedom. And the negation of this Being's existence is therefore, of necessity, as Hegel puts it, "infinite pain" (*Werke*, 10:25, §382). Taken together, that means that *ethical life must be the actuality of preserving itself as the capacity for self-negation*. Thus, the source and ground to which we attribute the formality of the "I" and the emptiness of the practical law is to be recognized as the absolute that at once transcends subjectivity yet is also substantially realized in the self-preservation of that subjectivity. Hegel makes this point as follows:

> Ethical life is the divine Spirit as indwelling in self-consciousness, as it is actually present in a nation and its individual members. [...] The two are inseparable: there cannot be two kinds of conscience, one religious and another ethical, which differs from the former in matter and content (Hegel, *Werke* 8:355f., §198).[38]

---

death. *Thus, it would do no harm to the law of freedom as such if this relation did not exist.* Constitutivism is barred from thinking that the capacity for self-negation belongs to the *definition* of spirit—and hence to the practical law itself. (That Kant himself is no Korsgaardian either is clear, among other things, in that he thinks the practical law, the law of our will, simultaneously as the law of the *divine* (*non-subjective, non-worldly*) will. He thus conceives of our own will, for which this law has an imperative character, as necessarily imperfect (see, for example, Kant 1990a, 414). Korsgaard is critical of Kant's analysis (see, for example, Korsgaard 2008, 51f.); in her criticism, however, she overlooks precisely the insight that moves Kant here.)

38 The idea of Hegelian ethical life is not the idea of a closed theocracy, as it might appear to be from this quotation alone. It is essential to the institutions of an ethical community of the sort described above that they demonstrate an understanding of their own finitude and the finitude of the persons who embody them. There are a number of examples of this: the institution of marriage includes the possibility of divorce (Hegel *Werke* 7:324, §172); the administration of justice includes the possibility of appeal (see Gans 2005, 178); the relationship between the constitutional bodies is generally conceived through the idea of "checks and balances" (see *Werke* 7:481, §312), etc. That ethical life is objectivity and thus the presence of the absolute means, for Hegel's characterization of ethical life as "the spirit of a people," that this sort of "national spirit [*Volksgeist*]" is essentially only possible as the preservation of its relationships to the other "national spirits [*Volksgeistern*]" (*Werke* 7:497ff., §330ff.).

3 Philosophy

3.1 Philosophy as Self-Knowledge

If ethical life is the presence of the absolute, then the determinacy that pertains to ethical life—since in ethical life, which is intrinsically concrete, universality must be "reconciled" with the particularity of actual individuals—is *the determinacy of the absolute itself*.[39] In the case of the ethical good, in other words, we cannot distinguish form from content in such a way that we could claim—or that it could show—that while the existence of *some* ethical good is necessary, the *determinate* good of one's own ethical life remains contingent.[40] No, to characterize the form of ethical life *means* to describe one's own ethical life. And to describe one's own ethical life *means* to present it as absolutely necessary. In short, ethical life makes it impossible to separate ethics from meta-ethics.

It follows from this that it is also impossible for us even to think a higher good apart from the good of our own ethical life. Accordingly, ideas for ethical improvement can only be possible as practical or political suggestions aimed at resolving concrete tensions in the actuality of our own ethical life. Utopia, taken literally, is nonsense. For the same reason, possibility and actuality cannot be pried apart in the case of the ethical good. Ethical life is *spirit* in the full Hegelian sense: its "possibility is [...] infinite, absolute *actuality*" (Hegel, *Werke* 10:27, §383).

This has consequences for the concept of philosophy. For in the description of my own ethical life, which is only possible as self-knowledge, I have an answer to the question of who I am. This answer is necessarily identical, for me, to the answer regarding what it means to be capable of asking this question in the first place. Thus, in the description of my own ethical life, I have a genuine answer to the philosophical question specified above: "Who am I, insofar as I am capable of asking who I am in the first place?"

Our previous characterizations of philosophizing could still seem like provisional answers to this question, since they could only be proffered, at first, as claims about what (since philosophizing is asking a question) I must be *in addition* to being a philosopher—namely, contingently determined, acting, self-determined,

---

[39] To this extent, the particularities that are internal to ethical life in its concreteness are essentially "ideal" in the Hegelian sense: "the Ideal is the finite [*das Endliche*] as it is in the truly infinite [*wahrhaften Unendlichen*],—as a determination, content, that is different as a *moment* but is not independently existent" (Hegel *GW* 21:137).

[40] Korsgaard, on the contrary, believes just this to be possible. See Korsgaard (2009, 23; see also 2n2) as well as Korsgaard (1996, 120–130 and 251–258).

subject to an ought, and in community with others. In the description of my own ethical life, however, I have an answer to the question of who I am that excludes the possibility of a separate answer to the question about my capacity to inquire in this way. Therefore, this description is no longer just a characterization of philosophizing as the struggle to gain the clarity the philosophical question seeks but a characterization of this clarity or *wisdom* itself. In other words, it is a characterization of *philosophy*.[41] Philosophy *is* the description of my own ethical life—and thus, in the first place and among other things, meta-ethics and ethics in one.

With this, we have also answered the question of the epistemological status of the clarity for which philosophizing strives. Because the description of my own ethical life is knowledge—objective self-knowledge—philosophy must be knowledge. Hence, the clarity sought with the philosophical question cannot consist in any alleged recognition that the person who asks it is incapable of answering it or that the question itself is a mere pseudo-question.

3.2 Philosophy as Dialectic and Reconciliation

Philosophy is ethical self-knowledge. As the description of our own ethical life, we might say it is the transparency [*Durchsichtigkeit*] of ethical life to itself. But is philosophy really nothing more than that? If this were the case, philosophy, in its character as knowledge, would go beyond ethical life just as little as it would go beyond the natural sciences if naturalism were true. But that is impossible, for ethical life is self-contradictory, and philosophy can only reconcile this contradiction if, in its character as knowledge, it exceeds ethical self-knowledge. This, in any case, is what the following reflections aim to show.

Ethical life is objectivity. As such, it is an actuality whose source and ground must lie at once in our subjectivity as agents as such and in the absolute that transcends this subjectivity. This non-identity in the ground and source of ethical life and thus in ethical life itself has the following implications. Ethical life is, on the one hand, the activity of preserving the existence of its members as the actuality of freedom. Yet, on the other hand, that freedom is to be defined as the capacity to negate this very existence. But as we have further seen, freedom must amount to more than the mere *capacity* for this negation. In the evil that is indispensable to self-consciousness—and thus to freedom itself—freedom has a necessary moment of activity that is *actually* directed at this negation. But this means that ethical life

---

[41] In retrospect, this also deprives our provisional answer to the philosophical question of its provisional character.

is an activity of self-preservation and self-destruction at once. This is its contradiction.[42]

The actuality of ethical life reveals this contradiction, for example, in the antinomic character of *education* [*Bildung*]. Insofar as it belongs to ethical life, education is an "immanent moment of the absolute" (Hegel, *Werke* 7:345, §187). As such, it has "infinite worth" (*Werke*, 7:345, §187). Education is the process by which the individual develops insight into the concrete universality of her ethical life.[43] It has its standard and its goal in this concrete universality, which cannot remain unattainable as the goal of an activity that is internal to ethical life. But as a consequence of the right of the subjective will, the individual person's interest in her education is at the same time essentially practical self-interest. And because practical self-interest as such can only be thought *in opposition* to other persons, this is also essentially an interest in our own advantage over others. Hence, competition and innovation are internal to the idea of education. But because universality is "brought into harmony" time and again with the particularity of the individual ethical agent in her concreteness, the discoveries and inventions (including scientific findings) which put individuals at an advantage in this competition must in turn eventually come to co-determine the general goal of education for everyone, thereby repeatedly deferring it *ad infinitum*. This means that education is a process that brings the individual to a goal that essentially withdraws from it by this very process itself. Hegel discusses the legal, economic, and political dimensions of this contradiction under the heading of *civil society* [*bürgerliche Gesellschaft*].[44]

---

[42] Korsgaard likewise discusses the *prima facie* possibility of a contradiction in the idea of practical reason itself, the so-called "paradox of self-constitution" (see Korsgaard 2009, 20, and compare Korsgaard 2002, 59 and 226). But for her, this contradiction only apparently exists. For she initially identifies the form of the practical law with the form of a law of mere animalistic self-preservation. For her, the idea of self-consciousness is only a dialectically inconsequential modification of this general concept of self-preservation (Korsgaard 2009, 41 ff.). Korsgaard errs in this way because she neglects to inquire about the conditions of the possibility of self-consciousness and necessitation. She thus misses the central significance of the struggle for recognition and the necessity of evil. It is a consequence of Hegel's conception of ethical life that there is a "paradox of self-constitution" that cannot be resolved in this way.

[43] "Thus, *Bildung* takes away the rough edges of a man's particularity until he conducts himself in accordance with the nature of the thing"; "[g]enuine originality, which produces the real thing, demands genuine *Bildung*" (Hegel *Werke* 7:345, §187).

[44] Hegel declares *Bildung* to be the *ideal*, the actual *purpose*, of civil society (*Werke* 7:343, §187). He lays out the legal, economic, and political dimensions of *Bildung*'s contradiction against the backdrop of the institution of private property, which he had explained before, under the heading of "abstract law," as an essential moment of the existence of freedom (*Werke* 7:102 f.). In effect, Hegel's representation of the "dialectic of civil society" (*Werke* 7:390) is thus an elucidation of the contradictory nature of capitalism as an "immanent moment of the absolute." Hegel's discussion of the

According to Hegel's theory of objective spirit, civil society is ethical life in its guise as the sphere in which individuals, as the ethical Beings that they are qua family members, relate to one another in their particularity. In its further shape as the *state*, ethical life is the concrete universal which is, for the individual agents, mediated with their particularity. But ethical life retains its contradiction even as the life of a state. To understand ethical life as state does not mean to resolve ethical life's contradiction, but rather to think the objectivity of that contradiction. The contradictory nature [*Widersprüchlichkeit*] of ethical life is always based on the fact that, as actuality, its ground and source must lie simultaneously in our subjectivity as agents as such and in the absolute that transcends this subjectivity. Hegel describes the manifestation of the contradictory nature of the state conceived in this way as *world history*. In world history, ethical life demonstrates its *finitude*. Thus, as Hegel writes in the *Science of Logic*:

> When we say of things *they are finite*, it is understood [...] that it is in fact non-being [*Nichtsein*] that constitutes their nature, their being [*Sein*]. [...] The finite [...] *passes away*, and it is not merely possible that it passes away, such that it could exist without passing away. [...] [T]he hour of its birth is the hour of its death (Hegel, GW 21:116).[45]

Ethical life's contradiction cannot be resolved ethically, practically, or politically. The contradiction is ethical life itself. Hence, this contradiction necessarily affects philosophy as well, in which ethical life itself is rendered transparent. Is philosophy thus ultimately nothing more than skeptical desperation in the face of ethical life's contradiction? Or can we, in philosophy, reconcile ourselves to this contradiction? Contradiction is the epitome of what ought not to be. To reconcile ourselves to a necessarily actual contradiction can therefore only mean to *know* its necessity.

---

economic and political dimensions of this contradictoriness opens into his strikingly clear-eyed analysis of the problem of poverty, the origins of the "rabble," and its consequences up to and including colonialism (*Werke* 7:386–393). Hegel discusses the legal dimension of this contradiction as the "antimony of the public code of law" (*Werke* 7:368f.). Admittedly, as the sphere of ethical life that it is, bourgeois society must also produce institutions that react to this problem—the police and corporations (*Werke* 7:382ff.). But these institutions cannot *solve* the problem (this is especially clear in Hegel *Werke* 7:390f.); rather, their necessity makes clear that this problem really is just one of the guises of the contradictoriness of *ethical life itself*.

45 This also explains why Hegel strictly differentiates the philosophical idea of *ethical life* from the idea of *holiness*, i.e., the conception of the presence of the absolute in the finite as the existence of a certain sort of *"finite rendered un-finite"* [*"ent-endlichtem Endlichen"*]: "But once the divine spirit introduces itself into actuality, and actuality emancipates itself to spirit, then what was a postulate of *holiness* in the world is supplanted by the actuality of *ethical life*" (Hegel *Werke* 10, §552).

And that can only mean to attribute its actuality to the same grounds that makes it a contradiction in the first place.

In the course of these reflections up to this point, however—i.e., in the course of philosophy—this has already been achieved. Or perhaps it is more accurate to say that the first step towards achieving it has been taken. For the characterization of ethical life we have arrived at here was the result of a reflection that took as its point of departure the question regarding the possibility of philosophical clarity about oneself. It is thus this clarity about oneself that demands the actuality of self-contradictory ethical life. At the same time, however, philosophical clarity about ourselves is also that in light of which ethical life is a contradiction in the first place. For the contradiction of ethical life is based on its character as self-knowledge. But this character, according to our reflections so far, rests on the fact that philosophizing, as clarity about its own inquiring character, demands the identity of the "I "of the philosopher and the "I" of contingent determinations. This means that philosophy—the transparency of ethical life to itself—*is* already reconciliation with the contradiction of ethical life. It is a reconciliation which philosophy itself, in its character as the asking of a question, necessitates. Thus, we can say, with Hegel: "Philosophy is [...] the reconciliation of the corruption [*Verderben*] that thought began" (*Werke*, 18:71 f.). And: "The movement that philosophy is finds itself already completed, when at its conclusion it grasps [*erfasst*] its own concept—i.e., it only *looks back* on its knowledge" (*Werke*, 10:37, §573).

But ethical life is the presence of the absolute. Therefore, philosophy (unlike this text) cannot limit itself to a demonstration of the necessity of ethical life (which is self-contradictory) for philosophical clarity alone. Instead, it is obligated (as this text implies) to designate the necessity of self-contradictory ethical life—in its character as a necessity *for* philosophical clarity—as *unconditional* necessity. It is for this reason that philosophy is only possible as *dialectics*, as the demonstration and sublation of absolutely necessary contradictions. And it is for this reason that philosophy must distinguish itself in its character as knowledge from ethical life.

Ethical life is the presence of the absolute. Practical self-knowledge, which is the guise in which we initially encountered ethical life, is therefore knowledge of the absolute. For this reason, as Hegel puts it, there "cannot be two kinds of conscience, one religious and another ethical, which differs from the former in matter and content" (*Werke*, 8:355 f., §198). But only philosophy, as knowledge of the absolute necessity of the contradictoriness of (among other things) ethical life, is self-knowledge that is, at the same time, knowledge of the absolute *as the absolute*. Philosophy is reconciliation in that it recognizes as unconditionally necessary the demise of the finite spirit of its age and, thereby, the unconditional necessity of this very recognition, i.e., the unconditional necessity of philosophy itself. And this is the reason Hegel describes the self-knowledge we attain by philosophizing as at once "knowledge of the truth of man" and knowledge "of truth in and of itself" (*Werke*, 10:9, §377).[46]

Hegel's philosophical strategy thus consists in demonstrating that the skeptical despair which initially haunts the philosophical consciousness of ethical life's contradictoriness is *knowledge.* He thereby overcomes this despair by bringing to it the unity of the system. By virtue of its completeness, this system constitutes the absolute knowledge that the absolute as such has of itself.[47]

Three lines of reasoning are united in this system. The *Logic* develops the idea of the absolute itself—i.e., the "idea in and of itself" (Hegel, *Werke* 8:63, §18).[48] As we saw in §2.1, it is the naturalness of its subjects that distinguishes finite spirit, which is actual in ethical life, from the absolute. But if this distinction did not ultimately come from the absolute itself, the absolute would be determined by something external to it—that is, it would be determinate, finite, and thus not absolute. Therefore nature, which accounts for this distinction, must itself be absolute.[49] Accordingly, Hegelian *Philosophy of Nature* develops the idea of nature as the "idea in its otherness" (*Werke*, 8:63, §18). Finally, the *Philosophy of Spirit* describes how the absolute in human beings, as the spirit that "comes from nature" and knows itself as such, arrives at knowledge of itself (*Werke*, 10:17, §381).

It is here that we learn what it means that in philosophy human beings bring skepticism—the recognition of our own contradictoriness—to "completion." In so doing, we know the identity of nature—as what distinguishes us from the absolute—with the absolute itself. So, the *Philosophy of Spirit* describes spirit as the "idea,

---

46 This introduces an asymmetry into the identity of "religious" and "ethical conscience": "Ethical life is the divine spirit as indwelling in self-consciousness, as it is actually present in a nation and its individual members. [...] But in point of form, i.e., for thought and knowledge [...,] the body of religious truth, as purely self-subsisting and therefore supreme truth, exercises a sanction over the ethical life which is located in empirical actuality. Thus for self-consciousness religion is the basis of moral life and of the state" (Hegel *Werke* 10:355, §552).
47 "God is only God to the extent that he knows himself; his self-knowledge is, further, a self-consciousness in man and man's knowledge *of* God, which proceeds to man's self-knowledge *in* God" (Hegel *Werke* 10:374, §564).
48 Compare: "According to this, logic should be conceived as the system of pure reason, as the realm of pure thought. *This realm is the truth, in its raw existence, in and for itself.* We can therefore put it this way: that this content is *the representation of God as he exists in his eternal being before he created nature and as a finite spirit*" (Hegel *GW* 21:44).
49 "[I]n the absolute truth of itself, [the idea] *resolves to release* [...] itself as nature [...] *out of itself*" (Hegel *Werke* 8:393, §244).

which returns to itself from its otherness" (*Werke*, 8:64, §18).⁵⁰ Thus Hegel shows that it is precisely in ethical life's passing away, from its own self, that it manifests its infinitude; and that the absolute is absolute in virtue of its presence as this infinitude in the passing away of the finite:

> But the thinking spirit of world history [i.e., the philosopher], having cast aside both the limitations of particular national spirits and its own worldliness, lays hold of its concrete universality and rises to *knowledge of absolute spirit*, as the eternally actual truth in which knowing reason is free for itself, and necessity, nature, and history are entirely devoted to the service of its revelation and are vessels of its honor (Hegel, *Werke* 10:353, §552).⁵¹

3.3 Philosophy as Dying and Reconciliation in the Ideal World

Philosophy, as insight into (among other things) the unconditional necessity of the contradictoriness of ethical life, is self-knowledge of the absolute as the absolute. As such, in its character as knowledge, it transcends ethical life. And not only that. Insight into the unconditional necessity of the contradictoriness of ethical life is not an insight that makes possible a *return* to ethical life. For with it, the philosopher recognizes tensions that, *as such*, cannot be resolved within ethical life—i.e., ethically, practically, politically. With this insight, it is thus impossible for her to continue to conceive of ethical life as her enduring Being. Already the very need for this insight, i.e., the requirement that we justify ethical life, can only emerge if the unity of inner and outer that is ethical life is broken in an (in principle) universally recognizable way. For the requirement itself is the need for reconciliation with an actual contradiction. This need can only emerge if the world that is ethical life has become alien to us. This means that reconciliation in philosophy is not reconciliation *in* the ethical world:

---

50 Compare: "Philosophy thinks its own concept in the end" (Hegel *Werke* 10:379, §573); "[t]his concept of philosophy is *the self-thinking idea*, […] the logical, but with the meaning that it is universality preserved in its concrete content as well as in its actuality. Science goes back to its beginning in this manner, and the logical is its *result*" (Hegel *Werke* 10:393, §574). It is *internal* to the absolute that it is *spirit*, or *self-thinking idea*: "The *absolute is spirit*; this is the highest definition of the absolute" (*Werke* 10:29f., §384).
51 In the *Metaphysics*, Hegel describes the most abstract logical form of this relationship under the heading "true infinity": "The finite is not sublated by the infinite as by a power external to it; rather, its infinity is to sublate itself" (*GW* 21:133). "This infinite, as a going into itself, a self-relation, […] *is* and *is there*, present, attendant" (*GW* 21:136). The threefold deduction that Hegel's encyclopedic system—which includes the *Logic, Philosophy of Nature*, and *Philosophy of Spirit*—ultimately proves to be (*Werke* 10:393f., §575) is the most fully developed shape assumed by the idea of "true infinitude" in Hegel.

> Where a people has departed from its concrete life, where separation and distinction between the classes has occurred, and a people approaches its end [*Untergang*], where a break has occurred between inner striving and external actuality, where the shape of religion no longer suffices, spirit makes known its indifference to its vital existence or tarries, unsatisfied, in this existence, and ethical life dissolves—it is only then that philosophizing occurs. [...] Philosophy begins with the end of a real world [*reellen Welt*]. [...] [A]nd its reconciliation is a reconciliation not in the real, but in the ideal, world (Hegel, *Werke* 18:71f.).

For this reason and in this sense, "the owl of Minerva begins its flight only with the onset of dusk."[52] And for this reason, philosophy, in its character as knowledge, exceeds the self-transparency of ethical life (which it initially is) to such an extent that complete transparency to our own ethical life is impossible prior to reconciliation, in the ideal world, with its contradictoriness. There must therefore be a sense in which "the ethical person" remains "unconscious of himself" (Hegel, *Werke* 7:294, §144, Addition).

Moreover, the "ideal world" in which philosophy is reconciliation is not a world in which one could really *live* as a determinate subject, as this "I." The life of the philosopher is her personality, her being [*Sein*] in ethical life. Thus, life is being [*Sein*] in the real world. There is no higher life for the philosopher. And philosophy is certainly not it. For philosophy is ethical self-knowledge. The philosopher does not have another being [*Sein*] as philosopher beside her being [*Sein*] as an ethical Being [*Wesen*]. Rather (as we saw in §3.1), as philosopher, she is an ethical Being [*Wesen*] and vice versa. Thus, it is the case that:

> Every philosophy [...] is a child of its time and is implicated [*befangen*] in its confinedness [...] It is the same universal spirit that is laid out by philosophy in thought; universal spirit is philosophy's self-thinking and is thus its determinate substantial content. Every philosophy is philosophy of its time (Hegel, *Werke* 18:65).

In other words, philosophy is immanent in ethical life and transcends ethical life *at once*. It is the self-transparency of an ethical life, yet it exceeds ethical life. It exceeds it in and through ethical life's own internal dying. How do these claims

---

52 "A further word on the subject of *issuing instructions* on how the world ought to be: philosophy, at any rate, always comes too late to perform this function. As the *thought* of the world, it appears only at a time when actuality has gone through its formative process and has exhausted itself. This lesson of the concept is necessarily also apparent from history, namely that it is only when actuality has reached maturity that the ideal appears opposite the real and reconstructs this real world, which it has grasped in its substance, in the shape of an intellectual realm. When philosophy paints its grey in grey, a shape of life has grown old, and it cannot be rejuvenated, but only recognized, by the grey in grey of philosophy; the owl of Minerva begins its flight only with the onset of dusk" (Hegel *Werke* 7:27f.).

fit together? Only thus: *Philosophizing is essentially this dying, too. It is this dying, from itself, of the ethical life in which philosophy has its time and the philosopher has her life as a determinate thinking being. Philosophizing is this dying as its justification.*

This characterization of the activity of philosophizing is not, of course, the claim that philosophy's completion signifies the natural death of the philosopher. For in persons, thought and nature form a *concrete unity* rather than a simple identity: they remain distinguishable in that unity.[53] That philosophizing is dying also does not mean that a new ethical life is impossible after the current one has come to an end. It means, rather, that philosophy is an activity that, *for itself,* cannot be oriented toward either the current ethical life or a new one, or toward the good in any sense. It means that, as the activity of knowing the demise of finite spirit in its age as the presence of the absolute, it participates in and deepens this dying. It means that in this activity, the philosopher, *at one with the spirit of her time,* "casts off [her] own worldliness" (Hegel, *Werke* 10:353, §552) and "gives herself up in reality and in fact [as] I in this singularity" (*Werke*, 16:186). As a consequence, philosophizing is, in the highest degree, the "activity undertaken by thinking reason [*der denkenden Vernunft*] and by the rational thinker [*des vernünftig Denkenden*] of positing oneself, as individual, as the universal, and, by sublating oneself as individual, of discovering one's true self as the universal" (*Werke*, 16:186).

It is enlightening to contrast this conclusion with the concept of philosophy that Wittgenstein puts forward in the *Philosophical Investigations.* Ethical life as such is not Wittgenstein's topic. But we can take what he says about philosophy's relationship to our everyday use of language as his elucidation of an element of Hegel's conception of philosophy as immanent in ethical life. He writes, "It is not our aim to refine or complete the system of rules for the use of our words in unheard-of ways" (Wittgenstein 1953, §133).[54] In contrast to Hegel, however, Witt-

---

[53] What was claimed as necessary in §1.1 is made possible on the basis of this distinction: that the philosopher remains the subject of contingent determinations even after casting off the determinations which are detrimental to the philosophical clarity at which she aims.

[54] Hegel does not just affirm this; one might say that he is a *much more systematic* "ordinary language philosopher" than Wittgenstein. "The forms of thought," as Hegel puts it in the introduction to the *Science of Logic,* "are first set out and stored in human *language*" and specifically in its grammar: they are set out in "prefixes and suffixes, inflections, and the like," in "prepositions and articles" (*GW* 21: 10). In contrast to Wittgenstein, however, Hegel also values the philosophical significance of the fact that natural language tends of itself towards the hypostatization of logical forms and thus simplifies the self-objectification of thinking which serves philosophical self-knowledge: "Much more important is that in a language the categories should be expressed as substantives and verbs, and thus be stamped into objective form" (Hegel *GW* 21:11). Above all, however,

genstein does not couple this thought with that of philosophy's transcendence of ethical life. For this reason, philosophy for Wittgenstein does not go beyond life in its character as knowledge: "The philosopher's treatment of a question is like the treatment of an illness" (Wittgenstein 2001, §255).[55]

Thus, for Wittgenstein, there is no standard for the *completeness* of the clarity we seek in philosophizing. For him, the idea of a completeness of this sort is as nonsensical as the idea of a complete list of all possible illnesses:

> [T]he clarity that we are aiming at is indeed *complete* clarity. But this simply means that the philosophical problems should *completely* disappear. The real discovery is the one that enables me to stop doing philosophy when I want to.—The one that gives philosophy peace, so that it is no longer tormented by questions which call itself into question.—Instead, we now demonstrate a method by examples; and the series of examples can be broken off.—Problems are solved (difficulties eliminated), not a *single* problem. There is not *a* philosophical method, though there are indeed methods, like different therapies (Wittgenstein 2001, §133).

On this point, Hegel disagrees with Wittgenstein. For Hegel, the philosopher has both her goal and the internal standard of completeness of the clarity she seeks in the "universal spirit" of her age. This "universal spirit" is the *one*—complex—problem that concerns her. As a consequence, her methods—which, as methods of absolute self-knowledge, are at the same time its content—must exhibit systematic unity and be knowledge in this unity. Philosophy thus has "its *justification* [*Begründung*] in its systematic scope alone" (Hegel, *Werke* 10:405). Therefore, it cannot be at peace with a discovery that can be demonstrated only in a series of examples. The peace we aim for in philosophizing cannot be a kind of peace that would enable us to arbitrarily stop philosophizing. *The basic philosophical speech act is the system* that lays out the universal spirit of its age in thought—i.e., *as such*—and hence as the presence of the absolute. And this universal spirit can only be laid out, as such, *in this way.* This is what the philosophical question calls for. Philosophical problems disappear completely in this system because the philosophical ques-

---

Hegel is not forced to treat the fact that natural language includes words with contradictory meanings exclusively as a source of likely confusion. On the contrary: "[F]or many of its words also have the further peculiarity of carrying, not just different meanings, but opposite ones, and in this one cannot fail to recognize [...] language's speculative spirit. It can delight thought to come across such words, and to discover in naïve form, already in the lexicon as one word of opposite meanings, that union of opposites which is the result of speculation but which to the understanding is nonsensical" (Hegel *GW* 21:11).

55 Compare: "The results of philosophy are the uncovering of one or another piece of plain nonsense and of bumps that the understanding has got by running its head up against the limits of language" (Wittgenstein 2001, §119).

tions are *answered* in it. But what remains in this system is no (ethical) life "after the recovery from illness." What remains is only the *truth*, which is *ideal*, of *real life*—which is *passing away*.

Philosophizing is dying. And because philosophy is self-knowledge, it must also know this about itself. It must know itself as the end of the philosopher's ethical life, and thus, since content and form are inseparable here, as the end of ethical life *as such*. Philosophy, in other words, must know itself as facing the *"absolute horizon,"* if you will. It must know itself as the presence of the absolute in the finite spirit that passes away.

But how is it possible for philosophy, as the knowledge of this dying (in which ethical life demonstrates its finitude), to know that it, too, belongs to finite spirit and its dying *without lapsing into a subjective idealism?* Is not the proposition that gives voice to this knowledge—"Every philosophy is a child of its time and is implicated in its confinedness"—the paradigmatic expression of the desperate attempt to achieve some sort of "sideways-on view"?

That depends upon *how* philosophy knows that it too belongs to finite spirit. If, as Hegel believes, philosophy *as such* is also the history of philosophy and thus, among other things, cognized world history (since all philosophy begins "with the end [*Untergang*] of a real world"), then its knowledge of itself as belonging to the finite spirit of its age would exist as historical retrospective.[56] In this retrospective, philosophy would just be itself and would not be in the position of desperately attempting to catch a view of itself from sideways-on. And, conversely, we could say precisely what Hegel says of the history of philosophy:

> It arises from the notion of the history of philosophy that, although it is history, it does not have to do with the past. The contents of this history are the scientific products of rationality [*Vernünftigkeit*], and these are not ephemeral. What was acquired in this field is the truth, and this is eternal—it does not exist at one time and then cease to exist in another (Hegel, *Werke* 18:57).[57]

---

56 That Hegel believes that philosophy *as such* is also the history of philosophy is apparent, among other things, in his saying that the conceptual development in the *Science of Logic*, in which thinking is purely "in its element," must be able to be reproduced in the history of philosophy, which, for its part, is the history of the truth that reveals itself in the course of world history: "We find the various stages of the logical Idea in the history of philosophy in the shape of a succession of emerging philosophical systems" (*Werke* 8:184, §86, Addition).

57 We should attend to the fact that Hegel only thinks the eternity of the existence of philosophical truth—i.e., of absolute knowledge—*prospectively*, not *retrospectively*. That something is *eternal* does not mean for him—as is actually the case in ordinary language use as well—that it *exists at all times*, but rather that it *abides*. If philosophy is essentially the history of philosophy, there must have been times at which one or another philosophic truth did *not yet* exist.

Philosophical knowledge is *achievement,* according to Hegel. World history is (among other things) the work of the struggle for it; the history of philosophy is the work of its elevation out of this struggle; and philosophy in a narrower sense (logic in particular) is the work of preserving it in memory. If this is correct, philosophy would know itself as belonging to—even as the pinnacle of—finite spirit. It would know this by understanding the work of elevating and preserving the truth of its time, which it is, as a moment in a process of "successive awakenings" of the absolute in the world-historical passing away of formations of finite spirit (Hegel, *Werke* 18:58).[58]

If philosophy knows itself as "successive awakenings" of the absolute in the world-historical passing away of finite spirit, and as the preservation of the truth of the same, then it contains, to be sure, an unconditional *hope* for a prospective ethical life at the same time. Hegel expresses this hope as follows: "Philosophy is thus a further character of spirit; it is the inner birthplace of the spirit that will later step forth towards actual formation" (*Werke,* 18:74f.).

But this hope, which is actual knowledge and no mere belief, nevertheless—or precisely for this reason—cannot be practical. It conveys nothing of the character of the ethical life to come or the manner of its emergence from the "inner birthplace of spirit" that philosophy is. It can neither move the philosopher in her actions nor make the movement that is her life more bearable. *Philosophy, as Hegel understands it, is nothing we can make something out of in life.*

To philosophize in the Hegelian sense means—or *would mean*—"to know [*erkennen*] reason as the rose in the cross of the present and to delight in it" (*Werke,* 7:26f.). The word "know" [*erkennen*] is crucial here. *Art* and *religion,* the other two forms of *absolute spirit* in Hegel's system, likewise refer to "reason as the rose in the cross of the present," but they refer to it in their capacity as *intuition* [*Anschauung*] and *imagination* [*Vorstellung*] rather than as *knowledge* [*Erkenntnis*].[59] And for Hegel, it would be inaccurate to extend philosophy's characterization as dying to the other two forms of absolute spirit. Only *knowledge* [*Erkennen*] of the presence of the absolute is dying. Intuiting and imagining are forms of mental activity that show no disposition to transcend the existence [*Dasein*] of their sub-

---

58 Compare: "In point of fact [...], the history of philosophy itself represents [the universal character of the nation and of the time and of the general state of affairs] [...], indeed, it represents their highest pinnacle" (*Werke* 18: 69). If philosophy as such is also the history of philosophy, then in knowing that its present is the end of ethical life, it also knows that it is the end of history *as such. For spirit holds nothing back:* its possibility is its actuality.

59 Hegel's play on the "rose in the cross"—Luther's Cross, which is taken from Martin Luther's crest—is in itself already a play on precisely these two other forms of absolute spirit. I am indebted to Sebastian Böhm for this observation.

ject (which is inherently determinate). For they are forms of consciousness of (possible) realities *in which the subject of this consciousness must still be (or be able to be) present as the determinate subject that it inherently is.*

Intuition quite obviously requires the presence [*Dasein*] of the subject vis-à-vis its object. And imagination is inherently directed toward possible intuitions. As such, imagination is a form of consciousness of possible realities in which we must still be able to discover the subject of this consciousness as the determinate imagining subject that it is. The imagining, in religious belief, of a reconciliation to (or redemption of) reality's corruption is therefore possible as the representation of a *life after death.* For such a life, as imagined, is a continuation of the life of *this determinate subject.* Dying that is merely an imagined survival, however, is precisely not dying in the proper sense of the word.

By contrast, in reconciliation as *knowledge* (philosophy), by "stripping away my own worldliness," "abandoning my individuality in reality and in fact," and "sublating myself as individual, finding my true self as the universal" I divest myself of my determinacy as *this* subject and, as such, as *intuiting and imagining* subject (Hegel, *Werke* 10:353, §552). In so doing, I divest myself of my (ethical) life.

Following upon the reflections that make up the main portion of this text, we can now understand to what extent philosophy, for Hegel, is the *"liberation* from the one-sidedness of the forms" of art and religion—that is, liberation from the one-sidedness of the form of reconciliation that defines them (*Werke,* 10:378, §573). And from the standpoint we have now reached, we can at least say this much about why Hegel characterizes philosophy as the "unity of art and religion" and hence as knowledge of the "necessity of the two [other] forms" (*Werke,* 10:378, §572). Philosophy can only be *self*-knowledge and dying at once if the life whose dying it inherently is likewise consists in forms of *clarity about itself*—where these (*living*) forms of clarity are distinguished from philosophical knowledge *purely as forms.* For only in this way can philosophical knowledge be the speculative reception and preservation of the ideal *content* of this clarity. Intuition and imagination [*Vorstellung*], which must belong to the spiritual reality of the human being as a sensible, living being, are precisely forms of this sort.

4 Conclusion

If to philosophize really means "to know reason as the rose in the cross and to delight in it," then the philosophical justification of the actual world cannot consist in the demonstration that it is, in fact, exempt from demise. This also means that philosophy cannot orient us in life; it cannot provide us a good to think practically—

not even a prospectively possible good.[60] And the delight that lies in philosophical knowledge cannot help us to endure the demise of reality. Philosophical self-knowledge, as we concluded in §§3.1 and 3.2, must appear on the scene with the claim that it is able to "reject the name of the *love* of *knowledge* and to be *actual knowledge*" (Hegel, *Werke* 3:14). Because of this, to philosophize (for Hegel and in fact) does not mean to learn to die, as it does for Plato. It means to die.

But precisely for this reason, Hegel's concept of philosophy cannot in the least be described as *morbid*. Philosophy is the knowledge of the expiring [*verderbende*] spirit of its age as the presence of the absolute. And *only* this knowledge is philosophy. To the extent that we *do not* have this knowledge, this conception of philosophy—and precisely this one—pushes us to take a stand in life, in ethical life.

Referencing Schiller, Ernst Cassirer formulates the motto for his idealism thus: "'Cast the fear of the earthly from you!' That is the idealistic position that I have always professed" (Cassirer 1995, 221). Hegel is the *opposite* of an idealist in this sense of "idealism." It is impossible to formulate this sort of imperative—which is directed at us as persons—within Hegel's conception of philosophy. As persons, we are living beings. Life, however, is being [*Sein*] in the real world. And here, life is finitude—and hence ultimately demise. For us as self-conscious Beings [*Wesen*], life *is*, therefore, anxiety and fear. Cassirer wants to render the knowledge of the expiring spirit of one's age into a kind of personal solace—the consolation achieved through an individual's ascension to a higher, detached standpoint, one which deprives the corruption of the finite of its fearsomeness. Thus, Cassirer's idealism is a form of just the "irony" that Hegel criticizes as the worst form of evil:

> The culmination [...] of the subjectivity which regards itself as the ultimate instance [...] consists in knowledge of ethical objectivity, but without that self-forgetfulness and self-renunciation that seriously immerses itself in this objectivity and makes it the basis of its actions. Although it is related to this objectivity, it distances itself from it at the same time and knows *itself* as that which *wills* and *resolves in a particular way* but may *equally well* will and resolve otherwise. [...] In this shape [*Gestalt*], subjectivity is not only [...] evil (evil, in fact, of an inherently wholly universal kind); in addition, its form is that of *subjective* vanity

---

[60] In *Critique of Rights*, Christoph Menke develops a dialectic of bourgeois ethical life that is meant to allow us to think a revolution that leads us "beyond bourgeois rights" (Menke 2015, 307). Menke thinks of this "beyond bourgeois rights" as *practical* to the extent that he gives it the form of possible "anti-rights" (Menke 2015, 369 ff.) whose establishment he recommends. This sort of revolution can only be thought, it seems to me, if we deny the full weight of the Hegelian idea of "absolute horizon"—i.e., the inseparability of philosophical form and philosophical content. To think their separability is precisely *not* to think ethical life (in the Hegelian sense), and thus a necessary condition of philosophizing itself. If my reflections bear up, it must be possible to show that Menke has not grasped the contradiction of bourgeois rights in its full profundity. I cannot provide proof of this claim here, however.

[*Eitelkeit*], in that it knows itself as this vanity of all content and, in this knowledge, knows *itself* as the absolute (Hegel, *Werke* 7:278 f., §140).

Hegel does not call us, as individual persons, to *renounce* the finite world in which we live. In Hegel, the call is rather like that which Franz Rosenzweig makes to his readers in the opening of his magnum opus, *The Star of Redemption:* "Man should not cast aside from him the fear of the earthly; in his fear of death he should—stay. He should stay. He should therefore do nothing other than what he already wants: to stay" (Rosenzweig 1930, 4).

But Rosenzweig does not address this call to us only as persons but also as philosophers. And here, following Hegel, we must contradict him. For with such an injunction, Rosenzweig evokes the possibility of a philosophizing—a "new thinking," as he calls it—that binds itself to remaining in the fear of the earthly.[61] In so doing, Rosenzweig exemplifies just what Hegel calls the "relation of reflection" and identifies as the "standpoint of our time" (*Werke*, 16:184). This is the position from which "finitude lies in the complete abstraction of pure thinking, which does not truly grasp itself as universal, but instead remains an I, a This One" (*Werke*, 16:186). And this standpoint, according to Hegel, is nothing more than another shape of evil:

> He says: in my finitude, I am a nothing that is to be sublated; but this sublation is likely not complete if this immediate individuality remains, and remains such that only this I becomes the affirmative as set forth by the standpoint of reflection. Finitude that raises itself to infinitude is only abstract identity, empty in itself, the highest form of untruth, evil and a lie (Hegel, *Werke* 16:186).

By contrast, the true philosopher in the Hegelian sense, in knowing the dying spirit of her time as the presence of the absolute, does not *simply* identify this dying spirit (or her own individual self) with the absolute. To *reconcile* the finite and the infinite is not to eliminate their difference. The philosopher does not, therefore, aim for the sort of infinite standpoint which would purportedly rob the finite of its fearsomeness by achieving an ironic distance toward it. Nor does she so closely identify the absolute with the fleeting spirit of her time or her own self that, in holding fast to fear, she denies the reality of this spirit's passing away—the reality of its end—to herself.

---

61 Referring to the Davos Debate in 1929 between Cassirer and Heidegger, Rosenzweig recognizes a confederate of the new way of thinking that he develops in *Star of Redemption*, which builds on the late work of Hermann Cohen, in Heidegger (and specifically not in Cassirer). Compare Rosenzweig (1930, 85 ff.).

> As the fulfillment [*Vollendung*] of spirit consists in perfectly *knowing* what *it is*, in knowing its substance, this knowledge is its *withdrawal-into-itself* [*Insichgehen*] in which it abandons its existence [*Dasein*] and gives its shape over to recollection (Hegel, Werke 3:590).

If, as I hope to have shown in this paper, true philosophizing is only possible as dying, then its standard cannot be the good, either for Hegel or for us. But for precisely the same reason, neither can a philosophizing that recognizes itself as a dying be outrageous.[62]

Abbreviations

Hegel's Works

Citations in the text refer to volumes and page numbers of the *Theorie-Werkausgabe* (Frankfurt am Main: Suhrkamp (1986)) and *Hegel's Gesammelte Werke* (Hamburg: Meiner (1984)). Citations of Hegel quotations from the *Theorie-Werkausgabe* have been abbreviated as "*Werke* Volume: Page." Citations from Hegel's *Gesammelte Werke* have been abbreviated as "*GW* Volume: Page." Paragraph numbers are occasionally added for the reader's convenience. What follows is a list of all the works cited from those two editions:

Hegel, Georg Wilhelm Friedrich (1984): *Wissenschaft der Logik. Erster Teil: Die objective Logik. Erstes Buch: Die Lehre vom Sein.* In: Hegel, Georg Wilhelm Friedrich: *Gesammelte Werke.* Vol. XXI. Hamburg: Meiner.

Hegel, Georg Wilhelm Friedrich (1986a): "Glauben und Wissen." In: Hegel, Georg Wilhelm Friedrich: *Jenaer Schriften 1801–1807, Theorie-Werkausgabe.* Vol. II. Frankfurt am Main: Suhrkamp, 287–433.

Hegel, Georg Wilhelm Friedrich (1986b): *Die Phänomenologie des Geistes, Theorie-Werkausgabe.* Vol. III. Frankfurt am Main: Suhrkamp.

Hegel, Georg Wilhelm Friedrich (1986c): *Grundlinien der Philosophie des Rechts, Theorie-Werkausgabe.* Vol. VII. Frankfurt am Main: Suhrkamp.

Hegel, Georg Wilhelm Friedrich (1986d): *Enzyklopaedie der philosophischen Wissenschaften im Grundrisse. Erster Teil: Die Wissenschaft der Logik. Theorie-Werkausgabe.* Vol. VIII. Frankfurt am Main: Suhrkamp.

---

[62] I wish to thank Irad Kimhi, James Conant, Markus Wolf, Matthias Haase, Pirmin Stekeler-Weithofer, Sasha Newton, and Thomas Wendt for conversations and discussions that resonated with me as I completed this text. My thanks to Eliza Little for her comments, Inga Siegfried for her questions, and Sebastian Böhm for references to relevant passages in Hegel's *Lectures on the Philosophy of Religion* and his remarks on the penultimate version of the text, which aided me greatly in clarifying some of its central passages.

Hegel, Georg Wilhelm Friedrich (1986e): *Enzyklopaedie der philosophischen Wissenschaften im Grundrisse. Zweiter Teil: Die Naturphilosophie, Theorie-Werkausgabe*. Vol. IX. Frankfurt am Main: Suhrkamp.
Hegel, Georg Wilhelm Friedrich (1986f): *Enzyklopaedie der philosophischen Wissenschaften im Grundrisse. Dritter Teil: Die Philosophie des Geistes, Theorie-Werkausgabe*. Vol. X. Frankfurt am Main: Suhrkamp.
Hegel, Georg Wilhelm Friedrich (1986 g): *Vorlesungen über die Philosophie der Religion I., Theorie-Werkausgabe*. Vol. XVI. Frankfurt am Main: Suhrkamp.
Hegel, Georg Wilhelm Friedrich (1986 h): *Vorlesungen über die Geschichte der Philosophy I., Theorie-Werkausgabe*. Vol. XVIII. Frankfurt am Main: Suhrkamp.

References

Anscombe, Gertrude Elizabeth Margaret. (1957): *Intention*. Oxford: Basil Blackwell.
Cassirer, Ernst (1995): *Nachgelassene Manuskripte und Texte. Bd. I. Zur Metaphysik der symbolischen Formen*. Hamburg: Meiner.
Gans, Eduard and Braun, Johann (Eds.) (2005): *Naturrecht und Universalgeschichte. Vorlesungen nach G.W.F. Hegel*. Tübingen: Mohr Siebeck.
Gobsch, Wolfram (2014): "The Idea of an Ethical Community: Kant and Hegel on the Necessity of Human Evil and the Love to Overcome It." In: *Philosophical Topics* 42. No. 1, 177–200.
Gobsch, Wolfram (2017): "Der Mensch als Widerspruch und absolutes Wissen. Eine hegelianische Kritik der transformativen Theorie des Geistes." In: Kern, Andrea and Kietzmann, Christian (Eds.): *Selbstbewusstes Leben*. Berlin: Suhrkamp, 120–169.
Haase, Matthias (2014): "For Oneself and Toward Another: The Puzzle About Recognition." In: *Philosophical Topics* 42. No. 1, 113–147.
Haddock, Adrian (2017): "Wahrnehmung und Gegebensein." In: Kern, Andrea and Kietzmann, Christian (Eds.): *Selbstbewusstes Leben*. Berlin: Suhrkamp, 190–208.
Hegel, Georg Wilhelm Friedrich (1991): *Elements of the Philosophy of Right*. Allen Wood (Ed.). Hugh B. Nisbet (Trans.). Cambridge: Cambridge University Press.
Hegel, Georg Wilhelm Friedrich (1997): *Phenomenology of Spirit*. Arnold V. Miller (Trans.). Oxford: Oxford University Press.
Hegel, Georg Wilhelm Friedrich (2007): *Hegel's Philosophy of Mind, translated from the 1830 Edition, together with the Zusätze*. William Wallace, Arnold V. Miller, and Michael J. Inwood (Trans.). Oxford: Clarendon Press.
Henrich, Dieter (2003): "Erkundung im Zugzwang: Ursprung, Leistung und Grenzen von Hegels Denken des Absoluten." In: Welsch, Wolfgang and Vieweg, Klaus (Eds.): *Das Interesse des Denkens—Hegel aus heutiger Sicht*. Munich: Fink, 9–24.
Kant, Immanuel (1900a): *Grundlegung zur Metaphysik der Sitten*. In: Kant, Immanuel: *Gesammelte Schriften*. Vol. IV. Preussische Akademie der Wissenschaften. Berlin: Georg Reimer.
Kant, Immanuel (1900b): *Kritik der praktischen Vernunft*. In: Kant, Immanuel: *Gesammelte Schriften*, Vol. V. Preussische Akademie der Wissenschaften. Berlin: Georg Reimer.
Kant, Immanuel (1900c): *Die Religion innerhalb der Grenzen der bloßen Vernunft*. In: Kant, Immanuel: *Gesammelte Schriften*. Vol. VI. Preussische Akademie der Wissenschaften. Berlin: Georg Reimer.
Korsgaard, Christine (1996): *The Sources of Normativity*. Cambridge: Cambridge University Press.

Korsgaard, Christine (2008): "The Normativity of Instrumental Reason." In: Korsgaard, Christine: *The Constitution of Agency.* Oxford: Oxford University Press, 26–68.
Korsgaard, Christine (2009): *Self-Constitution.* Oxford: Oxford University Press.
Kreines, James (2015): *Reason in the World: Hegel's Metaphysics and Its Philosophical Appeal.* Oxford: Oxford University Press.
McDowell, John (1996): *Mind and World.* Cambridge: Harvard University Press.
McDowell, John (1998): "Virtue and Reason." In: McDowell, John: *Mind, Value, and Reality.* Cambridge: Harvard University Press, 50–73.
McDowell, John (2009): "Hegel's Idealism as Radicalization of Kant." In: McDowell, John: *Having the World in View: Essays on Kant, Hegel, and Sellars.* Cambridge: Harvard University Press, 69–89.
Menke, Christoph (2010): "Autonomie und Befreiung." In: *Deutsche Zeitschrift für Philosophie* 58. No. 5, 675–694.
Menke, Christoph (2015): *Kritik der Rechte.* Berlin: Suhrkamp.
Nietzsche, Friedrich (1988): *Zur Genealogie der Moral.* In: Nietzsche, Friedrich: *Kritische Studienausgabe.* Vol. V. Berlin and New York: de Gruyter.
Pinkard, Terry (2002): *German Philosophy 1760–1860: The Legacy of Idealism.* Cambridge: Cambridge University Press.
Pinkard, Terry (2007): "Liberal Rights and Liberal Individualism without Liberalism." In: Hammer, Espen (Ed.): *German Idealism: Contemporary Perspectives.* London: Routledge, 206–224.
Pinkard, Terry (2008): *Hegel's Practical Philosophy: Rational Agency as Ethical Life.* Cambridge: Cambridge University Press.
Pippin, Robert (1989): *Hegel's Idealism: The Satisfactions of Self-Consciousness.* Cambridge: Cambridge University Press.
Rödl, Sebastian (2007): *Self-Consciousness.* Cambridge: Harvard University Press.
Rosenzweig, Franz (1930): "Vertauschte Fronten." In: *Der Morgen* 6. No. 6, 85–87.
Rosenzweig, Franz (1988): *Der Stern der Erlösung.* Frankfurt am Main: Suhrkamp.
Rosenzweig, Franz (2005): *Star of Redemption.* Barbara E. Galli (Trans.). Madison: University of Wisconsin Press.
Stern, Robert (2009): *Hegelian Metaphysics.* Oxford: Oxford University Press.
Taylor, Charles (1978): *Hegel.* Frankfurt am Main: Suhrkamp.
Wittgenstein, Ludwig (1922): *Tractatus Logico-Philosophicus.* Charles K. Ogden (Trans.). London: Kegan Paul.
Wittgenstein, Ludwig (1953): *Philosophical Investigations.* Gertrude E. M. Anscombe (Trans.). Oxford: Basil Blackwell.
Wittgenstein, Ludwig (2001): *Philosophische Untersuchungen.* Joachim Schulte (Ed.). Frankfurt am Main: Wissenschaftliche Buchgesellschaft.
Wittgenstein, Ludwig (2003): *Tractatus Logico-Philosophicus.* Frankfurt am Main: Suhrkamp.

Alec Hinshelwood
The Work of Human Hands: Marx on Humanity as Solidarity

Abstract: Marx seems to think that being human is a self-conscious activity which we humans realize only together with one another. We might say that for Marx, humanity *is* solidarity, and that this then bears on the ways in which we humans can coherently organize our living. In this paper, I argue for these ideas. I ask what conception of human living is internal to our taking ourselves, as rational agents, to be distinct individuals from one another. And I argue that whilst both neo-Aristotelian and Hegelian views fail to articulate that conception, Marx successfully does so with his conception of human living as an activity of self-maintenance which is itself mutually recognitive. In this activity of self-conscious living, then, we humans are, I think, as such oriented against servitude, and towards sharing the activities of production and care through which we all live.

Let us suppose we had produced as human beings [...]. I would have acted for you as the *mediator* between you and the species, thus I would be acknowledged by you as the complement of your own being, as an essential part of yourself. I would thus know myself to be confirmed in your thoughts and your love. In the individual expression of my own life, I would have brought about the immediate expression of your life and so in my individual activity, I would have directly confirmed and realized my authentic nature, my *human, communal* nature (Marx EJM 277–278).

1 Introduction

A striking idea in Karl Marx's writings is that being human is a self-conscious activity which we humans realize only together with one another. Marx seems to think, that is, that a human life is lived, and therein enjoyed, through an appreciation of the fact that being what one is, and so being well, is undertaken in mutuality with others. For him, our felt happiness ultimately resides in the acknowledgement of each other as fellows precisely within—amongst others—those productive activities where what is needed to keep ourselves in existence is procured or made. And however comforting we might find the semblances of community afforded by citizenship of a state, or by organized religion, Marx thinks that *if* a form of social organization—a distribution, ultimately, of control over the means of maintaining human life—requires any of us humans to further our own life at the expense of another's, then we will all suffer because of that form.

We might say that Marx insists on the *identity* of humanity and solidarity, and in this paper, I try to bring this identity into focus, arguing that Marx was right to insist on it. I do so by reflecting on the fact that as agents of intentional action, acting out of thought of what to do, we humans take ourselves to be distinct individuals from one another. I argue that if a neo-Aristotelian view about how our humanity figures in our thought of what to do were true, then this fact could not obtain; and calling this consequence the "problem of practical solipsism," I press that in order to avoid it, we need a better characterization of the self-conscious character of our human living. However, where a Hegelian alternative to neo-Aristotelianism might be thought to help here, I argue that it fails to avoid the problem, whereas in Marx's insistence that humanity is solidarity, we have a characterization of the self-conscious character of our human living on which the problem does not arise. So far, then, from being an optimistic expression of faith in an empirical claim about a capacity of ours for altruism, or about some need of ours for co-operative manual labor, Marx's basic thought should, I think, be seen instead as an articulation of that self-understanding which we humans have simply in being able to act intentionally.[1]

So construed, Marx is seen to hold onto a point emphasized by the neo-Aristotelian in the light of another point emphasized by the Hegelian. With the former, he thinks that as a manner of living, being human is an activity by engaging in which we individual humans maintain ourselves as such. And with the latter, he thinks that to be a self-conscious individual is to distinguish oneself from the others *with* them, in mutual recognition. For Marx, then, our activity of maintaining ourselves as individual human beings *is* our acknowledgement of each other as fellows, and we thus distinguish ourselves from each other *in* being human together.[2] Furthermore, by facing up to the absolute dependence on each other which is internal to the mutually recognitive character of our human living, we begin to clarify for ourselves, as philosophers, which forms of social organization we humans can coherently adopt as expressions of that living.

---

[1] See Kandiyali (2020) for a recent and very sophisticated example of the reading which I implicitly oppose here.
[2] I find this idea differently prefigured in Meiksins Wood (1972), Colletti (1972 and 1973), Gould (1978), Chitty (1993), Gourevitch (2011 and 2013), Read (2016), Julius (2016 and 2017), Balibar (2017, Chapter 2), Haase (2018), and Vrousalis (2020). A little further afield, see Theunissen (1984, Chapters 7–8), Løgstrup (1997, Chapter 1), Margalit (1998, Chapter 6), Weil (2005), Gaita (2011, Chapter 2), and Butler (2020).

In arguing this, I do not say that Marx explicitly presented his view—or how it differs from Aristotle's or Hegel's—as the way to avoid the problem of practical solipsism. I do think, however, that some of what he wrote may be helpfully so construed. And if Marx can, with his resolute embrace of "the standpoint of [...] social humanity," reorient our understanding of the questions of practical philosophy, then our approach to those questions should be no less informed by him than by his predecessors.[3] At any rate, my main aim is not to provide a full defense of all the argumentative steps towards which I shall gesture on Marx's behalf but rather to survey enough of the philosophical terrain in order that his distinctive contribution can begin to emerge, at least in outline, as an object of further inquiry.

The plan is as follows. In §2, I describe neo-Aristotelianism and then, in §3, argue that it faces the problem of practical solipsism. In §4, I describe a contrasting Hegelian position but then, in §5, argue that it fails to circumvent the problem. In §6, I begin to sketch out Marx's conception of humanity as the way forward.

2 Neo-Aristotelianism

An agent who is intentionally doing some kind of action, A, represents it as a goal, as to-be-done, and thinks themselves to be doing that kind, A, which they so represent.[4] More generally, such an agent thinks of what to do and takes themselves to act out of such thinking. I label this "practical thought." An agent of intentional action, being a practical thinker, thus takes themselves to be an individual, distinct from any other in the manifold of practically thinking agents. Practical thinkers, we could say, are such as to distinguish themselves from each other.[5] In the next section, I shall ask whether this would be possible if neo-Aristotelianism were correct; but I start here by describing neo-Aristotelianism.

Thought of what *to* do can be redescribed as thought of what is *good* to do. And one might represent an action-kind, A, as good to do because by doing A, one can do another kind, B, which one already represents as good to do; perhaps one makes a coat, for example, because one wishes to provide oneself with warmth. Or one might represent A as good to do because one would, in doing A, realize

---

3 See the 10th thesis on Feuerbach (Marx TF).
4 Cf. Marx (1976a, 283–284).
5 Cf. Müller (1977) and Williams (1993, Chapter 4) as well as Campbell's remarks on the conceptual role of "I" (1994, Chapter 4). Perhaps Parfit (1984, Part III) would deny that we humans, thinking practically, must distinguish ourselves from each other, but he would accept the weaker claim—which is all my argument actually relies on—that it is possible for us to do so.

something—happiness, say—which is good in itself.[6] Abstracting away from which action-kinds we represent as good to do, then, I think that we can say that goodness is the formal object of practical thought similarly to how truth—whichever determinate truths we happen to think—is the object of all theoretical thought.

The neo-Aristotelian seeks to elucidate the object of practical thought with the concept *goodness* which belongs to our thought of living things.[7] And elaborating the form which we deploy when representing an individual as a member of a general species, the neo-Aristotelian claims that our practical thought is an application of this form to ourselves and that *human being* is the species which determines this form in our case.[8]

The form can be characterized as follows. Within it, a species is understood as an interlocking set of specific activities, with engagement in each making possible and being made possible by the others. Together these specific activities constitute the single activity of living as an individual of the species in question. By engaging in this one activity as a whole over time, then, an individual maintains itself as an individual of its kind. For the living, to be is to live. This one activity will include taking in nourishment from the environment, in some determinate ways, and avoiding any threats it poses. Representing a species itself requires, then, grammatically generic propositions which exhibit the single teleological system formed by the specific activities which are comprised by the species—"the grizzly bear fishes for salmon in summer," for example, "and hibernates in winter"—whilst representing a given individual of the species involves representing the particular changes in which it participates, in the here and now, as expressing the structured activity characteristic of its species. Here, self-maintenance is not to be understood as a further activity in which a living individual engages, but rather in terms of the unity of that single, determinate activity by engaging in which the living individual exists over time as what it is.

In expressing the unified activity that is its living, then, an individual's doings are connected to each other teleologically, and the idea of goodness applies to that individual.[9] It will be good for a living individual to do something specific, that is, insofar it is done for the sake of doing something else which it is also good for that individual to do. This makes sense against the backdrop of that set of specific activities by which the species itself is constituted, engaging in the whole of which set

---

[6] Cf. McDowell (1998a).
[7] Prominent examples of this line of thought are Foot (2001) and Thompson (2004a, 2008, 2013).
[8] Some authors who have developed this conception of life as activity, whether in the service of neo-Aristotelianism or not, are Thompson (2008), Boyle and Lavin (2010), Boyle (2012), Haase (2013), Khurana (2013), and Rödl (2016a).
[9] Cf. Korsgaard (2009, Chapter 2).

is unconditionally good for an individual of that species. Again, then, maintaining itself as an individual of its kind is not a further end at which the living individual aims: actively being what it is over time, as the unity of all that it does, is for the living individual goodness itself—the medium, as it were, in which its doings are teleologically connected.[10] With a sentient animal, moreover, pleasure will attach to those of its doings which are, or which it feels to be, in conformity with its species.[11] As conscious living, we might say, being is being happy. Of course, though, a given individual can—in a particular case, due to outside interference—be acting in a way which fails to be fully in accordance with what individuals of its kind do. Such an individual then fares badly: unless it gets back on course, it will suffer and it may not survive.

Insofar, then, as the abstract idea of living as an activity gets determined by the species of an acting individual, it just is, according to the neo-Aristotelian, the idea of goodness as a measure away from which that individual can fall.[12] And in light of the fact that we humans are practically self-conscious animals, the neo-Aristotelian supposes that the goodness which is the object of our practical thought—the goodness which we intentionally enact—is an application of this abstract idea of living to ourselves. Here *human being* figures for us as the species which determines this idea in our own case, and our doings—related in our own thought as the taking of means to ends—must then be animated by a background representation of that species as the unified activity engagement in which is good for us without condition.[13] And of course, the claim is that the activity therein represented will include what are said to be virtues: being just and brave, say.

---

10 That self-maintenance is not to be construed as a *further* end at which a living individual aims is reflected in Marx's ironic comment that "[if] the silkworm were to spin in order to continue its existence as a caterpillar, it would be a complete wage worker" (1980, 203).

11 Cf. Newton (2017), and Reeves (2016). What a living individual enjoys are the specific activities engagement in which is characteristic of its kind; its enjoying of them *is* its engagement in them, its activity of living itself. For more on the distinction between the object and the act of enjoyment, see Owen (1986).

12 Moreover, in representing a living individual as such, one apprehends its parts precisely as those by possessing which it engages in the specific activities of an individual whose self-maintenance, whose living, takes the shape of its species. The idea of an individual's parts being as they "should be" is provided for, then, along with the idea that certain bits of its environment will nourish it (be good for it), whilst certain bits of an environment will enable it to engage in its kind-characteristic activities (be useful to it). Cf. Wiggins (2009).

13 Cf. Thompson's (2008, 8) idea that claims about "reasons for action" must always be indexed to a specific constituency of agents. See also Geach (1956), and Lavin (2017).

The representation of this unified activity must be first-personal, and we are supposed to be provided with it simply by being human: given what living a human life involves, it is supposed to be no accident that we humans are among the practical thinkers and represent just this determinate activity as the good way for us to live.[14] For the neo-Aristotelian, then, there will be a characteristic route through which we acquire this representation: namely, by getting initiated when young by our elders into the inter-connected set of practices in which being human is said to consist. Compare the non-rational life of meerkats, for example, in which the older ones must nevertheless train the young ones to live in the way that meerkats do. Moreover, since a human being's practical representation of their own species would not be the result of empirical inquiry, the neo-Aristotelian might claim that with that representation, so long as nothing has interrupted, the individual enjoys distinctively practical knowledge of their species.[15]

3 The Problem of Practical Solipsism

According to the neo-Aristotelian, being a practical thinker is not itself the activity by engaging in which any living individual maintains themselves as what they are. Rather, it is a determinable form—the abstract idea, self-applied, of living as an activity—that does not by itself settle the animal species which determines it in any given case. Compare, for example, how the abstract feature of being non-rationally sensate gets differently determined in sharks and bats.[16] For the neo-Aristotelian, then, members of two different species could each be practically self-conscious, but the difference between their species would mean that each of them only represents their own species as the good way for them to live. Indeed, whilst each of these individuals will be provided with a practical representation of their own species by that species itself, each could learn about the character of the other's species only empirically.

With this much in place, however, I think that a practically self-conscious individual would need empirical inquiry even to reach knowledge concerning their own species. After all, being able to act intentionally, and so think practically, such an individual would already know themselves to be a practical thinker.[17] However, to know themselves to be a practical thinker, on this view, would only be for them to know themselves to be alive and to belong to *some* species—even if they were to

---

14 Thompson (2004a, 2013) especially insists on this; see also Thompson (2004b, 376–378).
15 Cf. Thompson (2013), and Frey (2018, 78–79).
16 Cf. Ford (2011, 88–90).
17 Cf. Thompson (2004b, 353–354).

reserve the words "human being" for it—since no determinate knowledge concerning their actual species would be contained, just as such, in their knowledge of being a practical thinker. Although they would find themselves with a practical representation of a unified set of specific activities as their own species, then, the content of that representation would neither follow from their being a practical thinker nor be based on that empirical investigation into their species which, on this view, they know to be possible.[18] As the object of their practical representation, the actual character of their species would be grasped by them only formally: as whatever it is that explains, if nothing has interrupted, why they have the determinate representation of it that they have.

In that case, however, the content of that explanation, and so the actual character of their species, would not be grasped by the practical thinker simply in their having that representation. They could not, that is, take that representation to be practical *knowledge* of their species, for they would take themselves to be able to have and yet to be missing grounds for having a representation with that content. Rather, it would be for them a kind of guess about their good which they find themselves making. Moreover, it is irrelevant to this point if the practical thinker has got this representation from a conspecific—even a very powerful one—since the question remains what that other's basis for forming that representation could have been; in that case, the representation could only be for the practical thinker a bit of unverified hearsay about their good. As a practical thinker, then, the actual character of their species would have to remain an empirically discoverable aspect of themselves: something to which they stand in the same way, epistemically speaking, to how they stand to the character of species other than their own.

Here, to borrow Marx's words, the actual kind of the practical thinker must "be comprehended [...] as an internal, [mute] generality which *naturally* unites [...] many individuals."[19] And if this is so, then I think that there is a real question about whether the practical thinker could retain their grip on the possibility of enacting their own practical thought: of acting intentionally. After all, they could *rationally* determine the form of their practical thought only with an empirical investigation into their species, wherein they must suppose that their species' character —and so what they generically do—is fixed however they currently represent that. Rather than developing this concern, however, I want to press that the foregoing gives rise to the problem of practical solipsism. That is, I think that the possibility of a practical thinker's taking themselves to be a living individual, distinct from

---

18 Cf. Haase (2018, 124–125). I have been helped a lot here by Ometto (2022). See also Kitcher (1999) and Vogler (2006).
19 See the 6th thesis on Feuerbach (Marx TF). I have "mute" rather than "dumb" for the German *"stumm."*

other practical thinkers, has been undermined. By getting so much into view, my hope is that we shall be in a position to begin to appreciate, at least, Marx's contrasting conception of humanity as "the ensemble of social relations."[20]

Now, if a practical thinker can, in the end, only grasp the actual character of their species in empirical thought, then that species must be for them something to be recognized in sensibly presented members of the manifold which it comprises. They would, that is, have the idea of *a* human being as something which given objects of awareness are observed to be. In that case, the practical thinker's own individuality—here grasped by them, as a living being, only through a species—would have to be grasped in a thought which is based on their having been given to themselves as an object of awareness. The practical thinker would thus think something like "this living thing here is a human being; I, a practical thinker, am it." Doing so, however, they would answer for themselves the question which human being they are identical with from amongst the manifold of human beings. After all, they cannot be identical with more than one human being; and yet from within their practical self-consciousness alone, which one they are would no more be settled for them than the character of their species. By some mode of awareness, then, the practical thinker would have to be presented with that human with whom they *are* identical.

How, though, could they ever take themselves to know that they had got hold of the right one? They do not seek to identify the objects of two episodes of sense-awareness, each having already been brought by them under the same empirically recognized species. Contrast how one might identify a striped cat which one now sees walking out from behind a wall, for example, with the striped cat which one saw earlier walk behind that same wall. It is unclear, then, what possible grounds the practical thinker could take to bear on the question which they pose. Recognizable co-variation between the doings of a sensibly given human being and their own practical thinking could hardly serve for them, as practical thinker, as mark of their identity with that human being. Why should it? Here the formal "I live" of practical thought is completely indeterminate, and from within it alone—from within the practical thinker's thought of themselves as such—there could be no more reason for them to identify themselves with "this" rather than "that" sensibly given human being. From the standpoint of being a practical think-

---

[20] See the 6th thesis on Feuerbach (Marx TF). Schuringa (forthcoming) shows how the early Feuerbach partly embraced the problem of practical solipsism, and that Marx can then be construed as seeking to avoid it. See also Colletti (1973, 198) and Wolff (1988, Chapters 2–3). Of course, Marx acknowledged the importance of Feuerbach's repeated, countervailing emphasis on the communal character of being human; see, e.g., Marx (EPM, 381).

er, that is, they could only say of the humans: "*I*, for all that I could ever know, might as well be any of *them*."²¹

This apparently skeptical concern unfolds into the underlying conceptual issue: the problem of practical solipsism itself. After all, if a practical thinker understands the question which human being they are, then they have the idea of being some living individual, understanding the possibility of knowing themselves to be that one. Given neo-Aristotelianism, however, there can be no such understanding. For the neo-Aristotelian, if my argument is right, practical self-consciousness cannot contain any knowledge concerning our actual kind, and the practical thinker must conceive their identity with a particular human being as something to be known by them empirically. However, the possibility of this must be completely unintelligible to that practical thinker, and they could not have a grasp of what it is they would know should they know it. That is, they could not grasp what it would be for the thought of the form "this is a human being; I, a practical thinker, am it" to be true (or false).²² In the end, then, this practical thinker could have no grip on the possibility of being a living individual: at best, they could conceive of themselves as a practically thoughtful generality, set over and against a manifold of individual albeit practically thoughtless human beings.

This solipsism would not involve, then, the agent's thinking that they are, in fact, the only practically self-conscious individual, but rather would involve their lacking the very idea of a practically self-conscious *individual* in the first place.²³ Borrowing Marx's words: "instead of the ordinary individual with his ordinary manner of [...] thinking, we have nothing but this ordinary manner purely and

---

21 Cf. Strawson (1959, 90–94) as well as Anscombe (1981, 34) and Haddock (2019). It might be said that the practical thinker could be aware of a human being in *bodily awareness*, and that everything presented to a practical thinker in such awareness must figure as a part, so to speak, of a single space of feeling. This awareness could not then present to the thinker a manifold of human beings as such. Cf. Martin (1994). However, with such awareness being conceived here as a kind of structureless outer sense, the practical thinker would still have no reason to identify themselves with its object, since that could in fact encompass more than one human being. Cf. O'Brien (2007, 201–209). Of course, one might advance an alternative conception of bodily awareness, on which it affords no basis for such an identification because it is already a function, somehow, of practical self-consciousness itself. Cf. O'Brien (2007, 217), McDowell (2011) and Boyle (2018). However, I think that this then requires practical self-consciousness to *be* our activity of human living—cf. Rödl (2016b) and (2017a)—*pace* neo-Aristotelianism.
22 They precisely cannot, *pace* Evans, "make sense of identifying a person, conceived from the standpoint of [a world of objects of perception, *as* themselves]" (1982, 201). Cf. Wittgenstein (1976, §§4–5).
23 The worry seems be echoed by Gobsch in his criticism (2014, 189) of what he calls "naïve Hegelianism." See also Nagel (1986, Chapter 4) and Rödl (2017b, 292–294). I have been helped a lot here by Haddock's manuscript "Self-Consciousness and Form-Consciousness" and Haddock (2019).

simply—without the individual" (Marx 1967b, 163).[24] Of course, we practically thinking agents do take ourselves to be living individuals, distinct from one another.[25] And our own individuality could not, in that case, be something to which we must be *given access*, through awareness of a particular exemplar of an empirically recognized species. There cannot be, that is, any gap between having the idea of *a* practical thinker and knowing oneself to be the living individual that one is. Rather, one must be that living individual in knowing oneself to be a practical thinker, whilst knowing oneself to be a practical thinker—and so having that idea—in being that individual. Or, as we might put it: to be of the kind *practical thinker* is for one's own individuality as living being to be nothing other than the practical self-consciousness in which one is of that kind.[26]

Yet, if *practical thinker* is that generality in realizing which we, its individual bearers, exist over time, then it is itself our manner of living: the activity of living self-consciously. Knowing oneself to be a practical thinker must be, then, nothing other than living—maintaining oneself—as one; and in that case, our kind could not be a species of practically self-conscious animal which is defined against possible others within an overarching genus.[27] On the contrary, *human being* must be, as it were, the genus *practical thinker* itself: the activity of living through the very idea of that or, as Marx has it, "genus-being" (*Gattungswesen*).[28] There must be a use of "intentional action" on which it just refers to our, human action. And I think that we hang on to what we know to be possible—our own individuality as practically thinking agents—only by insisting on this in opposition to neo-Aristotelianism. How, though, are we to understand the idea that practical thinker—instead of being an abstract feature which, like being sighted, could get differently

---

24 Officially, Marx is criticizing Hegel here.
25 Cf. Williams (1981, 52, n. 8): "the aim of moral thought and experience [...] must primarily involve grasping the world in such a way that one can, as a particular human being, live in it."
26 Cf. the opening section in Khurana (2021).
27 I am not sure with which words a practical thinker could express their knowledge of their own individuality: "I am the one that I am" is empty, whilst "I am this one"—where "this" is a perceptual demonstrative of some kind—seems apt only for trying to express the impossible bit of empirical knowledge. Would the words "we are not the same human being" work? I think that by using them, one would not *tell* somebody something: one would rather oppose oneself to some confusion of theirs. At any rate, I suppose that a practical thinker can *show* what they know in their very living with others. Cf. Moore (1997, 225). Consider, then, Fanon's striking remark that the "fact that I am me is haunted by the existence of the other" (2021, 373); thanks to Rose Ryan Flinn for this reference.
28 As Schuringa (forthcoming) points out, "genus-being" is a better translation of Marx's use of "*Gattungswesen*" than is the typical "species-being." Cf. Colletti (1973, 234) and Khurana (2023).

determined by various animal species—is itself our manner of living: that activity our engagement in which just is our maintenance of ourselves as human beings?

4 Hegelianism

Since it involves the idea that being a practically thinking agent *is* our activity of self-conscious living, *humanity* itself, a Hegelian position is worth considering at this point.[29] Here, each practically self-conscious individual is said to oppose themselves to the others, of necessity, whilst their general activity of living is said to be an historically developed set of practices which, mediating those individuals' recognition of each other, is said to have determined itself. In §5, I shall argue that the proposed moment of opposition means that the Hegelian does not avoid the problem of practical solipsism. First, though, what is the view?

To begin here, we might note another apparent difficulty for the neo-Aristotelian. For them, the good thing for a living individual to do is just to fulfil their general role, as it were, within that interlinked set of roles which constitutes the species that the individual shares with others. Consider the fact that in the life-cycle of certain species of spider, for example, the male is eaten by the female after mating, or the female by her offspring after the latter hatch; that is how such individuals live well.[30] It is not clear, in that case, how the individual practical thinker is even to frame the idea of their own good as something which can conflict with the good of any of their conspecifics. How could their conception of life underwrite such an idea? For the Hegelian, however, it belongs to their being a practically self-conscious individual to have framed that idea, and the practical thinker's framing of it should be understood as an original choice of their own good over anyone else's.[31]

Now, for the Hegelian, conforming to the genus *practical thinker* is the unconditional good for any individual practical thinker; it is that activity engagement in

---

[29] Finding a single author who espouses all of what follows is not really possible, but for some papers which severally point in this direction, see: Haase (2013), Khurana (2013), Gobsch (2014), Rödl (2015), and Kern (2020). The interpretation of Aristotle which McDowell has developed over many papers—in, e.g., McDowell (1998)—also seems to count as Hegelian in my sense, at least to some extent. For what it is worth, the Hegelianism which I present is meant to be faithful to (what I take to be) Hegel's own thought, and so I include citations of Hegel's own texts and switch somewhat freely between describing the view of "the Hegelian" and that of "Hegel himself." However, I leave establishing the identity of the references of those two phrases for another occasion.
[30] Cf. Haase (2021, 478).
[31] Cf. Gobsch (2014, 2020).

which just is a practical thinker's being what they are. The picture is complicated, however, because without an empirically grasped species, the individual applies the genus directly to themselves. On this view, that is, each practical thinker is identical with a given subject of "sensuous desires," the satisfaction of whose desires that individual then represents as good. The individual practical thinker is such as to have framed, then, with the idea of the systematic satisfaction of *those* desires, an essentially private conception of how to be a practical thinker over time which is originally opposed by them to the shareable, general character of that genus.[32] Their being an individual practical thinker involves their having opposed, as it were, the generality of *practical thinker* precisely in thinking themselves under it.[33]

Equally, this is for them to have opposed themselves to all other practical thinkers. After all, opposing themselves to the shareability of *practical thinker* in thinking themselves under it, each individual practical thinker therein thinks of other practical thinkers as being precisely that to which they are opposed, thinking the others to have opposed themselves back in thinking the same. That is, each practical thinker takes themselves to be an individual—one amongst a possible manifold—precisely in purporting to exclude the same-thinking others from that genus, as if what is good in itself were only their own self-maintenance.[34] Each thinks, as it were, "*I*, being human, *am* humanity." However, whilst their distinguishing themselves from each other in this manner is, the Hegelian maintains, an essential moment in practical thinkers' mutual recognition, this aspect of being a practically self-conscious individual—what Hegel himself calls the "natural will"—cannot be the whole story.[35]

The genus from which a practical thinker would exclude any others must nevertheless be grasped by that individual as general: the shareable activity of self-

---

[32] Cf. Frege's idea (1997) that someone's "I-thoughts" involve a sense which is private to them alone and that such thoughts cannot then be shared with anyone else. On this connection, cf. Lavin (2014).

[33] Cf. Hegel (1991, §139): "When the will lets its content be determined by [sensuous] desires [...] and hence also by the form [...] of particularity, it thereby becomes opposed to universality as inner objectivity, i.e., to the good." See also Hegel (1991, §93, Remark). On this picture, we are, as Luther says, *incurvatus in se:* bent in on ourselves and thus such as to be originally in sin, and in need of being made right. Cf. Hegel (1991, §18, and 1971a, §24, 3rd Remark).

[34] Cf. Chitty (1994, Chapter 3, §5). And cf. Rousseau on the *amor propre* which makes "the whole universe necessary to each man," quoted in Meiksins Wood (2012, 208), as well as Engstrom (2013a) on Kant on self-conceit. It is striking how the first thought that McDowell (1998b) has his wolf think when it becomes rational concerns its own good and whether to free-ride on the activities of its pack.

[35] Cf. Hegel (1991, §11); see also Hegel (1977, §357).

conscious living, engagement in which is unconditionally good for *every* practical thinker.[36] After all, in thinking themselves under it—thinking it to be nothing but themselves—the genus can only oppose itself to the individual through their idea of the other: it must dissolve their self-directed individuality, as it were, since in thinking themselves under the genus, the individual distinguishes themselves from *other* practical thinkers and so must acknowledge their possibility.[37] Thus, the Hegelian maintains, individual practical thinkers must understand the genus, their shared activity of self-conscious living, to bring them into alignment with itself against their original opposition to its generality and thus against their opposition to the possibility of each other. Understanding this, individual practical thinkers recognize each other as such: as held together by the selfsame genus, their living essence.[38]

More concretely: the Hegelian thinks that self-conscious living is customary, claiming that it consists in those sets of practices which constitute different peoples' ways of life.[39] Having been habituated so to act, a practically self-conscious individual acts *from* such a set of practices, understanding themselves to do so. Practical thinkers thus develop in a way which is distinctive amongst living things. Practical thinkers are brought up against their original privileging of the satisfaction of their own "sensuous desires," through education, into ever greater conformity with the general practices of their people. They must be taught how to act, and their self-conception as individuals must be worked up into an identification of themselves with—and so, for the Hegelian, a kind of return to—the shared generality of their way of life. As Hegel himself says, "the habit of obedience is a necessary moment in the education of every man. Without having experienced the discipline that breaks self-will, no one becomes free, rational" (Hegel 1971c, §435, Zusatz).[40] To the extent that practical thinkers have "a nature," then, it is necessarily second: a manner of living which is won out of opposition to their "first."

It bears emphasizing how for the Hegelian, practically self-conscious individuality is a kind of necessary evil in rectifying which the general activity of self-con-

---

36 Cf. Hegel (1991, §8, Zusatz): "In so far as an end is still only ours, it is for us a deficiency, for to us, freedom and will are the unity of the subjective and the objective."
37 Cf. Meiksins Wood (1972, 108): "Insofar as individuality, as egoism, compels man to submit to community, that individuality is [...] self-contradictory, self-annihilating."
38 Hegel himself suggests that this complex illuminates his general idea of a "speculative identity" between general and particular; see Hegel (1971c, §436, Zusatz).
39 Cf. Hegel (1977, §§349–351).
40 Cf. Hegel (1991, §§151–153) as well as Lovibond on Wittgenstein (1983, §§14–16 and §20).

scious living sustains itself.[41] Individual practical thinkers become what they are in letting their self-conscious individuality be reconstituted. In getting brought up, such an individual becomes transparent, as it were, to the set of general practices which they self-consciously enact; and having been so rectified, individual practical thinkers can in their difference recognize each other as particular manifestations of the selfsame general activity of living.[42] Through self-conscious individuals, then, the activity of living is a power unto itself through which alone such individuals are made good; customary life is actual—and so efficacious—as something general.[43] I think that this is at least part of the reason why Hegel himself labels *humanity*, or *Geist*, the "concrete universal."[44]

In contrast with the general species of any non-rational animal, then, customary life itself is said to be *in* and to have changed over time: to have its own history as a generality.[45] Indeed, the Hegelian maintains that it must be seen as an activity which has developed *itself*: a form of living whose content is nothing other than its own self-development as a form. The history of customary life is then understood as culminating when that life distinguishes itself from—is articulated as a unified power which stands opposed to—the desiring individuals in rectifying whom it subsists. The Hegelian maintains that precisely this is the achievement of modernity.[46] Before this point, customary life's development should be understood as a cumulative series of attempts at becoming codified in overarching systems of law, wherein the equality of the systems' bearers to one another, and so those systems' common presence in their bearers, is made clear.[47] This is the process of self-critique through which customary life—humanity—has developed into itself.

---

[41] I think that "being rectified" is what Paul means with "justification" in, e.g., *Romans*, where justification is the Spirit's own work: we must, then, be faithful—anything more (or less) would be hubris, for to be in Spirit and thus truly to live, we must first "die in the flesh": relinquish being self-subsistent individuals in order to be together as members of Christ. Cf. Fredriksen (2017, 117–130). See also McCabe (2010, xi) and Luther: "the one task of faith" is "to crush the flesh," i.e., "the entire human person" (2017, 73 and 68). For Hegel himself, the genus as *Geist* subsists as general alongside its individual bearers by consuming them in habit during their lives, whereas in the case of animals, it subsists only in the replacement of old individuals by new ones. See Hegel (1971c, §§374–377, and 1991, §§151–152).
[42] Cf. Hegel (1977, §351; 1971c, §436; and 1991, §209, Remark.)
[43] Cf. Rödl (2015).
[44] See, e.g., Hegel (1971b, §376).
[45] Cf. Hegel (1971c, §548). Cf. Wiggins on languages (2022) and McCabe (2003a, 87–88).
[46] Cf. Hegel (1995, 209; 1991, §75, Zusatz; and 1991, §§349–350). See also Foster (1935, Chapter 4), Honneth (2015), McDowell (2017), and Khurana (2018).
[47] Cf. Stein (1999, Chapter 5) for some legal-historical background to the idea of codification here.

In taking the shape of the modern nation-state, then, and including within itself genuinely *public* institutions that are set over and against—whilst being reproduced by—manifolds of desiring individuals whose equal and inviolable rights against each other it defines and enforces, customary life as a form has liberated itself from its matter.[48] These individuals have been habituated to respect these rights—principally, to private property—but are otherwise free to pursue the satisfaction of their private desires.[49] Where, then, an animal expresses its activity of living *in* all its properly means-end ordered doings, the Hegelian thinks that our activity of living opposes itself to our desire-expressing, means-end ordered doings precisely as, in the end, the inviolable rights of other citizens.[50] Joined as potentially contracting parties within a free market, citizens of a state then recognize each other as such in lawful competition; and they are to see that state itself as the "spiritual organism" which holds them together as practically thoughtful human beings.[51] Its object—maintenance of itself—is then their own essential aim and unconditional good.[52]

5 The Problem of Practical Solipsism Again

The Hegelian fails to avoid the problem of practical solipsism, I said that I would now argue, because they take each practically self-conscious individual to oppose themselves to the others. In effect, the Hegelian thereby takes for granted a manifold of human beings, and ends up treating *practical thinker* like a general role which some members of that pre-given manifold play. In that case, however, the idea on which we must insist, as philosophers, in order to avoid the problem of practical solipsism—the idea that the individual practical thinker's thought of themselves can be nothing other than their living existence itself—has simply been passed over, and we are no further along.

---

48 Cf. Hegel (1991, §260). Contrast feudalism: custom itself was dispersed amongst competing institutions with overlapping jurisdictions—church and crown, for example. See Anderson (1979, Chapter 1) for how the publicity of modern political institutions is rooted in late feudal absolutism; for the suggestion that Hegel's political philosophy is to be understood against this backdrop, see Meiksins Wood (1991, Chapter 2).
49 Cf. Hegel (1991, §208). As *per* Hegel's definition of the ethical (1991, §141), these individuals have "a subjective disposition [...] of that right which has being in itself."
50 Cf. Hegel (1991, §§154–155). See also Velleman on Kant on reverence for the law (1999, 348).
51 Cf. Hegel (1971c, §432, Zusatz). For the Hegelian, then, the opposition of our kind to us individuals is more fully manifested in our having to conform our work and desires to market pressure. Cf. Hegel (1991, §189, §192, and §198).
52 Cf. Hegel (1991, §324).

The difficulty has to do with the so-called natural will, and the idea that each practical thinker originally chooses themselves, as I put it, in opposition to the shareability of the genus *practical thinker*. Here, we assume a practical thinker who, thinking themselves to be a given subject of "sensuous desires," thereby takes being a practical thinker to consist in the systematic satisfaction of *those* desires. However, those desires must be something of which the practical thinker is first aware, and the practical thinker's own individuality is then something to which they would have to be given access and which they would grasp by thinking: "this is a desiring subject; I, a practical thinker, am it."[53] Again, then, I do not think that they could find the possibility of making such an identification intelligible, and their grasp of themselves as an individual practical thinker could not get off the ground.[54] As "privately receptive," that is, and with the concept *subject of desire* having to be empirical in some sense, this putative thought of themselves could not *be* that activity by engaging in which the practical thinker maintains themselves as what they are, and so it could not really be their knowledge of their own individuality.

Now, Hegel himself depicts a fight to the death between self-conscious individuals, seeking to illustrate an aspect of being one, I think he thinks, by dramatizing a contradiction: namely, that (a) each individual practical thinker already thinks of the same-thinking others in thinking themselves; but (b) in thinking themselves to be practical self-consciousness itself, each rejects the idea of any other. And the problem here is with (b): it reverts to a characterization of the practical thinker as one who privately thinks themselves to be the indeterminate genus; that is just the self-choice.[55] Here, Hegel takes for granted a manifold of individuals

---

53 Cf. Hegel (1991, §14). See also Engstrom on Kant (2013b, 673–674) on inner sense and Meiksins Wood on the concept of private interest (1972, 111–112).

54 It might be said that in desire-awareness, conceived as a non-spatial mode of sensing, no manifold of subjects would be presented to the practical thinker as such. However, this would not enable the latter to identify themselves with the object of that awareness: it might yet encompass more than one subject of desire. Cf. Armstrong (1968, 338). I suspect that this is basically Hume's problem in his appendix to the *Treatise*; see also Martin (2006, Part III). I criticize this conception of desire from a different angle in my (2013).

55 I would propose (a) and (b) as renderings of the "twofold significance" which Hegel himself (1977, §179) attributes to how an individual self-consciousness has, of necessity, another one for its object. See also (1977, §184). Across this chapter, as I understand it, Hegel is working out the bare idea of an individual self-consciousness, which individual is only later specified as practically rational; see Hegel (1977, §177 and §349). This individual does not then identify themselves with a subject of "sensuous desire," so much as with their somehow brutely given particularity. In the drama of the fight to the death, this is a matter of their taking possession of their body as property the disposability of which entails destroying the other's, so that they might be by themselves self-

each of whom purports to think purely of themselves, thinking that to be a practical thinker just is to satisfy desires given to *them*.⁵⁶ And on the one hand, there should be no room for this: with (a), the idea that the shareability of *practical thinker* could be intelligibly opposed to begin with has already gone by the board; but on the other, with Hegel assuming (b) regardless, the problem of practical solipsism looms.

Of course, no Hegelian would happily claim that a purely universal practical self-consciousness abides over a manifold of living albeit practically thoughtless individuals and the view just is, *inter alia*, an attempted interweaving of the two sides.⁵⁷ With the foregoing (a) and (b), there is an unreconcilable opposition between practically self-conscious individuals taken by themselves, but this is meant to be resolved with the idea of customary life: a shared essence which is seen by those individuals to have a prior actuality as general and of which, in their recognition of each other as practical thinkers, they know themselves to be appearances. The Hegelian claims, then, that practical thinkers' being of necessity self-consciously together indicates that their individuality is, in the end, somehow a function of customary life itself. And the Hegelian thus seeks, in effect, to identify practical self-consciousness with the activity of living by imbuing a hypostasized conception of the former with a general life of its own, allowing each individual their own distinct, self-directed activity but insisting that all these activities must be mediated by that general activity as it realizes itself through them. This is reflected, then, in the picture of customary life as having come somehow to divide itself into the public institutions which define the role *citizen*, on the one hand, and of individual human beings as "naturally" able self-consciously to pursue means to desire-given ends, on the other.

However, it is hard to see how something general could *of itself* "use" one individual to act on another in time and, as before, an original identification would anyway have to lie, impossibly, at the heart of each natural will. Thus, neither of the related moments at which the Hegelian would bind self-conscious generality and our living individuality—the resurrection, as it were, or the preceding incarnation—really makes sense.⁵⁸ Despite avoiding an appeal to an empirically grasped

---

consciousness itself. Of course, that would be no resting place, hence the dialectic onwards towards the *Rechtstaat* and beyond.

56 That Hegel himself tacitly makes some such assumption is an old charge: cf. Frank (1989, 258–259).

57 See Hegel himself (1971c, §552, Remark): "the intrinsically concrete mind is just as essentially under the one of its terms (subjective consciousness) as under the other (universality)."

58 Cf. McCabe (2003b, 90): "The resurrection sets the seal on the incarnation." In his early essay on natural law, Hegel himself alludes to this theological motif as a way of characterizing, as he sees it,

human nature, then, the Hegelian leaves untouched the underlying issue: a conception of our individuality as something to which awareness originally gives us access. Here, our own individuality is, to borrow Marx's words, construed as an object of "observation" to which we are opposed as the "abstract" albeit active generality *practical thinker.* However, neither side is our own "sensuous human activity."[59] As *per* the underlying problem of practical solipsism, then, I do not think that the double-vision induced by the picture as a whole can be resolved: there is no way to grasp its two sides together as that single activity which is *our* self-conscious self-maintenance as human beings.

It is unsurprising, given this, if *practical thinker* should then seem like a general role which human beings play, with mutual recognition only obtaining between those who do.[60] Thus individual humans are said by the Hegelian to recognize each other as practical thinkers in the system of private right. After all, in contrast to feudalism's pairs of roles *lord/vassal* and *priest/laymen*, for example, private right has only one fundamental role, *legal person*, which indifferently binds in opposition all who play it, circumscribing with equal property rights which each has against the other the permissible means for their "naturally" self-directed activities.[61] Unifying a manifold every member of which acknowledges the others as the same, *legal person* and its supporting institutions are, as it were, the last custom: tradition's apotheosis, wherein it would ground itself and determine the naturally willful humans which it takes itself to confront.[62]

---

the moments of dialectical progression in general (1999, 151–152). For a helpful if critical discussion of how Hegel thinks of these two moments more generally, see Colletti (1972, Chapter 3).

59 See the 1st thesis on Feuerbach (Marx TF). I have "observation" rather than "contemplation" for Marx's *"Anschauung."*

60 Cf. the distinction which Thompson draws (2004b, 351–355) between the concepts *person* and *agent*, and Snowdon's (1990) likening of *person* to a phase-sortal like *adult*.

61 A practical thinker's individuality might then be modelled on the ownership of private property: "a body" of which they originally take possession. So it goes in Hegel; see Hegel (1991, §40, §§47–48, and §57). As a version of original, private self-identification, however, I do not think that such "self-ownership" makes sense.

62 Cf. Hegel's immediate association of "a universal principle of justice, by which each individual man, in virtue of his existence, has absolute value as a universal being recognized by all," with "the development of private rights relating to the property of individual persons" (1995, 376). See also Hegel (1971c, §§490–491) and then Hegel (1991, §192 and §207) for the idea that such recognition ultimately involves market participation and work within an "estate." Now, Hegel seems to allow that familial love is somehow mutually recognitive (1991, §158 and 1971c, §436, Zusatz). Given its claimed universality, however, only legal personality seems to involve, for him, the mutual recognition internal to being an individual practical thinker (Hegel 1991, §209). Indeed, by getting married, loving individuals are said by him not to contract but rather to "dissolve" themselves into one legal-personal unit (Hegel 1991, §40, §§158–159, and §167), largely to the advantage of the

This is reflected in the fact that *legal person* is not itself an activity by engaging in which its bearers maintain themselves as what they are. After all, it is not a generality whose inner articulation includes, just as such, those activities through which its living bearers interact with nature—working on it, for example, for the sake of getting food—or those activities through which those bearers care for one another. Indeed, whilst legal persons can contract with each other in order to obtain what they lack, from the standpoint of any given legal person, the need to realize this possibility in fact might appear to be an unhappy accident. What the generality then centrally includes are proscriptions *against* engaging in certain activities: trespassing, say, or stealing.[63] Thus the continued existence of a manifold of legal persons must be the work of an activity which goes beyond that generality: namely, that in which human beings as such engage, where those humans then can, by thinking of each other *as* legal persons, come to *count* as legal persons—or more fully, according to the Hegelian, as citizens of a state.

On this way of thinking about our recognition of each other, then, some of us human beings need never be included within it—who exactly and to what extent depending, in the end, on rights granted by states along with those states' concern to enforce those rights.[64] Of course, that sits in tension with the universalism contained in the idea—surely correct—that the sphere of our mutual recognition as practical thinkers must fully include each human being. Not for nothing, then, I think, can Aristotle be construed as reaching at this point for his concept of a "natural slave," and entering his remarks about women.[65] And despite the distance that Hegel himself places between his own thought and Aristotle's, it is in this gloomy region, I think, that we should locate his treatment of women and his remarks about those wage-laborers who at least *become*, as he says, unable to "feel and enjoy the wider freedoms, and in particular the spiritual advantages, of civil society" (Hegel 1991, §243).[66] Divisions are introduced between human beings, in

---

husband as the "genuine" practical thinker (Hegel 1991, §166 and §171). Only so is the family itself—or, I suppose, any woman—said to partake in the lawful whole of customary life. Cf. Aristotle's remarks at the end of Aristotle (1991, Book I) on how "natural slaves" are to partake in their owners' virtue.

63 Cf. Kant (1996, 86–87): the end of rational nature must "be thought not as an end to be effected, but as an *independently existing* end, and hence thought of only negatively, that is, as that which must never be acted against."

64 Cf. Hegel (1991, §62): *"freedom of personality* began to flourish under Christianity and became a universal principle for part—if only a small part—of the human race."

65 On "natural slaves," see Aristotle (1991, Book I).

66 Cf. Marx's discussion of Hegel's characterization of the landed gentry: "zoology is the secret of nobility" (CHDS, 174–175). One might also consider here Hegel's remarks on acquiescing to servitude (1991, §57 Zusatz). Cf. Macpherson (1962, 221–228) and Meiksins Wood (1972, 114–117) on

respect of their being practical thinkers, in order to reflect the fact that the sphere of our mutual recognition, so conceived, does not fully include those who are engaged in activities which are central to human living.[67]

Since we humans must exist over time as what we are in thinking ourselves to be practical thinkers, however, this thought of each other can be nothing other than our activity of living itself: that activity by engaging in which we maintain ourselves as human beings. Only by insisting on this do we, as philosophers, avoid the problem of practical solipsism, and comprehend that universality which is proper to the mutual recognition between us humans. I think that this is one of Marx's fundamental insights. By embracing it, we philosophers acknowledge that far from originally opposing ourselves to the shareable character of our living, and so to each other, we humans originally know that we maintain ourselves as what we are only through and for each other. Thus Marx says that "the *real, active* relation of man to himself as a [genus]-being, i.e., as a human being, is only possible [...] through the ['omni-operation'] of mankind" (EPM, 386).[68] And he says that if an individual's needs are *human*, then "the *other*, as a human being, [is] a need for him," so that "in his most individual existence he is at the same time a communal being" (Marx, EPM 347). I want to close, then, by sketching out some of Marx's thinking here in order to bring it into view as an object of further reflection.

6 Humanity as Solidarity

To begin with, we might note that the conception of living which the neo-Aristotelian makes available can perfectly well accommodate there being other kinds of animal, apart from us, that live "politically" in some sense.[69] An individual bee lives in a hive with other bees, after all, and that bee engages in its kind-characteristic activities only together with those others; a description of the specific activities which the species comprises must refer to this fact. So it is again with meerkats, for example, who live in packs but who nevertheless are—in contrast to bees

---

Locke on wage-labor and Nussbaum (1980) for an exploration of the intersection of a number of these themes in Plato and Aristotle.
67 On this general line of thought, see Depew (1991). See also Douglas (1966, Chapter 7).
68 I have used the completely artificial "omni-operation" as a much less misleading translation of Marx's "*Gesamtwirken*" than the translator's "co-operation." The latter wrongly suggests a series of contractual exchanges, which is a conception of our togetherness to which Marx was strongly opposed: cf. Marx (EJM, 266).
69 Cf. Depew (1995).

—such as to teach their young and whose body-parts do not reflect any of the specific roles, organized matriarchally inside a pack, that get played out within the pack's joint activities.

In each case, though, it is internal to the living individual's actively being what it is—its conforming to its kind over time—that the conspecifics with whom it lives are what they are. Their shared kind is divided, so to speak, into fixed but correlative roles that are distributed within circumscribed groups. The individuals in any such group then realize that kind in themselves only in their joint work. Each individual thus maintains itself as what it is only together with those others, and that is just to say that the well-being of each of them is interdependent with that of those with whom they live: being individual fragments of a limited but unified whole, as it were, their goods cannot conflict but rather complete each other. "A hive of bees comprises," as Marx colorfully puts it, "at bottom only one bee" (1973, 243). With *conscious* animals, moreover, this is a matter of pleasure and so happiness, and I think that this is on display when, for example, meerkats in pack act together or when, negatively, elephants in a pride mourn the loss of one of their young.

We humans are practical thinkers, however, and we are such in thinking ourselves to be such. In thinking this same thing, that is, thinking each other to think it, we distinguish ourselves from each other, and are thus under this same generality together.[70] What is such thinking, however, this distinguishing? I think that Marx claims that it is our activity, so to speak, of *self-conscious political living:* a single activity of living by engaging in which together we humans maintain one another as what we are. Here, our knowledge of own our individuality just is our continued engagement in this mutual activity, wherein each of us at once gives ourselves to and is given ourselves by the others. As Marx puts it: "Man is in the most literal sense a *zoon politikon,* not just a gregarious animal, but an animal that can individuate itself only [in community]" (1973, 84).[71] Being a practically thinking agent does not then involve originally opposing oneself to the shareable

---

[70] Cf. Fichte (2000, 45): "the concept of individuality [...] is a shared concept in which two consciousnesses are unified into one." See also Rödl (2014) and Julius (2016).

[71] I have "in community" for *"in der Gesellschaft"* rather than the translator's "in the midst of society" in order to stress the continuity between Marx's early and later thinking here. Cf. Marx's comments on direct democracy (CHDS, 87–89 and 189–190); and see Colletti (1972, Chapter 4) and Meiksins Wood (1972, 76–83, 120–123 and 160–173) on Rousseau's influence on this aspect of Marx's thinking. For Rousseau, in Meiksins Wood's fine words, "community [is] a fact of consciousness" (1972, 81). See Graeber (2013, Chapter 3) for a recent and congenial discussion of the concept *democracy* and some of its history.

character of one's kind: each of us humans distinguishes ourselves from the others, in practical thought, together with and not by opposing ourselves to them.

Marx seeks to capture this with talk of our *Durchsichselbstsein:* our being ourselves through ourselves.[72] Realizing *what* we are together in mutually recognitive living, that is, we practically self-conscious individuals realize *each other*, and we have then gone beyond even those other animals who, fulfilling distinct albeit correlated roles, jointly realize their species but that is all. Thus, our kind is not divided into fixed roles that are distributed within circumscribed groups: each of us *is* through and for the other their whole essence and felt happiness as a practical thinker, their humanity itself.[73] That is why Marx can say that man, "however much he may [...] be a *particular* individual [...] is just as much the *totality* [...]; he also exists in reality as the contemplation and true enjoyment of social existence and as a totality of vital human expression" (EPM, 351).[74] We humans are, it might be said, the cosmopolitical animal; and just as our kind, *humanity*, is not one species within a shareable genus—namely, *practical thinker*—neither is *humanity* itself a multiply specifiable genus.

Our general kind is seen to be, then, nothing other than each of us living individuals in our self-conscious interrelation.[75] Realizing each other as practically self-conscious individuals, that is, we resolve our humanity into each other without remainder: our essence is outside us just insofar as we are next to each other.[76] Thus, for Marx, our common humanity cannot reside in sets of institutions which bind us by reconstituting within themselves our supposedly self-directed individuality; and we do not belong together by being born into certain groups—nations unified by states, say—or by then playing any group-given roles—even that of *citizen*. We humans are together as such through one another, and the universality of our togetherness resides in our mutual interrelation as living individuals.[77] As Marx puts it:

---

72 See Marx (EPM, 356). For talk of self-distinguishing, see Marx and Engels (1998, 37).
73 Cf. Cohen (1966).
74 Cf. Marx (EPM, 327): "Man [...] looks upon himself as the present, living species, [...] he looks upon himself as a *universal* and therefore free being."
75 Marx thinks, then, that Hegel mistakenly treats "universality and individuality [...] as real antitheses," and that he fails "to regard the universal as the real essence of the finite real" (CHDS, 155 and 80). Colletti, rightly I think, attributes to Marx the contrasting view that with us, "[...] unity *is* the multiplicity in its interdependency" (1973, 273; emphasis added). See also Meiksins Wood (1972, 151–152), Gould (1978, 30–39), Bhaskar (2014, Chapter 2), and Balibar (2017, 28–35).
76 Cf. Marx (EPM, 330): "When man confronts himself, he also confronts other men."
77 Cf. Marx (EJM, 260): "man himself [is] the mediator for man."

> Since the essence of *man* is the *true community* of man, men, by [exercising] their own essence, produce, create this human community, this social being which is no abstract, universal power standing over against the solitary individual, but is the essence of each individual, his own activity, his own life [...] (Marx EJM, 265).[78]

Of course, the Hegelian is right to emphasize that in being a practical thinker, a living individual has the idea of their own good. Equally, the Hegelian is right to emphasize that in living self-consciously, each practical thinker's orientation towards their own good is already an orientation towards the others'. Again though, each of us *is*, as an individual, through and for the others what is good without condition, human living itself, and so rather than originally being an object of exclusion, the good of each of us is internal to the others': the satisfaction of our personal desires is as such of interest to all.[79] Thus, we are moved both to act and to feel by each other's happiness or suffering as immediately as by our own but *in* its being the other's. Any putative distinction between someone's private good and the general good gives way, then, to the distinction which we humans make between each other: we who, in our self-conscious interrelation as living individuals, are each then goodness itself. We thus recognize one another as human beings in mutual and immediate care, and this is the felt side of our shared activity of being human.[80]

Since, then, we grasp our action-kinds as what we humans do, as means or as ends, that grasp is sustained by our mutuality; doing them, we know ourselves to express our human living.[81] This does not mean that maintaining one another as living individuals is a *further* end at which we all aim in acting, but that how each of us feels bears immediately, when known, on the others' thought of what to do. Indeed, the refusal to allow that another's happiness or suffering *could*, as theirs, bear on one's feeling or action as immediately as does one's own just is a refusal of their humanity and therewith of one's own humanity.[82] We might label as "false,"

---

78 I have "exercising" rather than "activating" as a better translation of Marx's "*Betätigung.*"
79 Cf. Gould (1978, 55–56).
80 Cf. Meiksins Wood's idea that compassion is the "union of the intellectual and the emotional" (1972, 66), and that our "species-consciousness" then resides in our compassion for each other (1972, 76–80). Cf. Gaita (2011, Chapter 2), and Weil (1952, 64): "Belief in other human beings as such is *love.*" See also Marx and Engels (1975, 22): "[...] love does not separate humanity from the personal, individual man."
81 Cf. McCabe (2003a, 93–94).
82 The utilitarian cannot capture what is refused here. Along with their deontological opponent who claims the practical basicness of the concept *legal person*, the utilitarian conceives of happiness and suffering as states into which a patient is put. This reflects the underlying assumption that our own individuality is something to which awareness gives us access. Neither view can com-

then, any wish to do something with another human being to which that refusal is internal, for any such doing could only be a confused semblance of human action: the denaturing, so to speak, of an action-kind.[83] To have turned from another human in this way *is* to have turned against oneself, and it is then a kind of practical and so painful nonsense: an inherently distorted attempt to live, as it were, under erasure. Inhumanity thus goes beyond how other animals can, relative to their species, fare badly.[84]

For Marx, however, the system of private right—whose roots are ancient—would seem to be our inhumanity itself, since it involves "each man [seeing] in other men not the *realization* but the *limitation* of his own freedom" (OJQ, 230).[85] Thus it is, he thinks, a warped version of our togetherness: something within which we, distorting our internality to each other, present ourselves to each other as having been brought together as opposed, self-sufficient individuals: "the essential bond joining [man] with other men appears as inessential, in fact separation from other men appears to be his true essence" (Marx EJM, 266).[86] That is, thinking ourselves to be, in essence, privately needy owners of exchangeable property, we humans are turned against the absolute vulnerability to and responsibility for each other which is involved in our mutually recognitive living; and whilst our commodities then enjoy that self-sustaining internality to each other which is properly ours, we affect to exclude from the sphere of our recognition those who are engaged in activities on which our living existence as human beings depends.[87]

---

prehend that individuality, then, or how happiness and suffering bear immediately upon action. In fact, the self-conscious interrelation through which we exist as living individuals—in which the happiness of one is as such achieved in the deed of the other and *vice versa*—is itself neither action nor passion but what we knowingly express only together in linked action and passion. Cf. the 3rd thesis on Feuerbach (Marx TF).

83 There is nothing it would be for such a wish really to be satisfied, and a response to it could only aim at recalling its possessor to our common humanity. I think that we begin to understand the peculiar force of anger when we see it as responsive to one who is felt to have expressed such a wish. Cf. Améry (1980, Chapter 4) on resentment.

84 The characteristically human defect in action is not so much *Unrecht*, then, but a form of *Unsinn*. Cf. McCabe on "sin" (2003c, 32): "[it] has no point at all in the natural created world; for here it is as though the predator simply ate *itself*," and see his (2003a, 101–103). See also Laing (2010, 46–47), and Butler (2020, 25, 148–149, and 200–203).

85 Weinrib (1989) shows how Aristotle already had a developed picture of private right. Cf. Pashukanis (1978, 152–153).

86 Cf. Gould (1978, 30–39).

87 Marx advances the idea that we humans endow our commodities with our own mutually recognitive life in EJM. The topic returns in *Capital* under the heading "commodity fetishism." Cf. Col-

Acting this system out thus involves thinking in terms, reflected in Hegelianism, which induce the problem of practical solipsism. However, the mutual recognition in which we are practical thinkers *is* our human living, and it must be acknowledged by us as a sphere of fellowship which includes, *inter alia*, those who raise new human beings or care for old ones, and those who produce food, clothing or shelter. These activities are in fact already part of our common human living, and those who are engaged in them already recognize each other as fellows when undertaking them together.[88] As Marx says of communist workers: "association, conversation, which in turn has society as its goal, is enough for them. The brotherhood of man is not a hollow phrase, it is a reality, and the nobility of man shines forth upon us from their work-worn figures" (EPM, 365). Knowing our humanity, then, we humans are already set against inhumanity: holding fast to ourselves and thus to each other, we implicitly resist that confused self-conception internal to private right and avoid for ourselves the problem of practical solipsism.[89]

Marx says, then, that "a social revolution possesses a *total* point of view because [...] it proceeds from the point of view of the *particular, real individual*, because the *community* against whose separation from himself the individual is reacting is the *true* community of man, *human* nature" (CNKP, 419).[90] It is a good question, however, what this means for us in practice. Marx's idea is that maintaining our grasp of ourselves in our relation to each other, we humans are implicitly oriented towards sharing the whole range of activities through which we live, so that they become undertaken by all of us together. As he says, "if we regard these modes of man's social existence as the realization of his essence," then "these realities will also appear as man's *actual* universality and, therefore, as common to all men" (Marx CHDS, 99). And I think that we can at least begin to see how, for Marx, we humans can as such only oppose ourselves, together, to private control over the means of production since that requires us to live against each other.[91]

---

letti (1972, 76–92) and (1973, Chapter 12), and Silva (2023, 67–69). Ripstein and King make a similar point at the end of their manuscript "Did Marx Hold a Labour Theory of Value?"

88 Cf. Meiksins Wood (2008a, Chapter 2) on the sophists' democratic conception of knowledge of how to live a human life.

89 Cf. Graeber (2014, 94–102) and Meiksins Wood (1972, 80–83) on Rousseau.

90 Cf. Tronti (2019, Introduction); see also Butler on strikes (2020, 129–130) and Gourevitch (2015, Chapter 5).

91 I think that Marx would allow that our self-conscious interrelation as living individuals involves our drawing a distinction between each other's dwelling places, say, or each other's clothing. However, such "truly human property" (EPM, 333), internal to our self-conscious living, would not be— and is not, I think, ultimately compatible with—alienable private property in the means of production.

After all, it might be said that the very idea of a "natural slave" reflects a division between human beings who privately control the means of production—owners of factories, say, or large farms—and those who must work for them if they are to receive the food and shelter which they need to survive. With this idea, the former would affect to think that their being human just is the latter's not being such, as if our being human together could itself require some of us humans to be less human.[92] This makes no sense. For Marx, though, a legal person really is, in the end, one who either has private property in and so control over the means of production or, more ambivalently, one who must sell the "use of their labour-power" to them.[93] The former, represented by a state which enshrines and enforces their property rights, will affect to recognize each other without themselves living therein, whilst the latter must work for those property-owners if they are to be able to pay for the food and shelter which they need to survive.[94] Again, this class-divided structure cannot be a sound articulation of what we humans know our activity of living to be.

Knowing ourselves in practical self-consciousness, we humans know ourselves to live through and for each other. We oppose ourselves therein to any class division, and our history and so reality as human beings is then the history of such opposition: class-struggle.[95] Thus, for Marx, our being human requires us to abolish private property in the means of production, along with any state which supports it; and by then undertaking our humanity together without mediation, Marx thinks, we will have it lucidly in hand. We will all have each other.[96]

---

[92] Cf. Weil (2005, 188–190). By contrast, a drone is no less a bee than its queen, and neither really works *for* the other.

[93] For more on the control/ownership distinction, see Patterson (2018, 21–27) and Cohen (2001, Chapter 3).

[94] Cf. Marx (CNKP, 412). See also Marx and Engels (1998, 457), Colletti (1972, 92–97 and 102), and Meiksins Wood (2016, Chapter 7). See also Cicerchia (2021) and Leipold (2022).

[95] For an introduction to historiography as the study of human history so conceived, see Kaye (2022); for a stirring historical panorama of class-struggle, see Davis (2020, Chapter 1). Meiksins Wood (2008b) presents Marx's own views on human history both sympathetically and critically.

[96] I completed this paper whilst in receipt of a Study Abroad Studentship from the Leverhulme Trust. Thanks to the Trust for their support. My thanks also to participants of MindWork and to participants of the Bernard Williams Virtual Group—especially Jack Wearing—for commenting. Likewise, to participants of Professor Kern's Colloquium at the University of Leipzig. Many thanks also to the following individuals for reading drafts, and for helpful feedback: Julian Bacharach, Vanessa Carr, Rose Ryan Flinn, Sebastian Gardner, Matthias Haase, Adrian Haddock, Thomas Khurana, Martin McIvor, Steven Methven, Dawa Ometto, Edgar Philips, Craig Reeves, Sebastian Rödl, Christoph Schuringa, and Anna Lena Weyand. Thanks also to Chrysanthi Nigianni. I dedicate this paper to the ICU staff at Uniklinik Leipzig.

Abbreviations

Marx's Works

In the foregoing, I make reference to the following collection of Marx's early writings: Marx, Karl (1974): *Early Writings*. London: Penguin. A key for my references to the writings collected in this volume is as follows:

CHDS Marx, Karl (1974a): "Critique of Hegel's Doctrine of the State." In: Marx, Karl: *Early Writings*. London: Penguin, 57–198.
OJQ Marx, Karl (1974b): "On the Jewish Question." In: Marx, Karl: *Early Writings*. London: Penguin, 211–241.
EJM Marx, Karl (1974c): "Excerpts from James Mill's *Elements of Political Economy*." In: Marx, Karl: *Early Writings*. London: Penguin, 259–278.
EPM Marx, Karl (1974d): "Economic and Philosophical Manuscripts." In: Marx, Karl: *Early Writings*. London: Penguin, 279–400.
CNKP Marx, Karl (1974e): "Critical Notes on the Article 'The King of Prussia and Social Reform.' By a Prussian." In: Marx, Karl: *Early Writings*. London: Penguin, 401–420.
TF Marx, Karl (1974f): "Concerning Feuerbach." In: Marx, Karl: *Early Writings*. London: Penguin, 421–423.

For the reader's convenience, I cite the aforementioned texts by abbreviation and page number in the collection, e.g., "(CNKP, 419)."

References

Améry, Jean (1980): *At the Mind's Limits*. Bloomington: Indiana University Press.
Anderson, Perry (1979): *Lineages of the Absolutist State*. London: Verso.
Anscombe, Gertrude Elizabeth Margaret (1981): "The First Person." In: Anscombe, Gertrude Elizabeth Margaret: *Metaphysics and the Philosophy of Mind*. Minneapolis: University of Minnesota Press, 21–38.
Aristotle (1991): *The Politics*. London: Penguin.
Armstrong, David (1968): *A Materialist Theory of the Mind*. Oxford: Blackwell.
Balibar, Étienne (2017): *The Philosophy of Marx*. London: Verso.
Bhaskar, Roy (2014): *The Possibility of Naturalism*. London: Routledge.
Boyle, Matthew (2012): "Essentially Rational Animals." In: Abel, Günter and Conant, James (Eds.): *Rethinking Epistemology*. Vol. II. Berlin: de Gruyter, 395–428.
Boyle, Matthew (2018): "Sartre on Bodily Transparency." In: *Manuscrito* 4. No. 4, 33–70.
Boyle, Matthew and Lavin, Douglas (2010): "Goodness and Desire." In: Tenenbaum, Sergio (Ed.): *Desire, Practical Reason, and the Good*. Oxford: Oxford University Press, 161–201.

Butler, Judith (2020): *The Force of Non-Violence*. London: Verso.
Campbell, John (1994): *Past, Space, and Self*. Cambridge: MIT Press.
Chitty, Andrew (1993): "The Early Marx on Needs." In: *Radical Philosophy* 64, 23–31.
Chitty, Andrew (1994): "Needs in the History of Philosophy." DPhil dissertation. Oxford: Oxford University.
Cicerchia, Lillian (2021): "Why Does Class Matter?" In: *Social Theory and Practice* 47. No. 4, 603–627.
Cohen, Gerald (1966): "Beliefs and Roles." In: *Proceedings of the Aristotelian Society* 67, 17–34.
Cohen, Gerald (2001): *Karl Marx's Theory of History*. Expanded Edition. Oxford: Oxford University Press.
Colletti, Lucio (1972): *From Rousseau to Lenin*. London: NLB.
Colletti, Lucio (1973): *Marxism and Hegel*. London: Verso.
Davis, Mike (2020): *Old Gods, New Enigmas*. London: Verso.
Depew, David (1991): "Transfiguring the Polis." In: McCarthy, George (Ed.): *Marx and Aristotle*. London: Rowman and Littlefield, 37–73.
Depew, David (1995): "Humans and Other Political Animals." In: *Phronesis* 40. No. 2, 156–181.
Douglas, Mary (1966): *Purity and Danger*. London: Routledge.
Engstrom, Stephen (2013a): "The *Triebfeder* of Pure Practical Reason." In: Reath, Andrews and Timmerman, Jens (Eds.): *Kant's* Critique of Practical Reason: *A Critical Guide*. Cambridge: Cambridge University Press, 90–118.
Engstrom, Stephen (2013b): "Freedom and Nature." In: Hindrichs, Gunnar and Honneth, Axel (Eds.): *Freiheit: Stuttgarter-Hegel Kongress 2011*. Frankfurt am Main: Klostermann, 657–680.
Evans, Gareth (1982): *The Varieties of Reference*. Oxford: Oxford University Press.
Fanon, Frantz (2021): "The Meeting between Psychiatry and Society." In: Khalfa, Jean and Young, Robert (Eds.): *The Psychiatric Writings from* Freedom and Alienation. London: Bloomsbury, 363–382.
Fichte, Johann Gottlieb (2000): *Foundations of Natural Right*. Cambridge: Cambridge University Press.
Foot, Phillipa (2001): *Natural Goodness*. Oxford: Oxford University Press.
Ford, Anton (2011): "Action and Generality." In: Ford, Anton, Hornsby, Jennifer, and Stoutland, Frederick (Eds.): *Essays on Anscombe's* Intention. Cambridge: Harvard University Press, 76–104.
Foster, Michael (1935): *The Political Philosophies of Plato and Hegel*. Oxford: Oxford University Press.
Frank, Manfred (1989): "Schelling's Critique of Hegel and the Beginnings of Marxian Dialectics." In: *Idealistic Studies* 19. No. 3, 251–268.
Fredriksen, Paula (2017): *Paul*. New Haven: Yale University Press.
Frege, Gottlob (1997): "The Thought." In: Beaney, Michael (Ed.): *The Frege Reader*. Oxford: Blackwell, 325–345.
Frey, Jennifer (2018): "How to Be an Ethical Naturalist." In: Hacker-Wright, John (Ed.): *Philippa Foot on Virtue and Goodness*. London: Palgrave, 47–84.
Gaita, Raimond (2011): *After Romulus*. Melbourne: Text Publishing.
Geach, Peter (1956): "Good and Evil." In: *Analysis* 17. No. 5, 33–42.
Gobsch, Wolfram (2014): "The Idea of an Ethical Community." In: *Philosophical Topics* 42. No. 1, 177–200.
Gobsch, Wolfram (2020): "Autonomy and Radical Evil." In: *Philosophical Explorations* 22. No. 2, 194–207.
Gould, Carol (1978): *Marx's Social Ontology*. Cambridge: MIT Press.
Gourevitch, Alex (2011): "Labor and Republican Liberty." In: *Constellations* 18. No. 3, 431–454.

Gourevitch, Alex (2013): "Labor Republicanism and the Transformation of Work." In: *Political Theory* 41. No. 4, 591–617.
Gourevitch, Alex (2015): *From Slavery to the Cooperative Commonwealth*. Cambridge: Cambridge University Press.
Graeber, David (2013): *The Democracy Project*. New York: Spiegel and Grau.
Graeber, David (2014): *Debt*. New York: Melville House.
Haase, Matthias (2013): "Life and Mind." In: Khurana, Thomas (Ed.): *The Freedom of Life*. Berlin: August, 69–110.
Haase, Matthias (2018): "Practically Self-Conscious Life." In: Hacker-Wright, John (Ed.): *Philippa Foot on Virtue and Goodness*. London: Palgrave, 85–126.
Haase, Matthias (2021): "Anscombe on The Dignity of a Human Being." In: Haddock, Adrian and Wiseman, Rachael (Eds.): *The Anscombean Mind*. London: Routledge, 469–491.
Haddock, Adrian (2019): "I am *NN*." In: *European Journal of Philosophy* 21. No. 4, 957–970.
Hegel, Georg Willhelm Friedrich (1971a): *Encylopaedia*. Vol. I: *Logic*. Oxford: Oxford University Press.
Hegel, Georg Willhelm Friedrich (1971b): *Encylopaedia*. Vol. II: *Philosophy of Nature*. Oxford: Oxford University Press.
Hegel, Georg Willhelm Friedrich (1971c): *Encyclopaedia*. Vol. III: *Philosophy of Mind*. Oxford: Oxford University Press.
Hegel, Georg Willhelm Friedrich (1977): *Phenomenology of Spirit*. Oxford: Oxford University Press.
Hegel, Georg Willhelm Friedrich (1991): *Philosophy of Right*. Cambridge: Cambridge University Press.
Hegel, Georg Willhelm Friedrich (1995): *Lectures on the History of Philosophy*. Vol. II. Lincoln: University of Nebraska Press.
Hegel, Georg Willhelm Friedrich (1999): *Political Writings*. Cambridge: Cambridge University Press.
Hinshelwood, Alec (2013): "The Relations between Agency, Identification, and Alienation." In: *Philosophical Explorations* 16. No. 3, 243–258.
Honneth, Axel (2015): *Freedom's Right*. London: Polity.
Julius, Alexander J. (2016): "Mutual Recognition." In: *Jurisprudence* 7. No. 2, 193–209.
Julius, Alexander J. (2017): "Independent People." In: Kisilevsky, Sari and Stone, Martin (Eds.): *Freedom and Force*. London: Hart Publishing, 91–110.
Kandiyali, Jan (2020): "The Importance of Others." In: *Ethics* 130. No. 4, 555–587.
Kant, Immanuel (1996): *Groundwork of the Metaphysics of Morals*. In: Gregor, Mary (Ed.): *Practical Philosophy*. Cambridge: Cambridge University Press, 37–108.
Kaye, Harvey (2022): *The British Marxist Historians*. Winchester: Zero Books.
Kern, Andrea (2020): "Life and Mind: Varieties of Neo-Aristotelianism." In: *Hegel Bulletin* 41. No. 1, 40–60.
Khurana, Thomas (2013): "Life and Autonomy." In: Khurana, Thomas (Ed.): *The Freedom of Life*. Berlin: August, 155–194.
Khurana, Thomas (2018): "The Politics of Second Nature." In: Stekeler-Weithofer, Pirmin and Zabel, Benno (Eds.): *Philosophie der Republik*. Berlin: Mohr Siebeck, 422–436.
Khurana, Thomas (2021): "The Irony of Self-Consciousness." In: Finkelde, Dominik, Žižek, Slavoj, and Menke, Christoph (Eds.): *Parallax*. London: Bloomsbury: 145–158.
Khurana, Thomas (2023): "Genus-Being: On Marx's Dialectical Naturalism." In: Corti, Luca and Schülein, Georg (Eds): *Nature and Naturalism in Classical German Philosophy*. London: Routledge, 246–278.
Kitcher, Philip (1999): "Essentialism and Perfection." In: *Ethics* 110. No. 1, 58–83.

Korsgaard, Christine (2009): *Self-Constitution: Agency, Identity, and Integrity.* Oxford: Oxford University Press.
Laing, Ronald (2010): *The Divided Self.* London: Penguin.
Lavin, Douglas (2014): "Other Wills." In: *Philosophical Explorations* 17. No. 3, 279–288.
Lavin, Douglas (2017): "Forms of Rational Agency." In: *Royal Institute of Philosophy Supplements* 80, 171–193.
Leipold, Bruno (2022): "Chains and Invisible Threads." In: Dawson, Hannah and Dijn, Annelien (Eds.): *Rethinking Liberty before Liberalism.* Cambridge: Cambridge University Press, 194–214.
Løgstrup, Knud (1997): *The Ethical Demand.* Notre Dame: University of Notre Dame Press.
Lovibond, Sabina (1983): *Realism and Imagination in Ethics.* Oxford: Blackwell.
Luther, Martin (2017): *The Ninety-Five Theses and Other Writings.* London: Penguin.
Macpherson, Crawford (1962): *The Political Theory of Possessive Individualism.* Oxford: Oxford University Press.
Margalit, Avishai (1998): *The Decent Society.* Cambridge: Harvard University Press.
Martin, Michael (1994): "A Sense of Ownership." In: Bermudez, José Luis, Marcel, Anthony, and Eilan, Naomi (Eds.): *The Body and the Self.* Cambridge: MIT Press, 267–290.
Martin, Michael (2006): "In Praise of Self." In: *European Journal of Analytic Philosophy* 2. No. 1, 69–100.
Marx, Karl (1973): *Grundrisse.* London: Penguin.
Marx, Karl (1976a): *Capital.* Vol. I. London: Penguin.
Marx, Karl (1976b): *The Poverty of Philosophy.* In: Marx, Karl and Engels, Friedrich: *Marx and Engels Collected Works.* Vol. VI. London: Lawrence and Wishart, 105–212.
Marx, Karl (1980): *Wage Labour and Capital.* In: Marx, Karl and Engels, Friedrich: *Marx and Engels Collected Works.* Vol. IX. London: Lawrence and Wishart, 197–228.
Marx, Karl and Engels, Friedrich (1975): *The Holy Family.* In: Marx, Karl and Engels, Friedrich: *Marx and Engels Collected Works.* Vol. IV. London: Lawrence and Wishart, 19–54.
Marx, Karl and Engels, Friedrich (1998): *The German Ideology.* New York: Prometheus Books.
McCabe, Herbert (2003a): *Law, Love and Language.* London: Continuum.
McCabe, Herbert (2003b): "Easter." In: Davies, Brian (Ed.): *God, Christ and Us.* London: Continuum, 89–91.
McCabe, Herbert (2003c): *"Felix Culpa."* In: Davies, Brian (Ed.): *God, Christ and Us.* London: Continuum, 29–33.
McCabe, Herbert (2010): *The New Creation.* London: Continuum.
McDowell, John (1998): *Mind, Value, and Reality.* Cambridge: Harvard University Press.
McDowell, John (1998a): "Some Issues in Aristotle's Moral Psychology." In: McDowell, John: *Mind, Value, and Reality.* Cambridge: Harvard University Press, 23–49.
McDowell, John (1998b): "Two Forms of Naturalism." In: McDowell, John: *Mind, Value, and Reality.* Cambridge: Harvard University Press, 167–197.
McDowell, John (2011): "Anscombe on Bodily Self-Knowledge." In: Ford, Anton, Hornsby, Jennifer, and Stoutland, Frederick (Eds.): *Essays on Anscombe's* Intention. Cambridge: Harvard University Press, 128–146.
McDowell, John (2017): "Why Does It Matter to Hegel that *Geist* Has a History?" In: Zuckert, Rachel and Kreines, James (Eds.): *Hegel on Philosophy in History.* Cambridge: Cambridge University Press, 15–32.
Meiksins Wood, Ellen (1972): *Mind and Politics.* Los Angeles: University of California Press.
Meiksins Wood, Ellen (1991): *The Pristine Culture of Capitalism.* London: Verso.

Meiksins Wood, Ellen (2008a): *Citizens to Lords.* London: Verso.
Meiksins Wood, Ellen (2008b): "Historical Materialism in 'Forms which Precede Capitalist Production.'" In: Musto, Marcello (Ed.): *Karl Marx's* Grundrisse. London: Routledge, 79–92.
Meiksins Wood, Ellen (2012): *Liberty and Property.* London: Verso.
Meiksins Wood, Ellen (2016): *Democracy Against Capitalism.* London: Verso.
Moore, Adrian (1997): *Points of View.* Oxford: Oxford University Press.
Müller, Anselm (1977): "Radical Subjectivity." In *Ratio* 19. No. 2, 115–132.
Nagel, Thomas (1986): *The View from Nowhere.* Oxford: Oxford University Press.
Newton, Alexandra (2017): "Kant on Animal and Human Pleasure." In: *Canadian Journal of Philosophy* 47. No. 4, 518–540.
Nussbaum, Martha (1980): "Shame, Separateness, and Political Unity." In: Nussbaum, Martha: *Essays on Aristotle's Ethics.* Los Angeles: University of California Press, 393–438.
O'Brien, Lucy (2007): *Self-Knowing Agents.* Oxford: Oxford University Press.
Ometto, Dawa (2022): "Ethical Naturalism and the Guise of the Good." In: Kietzmann, Christian (Ed.): *Teleological Structures in Human Life.* London: Routledge, 135–158.
Owen, George (1986): "Aristotelian Pleasures." In: Nussbaum, Martha (Ed.): *Logic, Science and Dialectic.* London: Duckworth, 334–346.
Parfit, Derek (1984): *Reasons and Persons.* Oxford: Oxford University Press.
Pashukanis, Evgeny (1978): *Law and Marxism: A General Theory.* London: Pluto.
Patterson, Orlando (2018): *Slavery and Social Death.* Cambridge: Harvard University Press.
Read, Jason (2016): *The Politics of Transindividuality.* London: Haymarket Books.
Reeves, Craig (2016): "Beyond the Postmetaphysical Turn." In: *Journal of Critical Realism* 15. No. 3, 217–244.
Rödl, Sebastian (2014): "Intentional Transaction." In: *Philosophical Explorations* 17. No. 3, 304–316.
Rödl, Sebastian (2015): "Law as the Reality of the Free Will." In: Speer, Andreas, Hogrebe, Wolfram, and Gabriel, Markus (Eds.): *The New Desire for Metaphysics.* Berlin: de Gruyter, 207–220.
Rödl, Sebastian (2016a): "Acting as the Internal End of Acting." In: Alznauer, Mark and Torralba, José (Eds.): *Theories of Action and Morality.* Hildesheim: Georg Olms, 37–54.
Rödl, Sebastian (2016b): "Education and Autonomy." In: *Journal of Philosophy of Education* 50. No. 1, 84–97.
Rödl, Sebastian (2017a): "Selbsterkenntnis des Selbstbewegers." In: Kietzmann, Christian and Kern, Andrea (Eds.): *Selbstbewusstes Leben.* Berlin: Suhrkamp, 209–225.
Rödl, Sebastian (2017b): "The First-Person and Self-Knowledge in Analytic Philosophy." In: Renz, Ursula (Ed.): *Self-Knowledge: A History.* Oxford: Oxford University Press, 280–294.
Schuringa, Christoph (Forthcoming): "*Gattungswesen* and Universality." In: Luca Corti and Johannes-Georg Schülein (Eds.): *Life, Organism and Cognition in Classical German Philosophy.* New York: Springer.
Silva, Ludovico (2023): *Marx's Literary Style.* London: Verso.
Snowdon, Paul (1990): "Persons, Animals, and Ourselves." In: Gill, Christopher (Ed.): *Persons and the Human Mind.* Oxford: Oxford University Press, 83–108.
Stein, Peter (1999): *Roman Law in European History.* Cambridge: Cambridge University Press.
Strawson, Peter (1959): *Individuals.* London: Methuen.
Theunissen, Michael (1984): *The Other.* Cambridge: MIT Press.
Thompson, Michael (2004a): "Apprehending Human Form." In: *Royal Institute of Philosophy Supplements* 54, 47–74.

Thompson, Michael (2004b): "What is it to Wrong Someone?" In: Wallace, R. Jay, Pettit, Philip, and Smith, Michael (Eds.): *Reason and Value: Themes from the Philosophy of Joseph Raz*. Oxford: Oxford University Press, 333–384.
Thompson, Michael (2008): *Life and Action: Elementary Structures of Practice and Practical Thought*. Cambridge: Harvard University Press.
Thompson, Michael (2013): "Forms of Nature." In: Hindrichs, Gunnar and Honneth, Axel (Eds.): *Freiheit: Stuttgarter-Hegel Kongress 2011*. Frankfurt am Main: Klostermann, 701–738.
Tronti, Mario (2019): *Workers and Capital*. London: Verso.
Velleman, J. David (1999): "Love as a Moral Emotion." In: *Ethics* 109. No. 2, 338–374.
Vogler, Candace (2006): "Modern Moral Philosophy Again." In: *Proceedings of the Aristotelian Society* 106, 345–362.
Vrousalis, Nicholas (2020): "Free Productive Agency." In: *Philosophical Topics* 48. No. 2, 265–284.
Weil, Simone (1952): *Gravity and Grace*. London: Routledge.
Weil, Simone (2005): "*The Iliad* or the Poem of Force." In: Miles, Siân (Ed.): *Simone Weil: An Anthology*. London: Penguin, 182–215.
Weinrib, Ernest (1989): "Aristotle's Forms of Justice." In: *Ratio Juris* 2. No. 3, 486–503.
Wiggins, David (2009): "What is the Order Among the Varieties of Goodness?" In: *Philosophy* 84. No. 2, 175–200.
Wiggins, David (2022): "Languages as Things in their Own Right." In: Wiggins, David: *Meaning, Truth, and the Limits of Analysis*. Oxford: Oxford University Press, 118–128.
Williams, Bernard (1981): "Utilitarianism and Moral Self-Indulgence." In: Williams, Bernard: *Moral Luck*. Cambridge: Cambridge University Press, 40–53.
Williams, Bernard (1993): *Ethics and the Limits of Philosophy*. London: Routledge.
Wittgenstein, Ludwig (1976): *On Certainty*. Oxford: Blackwell.
Wolff, Robert Paul (1988): *Moneybags Must Be So Lucky*. Boston: University of Massachusetts Press.

Index

Anscombe, Gertrude Elizabeth Margaret   1f., 5–7, 9–11, 27–40, 45, 47f., 50, 52f., 74, 93f., 105, 114, 138f., 148, 158, 163, 282, 291, 329
Aristotle   3, 16, 20, 29f., 36, 43f., 46f., 54, 66, 72, 109, 138f., 167f., 252–254, 256, 284, 288, 323, 331, 339f., 344

constitutivism   137, 301f.
constructivism   2f.

desire   1f., 6, 8, 11, 15, 17f., 20, 22, 37, 49f., 72, 81, 94, 99, 101, 127, 148f., 157–165, 173, 179f., 182, 185f., 188f., 195, 198, 211–215, 217–232, 287, 291f., 294, 332f., 335–337, 343

empiricism   12, 61, 64, 296
end   10–13, 15–18, 27, 29, 37f., 41, 45–59, 61, 68–79, 81–85, 87–92, 94, 99f., 102f., 106, 108–110, 113f., 116, 119, 123–126, 128, 135–168, 184f., 190f., 196, 201, 211–214, 220f., 224–226, 228–232, 246, 255–257, 267f., 272, 300, 325, 328, 333, 335, 339, 343
– finite   11, 45f., 49–54, 311, 313f.
– infinite   10f., 27, 37f., 41, 45f., 48, 52, 69
Engstrom, Stephen   3f., 7f., 15, 46, 55, 74–77, 79, 138, 159–166, 215, 222, 227f., 332, 336
ethical life   3, 19–22, 179, 281, 284, 293, 298f., 302–314, 316, 334f., 337, 339

formal cause   9, 32–36, 58

Hegel, Georg Wilhelm Friedrich   3, 8, 19–22, 49, 58, 281–290, 293–303, 305–318, 323, 330–339, 342, 347
Humeanism   2f., 6, 14f., 104, 137, 148, 157f., 164, 166, 175, 179, 198, 200
Hume, David   2, 16f., 104, 172–174, 176–181, 200, 208, 336

instrumental reasoning   2, 14, 37f., 54, 69, 105, 109, 111, 119, 123, 135–154, 157, 159, 165, 167f.

intention   2, 4f., 9, 13, 20, 27–37, 41, 53, 61, 63–67, 76, 78, 82–86, 89–94, 105, 138f., 148f., 154f., 160–163, 177, 184, 200, 245f., 322f., 330

justice   15, 18f., 71, 92, 184, 190, 197, 239–242, 244–251, 253, 256, 258, 265–275, 277, 302, 338

Kant, Immanuel   3, 13f., 16f., 20, 45, 52, 54, 57, 73–76, 79, 82, 87, 91, 97–105, 107–110, 114–116, 118–122, 128–130, 138f., 159f., 163, 166, 168, 171–173, 175–178, 189, 197–199, 206–208, 211–220, 222–233, 257, 284, 293, 295, 298, 302, 332, 335f., 339
Korsgaard, Christine Marion   2, 14f., 103, 122–124, 135–137, 172, 174, 212, 216, 218f., 223, 227, 293, 295, 300–303, 305, 324

law   14, 17, 20f., 45, 52, 69, 74, 99, 101f., 104, 107, 114, 120, 128f., 171, 178, 182, 188–190, 198, 207, 211, 213, 215–217, 219, 226–229, 231, 249f., 252, 255, 274, 291–294, 296f., 299–302, 305f., 334f., 337
lifeform   8, 10, 21

Marx, Karl   3, 8, 20–22, 284, 321–323, 325, 327–330, 338–347

Plato   8, 18f., 173, 239f., 242f., 247f., 252, 256, 260, 272, 274, 277, 316, 340
practical cognitivism   3f., 6
practical knowledge   1, 3–7, 9f., 13, 15, 20f., 27–36, 50, 58, 67, 78, 99, 117, 138–140, 142, 149, 159–166, 200, 283, 291, 300, 323–328, 342
practical necessity   13f., 44, 97–105, 107f., 110, 114–116, 119–122, 129f.
practical reasoning   2–5, 7–13, 15, 27, 29f., 32, 35–41, 43–56, 58, 61, 63–66, 68–76, 80–84, 87–92, 94, 97, 104–107, 110–119, 123–125, 127f., 138, 140–142, 146, 153f., 163, 167

rational necessity   13f., 100, 109f., 112, 115–117, 119, 122–124, 130
Rousseau, Jean-Jacques   16f., 171f., 174–183, 185f., 188–209, 332, 341, 345

self-consciousness   4f., 7, 9, 19f., 27, 33, 35f., 39, 43, 53, 57f., 148f., 157, 160, 163–165, 186, 219, 225, 281–286, 288–292, 294–305, 307–313, 315f., 322, 328–330, 336f., 346
Socrates   18f., 239–249, 251–277

theoretical knowledge   2, 4, 6, 9f., 28f., 32–34, 58, 146, 163f., 290
theoretical reasoning   13, 40, 65, 86f., 97, 105, 108, 110f., 113–116, 124f., 130, 137, 141, 153
Thompson, Michael   14f., 21, 44, 49, 53, 92, 136f., 148f., 155, 166, 324–326, 338

virtue   3, 8, 18, 21, 168, 172–174, 177, 179, 189f., 197, 202f., 242, 245, 247f., 251–253, 267–270, 272–274, 276f., 297, 325, 339

www.ingramcontent.com/pod-product-compliance
Lightning Source LLC
Chambersburg PA
CBHW020219170426
43201CB00007B/259